Touring Prose

Touring Prose

Writings on Golf
by
Lorne Rubenstein

RANDOM HOUSE

Toronto

For Jim Fitchette,
a friend on the fairway
and in the rough

Published in Canada in 1992
by Random House of Canada Limited, Toronto

Canadian Cataloguing in Publication Data

Rubenstein, Lorne
Touring prose: writings on golf

ISBN 0-394-22286-5

1. Golf. I. Title.

GV965.R83 1992   796.352   C92-094649-6

The publisher would like to thank the following
publications for permission to reprint in altered form the
material presented herein: *Golf Digest, Golf Magazine, Golf
Monthly, Maclean's, SCORE, Toronto Life* and *The Globe and
Mail.*

Jacket design: David Montle
Front cover photo © Miguel Martin/
The Image Bank Canada
Author photo: James Fitchette
Typesetting: Tony Gordon Ltd.

Printed and bound in Canada

10 9 8 7 6 5 4 3 2 1

CONTENTS

FOREWORD

ONE SUMMER about the middle of the period covered by this spritely and graceful book, I invited Lorne Rubenstein to be my partner in a two-man best-ball at my own Briars Golf Club at Jackson's Point, Ontario.

This was a fairly presumptuous act on my part. My game was in its usual precarious state — I sometimes have to remind Lorne, when we play together, not *always* to say "20-handicapper" when he's referring to a feckless golfer — and, heaven knows, Lorne has opportunity enough to play in tournaments without extra invitations from me. But I happen to know he enjoys the Briars, whose original nine holes, laid out by Stanley Thompson along the edge of Stephen Leacock's azure Lake Simcoe (and since expanded) were the setting for my boyhood introduction to golf, and, as I reminded him when I called, it was too long since we'd had a game of any sort.

We played . . . well, *Lorne* was all right. He navigated our treacherous, 540-yard 14th with his customary, intelligent 2-iron, 2-iron, wedge, and, except for overreaching the difficult par-four second with a long, blind draw around the towering spruce that guards Thompson's banked green, gave our team a solid basis.

Me? Let's just say I failed to capitalize on the opportunities Lorne provided. But Lorne, God bless him, didn't seem to mind, and we had our usual pleasant time.

Afterwards, I asked if he'd like to stay the night and sneak in a dewy round at dawn, a time we both enjoy. He agreed — Lorne almost never turns down a round of golf. After a leisurely dinner, full of golf talk, we prepared for early retirement, and Lorne asked if he could borrow some bedtime reading.

Now, Lorne Rubenstein, as all his friends will testify, is a widely read and civilized man, a former master's student, committed to his beliefs — I remember that he wouldn't come to the Arctic one spring for our annual tournament on the ice until we helped him find the only family in Yellowknife that was holding a *seder* — a world traveller. So it was with some pride that I offered him a choice of our brimming cottage bookshelves, whose contents range from my daughter's old college English texts to Leacock and some other literary lapses, and from my collection of summertime thrillers to Gill's — my companion's — gardening library.

Lorne perused. We advised. He browsed. Finally, his eyes shining, he seized upon — I think — an old paperback Walker Percy.

"Do you know him?" I asked.

"There's a wonderful golf scene in it," Lorne said.

"Here, let me — "

I first met Lorne after I wrote him a fan letter at *The Globe and Mail*. This is not something I usually do, though I should — we all should. But I was so enjoying his literate, informed, thoughtful pieces in *The Globe* that I scribbled a note to tell him so. He wrote back. We became friends. He helped me start — and won the second of — the little tournaments I began at the Briars in 1986, which have now become a series of invitationals that reach, in Canada, from sea to sea to sea. We've played golf together all over the place; he well (he has a lovely, high-handed, vertical swing, and can *crush* a drive), I admiringly. He continues to write at least as well as he plays, with the same sense of controlled enthusiasm. He *loves* golf, and, as his introduction to *Touring Prose* shows, realizes how lucky he is to make a living from his pleasure. But, as several of the pieces herein also demonstrate, he does not let his passion for the game blind him to the occasional folly that surrounds it.

We're lucky too. To have him among us. And now, when other golfers come to visit Gill and me, there'll be no doubt which book we can send to bed with them.

PETER GZOWSKI

INTRODUCTION

IN SEPTEMBER of 1991, I and hundreds of other golf writers travelled to a new course at the eastern edge of South Carolina
where the Atlantic Ocean abuts the edge of America. This course
was called, simply, the Ocean Course, and it was designed by
Pete Dye for the Ryder Cup matches. Golfers and writers alike
wondered how this startling course that was built on a narrow
band of land between sea and marsh would stand up to three
days of intensely fought match play between teams of 12 professionals from the United States and Europe. We knew the verdict
a few days later: The Ocean Course had more than stood up; Dye
had shown that a new golf course could hold a major championship, indeed, the world's foremost team event. And in so doing
he had demonstrated again that change as the game's venues
might, alter as the game's equipment would, golf's timeless values prevailed. The Ocean Course on Kiawah Island was entirely
manufactured, as Dye didn't mind admitting. And yet to walk
there was to feel echoes of the windswept courses where the
game began, while at the same time being reminded that this
was a modern game, that the Ocean Course had more in common with PGA West's Stadium Course in Palm Springs, Califor-

nia, than it did with the Old Course in St. Andrews, Scotland. Golf covered the ages. The best courses existed in a sort of past present.

The 1991 Ryder Cup provided marvellously entertaining and even breathtaking golf, and it's hard to imagine an event that could have offered more opportunities for analysis and comment. The result of the matches was not decided until the final putt, after which the writers were nearly as drained as the golfers. We watched the closing ceremonies, then went back to our desks to try to capture the spirit of the event. I include my columns on the Ryder Cup in this collection. Indeed, although the event is still in recent memory, it gives me pleasure to go over the columns and relive the matches. That's why I enjoy writing, and reading, about golf. It's a game that invites reflection afterwards, but like baseball, its highlights occur in sudden, sharp bursts that follow a waiting period, as when Bernhard Langer stood over the par putt on the last hole at the Ocean Course that would decide the Ryder Cup.

The 1991 Ryder Cup was in some ways a summing up of all that has happened in the world of professional golf through the 1980s, the period, along with the opening years of the current decade, that this collection covers. The 1980s began with golfers from the United States clearly in a position of power. U.S. teams had won 19 matches, lost three and tied one since the Ryder Cup was inaugurated in 1927. Then the U.S. won the 1981 and 1983 matches, although the latter Ryder Cup went to the U.S. by the margin of a point.

It was clear that during the 1980s the balance of power in world golf was shifting. Spain's Seve Ballesteros had won the British Open and the Masters. Scotsman Sandy Lyle, Englishman Nick Faldo and West German Langer were about to show their talents to the golf world at large. So it was that the Europeans won the 1985 and 1987 Ryder Cups; the European win at Muirfield Village in Dublin, Ohio, outside Jack Nicklaus's hometown of Columbus, represented the first time a U.S. team had lost on home soil. And that team was captained by none other than Nicklaus himself. Meanwhile, Ballesteros was still winning majors, as were Langer and Lyle and, in 1987, Faldo. Golf was now perceived as an international sport from the professional side, as it had always been on the amateur side. This develop-

ment continued in 1989 when the European side retained the
Ryder Cup by halving the matches at the Belfry in England.

Then came the 1991 Ryder Cup at the Ocean Course, where
25,000 spectators a day tramped over the Dye-created dunesland.
Television took the game around the world with unprecedented
all-day coverage. This was indeed the Olympics of golf.

Here, then, was Langer, standing over his par putt at the last
hole after courageously holing putts at the 16th and 17th to prolong his match against three-time U.S. Open champion Hale
Irwin. And here, now, is Langer, anguished, his mouth open in
momentary horror as the six-foot putt slips by the right side of
the hole. By that margin of a missed six-foot par putt did the
Ryder Cup return to the U.S. But also by that narrow margin did
we all know that the golfers from the U.S. and Europe were
closely matched. It was apparent that if professionals from the
U.S. and Europe were to meet week after week, the result at the
end of the year would likely be a draw. The countries were
matched at the top in gifted golfers. Wherever you looked in the
U.S., Great Britain or Europe, you could see good golf being
played. The golf world was a feast, and the Ryder Cup its ultimate course.

It was a heady experience to have covered the game during
the 1980s, and into the 1991 Ryder Cup. And it is wonderful to
contemplate doing so throughout the 1990s, when golf continues
to put "a girdle round the globe," to use historian Robert
Browning's apt phrase from his 1955 classic work, *A History of
Golf*. The girdle only gets wider, as more and more people from
eight to 80, from Australia to Zambia, become enchanted by the
royal and ancient and often frustrating game.

The call of the game has led to a corresponding increase in the
amount of reportage and commentary. One need only examine
news and magazine stands and televisions everywhere. Golf
books are a growth industry; instruction books come out one
after the other; lavish coffee-table books depict beautiful golf
holes. Libraries of golf books fill rooms in private homes.

Then there's television. I watched in early November 1991 as
television brought into my living room the World Cup (which
Sweden won) from the new Le Querce course outside Rome.
Next came the Tour Championship from lovely old Pinehurst

No. 2. Soon after there was a special show in which Jack Nicklaus took viewers on a tour of his favourite nine holes of championship golf. Golf is always being played somewhere, because it's always warm somewhere. And television is usually there.

We live in a global village, of course, and have for some time. It is a global village that the golf writer in his fantasy enjoys thinking of as a global golf course. Certain that there is a golf story everywhere, he manages to find one everywhere. Having roamed much of the world, with much left to roam, I continue to marvel at the unlikely corners in which golfers can be found. Be it a settlement town in Israel, a lonely stretch of Indonesian Ocean shoreline in Bali, the veranda at Augusta National or a hilltop in West Virginia where Sam Snead lives overlooking 200 acres of surrounding mountainside, always there are golf and golfers. And always something to be written, happily enough for those of us who report on and comment about the game. We wander golf events while wearing badges that say "working press." Some people consider this a contradiction in terms, and I cannot argue. I have rarely considered what I do as work. Golf is a game and it is full of pleasure. This is not to say that problems and issues do not arise around the game, quite serious ones at that. Golf is getting too expensive for many people, who, unfortunately, will miss its lifelong charms. The game has been slow to grant blacks and women their full rights on the courses of the world. And it is all too easy to grumble about the money the best professionals are making, while forgetting about the game itself. The game has lasted for centuries. It must have something going for it.

This collection touches upon the many aspects of golf that I have encountered while covering the game. A majority of the columns and articles are drawn from *The Globe and Mail*, Canada's national newspaper, for which I have written since 1980. *The Globe* is a writer's paper, and the sports editors there have always encouraged me to range far and wide across the world of golf. Much of my work has been in the form of a column, in which I have been able to express my opinions and feelings while examining many aspects of the game. The brevity of the column has its virtues; the writer can concentrate on a single point and flesh it out within the confines of the space.

Herbert Warren Wind, now retired after years of writing his elegant golf essays for *The New Yorker*, once said something that has stuck with me. He was chatting with some newspaper writers when he said, "I really admire you fellows. You can tell a story in 800 words. Why, it takes me that long to clear my throat." Herb was being kind to all of us, for his essays are graceful and entertaining without being ponderous; the thousands of words he was given for his *New Yorker* pieces are required reading for any serious golf writer. Brad Klein, who contributes criticism on golf course architecture to *GolfWeek* magazine in the U.S., once called Wind up at his home in Manhattan. "How are you doing, Herb?" Brad asked. "I'm just polishing up a few sentences," the master answered.

That's what I like to think skilled golf writing is all about: Polishing up sentences until they sing, finding the words to convey feelings about golf. And as it happens, many fine writers are working at doing just that these days, during a period when golf is perhaps more popular than ever. As Dick Taylor, a former president of the Golf Writers Association of America, says, "It's better to cover golf than any other sport. The people are nicer, the ambience is nicer. I almost feel I've been stealing money."

One of the reasons Taylor feels that way is that golfers are, in general, accessible athletes. I can chat with a golfer at length during the early part of the week, prior to the beginning of the tournament. Anything goes then, but later in the week players are more likely to want to focus on the tournament itself. I can spend time with the player during those early days on the practice tee and putting green, when tournament policy permits. And during the tournament, I can walk along as he plays, often just inside the ropes. This enables me to observe closely how the player conducts himself on the course, his reactions to the good, the bad and the ugly circumstances that occur on a playing field so large, so open to the elements. There is no better way to learn about a golfer than to watch him in his natural environment.

Golf, then, gives the writer plenty of opportunities to find his voice. There's room to operate. A baseball writer can hardly sit on the field and watch the game. A football writer must content himself with being part of a crowded interview in a locker room after the game or, sometimes, participating in a mass press con-

ference. The spaciousness of a golf course, however, and the fact
that a tournament takes place over the course of a week, gives
the journalist a wide berth, one in which it's possible to develop
a rapport with golfers, professional and amateur alike.

That rapport is important. Gordon White reported on golf for
The New York Times for many years, until the fine young writer
Jaime Diaz took over recently. White knew that the relationship
between a player and a writer begins when rapport is established, when there's trust. The relationship ends if the rapport
doesn't develop, or if the trust is broken. "That doesn't mean
that you have to say he's the most important guy in the world,"
White says. "Most golfers are much too intelligent to think that
you're not going to say they hit a bad shot when they did. But a
baseball player might get mad at you if you say he struck out
three times."

Having never covered baseball, I can't comment on White's
latter statement. But I do feel golfers are about as decent a group
of people as one could hope to work with. It's hard to imagine
anybody more accommodating than Jack Nicklaus. He's had the
remarkable facility of being able to sign autographs for 30 minutes after a round, then come and talk to the press for an hour;
this after playing not particularly well.

The younger players are also for the most part comfortable
with the writers. Bobby Clampett says that his attitude is that if
somebody wants to talk golf with him, he'll find the time. Fred
Couples says that if he's approached properly — "and 99% of the
time I am" — then the encounter is fun. Paul Azinger is open to
real conversation, as is Tom Watson, perhaps the most thoughtful
golfer on the PGA Tour. Ray Floyd will chat at length, but is
likely to specify how long the interview will last. Once we met
over breakfast on Hilton Head Island, at 9 a.m. Floyd said he had
45 minutes. Forty-five minutes later he got up, without looking
at his watch. Nick Faldo and Payne Stewart are also quite willing
to sit down for a chat, though they may seem distant to the golf
fan. Of course a golfer needs to concentrate during the four
hours of a round. But during the 1991 Irish Open, Faldo and
Stewart sat and spoke candidly at the hotel where they were
staying.

As warm as the relationship between golfers and the writers can be, there is also another side. Golfers do get upset with writers, and writers with golfers. I found there was a distance to overcome when I started writing about the game in the mid-1970s. Golfers were wary of a newcomer, even if they were willing to talk. It wasn't until I had developed the rapport with golfers of which Gordon White spoke that the barriers started to break down. Maybe that's only natural, but it did make for some uncomfortable times.

I recall, for instance, an encounter with Johnny Miller in Las Vegas. The weather was steamy, and I had been trying to speak with Miller for some time. We finally arranged an interview, but when Miller came off the course one hot day, he decided he would rather do it another time. Feeling quite as hot as Miller, in every way, I told him that he and other golfers often complain that writers don't get to know the players well, and that we don't write enough interesting stories about them. I pointed out to him that we could understand them only if we spent some time with them, and that I was tired of running after him. I would write the story from what I knew, what I saw.

Miller told me to calm down, then invited me to talk in his room later. He asked at the beginning, rather diffidently, I thought, what I'd like to talk about. I said, "The swing." Miller seemed surprised. We were soon deeply into the subject and talked for two hours. The story worked out well, and a relationship that continues to inform my writing was established.

I mention this incident to point out that the relationship between players and writers should be a two-way street. Golfers too readily assume that writers are ignorant about the game. It's fair enough, I suppose, that the burden is on us to prove otherwise, but golfers might avoid strained relationships if they were not as quick to judge.

At the same time, many of the professionals' complaints are justified. David Graham, the 1979 PGA champion and the 1981 United States Open champion, has complained about what he calls non-ethical journalists. By non-ethical, he means the writer who will eavesdrop in the locker room to hear conversations between players, then write a story while taking the player's comments out of context. "If a guy wants to stick his foot in his mouth," Graham says, "let him. But *let* him. I appreciate honest journalism and the journalist who allows me to give bad press if I want to give it. But I think eavesdropping should be libellous. Unfortunately, it's not."

All pro golfers have experienced being misquoted or misrepresented. They wish they had more time after a poor round to cool down, or that writers wouldn't say they were angry when they refused to talk with them after shooting 75 while in contention. They don't appreciate talking to writers who don't know golf, even if they understand that a newspaper might be sending a football writer out to cover the one event in the area. And they certainly dislike leading questions that suggest the writer already has his story written.

Paul Azinger, for one, speaks for most golfers at one time or another when he says, "Sometimes I get so annoyed I never want to talk to the media again."

Azinger was asked during a tournament in Orlando in 1988, which he won, if he thought he could be the next dominant player. "I said I'd love to be the next dominant player," he explains, "but that it was tough in this day and age, what with so many good players." But Azinger's final words were chopped from the story that appeared. It came out as "I'd love to be the next dominant player." Azinger was concerned that he sounded cocky. And after the 1991 Ryder Cup, Azinger was accused in newspapers of comparing the U.S. victory over the Europeans to the U.S. victory over the Iraqis in the Gulf War. Azinger in his excitement had made a comment immediately upon entering the press room after the Ryder Cup that some people felt linked the events; he received hundreds of letters criticizing what he was quoted as saying. But Azinger claimed he never said that the U.S. thumped the Iraqis and now they thumped the Europeans. He spent some time and energy over the following months denying the statements attributed to him and apologizing for the way whatever he did say might have sounded. The power of the word is apparent.

This sort of occurrence is more common than we golf writers like to admit. Fred Wadsworth was doing well in the 1987 Memorial Tournament and was paired in the next round with Tom

Watson. Asked if he would be affected by the thought of playing with Watson, Wadsworth answered that he didn't think so, that he felt he would sleep well, and that the only player he would lose sleep over while contemplating playing with him the next day would be Jack Nicklaus.

"I cringed the next day," Wadsworth says. "It came out in the paper as a lack of respect for Tom Watson. I didn't mean that at all and felt badly. I have so much respect for Tom. I let it go, though, because I didn't know what to say to him. I hope Tom didn't take offence."

Watson probably didn't. Experienced golfers learn that they cannot control what is written about them. Says Bobby Clampett, once a golfer of much promise but now one who has not had the career expected of him: "I have never placed much importance on what is written about me. I'm more concerned about if I'm being the kind of person I want to be. My identity isn't dependent on what's written about me. Because I've held that view, I've been able to accept the good and the bad."

Clampett's point was that some golfers allow writers to mould their identity. He also points out that it's not surprising, though it is rare, that some golfers lose faith in writers. They become protective and sometimes withdraw. Even caddies sometimes withdraw from writers, though members of this generally loquacious group are more likely to speak freely. Yet Ian Baker-Finch's caddie, Pete Bender, has refused interviews since his experience after the 1986 British Open, when he worked for winner Greg Norman. Bender was quoted as saying some things that put other caddies down. He vowed never to talk to a writer again.

But Bender is by far the exception. Relations between writers, golfers, caddies, officials and the game at large, are for the most part pleasant. The game is just so full of incident; every player has a story, every tournament consists of story upon story, every course and place in the game is a library thick with rich material. In addition to *The Globe and Mail* pieces collected here, the reader will find longer stories from magazines, not all of them from golf magazines. Golf finds its way into many walks of life, precisely because a variety of people in cultures all over the world enjoy the sport.

This collection, then, represents the diversity of pleasures the game offers. Many pieces are entertainments, snapshots of a person or place, moments that caught and held my attention. Some pieces deal with the problems that arise in and around the game. There are articles that describe golf courses in faraway places, and the ways in which the people who inhabit these courses make travelling for golf an eye-opener.

Golf may be the finest game of all. As Ben Hogan concluded in his book, *The Modern Fundamentals of Golf,* "Whether my schedule for the following day called for a tournament round or merely a trip to the practice tee, the prospect that there was going to be golf in it made me feel privileged and extremely happy, and I couldn't wait for the sun to come up the next morning so that I could get out on the course again."

I feel the same way. As I write this, the snow has melted from the lawn in front of my home. The grass is beginning to turn green, birds are chirping and golf courses are preparing to open here. One week from today the Masters will begin at Augusta National, the loveliest place to be in April. Spring has arrived, the golf season is upon us and the Masters is here. That means more stories, more encounters around the game. I have enjoyed getting up every morning for the past 15 years because I never knew what the day would bring in the way of golf stories. The selection that follows is a record of what the days have brought. They have added up to a most agreeable life, and all because of golf.

Lorne Rubenstein
Toronto, April 1992

Chapter One

ARCHITECTS

THE PROFESSION of golf course architecture must be one of the most mysterious in the world. We golfers go out on a course and most of us simply play. Enjoying our round, we don't often stop to think that at one time this was not a golf course. We rarely consider the intelligence, more or less, that lies behind the lovely (more or less) course that we are playing. That doesn't stop us from making suggestions to our friends around the 19th hole; perhaps that bunker 15 yards short of the sixth doesn't belong, or why did the architect place a grassy hollow behind the green? You're not supposed to hit the ball over, are you? What purpose could a bunker have behind a green?

Golf course architects like to say that everything on their course was planned. Their signature is often apparent, of course, because one could no more hide a design style than a writing style. Still, Jack Nicklaus feels it's a compliment to him when a golfer can't be sure that he designed the course the fellow is playing; that means Nicklaus is showing variety in his work. At the same time, golfers these days collect golf courses in the sense that many enjoy playing, say, a Donald Ross course, or an A.W. Tillinghast course. It's sometimes fun to

1

play a course not knowing the architect, and then try to figure
out who designed it.

Course design is big business these days, and golf course architects are working at a dizzying pace. Jack Nicklaus has designed
courses in some 25 countries, from his beloved Muirfield Village
near his hometown of Columbus, Ohio, to Glen Abbey, the
home of the Canadian Open near Toronto, and on to courses in
Australia, Ireland, Spain and Zaire. He plays courses internationally, and he's a player in course design internationally.

Tom Fazio, meanwhile, turns down offers regularly from Japanese people who want him to design courses in their country;
but Japan is too far away for Fazio, who prefers not to be too far
from his wife and six children in North Carolina. He concentrates
on work in the United States above all and designed the amazing, flamboyant Shadow Creek course in Las Vegas for Steve
Wynn, the owner of the Mirage casino. He also designed with his
late uncle, George Fazio, Canada's top course, the National, in
Woodbridge, Ontario.

Golf course developers need not worry if Fazio won't travel to
build their courses far afield, however. There's Nicklaus, for one,
and many other architects willing to travel hundreds of thousands of miles in pursuit of their craft. Robert Trent Jones set the
tone by travelling some 250,000 miles a year. His son, Robert
Trent Jones Jr., as he is formally known, Bobby more informally,
has carried on where his father left off. He departed directly from
the 1992 Honda Classic at his new Weston Hills course in Ft.
Lauderdale for Paris, then on to Singapore before heading home
to San Francisco. His brother Rees doesn't travel as widely but,
like Bobby and his dad, has gathered a reputation for fine work.
Rees worked on restoring the Country Club in Brookline, Massachusetts, in time for the 1988 U.S. Open and did wonders to the
gracious layout. It was somehow old and modern at the same
time.

The articles included here touch on some of the architects in
the field. I write about Stanley Thompson, the Canadian who
took Robert Trent Jones in as a young man and who formed a
partnership with him. Thompson was boisterous and brash, and
he was Canada's most significant designer in the middle part of
this century.

I also take a look at Pete Dye, who designed the Tournament Players Club in Ponte Vedra, the site of the annual Players Championship, the PGA Tour's major event of its long season. Dye also designed the Ocean Course on Kiawah Island. Alice Dye is here as well; she's Pete's wife and an excellent designer in her own right, not to mention a fine player. There's a piece on Tom Fazio, who was voted top architect of the year in 1991 by his peers. There's a look at Tom McBroom, a Toronto-based architect who makes a point most years of studying some of the links courses in the U.K. He's a student of the game and the classic courses, as are all the best architects. And this chapter closes with a consideration of Desmond Muirhead, one of the most intriguing architects working today.

Robert Trent Jones

The Globe and Mail, **October 23, 1982**
Fifty years ago, golf began to evolve from a game of finesse into one of power. Steel had replaced hickory as material for golf club shafts; a golfer could swing hard without worrying that the shaft would twist in his hands.

The stability of the clubhead throughout the swing meant accuracy. The speed of the club head delivered squarely through the ball meant longer shots. Drives that went 220 yards with wood shafts travelled 250 yards. Scores fell as par, once good enough to win golf tournaments, no longer sufficed.

The trend to lower scoring accelerated in 1932 when Gene Sarazen fashioned and popularized the dynamiter, or sand wedge. That summer he won the British and U.S. Opens. Observers felt the club meant a difference of two shots a round. No longer was sand feared by competent golfers.

Courses weakened by equipment improvements were hardly a challenge to top golfers. Lesser players could drive into traps once reached only by the better golfers. Into the breach stepped Robert Trent Jones, in 1930 a 24-year-old golf enthusiast who had prepared for a career in golf course architecture by hand-picking a curriculum of studies at Cornell University in Ithaca, New York.

Upon an eclectic foundation of surveying, landscape architecture, hydraulics, agronomy, horticulture, chemistry, accounting, public speaking and journalism, Jones began to convert empty land into golf courses.

Jones believes a golf course should bring a "tingle of excitement" to the player. He should be able to stand on a tee, see the problem and choose a route by which he could traverse the hole, according to his abilities.

Jones initiated tier-trapping, a series of bunkers cut along the edges of fairways. Whether a golfer drove long or short, he was punished for an error. Should he be able to carry the traps, he was rewarded with a shorter approach to the green.

In line with the objectives of strategic golf, Jones began to use water hazards extensively. His namesake, the brilliant amateur Bobby Jones, once told him to be judicious in his use of water. "Remember, Robbie," Jones said while they inspected the site of the Atlanta Athletic Club, "that water is to a sand trap what an airplane accident is to an automobile accident. You can't recover from one, but you might from the other."

The apotheosis of Jones's work, and its first major expression, was the Peachtree Golf Club in Atlanta, designed with Bobby Jones in 1948. Tees as long as 80 yards and greens that averaged 8,000 square feet allowed flexibility in course setup. Pins could be placed in tight areas where they were defended by hazards; the better golfer could go for the pin, the lesser could use the entire green as his target. Jones attained his objective of each hole as a hard par, an easy bogey.

But wide recognition did not come to Trent Jones until he remodelled the outmoded Oakland Hills course in Birmingham, Michigan, for the 1951 U.S. Open. Donald Ross, an accomplished Scottish architect who did much of his best work in North America, had built the course in 1917. By 1951, the equipment changes made it too easy for major tournament play.

Jones pushed the sand traps out 30 yards from where they had been placed. Golfers didn't know what to make of a course that would catch their long, and often errant, drives.

That Oakland Hills would test the golfers' talents and nerves should have come as no surprise to players familiar with Jones's background. He seemed to have been born to build courses.

When Jones was 11, he spotted Walter Hagen coming up a dusty road in a white Packard to the Ross-designed Oak Hills Country Club in his hometown of Rochester, New York. Soon Jones was caddying for Hagen in exhibitions. When Ross visited the course, Jones picked his brain about design.

He also had a facility for playing. In 1927, he was low amateur in the Canadian Open at the Toronto Golf Club. He knew what made a course work and sensed the game was fun only if there were challenges. Soon he met Stanley Thompson, Canada's premier architect, and in 1930 collaborated with him on the Midvale Golf Club in Rochester. This soon led to the firm of Thompson and Jones, Ltd., with offices in Rochester and Toronto.

Thompson liked to stroll a course site before retiring to his study to mull it over. Fortified by a couple of bottles of the best whisky, Thompson's creative imagination would flower.

"Stanley was one of the most charming men I knew," Jones remembered while in Toronto to launch *Great Golf Stories*, a book he edited for Hurtig Publishers of Edmonton. "He could drink a tremendous amount of whisky and had the Hagen philosophy that you don't have to be a millionaire to live like one."

Thompson's methods worked. He built the Banff Springs course for the Canadian Pacific Railway and the Jasper Park course for the Canadian National Railway. Jones worked with him on the spectacular Capilano course in Vancouver.

Jones and Thompson dissolved their partnership amicably in 1938, the agreement being that each would work on projects that arose in their own countries. They continued to be friends, and when the American Society of Golf Course Architects was formed in the late forties, both were charter members. Ross was the first president, Thompson became president in 1949 and Jones in 1950.

At the 1951 U.S. Open at Oakland Hills, Jones watched the golfers take a beating from his work. Ben Hogan, the most accurate striker of the golf ball, was intimidated, as were all of the competitors.

In the first round, Hogan drove with a 2-wood rather than flirt with the traps in the landing zones. He was left with long-iron approaches into the target areas Jones had contoured into the greens. His first-round 76 suggested fear was not the correct response to the new Oakland Hills.

But in the succeeding rounds, Hogan changed his strategy. "Al Watrous [the head pro]," Jones said, "told him he had to attack the course."

Hogan pulled out his driver, shot 73 the second round, then 71 and 67 the last round. On the last hole, he carried the trap on the right side of the fairway at the dogleg and hit a 6-iron four feet from the hole to close with a birdie.

Hogan's win showed that a Trent Jones course could be handled. At the presentation ceremony, he acknowledged the struggle that must go on between the superior golf course and the superior golfer.

"I'm glad," Hogan said, "that I brought this course, this monster, to its knees."

Later that summer, Herbert Warren Wind profiled Jones in *The New Yorker* magazine. He gained wide recognition, and has since gone on to build more than 350 courses around the world. That adds up to more than 450 courses in 43 states and 24 foreign countries.

And there are lots more to come. At 76, the man shaped like Alfred Hitchcock seems years younger. His is a peripatetic existence. Thursday in Toronto, yesterday morning at home in Montclair, New Jersey, last night en route to Nice, France, where he is building three courses on the Riviera.

There is also a project near the Pyramids in Egypt, if Jones is granted the land, and one on the Red Sea from where the Sinai Desert is visible, and another on Mount Vesuvius in Italy. His latest Canadian work will open in the Kananaskis country of Alberta, in July. It is a public course, part of a project of the Alberta Department of Parks and Recreation, located 88 kilometres west of Calgary, 80 kilometres east of Thompson's masterpiece at Banff.

The years have done nothing to diminish Trent Jones's zeal. He is currently making changes at Oakland Hills again. "Those traps I put in for the 1951 U.S. Open," he said, "well, at the PGA Championship in 1979, the golfers were passing them. The long hitters like Dan Pohl and Tom Watson are driving the ball 270 to 280 yards now."

In 1951, Hogan's winning score in the U.S. Open was 287. David Graham won with 272 in the PGA in 1979, and then only after a playoff with Ben Crenshaw. Come the next major championship at Oakland Hills, it's likely the scores will be somewhat higher again, for this is Jones's mission and eventually will be his legacy: to preserve the challenge of the game.

Stanley Thompson

Score, Summer 1983

Nineteen twenty-two was a typical year for the golf course design firm of Stanley Thompson and Co., 24 King Street West, Toronto. That year the organization built or redesigned 11 courses in Canada: Elgin Golf and Country Club, London, Ontario; Thornhill Golf and Country Club, Thornhill, Ontario; York Downs Golf and Country Club, Toronto, Ontario; Uplands Golf and Country Club, Thornhill, Ontario; Cedar Brook Golf and Country Club, Toronto, Ontario; Briars Golf and Country Club, Jackson's Point, Ontario; Highland Golf and Country Club, London, Ontario; North Bay Golf and Country Club, North Bay, Ontario; Beach Grove Golf and Country Club, Walkerville, Ontario; Lingan Country Club, Sydney, Nova Scotia; and the Ashburn Golf and Country Club in Halifax, Nova Scotia.

That is how it was for the most highly regarded Canadian golf course architect, whose work can be seen and enjoyed across Canada. He designed some of the finest courses in the land: Banff Springs and Jasper Park, Capilano and Digby Pines, Kitchener Westmount and Kingston Cataraqui, Cape Breton Highlands and Anne of Green Gables. All bear his signature of pleasant opening holes, a routing that takes the player through what is best in the environment — streams, forest, sloping land — and on to a challenging finish. Thompson's layouts combine beauty with design inventiveness. One does not become bored playing his courses.

Thompson was born in 1894 and died in 1952. He came from a Canadian golfing family of five brothers, the likes of which has not been seen since. Frank won the Canadian Amateur in 1921 and 1924. Bill won in 1923. Nicol was head professional at the Hamilton Golf and Country Club in Ancaster, Ontario, for 50 years and runner-up in the 1913 Canadian Open. Matt moved to western Canada from Toronto and held a number of professional positions in Winnipeg and Brandon. And Stanley himself was quite a good player; most of the time he used only five clubs, and in the 1923 Canadian Amateur, when they were stolen, he merely borrowed a set and was a medallist with 72 in the qualifying round.

Thompson's real contribution to golf, though, was in his course design. He partnered Robert Trent Jones for eight years beginning in 1930, keeping offices in Rochester and Toronto. Later, they separated to take on work in their respective countries. In his own firm, Thompson worked with and influenced such Canadian designers as Howard Watson, C.E. (Robbie) Robinson, Norman Woods, Kenneth Welton, Robert Moote and Geoffrey S. Cornish. Along with Trent Jones and Scotsman Donald Ross — designer of Pinehurst No. 2 in North Carolina and Seminole in Florida — he was a charter member in 1948 of the American Society of Golf Course Architects. Ross was the president that year, Thompson in 1949 and Trent Jones in 1950.

In addition to those in Canada, Thompson designed courses in the Caribbean, the United States, Brazil and Colombia. He also left marks of another kind upon the people he came in contact with; he was an ebullient and joyous man who loved to live.

Thompson's zest for life took many forms. One is reminded of the wonderful British golf writer Henry Longhurst's lifelong philosophy he called "gap-filling," or trying anything at least once that he had not tried before. To this end, Thompson added a healthy disregard for money that would brand him an eccentric today, when course design, of necessity, has become concerned with high costs. Thompson was one to get the job done, and with flair. If that meant spending a few extra dollars of someone else's money, well, so be it.

On one occasion, Thompson was given a budget of $500,000 to build the Jasper Park course in Alberta, courtesy of the owners, the Canadian National Railway. Before the course was completed, Thompson ran out of money. Not to worry, though, for Thompson simply sat down with the Board of the CNR, waxed eloquent and came away with the necessary funds to secure completion.

Trent Jones, still as active as ever in course design, remembers his ex-partner vividly, and when he speaks of him, it is always with a smile and a chuckle. "Stanley was absolutely the most charming guy you could meet," he says. "He would meet guys ready to cut his throat, for he would have gotten them in financial trouble, but in 10 minutes he would have them right in his hands. He always had this little joke to break the tension. He'd take off on a tangent that would distract them, like 'Did you see that little bird land? Aren't the aerodynamics of bird flight remarkable?'"

According to Trent Jones, Thompson did not want to be a millionaire. He wanted merely to live like one. "He was a free spirit," Trent Jones says. "He had a tremendous personality. You couldn't dislike him. He was so generous he would lend money to people who needed it but then wouldn't pay the people he worked with. But he never meant any harm. He just loved to have a good time and to make people happy."

So healthy was Thompson's appetite for life that it becomes hard to separate what is real from what is apocryphal. One story that is true concerns the manner in which he contoured the ninth fairway at the Jasper Park course. As one stood on the tee, the full-bodied figure of Cleopatra came into view. Sir Harry Thornton, then head of the Canadian National Railway, was playing a round with Thompson and could not help but notice the adornments to the hole. However, he was not amused.

"Mr. Thompson," he said, "we have been friends for many years. I never thought you would have the audacity to do this to the Canadian National." Thompson smoothed out some of the curves, but the hole always kept the name Cleopatra.

So imaginative was this cigar-chomping, Scotch-loving bear of a man that he was not only more than willing to define and shape a hole with an outline of the female form, but he would build sand traps to call to mind other natural forms: a rose, a giant footprint, an artist's palette. He aligned greens with the peaks of surrounding mountains so that golfers could more easily line up shots.

Thompson once built a unique miniature golf course on the grounds of the Old Mill, just west of Toronto's Bloor Street bridge at the Humber River. The 18-hole course was built on two acres; each hole was from 50 to 200 feet. The greens were contoured, trapped and bunkered; shrubs and flower borders provided hazards. It took about 45 minutes to play, and the fee was 50 cents per round.

In the 1930s, Thompson went himself one better when he designed a golf course on three acres virtually in downtown Toronto. In conjunction with a Toronto syndicate of movie-house owners, he fashioned the Pinehurst Golf Course just a few blocks south of the intersection of Yonge Street and St. Clair Avenue. The property had a frontage of 328 feet on the west side of Yonge Street, 360 feet on Jackes Avenue and 185 feet on Woodlawn Avenue, for a total of 90,000 square feet. The shortest hole was 20 yards, the longest 65. Lunches, teas and dinners were served in the clubhouse. Glen Brydson, brother of Gordon, long-time pro at the Mississaugua Golf and Country Club, was the pro at Pinehurst.

It seemed that everybody sought Thompson's hand in their golf courses. One day, he was busily engaged in a sand trap on the Banff Springs course when a ball struck him on the shoulder. Soon there followed one Harry Oakes, an eccentric mine owner who later became a baronet and then the victim in a sensational murder mystery. Seizing the opportunity, he asked Thompson if he would build a golf course for him on his estate near Niagara Falls, Ontario. He wanted a 20-hole course with no fairway shorter than 900 yards, no traps, no doglegs, no rough, no ponds and no hills. Within a month, Thompson was at work, but when the project was nearly done, Oakes decided he wanted six extra holes. Thompson advised him this could call for building a peninsula into the Niagara River. Oakes dropped the project, paid Thompson $30,000 and put sheep to graze over the land.

Another time, Thompson designed the Cutten Fields course in Guelph, Ontario, for Arthur W. Cutten, a fabulously wealthy grain merchant from Chicago. Eventually, Thompson bought the course, solely on the rumour that Cutten had stashed a million dollars' worth of negotiable securities in the clubhouse walls. Thompson then pulled up boards, tore down walls and searched everywhere for the money, which was never found. However, the clubhouse did become Thompson's home, called Dormie House, and overlooked the course that spread below him. Many a day he would sit in his office with a selection of fine cigars and some excellent Scotch and gradually let his latest walk over a piece of property sink into his fertile mind. In this way, many of Canada's finest courses were born.

Thompson was truly a Renaissance man; he combined intimate knowledge of engineering and drainage principles with the artist's eye for shape, detail, background and land flow. "He had great feel for what I call movement of land masses," Trent Jones says.

In a booklet called *About Golf Courses: Their Construction and Up-Keep*, Thompson elucidated his philosophy of course design. He wrote: "Nature must always be the architect's model. The lines of bunkers and greens must not be sharp or harsh, but easy and rolling. The development of the natural features and planning the artificial work to conform to them require a great deal of care and forethought. In clearing fairways, it is good to have an eye to the beautiful. Often it is possible, by clearing away undesirable and unnecessary trees on the margin of fairways, to open up a view of some attractive picture and frame it with foliage . . . Oftentimes the natural beauty of many a golf course, which the average player assumes was always present, has been created by the skill of the engineer who can see opportunities for beauty in the rough woods, swamps or fields that mean nothing to the unskilled eye. The absence or presence of the above features, among others, will decide whether continuous play on a course becomes monotonous or otherwise."

Thompson felt a successful course was one that tested the skill of the low-handicapper without discouraging the high-handicapper. He believed both should enjoy themselves and attain from a round the same invigoration he felt when designing courses. He knew golf was played with all the senses, and in his courses like Capilano, with its views of Vancouver and Grouse Mountain, or a relatively unknown course like Uplands in Thornhill, Ontario, with its rolling hills, twisting par-fours and difficult finish through trees and chasms, he has attained all one could ask of a course architect. His courses are memorable; they are a privilege to play and constant sources of pleasure.

Pete Dye

The Globe and Mail, **April 6, 1984**
Amelia Island, Florida — A golf course designer's early work can be likened to a writer's first book or a director's first movie. It shows the form his abilities took when he was just beginning his trade. In the way it shapes and imposes structure upon a landscape, creates tension and builds to a conclusion or resolution, it suggests how well the designer handled the raw materials of his profession.

So it has been with all designers: Stanley Thompson, who designed Capilano in Vancouver and Banff in Alberta; A.W. Tillinghast, designer of Winged Foot in Mamaroneck, New York, where the U.S. Open will be played this June; Jack Nicklaus, who built Glen Abbey in Oakville, Ontario, and Shoal Creek in Birmingham, Alabama, homes of the Canadian Open and PGA Championship, respectively, this summer; and Pete Dye, the highly regarded and controversial architect of the Tournament Players Club in Ponte Vedra, Florida, and the 27 holes of the Amelia Links on Amelia Island Plantation near the Georgia-Florida border, where he did some of his first work in the early 1970s.

Amelia rates as one of Dye's favourite courses, perhaps because it tells him just where he was way back when. It shows an architect with a flair for the dramatic, as is so evident at the TPC. That flair, however, is only hinted at on the links at Amelia.

Mounds near the eighth green on the Oceanside nine, for example, are flowing, gentle arrangements rather than the tumbling bursts of earth that protect the right side of the 18th green at the TPC. A lake, around which are the final three holes of this nine, is more picturesque than penalizing. Certainly it is not the menace that the lake at the 18th at the TPC is.

Dye's concept of how a green should play is also evident at Amelia. Most putts have some sort of break, not always easily seen. A golfer is asked to co-ordinate the speed of the putt with the contour of the green, and although the greens are hardly as up and down as those at the TPC, they do demand a sense of touch.

Over the years, a Dye trademark has been a liberal use of railroad ties to shore up bunkers or ponds. There are many examples at Harbor Town Golf Links on Hilton Head Island, South Carolina, another Dye creation. At Amelia, Dye has used railroad ties in a recent reworking of the first hole on the Oysterbay nine.

The 290-yard, very narrow par-four hole originally played to a green hidden beyond clumps of rough ground that edged into the fairway. But the hole was too easy for better golfers. So Dye came in and, with course superintendent Ron Hill, added another green to the right, behind a pond that uses railroad ties as bulwarks. When the right-side green is in use, the hole is eminently more challenging on the approach shot.

That emphasis on the approach shot is quite apparent throughout Amelia. A tree near the green of the par-five, 540-yard second hole on the Oakmarsh nine requires the golfer to manoeuvre the ball. It would have been a simple matter to leave the green unprotected, particularly on a resort course that caters to all skill levels. But Dye introduced the element of shot selection and so built a stronger hole.

Dye's imagination at Amelia is another appealing quality. He had little formal training in course architecture and brings to his work an openness that rewards the golfer.

The seventh hole on the Oysterbay nine, for example, plays at 159 yards from the white tees and 163 yards from the blue. The difference hardly seems worth mentioning. But it is a perfect example of a principle: Never judge a course by its scorecard.

From the 159-yard tee, the golfer plays directly across the fairway to the green. The 163-yard tee is placed about 100 yards diagonally from the shorter tee. From there, the golfer must carry 155 yards across a salt marsh. The hole is an early version of the 17th at the TPC with its island green: Miss the green short, and it's a lost ball. At the TPC, of course, a lost ball is virtually any shot that misses the green.

In both cases, there is adventure. In both cases, the golfer feels an emotional high when he hits the green.

Dye courses are also noteworthy for the ways in which he blends holes with the environment. At Amelia, there is the wildness of the salt marshes and the beauty of oceanside holes.

There is a wonderful moment on the seventh hole at Oysterbay when the golfer emerges from the holes that play through dense forest of live oak and Spanish moss to the vastness of the salt marsh. On the Oceanside nine, there is an exhilarating moment when the golfer comes over the crest of a path to see sand dunes, whitecaps on the ocean and a long expanse of beach; the next three holes are threaded through the dunes.

This series of holes also includes two consecutive par-threes. Some architects have shied away from using land in this way, but Dye knew early in his career that if the landscape suggested that arrangement, there was no reason to ignore it. Mackenzie did the same with the 15th and 16th at Cypress Point in Pebble Beach, California. They are probably the most glorious oceanside holes in the world.

Given Dye's work at Amelia Island, it is no surprise to see that he has become such a force in the golf world. At the TPC, he did have problems with going too far in his contouring of the greens, but that was only his imagination knowing no boundaries. At Amelia, he allowed his imagination to trickle out and, in so doing, built 27 holes that, if it were possible, could one day be put in a museum of golf courses.

Tom Fazio

The Globe and Mail, **April 12, 1987**
Whether a golf course designer is a villain or a friend depends on the current fancies of the players who try his layouts. Coloured as their opinions are by the standards of their play, golfers' ideas are not always to be taken seriously. What matters more is the look of the course, how it plays and the ways in which it maintains the integrity of the environment without compromising the challenges of the sport.

Of designers getting plenty of work these days, none is more conscientious than Tom Fazio. Fazio, 42, has designed some 90 courses since he started as a teenager with his late uncle, former touring professional George Fazio. Young as designers go — Robert Trent Jones is 80 and still busy — Fazio has the reputation of a man who loves the land first. Next comes the course, and it's usually a beauty.

Yesterday morning, Fazio woke up in Jupiter, Florida, near Palm Beach, where his office has been located for 15 years. He then flew by private plane over his real offices — some courses he has been designing in the southeast, particularly South Carolina — and touched down at Kiawah Island, not far from one of his latest and most pristine courses, Osprey Point.

Just a few minutes after he arrived, Fazio was on the course. It won't open until the spring of 1988, but it is, as Fazio claimed, "a soft, gentle course." Riding around in a four-wheeler, Fazio demonstrated by the pure conviction of his word and the sweep of his views that he cares about his responsibilities.

Osprey Point is set in the midst of a 10,000-acre sanctuary for both golfers and wildlife. (Given golfers' temperaments, it's not always easy to distinguish the life forms.) The course is routed around four lakes, marshland and woods and vegetation so thick it's hard to believe a course could be built here.

But Fazio did build a course here, and golfers who tee it up when the course opens will enjoy the results, not to mention the peace and quiet. Osprey Point is far removed from the hurly-burly of those courses that are simply excuses for residential development.

"In my opinion," Fazio said, "anything done to a landscape or natural area is an encroachment. If you're not a golfer, what does it mean to you that we've built a good hole? All you want to know is why we cut down these trees. And I think that's good. The fact is that you have to take a piece of property and work with it."

In building Osprey Point, Fazio worked closely with a South Carolina environmental protection agency called the Coastal Council. Agents made random helicopter turns on a daily basis over the property to check on the development. They took aerial photos as the course progressed and compared them with photos taken when there wasn't so much as a vehicle on the land.

Standing on the par-three, 165-yard third hole, Fazio showed how he incorporated environmental features. The tee was set on one side of untouched marshland that extended east as far as the eye could see. The green was angled along an edge of the marsh and was framed by thick stands of live oaks. Your eye was drawn to the green, but also to the marsh and the wild, twisted trees sticking up from it.

Had Fazio wanted to build fairway turf in place of marsh, he couldn't have. Regulations required him to keep the marsh, just as they required him to build 11 wooden bridges to get the golfer from greens to tees to fairway. More than anything, Fazio has worked with the environment to maintain its natural feel.

The bridges also serve as viewing sites for bird-watchers. (Ben Crenshaw would be happy here; he's as comfortable with binoculars in his hands to watch birds as he is with a putter in his hands to sink putts.) Osprey Point seems to have more wildlife than a zoo; there are 140 different birds, 18 varieties of mammals and more than 30 examples of reptiles and amphibians.

Fazio, like most modern course architects, is more than happy to let the animal life be. Besides, he is dealing with law, "my friend and yours," he says, rather than the golfer's and course designer's enemy.

"Many times," Fazio said as he toured Osprey Point, "you hear that the agencies restrict us and complicate our courses or cause us to do things we don't want to do. I don't agree. Anyway, there isn't one way to do a course."

Fazio has designed 126 golf holes in and around Charleston alone. Not one, he's willing to bet, looks like another. That is in part because of the differing landscapes but also because of his handiwork. Recreational golfers are fortunate that there are people like Fazio in the business and that they are imaginative enough to design courses that meet environmental standards.

Dye's Approach to Tees Fashionable for Women

The Globe and Mail, **March 16, 1989**
Canadians who follow the PGA Tour may be watching this week's Players Championship at the Pete Dye-designed Tournament Players Club in Ponte Vedra, Florida. But they might want to cast their eyes farther south, to Casa de Campo in the Domini-

can Republic, where Alice Dye, Pete's wife and a course architect herself, is continuing her work of making courses more manageable for women.

Dye, 59, is the only female member of the American Society of Golf Course Architects. She's demonstrating that women need more than one set of tees at a course. That's the way it's been for years for men.

Dye reasons that a typical course might be, oh, 7,000 yards from the back tees. The pros and best amateurs will play these tees. The next set of tees might be 6,600 yards, from where most male golfers will play. Another forward set may be 6,100 yards, from where high-handicappers, older golfers and women will play.

The problem is obvious, though nobody before Dye has addressed it. Men usually have three sets of tees from which to choose. A low-handicap male can compete against a higher handicap male if each plays tees appropriate to his ability. But women of varying abilities and strengths have but one set of tees.

According to Dye, who plays to a two-handicap and has won numerous amateur tournaments, the problem wasn't addressed in the past because it didn't need to be. Courses weren't overwatered. The ground was firm. A woman could drive a ball down the fairway and watch it roll another 50 yards.

"Women and older guys could hit two shots on a par-four and get in the vicinity of the green," Dye said yesterday from Casa de Campo, where she and her husband have a winter home. (Pete Dye designed two fine courses there, both of which have two sets of women's tees.) "And nowadays all the fairways are also bent grass instead of bluegrass. Bent is softer, so the ball doesn't go as far when it lands."

Dye didn't say so, perhaps because she was being diplomatic, but it's also true that nearly all courses in the history of the game were designed by men for men. Women's needs weren't considered.

Dye's elegant solution is to introduce at least two sets of tees so that the holes set up well for them. She's produced a poster that explains the principles. She also spoke at a recent summit on the state of the game and last month addressed 2,000 people at the Golf Course Superintendents' Association of America meeting in Anaheim, California. A few women are following her lead by apprenticing themselves to course architects.

Dye's point of view makes sense. As she indicated, at least a third of the game used to be along the ground before courses were overwatered. And women drive the ball only 130 yards in the air on average. Courses are virtually unplayable for all but the longest-hitting women.

"The average course for women is 5,800 yards in the U.S.," Dye said. "It should be 5,000 yards."

Dye's thinking also applies to men. Typically, a group of golfers will play the same set of tees, even if they vary greatly in the distance they can hit the ball.

"Suppose you built a 400-yard par-four," Dye said. "Three fellows who drive within 40 yards of another play it. The first guy drives 240 yards and has a 160-yard shot left. That's an 8-iron for him. The next fellow drives 220 yards and hits a 4-iron for his 180 yards. The guy who drives 200 yards has 200 left and can't reach the green. He'll say we built an unplayable hole for him. The longer hitter will feel the hole doesn't challenge him. All three should play different tees."

Men at least have those different tees. Women usually don't. Oddly, Dye hasn't had the easiest time convincing women that her ideas are workable. They're concerned that their handicaps will decrease if they play forward tees, i.e., shorter courses. Then they won't be able to win prizes at tournaments.

"But their handicaps won't change," Dye explained. "The course rating will change, so the relative differences between scores and ratings, which handicaps are based on, will remain the same."

Dye's ideas are taking hold. Most new courses include more than one set of tees for women, and women who understand that their handicaps won't change are playing the appropriate tees.

"I've had a real good response to this," Dye said. "I don't want to ram it down people's throats. I want them to see that it will work."

Dye and her husband recently designed a new course at Mission Hills in Palm Springs, where the Nabisco Dinah Shore LPGA event is played each winter. The course, known as the Dinah Shore course, has three sets of tees for women. It's meant to be the new site of the LPGA event.

This means that women will be able to play the same course as the LPGA pros without partaking of four or five hours of masochism. All a woman need do is pick the right tees for her game.

That's the key — choosing the proper tees. Alice Dye is doing the game a service by pointing out that course designers should take women's golf into account. The American Society of Golf Course Architects should be pleased that she has taken up membership in their group.

Tom McBroom

The Globe and Mail, **April 3, 1990**
Sometimes it seems that Canadian golf course architects are taking over the landscape. From sea to shining sea or, more properly, from tee to tee, they're creating private and resort courses, along with a few public ones. "The times have never been busier," said Tom McBroom, a respected Toronto-based designer.

Among other major Canadian designers are Graham Cooke and John Watson in Quebec; Doug Carrick, Bob Moote and Rene Muylaert in Ontario; and Les Furber, Rod Wittman and Bill Robinson out west. All are about as busy as they want to be, but 37-year-old McBroom seems to be emerging as spokesman for the profession in Canada.

He began his company in 1978 and has had the good fortune in recent years of working closely with Atlanta designer Bob Cupp on Beacon Hall in Aurora, Ontario. Beacon Hall is a private equity club in which members own a transferable share, and it has a reputation as a top-notch course, retaining a natural feel while providing the exciting golf that sensitive designers can produce with their efforts.

"Beacon Hall was a tremendous experience for me," McBroom said. "It was an opportunity to co-design and build what I think is a world-class course."

Building that kind of course is every designer's dream. But, just as the best jockey cannot win on a poor horse, the finest architect cannot make an Augusta National course from poor ground. Young designers especially must take on projects on less-than-attractive ground if they are to get ahead.

McBroom learned a lesson when he worked on Millcroft in Burlington, Ontario. The club has a fine junior-development program, but the course was really only an excuse for a real estate development. McBroom said he did what he could, but the holes are wedged in between homes. McBroom does not like the feeling of confinement at Millcroft or at short executive courses that are usually 5,000 yards or fewer.

"Golf is a game steeped in tradition. It has certain dimensions, a usual balance of par-threes, fours and fives. I think people want traditional golf experiences. That's why they go back to England and Scotland."

McBroom went on to design Cranberry Village and Monterra in Collingwood, Ontario. As well, he has been involved in the public Hockley Valley course northwest of Toronto, scheduled to open this year; Camelot, an equity club in Ottawa; renovations at the Ottawa Hunt club; and other projects.

"The Ottawa Hunt project is a major renovation of a Willie Park course. I like to say Willie Park and I are doing it. You have to pretend you're him, that you've been reborn. It's the only way to retain the character of the course. I see a renewed appreciation of the work of the early designers — Willie Park, Donald Ross, A.W. Tillinghast, Stanley Thompson. That's a good sign."

McBroom has worked on land that sweeps through both forest and open links-like land, as at Beacon Hall. Deerhurst is in rock country on a site so barren that all the fill and topsoil needed to be imported. Hockley Valley is virtually treeless and plays up and down and over natural hollows, with an elevation change of 350 feet.

McBroom was steeped in the game. His grandfather played at Rosedale in Toronto, an exclusive club that Cupp is remodelling (with Donald Ross, as *he* says) by putting in bunkers and reshaping greens so that it resembles the original design. McBroom also played at Credit Valley in Mississauga, is a member at Beacon

Hall and carries a five handicap that, like all busy golfers, he sometimes plays to.

But he also has a feel for the public golfer. "The wave of the future is in good, public courses. We're finding a more sophisticated golfer today. The result is that the whole notion of resort and public courses is changing in Canada. Before, we had mediocre turf, short courses. We're catering to a different golfer now."

The development is working its way into municipal courses. McBroom is rebuilding the Humber Valley course for the Metropolitan Toronto Parks and Property Department — nine holes last year and nine this year.

"The course was not in good shape. The greens were too small for the amount of play, plus there was a problem with safety due to congestion. Our objective is to improve the conditions so that we can provide good, basic golf at a reasonable price."

But it's not always easy to create the desired result. For one thing, land costs are prohibitive these days. And when land is found, architects are faced with strict environmental controls.

"Golf course design must respond to the natural environment," McBroom said in an address to a recent Canadian golf summit in Toronto. "That is as it should be. We must preserve wildlife habitats and wetland marsh areas. Water is a key issue, so we must use grasses that respond to less water.

"The environmental-approval process is going to get more complicated, not less. The regulatory people are looking closely at us. We have to deal with this thoughtfully, to hire wildlife biologists and hydrolists, among other experts in the area."

McBroom is also worried that golf may be moving away from its traditions, what with mandatory carts instead of walking, high-tech equipment and clubs so expensive to join that only wealthy golfers or those willing to make extreme financial sacrifices will be able to play.

What of the future?

McBroom thinks golfers will drive farther to play, two hours or more, as they do to ski. He envisions more naturalness in design to keep costs down, while working with environmental agencies.

"The costs of golf course development tend to be astronomical. Something will have to give. I think it will be the clubhouse. The days of the 30,000 to 40,000-square-foot clubhouse will disappear. You're looking to a traditional course, minimal clubhouse. Change your shoes, play, then have a beer. This might help us get back to the roots of the game."

Desmond Muirhead

The Globe and Mail, **October 31, 1991**
Sports fields are not often perceived as environments in which designers can create exciting forms. Baseball diamonds and tennis courts are essentially static areas with fixed dimensions. Designers work more with the stadia that surround the playing fields than the centres of action themselves.

But one playing field, a golf course, differs: Its 18 holes wander over 150 acres or so and can assume a remarkable variety of shapes. Hence the need for a course architect or designer. Some architects earn upwards of $1 million per project.

Of golf course designers working today, none is more imaginative than Desmond Muirhead, who expresses philosophical ideas in his courses by the use of symbolic land forms. Muirhead, 68, spoke Monday at Harbourfront in Toronto as part of Virtu's Centrifuge design lecture series.

Muirhead, who was born in London and was educated at Cambridge University, later studied horticulture at the universities of British Columbia and Oregon. He eventually designed the Muirfield Village course in Dublin, Ohio, with Jack Nicklaus, probably golf's finest player ever.

Muirfield Village opened in 1973 and ranks as one of North America's finest courses. But Muirhead and Nicklaus had a falling-out while working on it. Muirhead left course design in 1974 and did not return until 1984, when he created Aberdeen in Boynton Beach, Florida.

Muirhead, who describes himself as "mercurial," had in the meantime opened an art gallery in Costa Mesa, California, which he said was "like shooting yourself in the foot, a self-inflicted wound." He also designed four new towns in Australia, of which one has been built. Inevitably, perhaps, he found his way back to course design, this time with renewed energy and purpose.

While walking the site at Aberdeen, he saw that a golf course was symbolic, in that so much happened to a player during a game. So, he thought, why not represent themes of beginning and end, danger and reward, in the course? Why not link holes to create a narrative?

"The idea was not new," Muirhead said at a Toronto hotel Monday prior to his lecture. "The Old Course in St. Andrews, Scotland (home of golf for centuries), is the genesis of course design. It's full of symbols, holes called the Hole O'Cross and Ginger Beer and bunkers named the Principal's Nose, the Grave and the Valley of Sin," the latter being a deep hollow at the front of the final green from which only the rare golfer emerges un-scathed. "The Old Course is sacred ground. The moment you step on it you feel it. And much of the symbolism is religious, from the Calvinist town."

His symbols at Aberdeen are apparent everywhere, although best appreciated from aerial shots of the course. One hole takes the shape of a dragon snorting smoke. There is peril here, but also reward for reaching the target across a lake.

"A symbol tells you about something in a way that is different from how you see it normally," he pointed out. "It's more stimu-lating to do it this way than just putting a hole in the ground."

Aberdeen has been received sceptically by architects, many of whom scorn Muirhead's use of symbolism. But golfers enjoy Ab-erdeen, and other architects, such as Canadian designer Thomas McBroom, say that golf needs Muirhead.

Muirhead's new Shinyo course in Japan incorporates the ge-stalt psychology principle of closure. Surrounding mountains frame a hole and turn it into a theatre. Here he has also used the Japanese principle of "borrowing on distant space," whereby the mountains beyond the course make the course seem more spa-cious.

"I think of [John Stuart] Mill writing *On Liberty*. Nothing is more emancipating than being on a golf course. It's like going into a nursery. It's soothing to be surrounded by green grass and water. You're in haunts where beauty dwells."

Chapter Two

COURSES

MICHAEL MURPHY wrote in his delightfully wise book, *Golf in the Kingdom*, that the golfer begins at the tee, a wide and open place, and ends up at the hole, a small and dark place. We golfers repeat this sequence 18 times a round; it's our journey. Murphy suggests the trip is an analogue of life, for we begin with all the world ahead of us and finish under the ground. But in golf there's a difference: We pick ourselves up from our burial spot and continue. We have chances to redeem ourselves in our sometimes dangerous, sometimes peaceable trek over 18 holes.

To travel from course to course is similar, except on an even broader scale. To a golfer, the world consists of places to visit, distant beacons whose signposts have familiar and not so familiar names: Pebble Beach, the Old Course, Royal Portrush, maybe the Homestead or the Sagamore or little-known Wawashkamo, a peaceful nine-holer on Mackinac Island on Michigan's Upper Peninsula. We visit these places, yet at the same time we also have our home courses in mind. They are reference points, and it is to our home course that inevitably we compare all others. We come to endow our home course, be it grand or humble, with special qualities. We may like a feature there that we belittle elsewhere.

The golf journey I have taken is hardly complete, but I, like all players, have my favourite courses. I begin this selection at home, where my heart is, at the National Golf Club in Woodbridge, Ontario, just outside of my hometown, Toronto. This is the toughest course in Canada, rated at 77.0 from the back tees, though it is under 7,000 yards; golfers also rate it the country's number one course. I don't put much stock in top 25 or top 100 lists, but somehow, illogically, it's pleasing to play most of my golf at the course rated the best in Canada. Yet it's not the National's severity off the tees or into the greens that ultimately keeps me there. No, it's the feeling I get as I drive along the road to the course that parallels the 12th hole, a par-five shaped like a figure eight deep into the wooded valley portion of the course. I like to drive by early in the morning when the dew is still on the fairway and the course is still untouched. My pulse quickens, I come alive to the day. I'm entering a beautiful place.

Anticipation accounts for a substantial amount of the excitement we can feel when we think about playing a new course, or returning to a much-loved favourite. The National is my touchstone, but other courses have beckoned and continue to do so. I write here of learning how bentgrass works in the heat of southern Florida on the Jack Nicklaus-designed Loxahatchee course. Nicklaus and other architects often refer to a Scottish feeling in the courses they have been building; by that they mean a rumpled look to the fairways, an open-to-the-wind atmosphere on the course. But still there's nothing like visiting the links of Scotland, and especially at old Prestwick does the feeling of the game as it was played a century ago prevail. Blind shots, mammoth bunkers, smallish greens nestled in hollows: Prestwick has them all. The old lives, and we know it's pure golf.

Pure golf is also available at the Sagamore in upstate New York and The Orchards in South Hadley, Massachusetts. Both are Donald Ross courses, and both are challenging while offering leisurely golf in pristine environments. They get the juices going. They represent the gems that await any curious golfer.

Maybe that's the main ingredient that wandering golfers share: They are curious, and so they end up in unlikely places that in memory evoke pleasant feelings. Never would have I imagined that I would one day golf in West Africa and combine my visit with a safari; or that I would hear the kind of story that my caddy Larry told me one day while I played Royal Portrush in Northern Ireland; or that the summer of 1991 would find me with my wife, Nell, walking quietly, the two of us the only people on the nine-hole Wawashkamo course in her native Michigan. We learned of the history of this gentle course that had deteriorated until a gentleman who cared came along and began to put it back together again. I write that the name of the course came from the verb wa-wash-kamo; an Indian chief noted that the golfers wa-wash-kamo, walk a crooked path, that is. All golfers do that, for it is a crooked path indeed that leads us to courses.

THE NATIONAL

The Globe and Mail, **October 28, 1983**
It is a jewel of a golf course, known simply as the National.

And national it is, this masterwork of design in Woodbridge, Ontario, that is becoming recognized, one-two with Glen Abbey Golf Club in Oakville, Ontario, as Canada's finest course. Yet this unofficial ranking has emerged without the fanfare generated from the presentation of major golf championships.

The only tournament of consequence held at the National so far was the 1979 Labatt's International for the Canadian Professional Golfers' Association championship, won by Lee Trevino.

The National is everything a great golf course should be. It has variety, as conceived by owner Gil Blechman and created by architects George and Tom Fazio. It has difficulty, as attested to by anybody who plays it at any length from the 7,015 yards off the back markers to the 6,142 yards off the front ones.

The National is a dramatic golf course, as underscored by golfers who come to the par-four 17th and 18th holes needing pars or birdies to win matches. Both holes are separated by a lake that seems too calm to send a golfer's heart racing with anxiety. Both greens are set on promontories that remind an observer of Point Garry In and Point Garry Out at North Berwick in Scotland. There is flavour in these holes, and there is character.

George Knudson, who plays the National on those rare days that he leaves his teaching duties at Buttonville Fairways, has seen the havoc wreaked by the National's final holes.

"It doesn't matter how many shots I give guys I'm playing," Knudson says, "when the money's on the line and they're looking at 17 and 18, if they aren't sure where their ball is going, I'm a winner."

Still, the National, like all the best courses — Augusta National, Glen Abbey, Pebble Beach, St. Andrews — does give up low scores, when the quality of the golf is high. When Trevino shot 67 during the 1979 CPGA, he closed with four consecutive birdies. And he had to play different types of shots to each hole: a slinging, low 3-iron that faded near the pin at the front of the green on the par-three 15th; a high drop shot that floated on to the wavy 16th green; an arrow of a 7-iron within a few feet of the 17th hole; and a 4-iron to the 18th that seemed to stay in the air forever as it rode the up escalator to the home green.

In those last holes, Trevino not only defined his character but stamped the National as a supreme test of golf. That it would succumb to wonderful golf strokes may have surprised observers who felt the course was simply too hard.

For there is much more than harshness to the National. More than being a relentless exploration of a golfer's talents and more than providing a stage for the emotions, it is a course concordant with the values of a centuries-old game. It seems to have always been there.

The National fits with the landscape. Its shadings of green delight the eye; its tightly knit fairways join seamlessly with the fringes of greens. It runs downhill and uphill and sidehill. Around the fifth and sixth holes, there is the sense of open space common to Scottish links. At the edge of the course, in the corners of the 11th and 12th holes, there is the feeling of privacy one gets around Amen Corner at Augusta National.

That these elements of the game are combined in one modern golf course comes as no surprise when one meets owner Blechman. He is a man of vision, born in Brooklyn, New York, never a golfer until he came to Canada in 1951.

Blechman jokingly calls himself the worst kind of Canadian, "one who came here by choice." He is the sole owner of a company called Design Dynamics in Oakville, Ontario, which manufactures auto seat covers. But the National is his first love, though he has lost substantial amounts of money on it every year since 1977, when he bought out partners Harvey Kalef and Irv Hennick.

But there is no bitterness in Blechman's voice when he discusses the National. How could there be? He has shaped something beautiful with the force of his convictions.

Before the course was opened for play in 1974, Blechman often drove with his wife in the middle of the night to the lookout over what later became the 17th and 18th holes. "I would shine my headlights down there," he says, "and say, 'See, honey, that's a lake, and that's going to make these finishing holes special.'" As indeed they are.

Blechman, however, is quick to point out there is much more to the National than his own contribution. In recent years, he has assembled a management team that is gradually making the club economically sound as well as enjoyable to play. He knows the club simply cannot go on losing money.

To that end, Blechman's team includes Ben Kern, the director of golf, course superintendent Kenny Wright — hired when Northwood Country Club folded a few years ago — clubhouse manager Larry Montpetit and club secretary Audrey McHarry. Kern also employs four assistant professionals and first-tee host and bon vivant, Joe Rice.

"I'm operating the National," Blechman says, "as I run my business. I believe I have a top management team in both places, and I give them responsibility to attain our goals. The people at the National share my feelings for the place."

Kern is a case in point. He has not only put together a group of assistants committed to the efficient running of a first-class club, but has also ensured they have ample opportunities to develop their games.

To breed a competitive spirit, Kern holds qualifying competitions for the assistants' tournaments. These are 36-hole events from the pro tees. Kern designates how many spots the assistants will play for. "It's not unusual for par to be the qualifying score."

Come winter, the four assistants will also benefit from the generously good feeling of the National's members. They contribute to a fund that is used to send the golfers south for competition. And there is an added benefit to Kern and the clubs. The assistants see other pro shops and often return with ideas for handling the problems of cart control, signing members in and out, arranging tournaments — all the little things to go into making a first-class club.

"It all lends to the concept of the club," Kern says. "It's the whole feeling of the National. The staff dresses the same way so that members can always pick them out. Personally, I feel I'm at the nicest place in Canada."

Evidently, the National's members feel the same way. In the past, golfers might have wondered — given the financial problems — whether the club was going to be sold or be semi-private; perhaps it would become a real estate development. But now, the membership has settled at about 300 senior men; 50 corporations have also joined, each holding three memberships.

Perhaps the best evidence of the members' satisfaction is that at the end of the year, a group of about 100, known as the Rounders, takes Blechman and the staff to dinner, so much do they appreciate their efforts.

It is also apparent that these efforts will continue. In September, Tom Fazio made his annual visit to the National. He, Blechman, Kern and Wright toured the course. Since then, modifications have been made to some greens and tees; mounds have been incorporated to give more of the Scottish dimension that Blechman understands is vital to fine courses.

These changes are indicative of Blechman's enduring philosophy. "I want a club and a course that members are proud to belong to, and that the staff is proud to work at. And I want a golf course where we could play the United States Open with a week's notice, without adding rough."

Blechman will obviously not get the U.S. Open for the National. The Canadian Open is ensconced at Glen Abbey. However, Blechman is not pushing hard for a big tournament.

"I don't care if we're hidden and nobody knows about us," he says, "but I do care that we're a jewel. If we show the gem in the right setting, fine. Otherwise, I won't have a major tournament here."

That right setting could be available. Blechman says he would consider holding the World Cup at the National. This year, the tournament is being held at the Pondak Indah Golf Club in Jakarta, Indonesia. Thirty-two two-man professional teams compete annually in the event, begun in 1953 by industrialist John Jay Hopkins in Montreal as the Canada Cup. And the tournament — mired for a few years in administrative and financial troubles — is again emerging as a major world event.

The World Cup would be just the tournament — just the setting — in which to unveil the National to the world.

LOXAHATCHEE, FLORIDA

The Globe and Mail, **February 16, 1985**
The course looks as though Jack Nicklaus created it after a journey to the Old Course in St. Andrews, Scotland, Portmarnock in Ireland and Pebble Beach in California. It seems to belong in Florida about as much as raw, cold weather, which the Loxahatchee Golf Club got yesterday for its official opening.

When you first approach the Loxahatchee club, you notice not the individual holes, but what Nicklaus calls the "façade," or background: cones of earth that point skyward from the once-flat earth like a birthday hat on a kid's head. They run down the sides of the fairways and behind the greens in series, framing and defining what they enclose.

This is a course that was once dead flat. By building the mounds, Nicklaus shaped a landscape with more sides and angles than the Pythagorean theorem.

Loxahatchee's mounds made it seem a moonscape in yesterday's gloomy conditions. They caught the eye in a dramatic way, but also suggested routes to play the holes. At the same time, they separated one fairway from the next, thereby secluding holes one from the other. The mounds have functional as well as aesthetic value.

The mounds also add a certain sublimity to the course under the right conditions of light and shadow. Late Wednesday evening, the sun flickered on the mounds. When the sun was quite low, the contours took on the many shades of green that can make a course such a delight merely to see, never mind to play. In fact, that evening, Loxahatchee was strongly reminiscent of Portmarnock, perhaps the purest and simplest course in the world.

Of course, Loxahatchee is hardly in the class of a Portmarnock yet. Such stature takes time to be conferred, if it ever is. There's also another point to consider: Nicklaus's experiment at Loxahatchee with bentgrass greens.

Bentgrass greens usually have been used only in more northerly climates. Most Canadian courses use them. Conventional wisdom has it that they can't withstand the stress imposed upon them by the south's summer heat and humidity. However, they are considered a far superior putting surface to the bermuda grass used in most southern greens.

A few years ago, the Augusta National Golf Club, site of the Masters, switched to bentgrass greens. The club had to rebuild most of its greens to put the bentgrass in. Underneath the 12th green, shaded as it is by trees, the club installed a heat-pump arrangement to cool the green in hot weather and to warm it in cooler winter weather, which Augusta can get.

The greens at Augusta have provided finer putting surfaces, but the course is also closed from May 15 until October 1. As Ed Etchells, the man in charge of the maintenance side of all Nicklaus courses, says, that reduces the abrasion to the bentgrass caused by the heavy patter of golfing feet.

Loxahatchee, however, isn't meant to be an Augusta National. About 325 people will be buying homes here, and they will want to play golf year-round. With bermuda greens, Florida courses have traditionally overseeded in the fall with bentgrass; it takes six weeks for the seed to have taken enough so that the greens can be cut down to make them reasonably playable. In the spring, when the overseeding is going out, there isn't much grass to putt on for another six weeks, until the bermuda comes back in.

Pure bentgrass greens, though, will extend the golf season. That's what Nicklaus and Etchells find most attractive about the experiment. Besides, as Nicklaus said, "The stress period on bent is in the summer, when we're not going to have much play here anyway."

Nicklaus and his organization have used bent greens on courses in hotter and more humid climates. They worked fine at Shoal Creek in Birmingham, Alabama, last summer, where the PGA Championship was played. They've got bent greens at courses in Houston; Austin, Texas; Jackson, Mississippi; and Baton Rouge, Louisiana.

In truth, bentgrass at Loxahatchee is more of an investment in what a golf course should be than it is a gamble. Small misting systems have been installed in the greens to cool the air when it gets sultry. The better fungicides available today should ward off any diseases that stress could cause. Should it, for some unexpected reason, prove impossible to use the bent greens, Nicklaus can always revert to bermuda.

But nobody believes that will happen. Nicklaus isn't a man to live in the past, which in this case is spelled "bermuda." He's as serious about his course design as he is about going after a twentieth major championship this year. Too bad one can't go far into the future to see if his course work will stand up as long as his record will.

The Prestwick Golf Club

***The Globe and Mail,* September 19, 1986**
Prestwick, Scotland — The stone cairn in a field at the corner of the course is a reminder that there were great golfers before Bobby Jones and Jack Nicklaus. At the Prestwick Golf Club, where the British Open began in 1860, the names that come to mind are Willie Park, the father-and-son duo of Old Tom Morris and Young Tom Morris, and Freddie Tait.

These names are memorable because 125 years ago, Prestwick members held a notable tournament. Park travelled from the Musselburgh Course near Edinburgh and beat seven golfers on a blustery mid-October day to win the tournament that eventually became the British Open. It was played at Prestwick from 1860 to 1870.

Prestwick then had only 12 holes. The first began from the cairn and covered 578 yards to what is now the 16th green. That was long then and it's long now. One year, though, that didn't bother Young Tom Morris.

Morris hit two shots across the sandhills. His long third caught the wildly undulating green and rolled in the hole for an eagle. He used a hickory-shaft club and a gutta-percha ball and won three consecutive Opens beginning in 1868.

Those days are long past, but the feeling of golf in another century remains at Prestwick. The course is now 18 holes and directly underneath the routes taken by planes that use the international airport across the road. The original 12 holes are still there, though, lost in the sandhills but in view for those who care.

To see those holes and to play their modern counterparts, which incorporate some of the original greens and shots, is to remember a period when "blind" golf was considered real golf. On both the 206-yard fifth hole, known as the Himalayas, and the 391-yard 17th, known as the Alps, the golfer must hit to greens he can't see. He fires away over the hills and then walks across them with anticipation to see the results of his shot.

Such blind holes have all but disappeared from modern golf. At Prestwick, though, it's still play the land as it lies — not as it is manipulated. North American architects design holes between condominiums, and golfers drive small cars from hole to hole, and people still have the nerve to call the game golf. Over here, that seems like a different sport.

The folks at Prestwick agree. The most historically minded can recall when Tait, playing in the 1899 British Amateur, hit a shot out of the waterlogged Alps bunker in front of the 17th hole. That's playing it as it lies. That, say died-in-the-hickory Prestwickers, is golf.

In North America, architects and golfers despise blind shots. Here, there are many holes where the green is hidden or the target — the flag — isn't really the target. You play the course as the landscape dictates or you drop shots.

For instance, Prestwick's landscape includes a wall beside a railway track. The first tee is up against that wall, which runs a full 346 yards along the right side up to the green. Miss over the wall and you might never retrieve the ball — unless you take one of the trains to Glasgow. Meantime, the line to the flag is usually to one side of the hole — the better to take the slope.

This kind of hole makes Prestwick a museum piece. However, it does not make it an anachronism. Many knowledgeable golfers such as Ben Crenshaw and Tom Watson feel there is a place in golf for both indirect lines to the flag and blind shots.

Blind holes offer a timeless pleasure lost in North America. Golfer and writer Horace Hutchinson captured their appeal in an 1890 article about Prestwick.

"The holes," Hutchinson wrote, "lay in deep dells among sandhills, and you lofted over the intervening mountain of sand and there was all the fascinating excitement, as you climbed to the top of it, of seeing how near to the hole your ball might have happened to roll."

That excitement lives on at Prestwick, where the British Amateur will be played next June for the first time since 1925. Playing the course now, one wonders if and when North American architects — many of whom claim they are building Scottish-type courses — will bring back the blind hole to golf. Tomorrow wouldn't be soon enough.

Sagamore Golf Club

The Globe and Mail, **August 6, 1987**
Bolton Landing, New York — There's treasure in the Adirondack Mountains. It's in the grassy chipping mounds and the knobs and ridges on the greens of the Sagamore Golf Club, designed by Donald Ross in 1928 and now restored to its original look. This course makes the word classic mean something.

It's not easy to restore a treasure, be it a waterlogged Monet or a neglected Ross. Just a few years ago, horses cantered on up-and-down land where golfers walk today. The grass in the fairways was then knee-high and the treasure was buried under the litter.

However, the entire course was reseeded, and today's Sagamore is a testimonial to those who cared about Ross's work.

Ross, then 27, arrived in New York in 1899 from his home in Dornoch, far in the north of Scotland, where golf has been played since the 15th century. He caddied and golfed at the Royal Dornoch course as a teenager, studied club making in St. Andrews, Scotland, and worked at the Old Course under professional Old Tom Morris. How's that for an apprenticeship?

Ross then became the professional at Dornoch for seven years, until he met Harvard professor Robert Wilson, and U.S. golf course design improved forever.

Wilson was an astronomer who studied the history of golf in Scotland when not investigating deeper mysteries of the universe. He told Ross golf had a future in the United States and so might he. Ross came over at Wilson's invitation, and by the turn of the century was designing Pinehurst No. 2, the course he is most identified with.

But Ross also designed Scioto in Columbus, where Jack Nicklaus learned to play. He did Seminole in Palm Beach, "the only course," Ben Hogan once said, "where I could be perfectly happy playing every day." And he did Essex in Windsor, Ontario, where the 1976 Canadian Open was held and where PGA Tour pros Ben Crenshaw and Craig Stadler wish it would return.

Ross built his courses around the greens. When he found the right site, he and a workman used a mule and a drag pan to move dirt and contour the surface. A note on a sketch page might read "Raise green four feet. Three undulations three feet above green at outer edge and blend smoothly into fairway. All form one undulating mass."

"One undulating mass" is right. Sagamore's greens are so subtly contoured that a chip shot or putt hit slightly off line can roll off the green. The greens blend so well with the fairways that the slopes aren't easily seen even on a first or second reading.

There is solace in these open spaces. One's eye is never jarred; almost magically, white birch trees loom in the pine forest as targets for approaches to greens.

At 6,700 yards, Sagamore has enough length for the modern golfer. There was no need to add yardage; the mandate, as talented grounds director Mark Graves said while playing, was to preserve the course as Ross designed it.

The restoration that began in late 1984 attracted head professional Tom Smack to Sagamore from a six-year posting at the Castle Harbour course in Bermuda. Norman Wolgin, a non-golfer from Philadelphia, owned Sagamore — part of the resort of the same name — and was aware he had something special that needed work. Smack accepted the challenge.

"I'd seen what had been done at Mid-Ocean in Bermuda," Smack said, "where they took bunkers out and changed the original design. I'd also seen Ross courses like Inverness (in Toledo, Ohio) altered. The first time I walked this course, though, I knew it was a masterpiece, and that we should retain its tradition."

Graves, Smack and their co-workers have done that. They've added ponds at the fifth and sixth, but only to improve drainage in boggy areas. They've extended some tees to cope with increased play — there are more golfers today than in 1928 — and they will re-establish a few tees of old that have been moved over the years. Beyond these changes, they plan nothing but loving care of the Sagamore that Ross designed.

Best of all, the preservationists will retain Ross's greens. There's not a bunker in front of any, not a forced carry to a tucked pin anywhere. The greens are so inviting that a golfer can run the ball up if he wants. But he risks an awkward bounce if he doesn't hit his shot just so. The rewards make the risk worthwhile.

It must have been a treat to play Sagamore 60 years ago. Thanks to a few people who love golf and appreciate Ross's work, it's also a treat to play it today. Golf course collectors should add this one to their list of must-plays, right up there with Pebble Beach and Merion.

The Orchards

The Globe and Mail, June 27, 1988

South Hadley, Massachusetts — By the time the most aptly named course in Massachusetts opened on a morning last week, the most aptly named head pro in the United State had already been on the scene quite a while. The Orchards, designed by Donald Ross in 1922, was under the supervision of Bob Bontempo, and everything was in order.

Bontempo was on the tee, making sure the golfers got off in good time, as is his responsibility, and that they were swinging with good tempo, as he teaches. The time at this gem of a course in middle Massachusetts was 8 a.m., and when the first ball soared down the fairway of the 416-yard opener, another day's play through the apple trees had begun.

The Orchards is a little-known sweetheart of a course, 18 holes that swing in and out of primary pine forest, the greens small and undulating, the pleasures of the game many. Members pay $850 (U.S.) to belong here — the same price for men and women, the course available to them at all times. There's no such thing as Ladies' Day at The Orchards. They play anytime, which is as it should be.

Indeed, the course is gaining a reputation as an ideal site for women's tournaments. The national women's intercollegiate championship was held here in 1973; the U.S. Golf Association held its girls' junior championship here last year. Bontempo figures the U.S. Women's Amateur could be next, particularly since senior USGA official David Fay told him recently that The Orchards is suitable for any USGA event except for the men's Open, for which it's too small and intimate. That, however, is also its charm.

The Orchards began when Joseph Skinner, a silk-and-satin magnate in the area, commissioned Ross — the Scotsman who built Pinehurst No. 2 in North Carolina and Oak Hill in Rochester, where the U.S. Open will be held next year — to design a course on 200 acres across the road from his estate. The course was Skinner's gift to his daughter, Elisabeth. She was a talented golfer, and he figured she would improve if she had a place of her own to play.

Ross completed nine holes in 1922 and did the other nine five years later. The course is vintage Ross — crowned greens that fall off on the sides, bunkers that flow with the land. It's a gentle course, but at 6,477 yards long it can test all but the long-hitting touring professionals.

The most stimulating hole is the 446-yard 13th, where the fairway cants sharply to the right. It's a narrow band between wildflowers to the left and forest to the right. The green sits on a high point from where one can see the mountains of Holyoke Range.

As good as The Orchards is as a course, its history is as impressive. Skinner sold it to neighbouring Mt. Holyoke College in 1941 for $25,000, with the proviso that his daughter be granted a lifetime membership. The all-women's school decided in 1977 that The Orchards' members should run it as a separate financial entity, which it has since. The college generously lent the club $200,000 last year, at 5% over a 20-year period, thereby signifying its continuing commitment to The Orchards.

The club is thriving. Course superintendent Paul Jamrog worked with Bontempo to restore the condition of the holes. The traps, for one, now look properly old, scraggly and wild at the edges. They're fine to play from, but the grass is allowed to grow around them. This is golf in a natural state, just the way Bontempo and his members like it.

Golf is in Bontempo's blood. His dad was a club pro for 59 years and once beat the legendary amateur Bobby Jones one-up in a casual match at the Longmeadow Club down the pike. Jones signed a dollar bill for the elder Bontempo. The son, a sentimental man, who is the man for the job at The Orchards, carries it in his wallet.

"I remember Elisabeth Skinner's last days so well," Bontempo said yesterday before bidding good day to a visitor. "It was a hot August day last summer, just before the final of the junior girls'. She had her butler drive her across the road to the club. He pulled up to the circle around the putting green, and she got out, wearing a blanket around her, and shook hands with the two finalists before they teed off."

Elisabeth Skinner died a month later. She was 95. The Orchards is 66, a hidden treasure of American golf that should last forever.

Côte d'Ivoire

The Globe and Mail, **February 7, 1990**
Yamoussoukro, Côte d'Ivoire — Two unusual species — the golfer and the white rhinoceros, the former found everywhere, the latter less frequently encountered — are without each other's knowledge part of a plan to help the economy in Côte d'Ivoire recover from hard times.

Evidence of this was discovered one recent morning in this country in West Africa. A group of golfers — myself included — looked for birdies at the Yamoussoukro Golf Club, then sought bigger game in the nearby, yet-to-be-opened game reserve of Abokouamekro.

It was a moment unlike any the golfers had experienced. They saw antelopes in their natural habitats of open grassy plains. Later, they came upon the white rhinoceros, three to four tons of beast, and so awe-inspiring that the golfers stopped blathering on about their games.

The rhino was the only one in Côte d'Ivoire, having been brought here from South Africa to help develop the new game reserve as surely as the Ivorians have imported golf to assist their economy. Time will tell if they will succeed.

Both the big game and the royal and ancient game are part of President Felix Houphouet-Boigny's plan for the republic over which he has ruled since it gained independence from France in 1960. Now 84, Houphouet-Boigny has long hoped Côte d'Ivoire would be successful in its own right, reliant on its own resources.

The president had made excellent progress through the mid-1980s, by which time the Ivorians had established an agriculturally based economy second to none in Africa. David Lamb in his book *The Africans* noted that Côte d'Ivoire was one of only four non–oil-exporting African countries in which meaningful economic development, political stability and an emerging middle class existed.

Côte d'Ivoire's economy was based on cocoa and coffee, its main items of export. But world prices for these products dropped sharply in recent years. The Ivorian economy suffered, as did the Ivorians, and worry replaced optimism.

The government called for diversification, and the Ivorians were soon producing cotton and rubber. The French, having colonized Côte d'Ivoire in 1917 — the country was called Ivory Coast until recently — were still settled in key advisory positions. And Houphouet-Boigny had completed the first sequence of his dream, or what some people call his expensive folly — Yamoussoukro, the new capital city on the site of the ancestral village in which he was born.

Yamoussoukro is Houphouet-Boigny's brazen attempt to introduce modernism in a society still rooted in tribalism. Wide boulevards unlike any in the country gleam under thousands of light standards, but there is very little traffic since most Ivorians can't afford cars. A new basilica that the Pope has yet to consecrate is the biggest in the world and was featured on CBS's "60 Minutes" in last fall's opening segment.

Meanwhile, fires flicker on outdoor cooking pots as Ivorians who live without electricity prepare their evening meal from the food that they grow. We watched one afternoon at the presidential grounds as a feeder tossed a live chicken to crocodiles that swim in the moat surrounding the president's palace.

V.S. Naipaul has written about this ritual that is grotesque to Western eyes. We could hardly bear to watch as the crocodiles crept up the bank towards the chicken. "A public ceremony of kingship outside the big blank wall of the presidential palace," Naipaul called it in his 1984 essay "The Crocodiles of Yamoussoukro."

Ancient ritual full of symbolism or simply a demonstration of paganism, the feeding of the crocodiles cast a sense of mystery over our journey. What was this place — Côte d'Ivoire?

Naipaul also wondered whether a villager who had fallen over the iron rail into the lake, there to be mangled by a crocodile, was a victim of an accident or a voluntary sacrifice. Perhaps he had chosen the role of martyr to save his village from evil.

"So the crocodiles," Naipaul wrote " — seen in daylight, by a crowd with cameras — became more than a tourist sight. They become touched with the magic and power they were intended to have . . . and the symbolism remained elusive, worrying."

We felt shaken and soon sought a more familiar environment. The Yamoussoukro Golf Club was nearby, "a great creation," Naipaul wrote when first he saw it, "perfection in a way."

Perfection it is not, although the course is fine enough. The Golf Open de Côte d'Ivoire was played here last November. Fiji's Vijay Singh won this stop on the Safari Tour. Along with the money, Singh took the Trophy Felix Houphouet-Boigny. Yamoussoukro is, after all, the president's choice, and he wants the world to know there is golf here. Indeed, as Naipaul wrote, he sees golf as a symbol itself. He believes it can help lead Côte d'Ivoire to the promised land of wealth.

"To attract visitors," Naipaul wrote, "there is a great golf course, beautifully landscaped and so far steadfastly maintained against the fast-growing bush. It is the president's idea, though he doesn't play golf himself. The golf idea came to him when he was old, and now in his benign, guiding way he would like all his people, all the 60 or so tribes of the Ivory Coast, to take up golf."

The golf at Yamoussoukro is rather good golf, if not as challenging as that available at the Ivoire Golf Club 200 kilometres to the south in the big city of Abidjan. Ivoire is superb, as good a course as I have seen anywhere, with the exception of the world's finest. Yamoussoukro, meanwhile, has tight driving holes and nifty par-fours that curve around water. There's an island green that U.S. designer Pete Dye would have surrounded with railroad ties but that here retains an appealing wilder feel. And there's the bush — tangled sections of stately bamboos shooting so high, the songs of birds in the trees, anthills three metres high and as wide again.

Both Yamoussoukro and Ivoire hosted a big pro-am recently. Many French golfers competed in this country where French is the main language, and they were accompanied by local caddies dressed in the club uniform. But the Ivorians want more. They covet golfers from around the world and so have started to make it known that their two 18-hole courses are open to all. They are contemplating a course in the mountains northwest of Abidjan to add to those in Abidjan and Yamoussoukro. These courses seem well-run, although the latter's fairways could be in better shape.

Yet golf alone will hardly resuscitate an ailing economy. One travels to a place so far away in distance and culture for additional reasons.

"I travel," Naipaul wrote, "to discover other states of minds." And other states of minds are easily found in Côte d'Ivoire, states of minds that belong not only to the Ivorians, but that we might discover in ourselves.

Hence our trip to look for the white rhinoceros at Abokouamekro. The government has introduced the rhinoceros here because it hopes by this and future moves to compete for the tourist dollar with such countries as Kenya and Zambia. It may prove to be a crafty move. Or it may not work. It's not as if there are no other animals in Côte d'Ivoire.

We ventured out one morning before dawn to the Comoe game reserve northwest of Yamoussoukro. There we came upon antelopes in the wild — springboks scampering about in their natural habitat. And later at the edge of a river, we happened upon three elephants. And in villages close by Yamoussoukro's wide boulevards, we watched ancient tribal dances, visited a mud hut that served as a morgue where a group of women — members of the Senoufo tribe — were protecting the body of an elderly woman who had just died. They waited until they learned from the woman's soul that any evil spirits had departed. Then she could be buried.

We saw all this, and then we golfed. The conjunction of time, place and culture threw me off balance for a couple of weeks after I returned. I had dinner in Abidjan and breakfast the next morning in Manhattan.

We travel to discover other states of minds, Naipaul wrote. Houphouet-Boigny must know this. He cherishes his dream of rebuilding Côte d'Ivoire's economy. Ivorians know him affectionately as Le Vieux — the Old One — but the fact that he doesn't seem to have groomed a successor is worrying. Yet he has helped make Côte d'Ivoire one of Africa's more stable countries and may yet subdue the tensions that a slumping economy brings.

It's a long shot, and only one small segment of a larger strategy. But some Ivorians wait to see if Houphouet-Boigny can make his plan work and thereby help stabilize the economy of this enterprising country that stimulates feelings alternately sad and hopeful. I, for one, came away stunned.

The Old Course

The Globe and Mail, July 14, 1990
There's no telling who might play well during next week's British Open at the Old Course in St. Andrews, Scotland. But one thing is certain: The auld grey toon by the sea and the course will cast their collective spell not only over the visitors and players, but across the golfing world.

First, and above all, there's the course. It seems nothing but a flatland between an ancient town and an often harsh sea. So what if golf has been played there since 1552, and probably earlier? So what if the course enchanted Bobby Jones, Sam Snead and Jack Nicklaus? There just doesn't seem much to it.

Ah, but that's just it, the locals will say. Even Jones and those who followed him to the Old Course felt nothing but distaste at first. But the subtleties gradually revealed themselves to the golfers. Jones eventually said he could take everything out of his life but his experiences in St. Andrews and it would have been a full life.

The Old Course, Jones learned, has a way of calling golfers, even of implying to them that golf should be played its way: along the ground sometimes, in the air other times, traversing various angles to the greens. Nothing is straightforward at the Old Course. Thoughtfulness counts more than strength.

Now these factors on their own could mean only that the Old Course is an interesting anachronism. But the Old Course is a model for many other courses, though nobody knows who first laid it out. Its first influence, perhaps, was that it set the standard for a round at 18 holes when in 1764 it reduced its number of holes from 22.

But the Old Course has also encouraged other courses to adopt its pattern of strategic design, where a golfer is given options rather than being forced to play over lakes and bunkers. Most notable is Augusta National Golf Club, site of the annual Masters.

Augusta National was co-designed by Bobby Jones and Alister MacKenzie. Jones said they were both "extravagant admirers" of the Old Course. And so they would have rolling fairways and wavy greens that followed the ground's contours; few impositions on the land, that is.

Nobody needs reminding of how popular Augusta National is, though few golfers other than its members play it. But every spring, we watch the Masters and marvel at the course. There wouldn't be an Augusta National had there not been an Old Course.

Other courses, mind you, have also tried to emulate the Old Course. But few invoke its essence as well as Augusta National. Oddly, or perhaps not so oddly, considering the influence of the Old Course, many courses have called themselves St. Andrews, as if the name would confer instantly a reputation that cannot be duplicated.

The U.S. started the process in 1888 with its first permanent club, St. Andrews in Yonkers, New York. Transplanted Scot John Reid founded the club and St. Andrews was the name the original members wanted.

"St. Andrews in Scotland had been the cradle of golf," Herbert Warren Wind wrote in *The Story of American Golf,* "and who knew, perhaps this new St. Andrews would assume the same role on the American continent."

The name stuck and spread. Nicklaus designed a St. Andrews course in Hastings on Hudson, New York, near the site of the first U.S. club of the same name. But it was more of a housing development, and never really got anywhere.

There are also courses named St. Andrews in Japan, and in California, Missouri, Illinois and Trinidad. And there's a Sintendreze in Germany. They have the name, but they don't have the land or the town or the history.

Still, the flattery goes on. There's a St. Andrews-by-the-Sea in New Brunswick, and many Toronto golfers remember the old St. Andrews near the present area of Yonge Street and Highway 401. Bill MacWilliam, whose father was the pro at that St. Andrews, has honoured his father and the town by founding two courses of the same name north of the city.

But there is only one authentic Old Course, and one St. Andrews. And to be sure, a genuine Canadian connection to the Open at the Old Course exists in the person of Toronto businessman James Kidd.

Kidd's great-grandfather, Tom Kidd, won the first British Open held at the Old Course, in 1873. Tom Kidd, like all Open winners, received a gold medal. His great-grandson, however, has yet to find the treasure, although he has immersed himself in the history of the event. And next week, finally, the world will see the just-opened golf museum next to the Old Course. Maybe Kidd's medal will turn up one day.

In the meantime, attention will focus on St. Andrews for the Open, and rightfully so. The U.S. PGA Tour has, for the first time in recent history, not scheduled an event opposite the Open, as if to say, what's the point, nobody will care about golf anywhere but in St. Andrews. And guess what? The PGA Tour is right.

Shorter Courses

The Globe and Mail, **May 2, 1991**
Hot Springs, Virginia — Many modern golf courses are more than 7,000 yards from the back tees. Yet most golfers are incapable of playing that long a layout. That's why it's instructive to play a layout less than 6,000 yards, as is the Homestead course here — all the way back.

The course is the oldest of three in the area that are owned by the resort of the same name. Sam Snead learned to play in the hills here. At 5,957 yards — all the way back — the Homestead gives higher-handicappers the chance to play a course as the touring pros play a longer layout; they can hit shorter clubs in.

It's too bad that there aren't more decent short courses. Touring pros represent a minuscule percentage of golfers, yet courses are designed for them. Architects say they design courses for all golfers, but most admit when pressed that they design with the back tees in mind. They force the forward tees into the plan, of necessity.

"You can build a course for all varieties of players," Robert
Trent Jones Jr. said in a recent interview while playing Palmetto,
an exemplary shorter and older course in Aiken, South Carolina.
"But it's not easy to do."

Courses around 6,000 yards were once the norm. The Homestead course started in 1892, and its first tee is the oldest in use
in the United States. The hole itself is but 342 yards from the
back tee, and that, according to head pro Don Ryder, may be a
few yards longer than it was originally.

As short as the Homestead is by conventional standards, it offers enough golf for most amateurs. Cart paths are an unfortunate concession to modernity and the lack of caddies, but the
course is still hilly, full of blind tee shots and crowned greens
that fall off to the sides.

The course is in a tradition fast disappearing — the challenging
short course. It's in the same category as was Uplands in
Thornhill, Ontario. Only imaginative addition stretched the Uplands scorecard beyond 6,000 yards. But golfers learned to play
from a variety of lies. Now Uplands is an awkward nine-holer, its
original layout mauled for estate housing.

Courses such as Uplands and Cataraqui in Kingston, Ontario,
or Marine Drive in Vancouver, didn't and don't need length.
They're tricky around the greens, which is where the pros are
most tested today. That's the way it is at the Homestead; that's
not the way it is for amateurs who play long, watery courses.

Glen Abbey, the home of the Canadian Open in Oakville, Ontario, exemplifies the problems of which the Homestead is a
counterpoint. The Abbey tests anybody's game and mangles most
amateurs. It's just too tough and too long for the many water
hazards.

A shorter course is more enjoyable, invigorating rather than
enervating. The ninth at the Homestead is only 311 yards, but it
plays into a deep valley and then up to a green so sloped at the
front that a misplayed shot can roll all the way down the hill. It's
reminiscent of the shape of the ninth green at Augusta National,
though not as fast.

Yet many developers of new courses demand both contour
and extreme speed in their greens. Again, they want to emulate
courses built for touring pros, and so add lunacy to length.

Natural slope on greens such as the Homestead's means that the speed doesn't have to be barely manageable. Less speed also means that greens won't suffer from bacterial wilt or, as architect Pete Dye calls it, the "rich man's disease" that comes from private clubs that want overly fast greens.

"You think of Donald Ross building Pinehurst [Pinehurst No. 2 in North Carolina] in 1901," Dye said in a recent phone interview. "He could not conceive people hitting the ball so far; he could not conceive greens that would putt at 11 on the stimpmeter [the distance in feet a ball dropped off an angled board will roll]. He built his greens for a speed of maybe five on the stimp. We should agree on a speed for greens, maybe eight or nine on the stimp at the most."

That's as fast as the Homestead's greens get, and that's as fast as most amateurs can handle on contoured greens. Contoured greens also go with shorter courses, where amateur golfers hit less club into greens and can enjoy the challenge of placing the ball on them.

Modern courses prevent amateurs from doing this. But golf was not created for touring pros. It's a game for amateurs, most of whom don't hit the ball far or deal competently with contour and speed in the same green.

Amateurs would enjoy the game more if they could play courses meant for them — short courses, that is. Somebody should build them, and from the back tees.

Wawashkamo

The Globe and Mail, **July 31, 1991**
Mackinac Island, Michigan — Golf's centuries-old history means that some courses inevitably lie fallow and therefore need restoring. Restorations can sometimes be contrived, but it also happens that the right person can come along to do the job.

That's the case at Musselburgh Golf Club east of Edinburgh, where local links-lover Peter Cunningham is restoring the old course that held six British Opens between 1874 and 1889. And it's the case here at Wawashkamo Golf Club, a nine-holer on a high point of Mackinac Island.

Wawashkamo is of another time, having opened in 1898. Visitors from the mainland take a ferry to the island, then walk or bicycle to the course. Alternatively, they take a horse-drawn taxi, because no motorized vehicles are allowed on the island.

The result is that golf here is in many ways a trip back to a vanished period of American history. But there might not be much of a course at all, were it not for the interest of professional cum superintendent Larry Grow, and the forbearance of the club members who hired him.

Grow hails from Traverse City, southwest of Mackinac. He taught school for 20 years and first visited Wawashkamo in 1974. He felt an immediate attachment to the course, an attachment that developed as he visited during the next decade. But he worried that the course was deteriorating.

Grow learned that Wawashkamo was founded at the turn of the century when Chicagoans who summered on Mackinac commissioned Alex Smith to design a course. Smith was born in Carnoustie, Scotland, and had been involved in a course called Washington Park in Chicago; oddly, it was inside a race track, as Musselburgh was and is.

So Smith designed Wawashkamo. It's a state and national historic site and Michigan's oldest course. Smith laid the holes out on and around the grounds where the 1814 Battle of Mackinac Island between the U.S. and Britain occurred in the aftermath of the War of 1812. Thirteen U.S. soldiers are buried in woods off the sixth green.

Chippewa Chief Eagle Eye made an observation that led to the course's name. He noted that the golfers *wa-wash-kamo* — walk a crooked path. A century or so later and the chief might have qualified as an analyst on golf telecasts.

But the crooked paths became overgrown. Original bunkers were lost. The circus ring — Smith's inventive 18-inch-high braided wall of rough that surrounded most of the third green — had pretty well disappeared. But Grow sensed that what time had eroded could still be recovered.

"I felt there was something here," Grow said the other day while working on the course, which he takes care of, along with his son Andy and two other staff members. "It gave me goose bumps."

Grow's fascination with Wawashkamo grew — pardon the pun. He kept in contact with the club, whose annual dues are $250. The original pro, Frank Dufina, had started at the club in 1902, retired in 1969 and died in 1972 in his nineties. The club didn't have a pro or real maintenance crew from then until Grow arrived.

Bob Milton, the club president then and now, listened to Grow's proposals in 1985 and, sensing his vision for the course, hired him. Grow lives on the course and his 15 hours a day are showing results. His course is becoming a small gem.

Grow thrives on his work. He still feels the abiding history and mystery of the place and marvels at how a simply laid-out course can capture a golfer's imagination.

And capture it Wawashkamo does. Two sets of tees on each hole make up a round of 18 holes. The fourth on the front side is a 130-yard par-three to a green partially obscured by a hill. The last hole is 465 yards and swings around in front of the clubhouse to a green left of the modest, yet lovingly redone, structure. Grow's son Andy lives in the original caddyshack opposite the pro shop.

Grow has assembled in his shop a small but interesting collection of golf artifacts. A fellow in California sent him Alex Smith's 1907 book *Lessons on Golf*. Bob Lucas of the Golf Collectors' Society sent clubs that Smith made.

Grow has done his homework. He visited Carnoustie in 1987 to learn more about Smith, who won the U.S. Open in 1906 and 1910. He's also corresponded with Cunningham of Musselburgh and may visit there in the fall to help with his restoration. They're birds of a feather.

People such as Grow and Cunningham are curators of golf's history. Their courses are playable museums. Their love of the game is pure, and their works of restoration are treasures.

High Links in Northern Ireland

The Globe and Mail, **March 11, 1992**
Newcastle, Northern Ireland — There are courses every golfer dreams of playing, and now our party of eager pilgrims has ar-

rived at one of them. We are standing on the elevated 10th tee of the Royal County Down Golf Club, which no less an esteemed critic than British golf writer Peter Dobereiner believes to be the finest course in the world. We survey the wild dunesland that lifts our spirits higher and higher. We think of tomorrow morning, when we will walk and play these ancient, romantic links.

Now, as we stand on the tee, we become quiet. The silence is sudden after our opening exclamations at the vastness of the course, at the ways in which the land rumbles, rises and crests, at the sound of the sea so near — there, over the grassy dunes, along the first hole. We are excited, rhapsodic, and now we are quiet. That's because we have been overwhelmed by the grandness of the view that presents itself; we turn around on the 10th tee and face away from the course.

Here is where the Mountains of Mourne come down to the sea. The mountain range hovers over the course and seems somehow to protect it from the political problems of Northern Ireland. We have travelled across the checkpoint into the country without difficulty, having wondered what might ensue in this land of The Troubles. Not to worry, we are calmed. Friends have told us not to worry, the golf is quite safe.

Indeed, it seems to be; so we look forward to our morning round. Down the road just out of town, we settle in to the Burrendale Hotel, a comfortable, modern place. Soon we are drinking a glass of Guinness at the bar. Royal County Down's club secretary Peter Rolph is here as well, and he joins us as we drink this Irish elixir and talk of golf at County Down. Old Tom Morris won the 1861, '61, '64 and 1867 British Opens and later designed the course.

That was a century ago, and Old Tom's fee was £4. Rolph confirms that the course can be tough, especially when the wind blows. But he reminds us that this is part of the game at an authentic course, and besides, there's no sight lovelier than the sun over County Down. He assures us that this occurs frequently. And we rest assured.

Now it's morning, and we are on the first tee. The par-five swings along a valley, and the green is set in a hollow far down the fairway. It's visible from the left side of the fairway. My caddy, Anthony, tells me to hit a "nice, quiet one" for my third, a

6-iron into a breeze. I pull it slightly left of the green. No problem, because it's possible to putt from the sides of the greens at County Down. Two putts later, I have my par.

On we go, and soon we are on the fourth tee high above the ground and back behind the gorse bushes. We can see the town and the looming Mountains of Mourne. The hole is a par-three, but I'm not sure I want to play. I would like to savour the vista for a while.

That's the way it is all round County Down. From high tees with views we drop into meadow, then scramble along the rugged terrain to greens tucked away. We stand on the famous ninth tee and stare directly at the mountain, and the Slieve Donard Hotel at the edge of the course. It's a scene out of *Wuthering Heights*, but we are in Northern Ireland. We are in the country where the musician Van Morrison was born, and of which he writes and sings with passion.

One song is called *Queen of the County Down*. And while Morrison certainly was not writing about the golf courses here, it's fair to say that Royal County Down is the queen of the numerous courses in the area. Then there's Royal Belfast, another exceptional course. It's the only one where visitors require a letter of introduction, perhaps from their home club professional.

If Royal County Down is the jewel in one crown, Royal Portrush in County Antrim north of County Down is the gem in another. The Dunluce course here was the site of the 1951 British Open. That was the last time the Open was held outside of Scotland and England. Like Royal County Down, Portrush is a century old.

Portrush presents itself to the approaching car driver in what must be one of the most arresting manners possible. We drive along the curving A26 road towards the town of Portrush, and then hold our breath as the three courses of Royal Portrush reveal themselves below as heaving masses of earth covered by shaggy, blowing grasses.

Along with County Down, Portrush was one of eight founding clubs of the Golf Union of Ireland. We are introduced to Wilma Erskine, the only female club secretary at a Royal club (of which there are many). She takes us through a clubhouse that is as much a museum of golf, and then we move out to make our way around the links. The standard scratch, or course rating, is 73 from the back tees. That's a shot higher than par, always an indication that the golf course is strong.

That Portrush is, and so it's no wonder that the 1993 British Amateur will be held here, or that famed U.S. architect Pete Dye is a member. He shows up from time to time as if in need of inspiration for one of his new designs. And he always gets what he comes for at Portrush.

Larry, my caddy, takes me through the course. We walk along a path to the third tee, from where the links spread out on all sides. Our invigorating walk continues through the front nine and eventually on to Calamity, the 14th hole, one of Dye's favourite holes and surely one of the best par-threes anywhere. It is 200 yards of fright. The green is perched on what appears to be a shelf, with a severe fallaway to the right. Miss down there and you are on ground where it's difficult to take a decent stance, let alone to make a reasonable shot. I hit my tee ball here and am nearly standing on my head for my next shot.

Better to miss to the left and maybe find a haven called Bobby Locke's hollow. It's so-named because the South African golfer managed to make his par from here every round of the 1951 British Open. Later comes the par-five 17th, where an enormous bunker to the right stares the golfer in the eye as he stands on the tee. It's forbidding.

But never mind. Both Portrush and County Down are tough, yet they do finish with milder holes. The finishes don't really detract from the overall impression; it's just that the rest of each course is exceptional. And if you play well, who knows, you just might find that your caddy says something that will stay with you forever.

"I always know when I'm with a fair golfer," Larry says to me after our round, "because I get 'round with my feet dry."

But Larry also had said something else during the round, and I don't think I've ever come across a story in which romance and golf are more closely linked.

"My girlfriend was walking around Portstewart with me last night," Larry, 37, told me as we went around Portrush. (Portstewart is another fine course in the area.) "She was taking a swing here and there. We were on the tee, and I asked her to take a swing with her eyes closed. When she opened them and looked down, I'd put an engagement ring on the tee block. She wasn't expecting our engagement for months."

Nobody in our group got engaged at County Down or Portrush, but we did commit ourselves to returning. How could we not, when the attraction we felt was so strong?

Chapter Three

EQUIPMENT

IN MARCH of 1992, while covering the Honda Classic in Ft. Lauderdale, I found myself engaged in a frantic search for the perfect putter. I was surprised, since I consider myself a rational man. However, I had recently come unglued because of a stretch of truly wretched putting and so figured against all logic that a new and completely different putter could help. I wasn't out of the airport more than 15 minutes before I pulled into a golf shop and, having sunk a few short putts on the indoor carpet, purchased a Zebra putter. It was slightly longer than standard, and it seemed heavier. I also liked the upright lie. That evening I was putting balls on the living-room rug in the condominium where I was staying, along with a friend's daughter, the darling five-year-old Emma. She held a small pail in front of her as I putted. Emma thought I was putting well enough, but then again she was kind enough to move the pail when I was off line. Most putts, therefore, found their mark.

The Zebra is still in my bag, but so is something called the PLOP putter that I found in Florida; PLOP, that is, for Physical Laws of Putting. A computer expert in California has come up with what he says is about as close to a perfectly balanced putter as is possible. But what does that say about counterbalanced putters? A new theory was going the rounds last spring that a putter should be as heavily weighted throughout the shaft as at the clubhead end. That is, the putter would feel heavy when the golfer turned it upside down; the idea was that a golfer could better achieve the supposed ideal pendulum stroke on fast greens if the putter would do most of the swinging itself. Mass, apparently, would do that.

What can I say? I have just gone into my basement room and counted 25 putters. That includes two left-handed putters. You see, somebody told me that I should putt left-handed, since I am left-handed and left-eye dominant. My dominant eye would then be behind the ball. I've tried and I do feel comfortable over the ball. The ball rolls smoothly, but it doesn't seem that I am making more putts. Maybe I should try another left-handed putter. A PLOP maybe? Then again, I have putted well right-handed from time to time. Maybe I just need more practice with the Zebra.

Here's some advice: Don't ask me about equipment. I only know that golfers are willing to try anything new, anything that they think could improve their game. Of course, the equipment manufacturers know this and so their research and development people are forever working on the next innovation, the next longest ball, the next wonderful shaft, the next generation of perimeter-weighted, investment cast clubs guaranteed to minimize error. Even shoe manufacturers are in on it. "Time to pump up," long-hitting 1991 PGA champion John Daly said in a blatant advertisement for Reebok during a made-for-television event.

But I love it all, every last tacky appeal to our dream of the perfect piece of equipment. That's why I have included this selection of stories about the mad search for something that will help. How could I resist writing about The Secret Weapon, or the PuttOScope, or J's Professional Weapon? Then again, I look at the collection of clubs in my basement and I think, How could I be duped? Never mind. The variety of equipment available is mind-boggling, dizzying. I'm bewildered, but you never know what might help.

Philp to Nakamats, the Putter Passes

The Globe and Mail, **October 7, 1983**

In 1931, British writer H. Newton Wethered deliberated upon the perfect putter, as made by master Scottish club maker Hugh Philp. The wooden putter was "a thing to be coveted on the green by any natural expert, especially when its shaft may have been cut from the lemon, or some equally appetizing tree."

Wethered also noted that the putter "encouraged slowness . . . removed the besetting sin of straining after unnecessary effort." It did so by its heavy weight; it also had "too substantial a grip to permit any hurrying of the stroke."

Philp was born near St. Andrews, Scotland, in 1782 and made fine golf clubs until he died in 1856. In 1819, he was appointed club maker to the Society of St. Andrews Golfers, which became the Royal and Ancient Golf Club of St. Andrews in 1854. His clubs were valued for their graceful lines. To own one today is to own a masterpiece.

Although Philp's putter was the state of the art, he still had to face a problem as old as golf. Those who play the game — Royal and Ancient or Common and Modern — are human beings. Fragile, vulnerable and nervous, we twitch over four-foot putts. The fault, dear Mr. Philp, one might say, lies not in our putters, but in ourselves.

Human fallibility has led to no end of putters designed to control our putting maladies. Ping, Potato Masher, Bullseye, Zebra, Basakwerds or T-Line, they have come forward to help us on the greens. Nevertheless, putts are still missed from Kasumigaseki in Japan to Muirfield in Scotland.

Three weeks ago at the West Coast Merchandise Show in Industry Hills, California, a new putter called The Secret Weapon was introduced. Designed by Dr. Yoshiro Nakamats of Tokyo, it features a 1 1/2-inch square grip that enables the golfer to clasp his hands around the putter and place both thumbs on the grip beside each other. The stroke becomes more arms and shoulders; manipulation by the wrists is reduced.

The Secret Weapon has another feature that Nakamats (as he prefers to spell it in English) considers as important as the wide grip. The head of the putter acts as a tuning fork. When the head strikes the ball, an audible sound is given off; the frequency of the sound is related to the solidity with which the ball is hit and the distance it is hit.

When a putt is improperly struck, the golfer senses a vibration. This encourages a subconscious learning that will have the golfer hitting more and more putts on the putter's sweet spot.

If anybody can bring science to what Philp construed as art, Nakamats may be the man. Bob Delvecchio, president of New World Concepts International in West Springfield, Massachusetts, distributors of the Japanese-made putter, says Nakamats is a "genius. He is the No. 1 inventor in the world, with 2,360 patents out."

Nakamats, 54, is president of Naco Corp., a high-technology company in Tokyo that specializes in audio, optics and computers. After putting inexpertly for 30 years, he built a machine to test putters. Aware that some sort of feedback system would encourage learning, he incorporated the tuning fork and wider grip applications. The grip takes the golfer back to the way he might have gripped a putter as a child. The tuning fork brings a sense of feel into the stroke.

The Secret Weapon won the Grand Prix Award as best invention for 1982, selected at a meeting of the International Inventors Association. Delvecchio, a former studio drummer with such musicians as Edgar Winter and Chuck Berry, is using Chubby Checker — he of The Twist — to market the putter. The idea is that if it won't twist in his hands, it won't twist in anybody's.

The least expensive model of the putter sells for $175 (U.S.). A sterling silver model goes for $250 and an 18-carat gold version for $350. "The gold putter isn't for gimmickry," Delvecchio says, "but because gold is the best conductor of frequencies."

Next week, Delvecchio and Nakamats are off to California to tape a television show. *Newsweek*, *Time* and *People* magazines have called. Professional Pat Lindsey, winner of the recent B.C. Open in Endicott, New York, (without the putter), has also called, saying he would like the putter shipped immediately to him.

Where will all this lead? A possible scenario: Next July, Jack Nicklaus, seeking his first major championship since 1980, is at

St. Andrews ready for his first round in the British Open. In his hands, he holds The Secret Weapon.

When he tees off, tradition, science, Nakamats's ingenuity and Nicklaus's genius for golf all merge.

Supercharged, Nicklaus hits his opening shot down near the legendary Swilcan Burn and pitches into the hole for an opening eagle. Seventy-one holes later, he walks through the Valley of Sin on the 18th green a clear winner of his fourth British Open, his third at St. Andrews. Nobody, but nobody, has come close. He has been in a world of his own for 72 holes.

Many Gadgets Designed to Aid Golfer's Swing

The Globe and Mail, **April 21, 1984**
In the late-nineteenth century, a logic teacher at Oxford University who had been introduced to golf described the game as one of "putting little balls into holes with instruments very ill adapted to the purpose." He might have added that the people who used these instruments also seemed ill adapted to the purpose; had he accepted that as fact, he would likely have run out and purchased one of the many training aids that promoters and manufacturers have always been eager to sell golfers.

Generations of golfers have seen these aids come and go. In one form or another, a very popular item has been a gadget intended to help golfers achieve a fundamental of the effective golf swing: a firm left wrist at impact (for right-handers). It is there that most golfers break down and lose control and power.

The Blake Swing-Check sold for $2 in Toronto during the summer of 1927. It was an early model, as was the Denman Rite-Grip, available for the same price that year out of Toledo, Ohio.

The Canadian version was a fingerless grip with a strap running across the palm. The grip end of the club fit into this strap. An advertisement in *Canadian Golfer* magazine said the device "corrects faulty habits, prevents overswinging, slicing, hooking" and, of course, "reduces your score."

The Denman affair, meanwhile, was designed to lower a golfer's left hand and turn it downward, "à la professional." Its firm backing was said to increase left-hand strength, "thus ensuring full left hand control."

In 1962, a device called Remind-a-Sleeve was sold through golf magazines. The adjustable plastic sleeve was said to keep the left arm straight. It was available at $3.93 out of Newton Centre, Massachusetts.

About a decade later, professional Tommy Bolt advocated the Tone-O-Matic Hit-Tru Golf Aid. This was also a fingerless, stiff-backed glove. Bolt, who often taught golfers to swing through the ball with their left hand alone, felt the Hit-Tru glove would teach the golfer the hand's proper function.

Before the 1970 Canadian Open at the London Hunt and Country Club, Bolt gave Kermit Zarley the glove. Zarley used it in practice and won the tournament. He credited the Hit-Tru glove for helping him hit through.

The Hit-Tru gizmo was invented by Gil Smith of St. Petersburg, Florida. Eventually Smith sold out his Tone-O-Matic company to Fabergé. Bolt was hired to do nationwide commercials on behalf of the new owners.

Not to be outdone, and perhaps feeling sorry for the neglected right hand, former PGA tour player John Schlee came on the scene in the early eighties with what he called "The Secret." Schlee claimed in advertisements that he had known the secret since 1969, when Ben Hogan unveiled it to him.

Hogan's secret, apparently, was a cupped right hand at impact. Schlee turned that into an instrument that fit over the back of the right hand and up the forearm. A strap fit around the fingers and grip end of the club. The mechanism locked the right hand into place so that every golfer seemed assured of looking like Hogan at impact.

David Ogrin used Schlee's device in practice last summer. He tied for thirteenth at the U.S. Open and was only three shots out of the lead at the halfway mark of the Canadian Open before slipping. Nevertheless, he saluted the virtues of the training tool, which sold last year for $24.95 (U.S.), postpaid from the City of Industry, California.

These tools, however, cannot teach the golfer the proper swing or stroke. Their originators assume that the golfer will somehow manage to launch his clubhead into the atmosphere on his backswing, and that the gadgets will take care of the rest. But that's patently not the case, though the aids do at least try to teach the golfer what certain positions at impact feel like.

Realizing golfers want and need more, some people have recently been working on equipment to enable the golfer to sense and therefore understand an effective full swing and a correct putting stroke. Inventors of the equipment say the most effective way to learn is through developing the right muscle memory.

Last summer, an Irish engineer named Michael O'Flanagan came up with an optical instrument he called PuttOScope. This is essentially a twin-mirror device that is positioned on the putter head. While looking at a horizontal mirror the golfer can locate the image of his eyes. That tells him if they are directly over the ball. He can also fix his line to the hole properly by setting himself so that he sees the flagstick reflected in a second angled mirror.

The PuttOScope was used by Irishman Liam Higgins when he won a professional tournament last August. He told a reporter for the *Irish Times* that the PuttOScope improved his putting. It has recently come on to the Canadian market.

At last month's Tournament Players Championship in Ponte Vedra, Florida, inventor Fred Slagle of Madison, Ohio, demonstrated his Pro-Gressive Putting Technique, using a training putter on a roller and a playing putter. His sidekick, a young woman in her early twenties whose good looks caught the players' attention as much as her stroke, actually did the putting while Slagle placed balls on the ground and explained.

Slagle's system is based on the idea that the putter must be taken back low to the ground, which is accomplished in practice when the golfer sweeps it back with the roller. A very short backstroke is used, while on the forward stroke the golfer keeps his eyes one inch in front of the ball to help him accelerate through it.

Once the golfer has grooved this stroke by putting ball after ball in rapid-fire succession, he is asked to learn how to impart topspin to the ball. He does this by putting over a spin bar set on the ground and just behind the ball so that his putter head must rise at impact.

Slagle claims the most efficient way a right-hander can do this is by lifting the putter sharply at impact, using the left elbow as a piston. At impact, the elbow flares up and out as if it were a chicken wing.

Difficult as this seems, Slagle's assistant holed 15 six-foot putts in a row with the roller putter, then 16 in a row without paying attention to whether or not she contacted the ball on the putter's sweet spot. She also made 10 consecutive putts using the toe of the putter, thereby emphasizing the importance of overspin rather than point of contact of ball against putter face.

Slagle owns a golf course in Ohio and he developed his system after golfing in Costa Rica last year with a 70-year-old man who four-and-five-putted regularly because he picked the putter up on his backswing and decelerated through impact.

By mid-week at the TPC, Slagle had sold his Pro-Gressive Putting Technique to Hal Sutton, Bernhard Langer, Mark Pfeil, John Cook, Gary Hallberg and Jim Nelford. Nelford had to pay $600 to have a left-handed model made up. The normal price for the roller putter and the trainer is $258.

While Slagle demonstrated his inventions on the practice green, a fellow named Dennis Cone discussed what could well turn out to be the most useful piece of equipment of all: a machine into which the golfer places himself to learn the feel of the path of the clubhead during the swing, otherwise known as the plane.

Hogan thought the plane was a fundamental of golf, but teachers have always had difficulty communicating just what swing plane means. The Swing-O-Sizer, as the machine is known, is meant to offer golfers a reference system.

The Swing-O-Sizer was designed by a 12-handicap golfer in Orlando named Richard Ohly, with whom Cone is now a partner in a company called Swing Plane Systems. In its original form, it consisted of two connected, tilted, circular pieces of wood that form a track for the shaft to follow as the golfer stands inside the doughnut middle. The machine is supposed to trap the shaft and control the plane while allowing the clubhead freedom of movement.

The machine costs less than $2,000 to build and will remain relatively inexpensive even when the final product is made from a plastic material. Ohly and Cone plan to lease the Swing-O-Sizer to pro shops and hope to secure the approval of the Professional Golfers' Association of America.

Cone is president of the Orlandoland Junior Golf Association. He and Ohly recently opened what they have called a Muscle Memory Training Center in Orlando with three Swing-O-Sizer units. They hope to have 20 such locations in Florida within the next two years.

With this latest influx of high-tech equipment to the golf world, it's only natural that there should also be a sophisticated computer to tell the golfer via hard copy exactly what he is doing, once he has learned how to do it. At the TPC, a $20,000 golf-swing analyzer made by a company in Illinois called Sportech did just that.

The machine told Bobby Clampett what proportion of his weight was on his right side at the top of his swing and how much he had shifted to his left at impact. It told Tom Watson his clubhead speed when he hit the ball with one of the new light-weight shafts and even indicated how many degrees the face of his clubhead was open or closed upon impact.

These measurements were taken via sensors upon which the golfer stood and over which his clubhead passed. The readings showed on a monitor and were printed for the golfer.

How helpful the latest swing aids prove to be remains to be determined. Should they go the way of the Blake Swing-Check or the Denman Rite-Grip, however, golfers can always follow the advice of six-time British Open champion Harry Vardon.

"No matter what happens," Vardon advised, "keep on hitting the ball."

Golf Balls, Frisbees That Light Up in the Dark

The Globe and Mail, May 7, 1987
There is no doubt about it. Golfers are definitely a wacky bunch. They're proving it again these days by playing golf at night, with golf balls that glow in the dark.

The Nitelite ball, as it is called, was developed in New Hampshire last August by the father-and-son partnership of Nelson and Corky Newcombe. Their Pickpoint Sports Co. specializes in evening sports products, and the golf ball is just the latest in a series that began a dozen years ago and includes lighted footballs, tennis balls, Frisbees and fishing lures.

"The golfers came to us," Corky Newcombe said, "and told us they were tired of having to walk off the course after 15 or 16 holes because of the dark. There was a definite need there, and so we invented the product."

The product produces, up to a point. The Nitelite ball is translucent, all right, and can be seen for hundreds of yards in the dark because of a light match inserted in it. It is also official golf-ball weight and size, but it does have a hard feel and doesn't go as far as a regulation ball.

According to Don Webb, the pro at the Hollinger Golf Club in Timmins, Ontario, where he has run Nitelite tourneys, the ball has been a "roaring success." He said yesterday that it can't be lost unless a player hits it in the water. "It's like taking a flashlight and throwing it."

Night golfers have learned a thing or two about their game. They don't use a driver from the tee because the ball is so hard that it cannot be compressed easily and so does not get up very high. Instead, they use 3-woods. They also take an extra club or two on iron shots.

One golfer who tested the Nitelite found that it tends to skid rather than roll on chip shots. Others have noticed how difficult it is to putt well. It is not easy to line up the ball with the centre of the blade.

But the limitations don't seem to matter to golf addicts. They pay their six or seven dollars a ball, plus another buck or so for the light match, and then take their night shifts on the course. The golf world isn't exactly being overwhelmed by night golf, but there are enough events to keep any player smiling, or glowing, as the case may be.

A National Nitelite Tournament is being held this summer in the U.S. It will benefit the American Cancer Society and culminate in two nine-hole rounds at the Doral golf club in Miami.

Meanwhile, the first night game in pro golf will take place on June 3 at the Urbana Golf and Country Club in Champaign, Illinois.

There is also plenty of late-night activity in Canada. Twenty-one teams of four players will play a scramble format tomorrow night at the Dundee Country Club in New Dundee, Ontario. There is supposed to be a tournament at the Kleinburg Golf Club north of Toronto next Wednesday night, though as of yesterday the club hadn't received a single paid entry.

Moonlight golf has really caught on up north. Webb will run one tournament a month this season. Starting times begin at 10:30 p.m.

He's also sold 100 Nitelite balls that will be used for the Midnight golf tournament on the first day of summer in the Yukon. "It does get dark there sometime," Webb pointed out.

Golfers who have played night golf report that the scenes are right out of *Star Wars*. "If your group hits its shots down in a hollow or over a hill, when you get there you see four balls shining," said Webb yesterday from Timmins. "When you whack it in the bush and it bounces off trees, you can see every branch it hits because of the glow."

The glow also has attracted outsiders. The Hollinger course runs along a highway and last year the police stopped by. What were those unidentified flying objects anyway? Webb said the police were curious and very understanding.

There seems to be no end to the golfing madness. A few years ago, a ball showed up that was guaranteed not to hook or slice. (And where are they now?)

Then came coloured golf balls that were supposed to take over the market. (And where are *they* now?)

A couple of years ago it was the Cayman Ball that went half the distance of the regulation ball. (And where is *it* now?)

Never mind. The latest and trendiest is a golf ball that will brighten up the night. Could Thomas Edison have imagined it would come to this when he invented the light bulb? Is this an incandescent development in golf, or a bright idea that will become dull and fade out?

Let there be light, the golf-mad populace said, and there was.

Groovy Clubs Spark Debate

***The Globe and Mail*, January 23, 1988**
It was a shot that compelled some major players in the normally conservative world of golf to come out swinging.

When Mark Calcavecchia hit a 7-iron on the 70th hole to a small green surrounded by water, with a wind behind him, and was able to stop the ball within eight feet of the hole on his way to a birdie to win the 1987 Honda Classic in Coral Springs, Florida, he brought to a head a controversy that had been simmering for months.

By anyone's standards, it was a miraculous shot and it called attention to a great leap in technology that was beginning to change the game. Calcavecchia had used a new type of iron with a design that gave him extraordinary control over the spin of a ball — especially on shots made from rough circumstances. His ball had landed as if it were in molasses.

The new clubs — equipped with square grooves rather than the usual V-shaped indentations on their playing surface — make the game easier, but they have also forced golf into a dilemma: Should a sport be obliged to accept all technological innovations or should it make rules that define things forever?

Golf has accepted many technological innovations in its long history: Hickory shafts have given way to metal; and leather balls stuffed with feathers have been outmoded by modern rubber-core balls.

It's not clear that the sport's governors are going to be as receptive to innovation this time around.

Next weekend, the United States Golf Association, the rule-making organization that is one of two recognized golfing authorities, will finally have something to say on square-groove clubs. The decision could have extensive repercussions because most governing bodies, including the Royal Canadian Golf Association, follow the lead of the USGA and golf's other major organization, the Royal and Ancient Golf Club of St. Andrews, Scotland.

"Groovegate," as the controversy has come to be known, has focused on the USGA's right to make policy. It also involves Karsten Solheim, founder and president of Karsten Manufacturing Co. of Phoenix, Arizona. The company manufactures Ping

Eye2 Irons, the most popular club in the world and, according to the USGA, an implement too helpful to the golfer.

Greg Norman, one of the top money winners on the PGA Tour, figures square grooves can trim as many as two or three shots a round. "It's not hard to improve that much if you've got an easy shot each time you miss the green purely because of the new equipment."

But many pros, including Jack Nicklaus, are calling for the clubs to be banned.

Solheim, 76, says the clubs are "a real breakthrough in improving golf-club performance. Just as the tread on a tire improves the ability to control an automobile, so do the grooves on a golf club improve a player's ability to the control the ball."

His clubs are used in 66 countries and are back-ordered for months in pro shops in Canada and the United States. His company, which employs more than 1,500 people, has 22% of the $525-million (U.S.) annual golf club market. Solheim said more than 500,000 sets of Ping Eye2s (at about $1,000 a set) have been purchased since their introduction in late 1984.

But the USGA is concerned that the clubs reduced the element of artful shotmaking that it deems so much a part of golf. The association's certificate of incorporation of 1894 obliges it to promote and conserve the "best interests and true spirit of the game of golf as embodied in its ancient and honourable traditions."

The USGA changed its Rules of Golf in January 1984, effectively allowing any observant manufacturer to develop iron clubs with square grooves, known also as U-shaped or box-shaped grooves.

Iron clubs had long incorporated V-shaped grooves on their faces. The rules required that the grooves be no more than 0.035 inch wide from edge to edge, and no nearer to one another than three times the width of the adjacent groove. The triple-tiered rule was meant to set a standard for manufacturers and to ensure that ability counted more than equipment.

By the late 1970s, though, golf-club manufacturers had become involved in the so-called investment-cast method, in which a single mould could be used to produce vast numbers of irons, many of them unconventional in design, like the Ping Eye2. Clubs that were made by the old forging method took much longer to produce; it was also difficult to design anything other than a conventionally shaped clubhead.

Investment-cast clubs soon became the clubs of choice for the majority of golfers, but the procedure meant that grooves lost definition and became U-shaped rather than V-shaped. So, the USGA simply changed the wording of the rule to allow U-shaped grooves; it had no reason to believe U-shaped grooves would enhance performance.

Solheim, though, knew that square grooves could very well give a golfer more control over the golf ball. He had already proved this to himself with his Ping putters, which many Tour golfers were using successfully. He had a waiting clientele when he came out with his Ping Eye2 square-groove clubs.

Golfers soon found out what Solheim knew — that square grooves allow them to put more spin on the ball, thus generating more control.

They are particularly effective from greenside rough. It has generally been more difficult to control the ball from the rough because grass blades intervene between the ball and club face, but square grooves (because they can trap more water and material) cut through the blades and grab the ball.

Tests conducted eventually by the USGA showed that spin rates and, thus, ball control did indeed increase with Ping Eye2 clubs. The increase in spin rate was particularly dependent on the distance between grooves. The USGA also concluded that square-groove clubs might produce more spin than V-groove clubs.

The USGA decided it would have to come up with a new formula for measuring groove width and that the formula that worked with V-grooves was no longer useful.

So, last June, the organization adopted a means of measuring the width between grooves that effectively banned Ping Eye2 irons, but it did not confront head-on the issue of square grooves. That will come next weekend.

The June ruling "grandfathered" the use of Ping Eye2 irons — the new irons will not be declared illegal for all golfers until January 1, 1996. However, the USGA has banned them for its own competitions, such as the U.S. Open, U.S. Amateur and U.S. Women's Open, starting in 1989.

Meanwhile, about 20 manufacturers are making clubs with square grooves that meet the width requirement. Solheim has refused to retool, saying his clubs were legal when he made them, and he has advertised heavily in golf publications in an attempt to influence the USGA to reverse its position.

"I feel the USGA," Solheim said, "has no choice but to reverse its measurement rule."

But this is not likely to happen, so attention now is centred on the larger question of square grooves themselves.

The association recently observed tests conducted by the PGA Tour, set up for pros, in Palm Springs, California, to determine the influence of square grooves.

"Our decision will depend on what the numbers show," Frank Hannigan, the USGA's executive director, said in an interview from USGA headquarters in Far Hills, New Jersey

Some players feel the USGA is within its rights to control technical developments. Tom Watson calls the USGA the "guardians of the game, absolutely necessary."

"There's got to be a time when you say, 'No more.' If you took a poll of the players, I think a majority of them would say we should not play with boxed grooves."

Frank Thomas, technical director for the USGA, agrees that the square grooves inordinately influence control of the golf ball. But he emphasizes that the real benefit accrues only to fine players, not the average golfer.

"The very best players in the world benefit the most," Thomas says. "There are golfers who will realize some extra spin, but it is maximized among golf professionals."

Whatever the USGA and the PGA Tour decide, it's clear that golf has entered a new age. It's an age where sophisticated equipment could influence a player's ability to control the flight of the ball. It remains to be seen how dramatic the effect is, and what its long-term repercussions for the game at large will be.

USGA Comes Up Short on Long Putters

The Globe and Mail, **February 14, 1990**
The commotion about the legality of Ping Eye2 square-groove irons has obscured another issue that has more to do with whether equipment innovations reduce the skill required to play

the game. The issue is that of long putters of the sort that Orville Moody used to win the 1989 U.S. Senior Open and that many golfers, both pro and amateur, are using today.

To settle the Ping Eye2 issue first. The USGA ruled that anybody who already is using the Ping Eye2 irons with their wider grooves can continue to use them, but that no new such irons can be made. Karsten, the company that manufactures the Ping Eye2 irons, agreed to retool and come up with a means of making irons that conform to the USGA's method of measuring grooves.

Case closed, then. No money exchanged. The end, one hopes, of golf's protracted and most boring controversy. After all, the difference between what was legal and what was illegal amounted to the width of one human hair in the measuring of groove width. Does anybody really believe that helps a golfer?

But the longer putter. Now there's an area for debate. There's a forum for discussion. Rule 4-1 of the USGA's code points out that a golf club "shall not be substantially different from the traditional customary form and make." The long putter appears substantially different. But is it?

The long putter is 53 to 55 inches, stem to stern, some 18 inches longer than most putters. The golfer can stand up nearly straight while using it. More important, the putter is designed so that the player can lock one end against his upper body. Wrist break becomes negligible, and short putts are easier to make when there's but one fixed pivot point.

"The length and method allow a golfer to swing the putter almost through its natural arc," USGA technical director Frank Thomas said yesterday from his office in Far Hills, New Jersey. "Without the wrist action, the putter is more easily guided along the line. So you don't get nervous over those little putts that cause the yips, the ones you think you should make. I don't know if the longer putter makes a good putter better, but it does seem to make a bad putter better."

That's for sure. Moody couldn't sink a four-footer into a bathtub when he used a conventional putter. But he became Bobby Locke incarnate when he stuck the longer putter against his ribs. Okay, he didn't turn into the magician Locke was on the greens years ago, but he did become a more-than-competent holer-outer, as they used to say in Scotland. His fears dissolved. His money winnings expanded.

Enter the USGA, worried over the legality of the long putter. Did it deviate too far from traditional style? Was it a great advantage to the skilled player? The USGA's equipment-standards committee met and then ruled.

"The committee felt, and the executive committee agreed, that the use of longer putters introduces a new element but does not change the essential nature of the game." These are Stuart Bloch's words, and he is the chairman of the equipment-standards committee and a USGA vice-president.

This recent decision was progressive. It meant that the USGA acknowledges that change is inevitable, as it always has been. After all, the USGA has allowed metal woods, graphite and boron shafts, etc. Besides it has never had a length limitation on clubs, although no club can be shorter than 18 inches.

Still, the decision wasn't easily come by.

"Every person involved in the decision struggled within himself," Thomas said. "But we also had letters from older players saying they couldn't play without it any more. At times we were torn between our hearts and what is good for the game. In the end we decided that the long putter, while it may not be in the traditional style, was not un-traditional enough for us to disallow its use."

Older players won't be the only ones to use the long putter, which most manufacturers now make. Tom Kite has fiddled with his grip to improve his stroke and has also practised with the longer putter. Reports from the field indicate that he can't miss from within 15 feet. Craig Stadler put on a horrifying display of putting during Sunday's final round of the Hawaiian Open when he missed five short putts on the last few holes. He may well be using the long putter this very minute. He should be.

The long putter did come with one unexpected liability. It's too long to carry in the cabin of an aircraft. Thomas said that airline officials considered it a weapon and wouldn't allow it aboard. The USGA has solved this problem by approving the collapsibility of the putter as long as it isn't made of two separate components, and as long as it is used only in the fully extended position. Golfers can take their long putters with them inside the cabin if they so desire. Why anybody would want to is another question.

So you can use your old Ping Eye2 irons to spin the ball to a stop nearer the hole. You can use long putters to make short putts. The game is becoming too easy. Surely you agree.

When It Comes to Clubs, Loyalty Isn't Ironclad

The Globe and Mail, **January 22, 1992**
Somebody will unearth a Ping iron hundreds of years from now at the Crooked Stick Golf Club in Carmel, Indiana, long after the club has become an estate housing development. John Daly will have used that iron in winning the 1991 PGA Championship at Crooked Stick and will have given it to what was once the club's museum.

Really, though. How much can Daly have valued the irons? Five months later he isn't even playing Pings. Daly recently signed a five-year $5-million contract to play Wilson's Ultra irons. Our golfing archaeologist of the future might as well use Daly's crooked stick — that iron — to weed in his organic vegetable garden.

This scenario comes to mind because so many top players are changing equipment today. Even Jack Nicklaus has left the MacGregor Golf Company after some 30 years. It's a wild time in the biz, and smaller companies are feeling the effects.

Run the list down. There's Daly. Fred Couples, the hottest player in golf with 15 top-six finishes in his past 17 tournaments, including three wins, has left the Tommy Armour company for Lynx and $1 million a year. Meanwhile, Joey Sindelar has left Toronto's Accuform to sign with Tommy Armour for a contract rumoured to be in six figures annually. Accuform can't match the bonanza, so Sindelar has left the company after 10 years.

The changeable situation will come more into focus when the thirty-ninth annual PGA merchandise show begins Friday in Orlando. Accuform will display its clubs. Players and other manufacturers know that Accuform makes perhaps the most precise irons in the game, a consequence of the 15-year-old company having evolved out of a respected airplane-parts manufacturing business that is still thriving.

But the current marketplace is such that Accuform can't focus on the PGA Tour. Accuform depended on the quality of its product rather than bloated contracts to sell itself. That's why Sindelar played Accuform for a decade. It's why Davis Love III played the clubs for 18 months in 1989 and 1990 before going to Hogan and now to Armour, and why Canadian Dan Halldorson has played the clubs for years.

Now Sindelar is gone. Accuform's highest-profile player has won six PGA Tour events since 1985 and finished as high as third on the money list in 1988. The company feels his loss.

"We've had a tremendous relationship with Joey," Accuform vice-president John Saksun Jr. said yesterday. "If we could pay him the money, he would still be with us. There were a couple of years where he had better offers, but he played our clubs for less money."

Saksun pointed out that selling clubs is all marketing. He mentioned that people in the industry realize that players don't switch because they suddenly like another club.

But switch they do. Ian Woosnam left Dunlop for Maruman a few years ago after a tremendous year. He played terribly for a long time. Wayne Levi switched to Yonex last year and went from winning four PGA Tour events and finishing second on the money list in 1991 to winning none and finishing eighty-seventh. It's also true that Sindelar fell to ninety-fourth spot last year while still playing Accuform.

It should be obvious that form has more to do with one's performance than one's equipment. But the public buys the dream that the club can create the swing. And who better than tour players to suggest the illusion? Never mind that they can shoot 66 with any properly made and fitted club.

"As a company you're rolling the dice when picking players," Accuform's director of marketing, Brad Turner, said this week. "It will be interesting to see how Daly and Couples do with their new clubs."

Meanwhile, PGA Tour player Bill Britton has come on board for Accuform. He's finished thirty-fourth, fifty-first and fifty-seventh on the PGA Tour the past three years. Britton can play. But will the Staten Island, New York, pro stick with the company no matter how successful he becomes? That remains to be seen.

In the end, it was disappointing to watch as Sindelar promoted the Armour clubs during the Bob Hope Chrysler Classic telecast on the weekend. He said he was struck by how many golfers were talking about the 845S irons. He said he had never seen that amount of excitement over a set of irons.

But there was more to the story. You can't blame Sindelar for taking Armour's money, but you can feel turned off by his words. Sindelar might have said, more to the point, "Armour is offering players more money than Accuform, and that's one reason why the touring pros are so excited about them."

Couples, Daly and others could say the same thing. They would be more accurate, but such straightforwardness wouldn't sell clubs to the public.

Chapter Four

INSTRUCTION

HERE IS one reason among many that golf works as a lifetime sport. It's because we can always improve, and that's no illusion. It's promised in all the golf magazines and instructional videos. Golf schools make a living out of every golfer's belief that his best golf is ahead. And who is to say it's not? That's especially true for golfers who have never really applied themselves to learning the fundamentals of the swing. It's true: There are fundamentals.

But that doesn't mean that we learn well. How could we? There's too much choice, and besides, we amateurs don't have a teaching professional watching over our every shot, video-taping our moves away from, into and through the ball. Most golfers, in fact, have never given themselves the opportunity to play to their potential. That would mean sticking with a sensible system for some time, playing through the bad times with confidence that things will turn around. Instead we come from the course slightly distraught. Somebody asks, "How did you play today?" And we answer, wryly, "I don't know. I just didn't play my usual game today. Now that I think about it, I rarely play my usual game."

Precisely. What's usual is our flubs. But not to worry. We only have to get some handle on the swing. And for that the machinery of instruction is out there. We have already dealt in Chapter Three with the gadgets and instructional aids that are meant to help us become the golfers we are meant to be. Now I'd like to take you into the world of instruction itself. It's as bizarre as the equipment world, that's for sure. But it's all in the interest of finding a perfect swing, or at least a better swing.

Start with "The Golfing Machine," in which G.O.L.F. stands for Geometrically Oriented Linear Force. I attended a school that taught this method that Bobby Clampett once swore by, and to which in large part 1991 Players Championship winner Jodie Mudd subscribes. Why not? It has all the answers, tells you where you need to be every part of the swing, and gives you choices. But is it science or is it just theory? You decide.

I went to a university library once to really study the swing. There I found some 40 doctoral dissertations on golf, some of which I discuss in a column here for your eternal edification. (That doesn't mean confusion.) Failing that, try the books and magazines; they're full of the latest information on the swing. I took a look at some of the theories in a column and then couldn't take the club back without having a long discussion with myself first. But I did enjoy the reading.

Even the touring pros have troubles. They're constantly overhauling their swings, searching for the better way. Ray Floyd has done it, Jack Nicklaus has done it, Greg Norman and Nick Faldo have done it. Maybe nobody has done it better than Faldo, to whom I refer frequently in this chapter. He works, of course, with David Leadbetter. Leadbetter's book, *The Golf Swing*, came out in 1990 and had sold some 200,000 copies at last count. His video on the full swing has been the best-seller for some time. And there's no doubting the value of his work. The 30-minute lesson I took from him as part of some original research was well-spent time. The trouble is, I need further work. Faldo works with Leadbetter for 10 hours a day from time to time. How can I expect to improve in 30 minutes? This question brings me to another: How has United States vice-president Dan Quayle done after his work with Leadbetter? I include a column that considers Leadbetter's work with Quayle.

But Leadbetter isn't the only teacher. Not by a long shot. Canadian master George Clifton had a look at my swing a few years ago. He thought I needed more extension on my backswing. Then there was the session I had with Jack Grout, Nicklaus's only teacher. Grout died May 13, 1989, and Nicklaus has said that he misses him as both teacher and friend, probably more of the latter since the best teacher is also a good friend. Grout expressed some deep feelings towards his protégé Nicklaus in his will. That section of the will was made public; I include his words here because they were the feelings of a kind and decent man who felt there were many fine teachers in the game. Grout was right. I am sure of that. Teaching is an art as much as it is a science. It's all about communicating and relating to an individual about something quite personal — his golf swing. I'm convinced that most golfers would do well to find a teacher whose company they enjoyed and then commit to a program over a significant period of time. The student might then be able to play his "usual" game more often. That's the goal of instruction; it's not often realized, but then again what would golf be without the continual search for the magic? I've searched, too much probably. That was apparent to me as I compiled the pieces that follow.

The G.O.L.F. MACHINE

Toronto Life, **August 1983**
January 20, 1687. Thomas Kincaid, Edinburgh medical student and incipient golfer, writes in his diary the first known words of golf instruction: "After dinner I went out to the golve. I found the only way of playing at the golve is: 1, to stand as you do at fencing with a small sword, bending your legs a little, and holding the muscles of your legs and back and armes exceeding bent or fixt or stiffe, and not at all slackening them in the time you are bringing down the stroak."

Amen. And the flow of instruction has not abated in the 300 years since, as golfers endeavour to solve what writer Paul Gallico once called "a mystery as much of a one as the universe and solar system, electricity or ionic affinities."

The idea that the swing can be understood and mastered appeals to most competent golfers, but to none more than Bobby Clampett, a 23-year-old professional from the U.S. who is expected to play in the Canadian Open at the Glen Abbey Golf Club from July 28 to 31. Clampett is the embodiment of a system set down in a book called *The Golfing Machine*, a confusing tome replete with diagrams, photographs, cross-references and strange terminology.

The book was written by Homer Kelley, a problem-solver by inclination (he once turned down an invitation to join the Mensa Society) and an engineer by profession (he worked for both the U.S. Navy and Boeing aircraft). Kelley, who died in February at the age of 75, believed that the swing was subject to universal laws of force and motion, and in 1941 he took it upon himself to study it. Twenty-eight years later, *The Golfing Machine* was published under the imprint Star System Press, so named because Kelley had once come across a definition that said a star was a vision of distant truth, and Kelley felt he was writing the *truth* about the golf swing.

Kelley's first disciple was Ben Doyle, whom he met in 1969 while Doyle was a golf pro in Bellingham, Washington. Three years later, the Vancouver-born Doyle had become the "machine's" first authorized instructor and the teaching professional at a course in Carmel Valley, California, which happened to be the home course of 12-year-old Bobby Clampett. Doyle has been Clampett's only teacher since, and while Canadian golfer Jim Nelford and U.S. players Johnny Miller, Pat McGowan and Mac O'Grady have been exposed to the system, only Clampett has had what amounts to lifelong immersion. He has also used his knowledge to advantage: In 1981 and 1982, his first full years on the PGA Tour, Clampett earned nearly $400,000 (indeed, last year he won the Southern Open and came very close to winning the U.S. and British Opens).

Although it's self-evident that the golf swing is nothing more than angles, lines, arcs, planes and alignments, the idea that it could be looked at so scientifically would have been heresy to me a few years ago. I believed then that the best anybody could do was to play by feel. I attributed problems of even the top players to natural fluctuations in human performance. I did not

consider that incomplete understanding was the culprit. However, I began to see that players such as Ben Hogan, George
Knudson, Jack Nicklaus and Tom Watson — golfers who stayed
in the game the longest — could analyze their swings intelligently.

There is no question that *The Golfing Machine* is complicated,
but, as Kelley wrote: "Treating a complex subject or action as
though it were simple multiplies its complexity because of the difficulty in systematizing missing and unknown facts or elements. Demanding that golf instruction be kept simple does not make it
simple — only incomplete and ineffective." In other words, simple
ideas don't produce free swings; they freeze swings.

Clampett agrees: "Mr. Kelley has brought us something that
we can really base our swings on. He doesn't say it's the only
way to play golf. It's a basis to understanding your swing, and it
allows for all variations in the swing. It explains all the components in the swing and then leaves it up to the player to choose
his variations. People who understand the system can become
more consistent because they understand what they are doing."

The Golfing Machine begins by redefining golf. It becomes
G.O.L.F., or Geometrically Oriented Linear Force. Kelley asserts
that there are precisely 24 components to the golf swing, and
while the terms sound difficult, they simply relate to what goes
on in the efficient swing. Recently I attended a four-day school
on the "machine" held by authorized instructor Tommy
Tomasello at the Lake Marion Golf Club in Santee, South Carolina, and found that my own swing could be improved.

Each of Kelley's 24 components has variations — to a total of
144. Together, they account for all the individual differences in
the golf swing and the relationship between what happens to a
golfer's swing when he chooses one variation over another. Consider, for example, the component called knee action. Says
Clampett: "We could talk about right-anchor knee action as opposed to standard knee action. Right-anchor knee action really
doesn't produce a structured enough backswing. It tends to restrict the shoulder turn, then to restrict the hip and back turn. It
makes your hands want to go behind your head. But if you go to
standard knee action it can help promote where you straighten
your right knee. It can make your hands come farther out at the

top of your backswing, and give you a more structured feel. It can also help you set up behind the ball more on the backswing. There are a lot of advantages to it, but if somebody is real comfortable playing with right-anchor knee action then he should use that."

The 24 components, operating effectively, produce an efficient and precise stroke. When Clampett is playing well, he does seem machine-like, and he has been criticized for being more a mechanical man than a golfer. The truth, though, is that his knowledge liberates rather than suppresses his creativity. He can invent shots simply by selecting variations of components.

Such was the case during the final round of the World Cup near Acapulco, Mexico, last December when Clampett faced a delicate chip shot from 3 feet behind the 17th green to a hole cut only 20 feet away from and below him. The sod was fairly new, and his ball could have bounced every which way. For a minute or so Clampett bent near the ground, examined its minutest details, then settled on his putter for the shot. He came within an inch or so of holing it.

"I had all sorts of opportunities there," Clampett told me after the round. Opportunities, mind you, not shots. "I was looking for the stroke that would give me the purest roll to the hole, one that wouldn't be affected by inconsistencies of the ground." Clampett could have chosen vertical hinging for the shot, with the clubface laid back, to pop the ball and let it land softly on the green. Or he could have used angle hinging, letting the clubhead rotate to the left through the ball, thereby hitting a lower shot that would run down to the hole. But because he had so little space to work with, he chose to putt the ball. Similarly, on full shots, he can decide what to do by running through the permutations or combinations available to him.

While Clampett is always trying to be machinelike, he *is* aware of human frailty. "None of us," he says, "will ever know exactly what went wrong every time we make a golf swing. We'd like to think we could, but we'll never know that. Ideally, the execution of a golf shot should be non-emotional, filled with positive programming. When the machine is in running order, and the computer is feeding the machine positive reinforcement, you should hit nothing but very good golf shots."

Another situation at the World Cup showed just how powerful a machine-like approach can be and also how it is limited by the unknowns of human nature or impulse. On the last hole of the tournament, Clampett needed to hit the ball close to the hole, if not sink it, to give him and partner Bob Gilder a chance to tie Spaniards Manuel Pinero and José-Maria Canaizares, with whom they were playing. Clampett was 149 yards from the hole. As he prepared for the shot, he was reminded of a similar circumstance a few months before at a tournament at Pinehurst, North Carolina, when he felt he needed to hole his final shot to have a chance at a playoff.

"When I hit that shot at Pinehurst," Clampett told me after he had finished the World Cup, "I had the same yardage to the hole. I was focused right in on what I had to do. I had perfect tunnel vision where I saw nothing but where I wanted the ball to go. I had such good programming there, and when I hit the shot, I actually thought it might go in. But it landed just short of the hole and stopped quickly." Clampett had been stymied by the manner in which the ball reacted when it hit the ground, an imponderable from that distance.

Back on that last hole at the World Cup, Clampett had the same feeling. He saw only his target. But then he hit the ball 30 feet to the right of the hole, a poor shot when his thoughts were so concentrated. I wondered what had gone wrong. Clampett, his wry smile giving away his acceptance of the game's enigmas, had a perfectly acceptable response, though he was as befuddled as I. "Golf's a funny game," he said. "Sometimes you feel you've put the same thoughts on two shots, but they go entirely differently. I felt so sharp, so precise on that shot. But the results weren't there. It's frustrating to think that if I program myself so precisely, that the results still might not come out. But I know there are so many things that happen from analyzing the shot before you swing to the finish. You can't possibly break everything down. All you can do is look at yourself as a machine, and try to create a golf swing based on law."

Yes, that's all anybody can do, and at least the "machine" gives the player a means of understanding the swing. Its comprehensiveness is its great virtue; it's hardly a defect that it does not explain the mysteries of our psyches and nervous systems. Let that task fall to the psychologists, the neurologists and the philosophers. Homer Kelley was an engineer, and *The Golfing Machine* and Bobby Clampett are his legacies.

A Time for Theories on Stroking the Golf Ball

The Globe and Mail, **April 27, 1984**
Lead with the left. Hit with the right. Lift the left heel going back to facilitate getting onto the right side. Turn your hips in a barrel. Hold your arms tightly together, as if they were cast in plaster. Swing to a reverse C position. Guard against reverse pivoting.

Next: Absorb these and other seemingly endless golf maxims and try to swing a golf club. Then, send your caddy on an expedition into the rough if you're in North America, the heather and gorse if you're in Scotland, or the jungle if you're in Thailand. Best also to have a flask of whisky along to calm your nerves, especially since all you've done is try to follow somebody's idea of golf instruction.

Maybe it's not good form to make light of our agonizing efforts to master golf, but it's the beginning of the season across Canada and, undoubtedly, every golfer is certain he has some new and useful idea that will help him improve. Come October or sooner — tomorrow? — most of the ideas will have proved worthless.

Nevertheless, it is one of the charms of the game to sit on the balcony in the evening and contemplate some of the thoughts, sayings and pseudo-principles that pass through like so many weather systems. If nothing else, they can help develop in the golfer a sense of humour that British champion Joyce Wethered said was the quality that helped her most overcome both her own and the game's vicissitudes.

Consider, for example, some of the instructional material that has appeared in golf magazines over the years. A Delaware professional named Rick McCall once wrote that golfers could correct excessive arm action in the chipping stroke by crossing one foot over another when practising. Ken Venturi has just suggested that on the downswing of a chip shot the golfer should move his right shoulder towards his chin "to promote a raking action, returning the clubhead to a square position at impact."

In 1967, a man named Benito L. Lueras from Miami advocated in a golf magazine that golfers place a sheet of rolled paper in their mouths and point it at the ball before swinging. If the paper moved, that would indicate head movement. He didn't advocate the paper be flavoured for extra taste.

Recently we've had Jim Simons telling the golfing public to start the swing by pulling or turning the right hip off the line. If that gets too complicated for the higher-handicap player, Simons suggests, he should focus more on swinging his arms. But where oh where do the hips go if the arms lead?

Golfers have an apparently insatiable appetite for tips. An editor for a leading U.S. magazine recently wrote that rather than in-depth studies of the psychological side of golf, "the readers much prefer, according to all surveys, 'hit the hell out of your 5-iron.'"

To do exactly that, golfers have been told to rotate their wrists through impact for more hand action. They've been advised to keep the right hand from passing the left at impact. They've been encouraged to hit up against a firm left side. For some, the rule of thumb is to stay behind the ball at impact, which is where most of us are naturally — behind the eight-ball.

Smiting the ball is, of course, a great thrill for golfers. No surprise, then, that it's been a source for much discussion. In 1923 Seymour Dunn wrote that power is transmitted to the clubs by the use of the hands, thereby preventing "leverage collapse." Homer Kelley wrote in his book *The Golfing Machine* about "power accumulators," the first such factor being a bent right arm striving to straighten itself through impact.

The main factor for power, post-doctoral students of the golf swing agree, is clubhead lag or delay. This occurs when the clubhead is well behind the hands just a split second before impact. Then, supposedly, the clubhead catches up as the golfer releases through the ball the energy he has stored during his swing.

The position is evident in any stop-action photographs of better golfers. It's also been hailed as the secret of good golf for years, for it allows the golfer to swing not only with power, but with rhythm, which creates accuracy.

The real question is how to achieve this position. It happens because of centrifugal force. But centrifugal force is abstract. The eye can't see it in another golfer, though the player can certainly feel the pull when he's performing. However, explaining it must go a lot further than "hit the hell out of your 5-iron" idea.

Naturally, there's no shortage of explanations, analogies, metaphors and aphorisms, all meant to catch a sense of clubhead lag.

Hopeful golfers might try to feel the force. Or they might try to hit the ball with the butt end of the club, as George Knudson was told to do years ago but which he vehemently rails against today. The golfer might think of pulling down on the church bell from the top of his swing, or, as Knudson now suggests, he might simply transfer his weight from his right to left side when he begins his downswing, a move that he feels will create clubhead lag.

Should any golfer find the secret to good golf, along with the ability to communicate it, he is advised to go to the British Museum in London, where he no doubt will be immortalized somehow.

Not to preach to the converted who believe there are answers once and for all to the riddles of the golf swing, but a word of warning is necessary in these first days of spring. Perversely, the harder we try in golf, the more we seem, as Walter Travis wrote in 1901, to introduce "a jerk in the swing." Horrible to say, but could that jerk not be you, or me, hopeful golfers all?

Masterly Golf Mentor Is the King of Swing

The Globe and Mail, **February 1, 1985**
Anybody looking for the ultimate in golf instruction should hop a plane today and visit Torontonian George Clifton. He can be found at the Turnberry Isle Country Club in Miami, often sitting on a chair behind Ladies Professional Golf Association touring pro Nancy White-Brewer, the newest Canadian on the tour.

Should the visitor in quest of real knowledge of the golf swing journey to Miami, he will find a man who has been teaching golf for nearly 50 years. In his quiet and dignified way, Clifton, 67, has placed himself in the honour roll of golf instructors. In any roll call of master teachers, he belongs with Stewart Maiden, Tommy Armour, Ernest Jones, Jack Grout and Canadians Bob Gray and Gordon Brydson.

Clifton has worked with such Canadian pros as Jerry Magee, Jim McKitterick and Irv Lightstone. "He's been like a godfather to at least 25 of us," says Lightstone, who worked as an assistant under Clifton at Maple Downs, north of Toronto, 30 years ago. Lightstone eventually took the head pro job there, a position he still holds.

"George had a way of getting you on the right track," Lightstone says. "That's because he was really so much more than a teacher. He made you feel like the most important person in the world for the time you were with him."

Thirty years ago, Clifton taught a boy named Norm Mogil. Mogil, now 40, went on to win the club championship at Maple Downs four or five times and won the Canadian Junior title in 1962. Clifton taught Mogil the basics of the swing; Mogil has not vacillated since and, according to Lightstone, has a wonderfully repetitive swing.

"George had and still has a thorough understanding of the golf swing," Mogil says. "He's thought it through, acquired it over the years rather than repeating what he heard."

Clifton's methods were evident last week at Deerfield Beach, Florida where he was working with White-Brewer. She would hit a few balls and ask a question. Clifton would rise from his chair, walk beside her on the tee and make sure she understood exactly what he was saying. When he would sit down, he would be confident that he had got his point across.

"I have always believed that a golfer has to get the basics down," Clifton says. "I've tried to teach Nancy so that, when I'm not there, she can still look at her game and make the necessary changes."

Clifton's greatest asset is that he allows players to be themselves. He believes that all top golfers have one move in common — "they must set the club on the inside coming down

through the ball and allow their club to collide with the ball" —
but feels they can achieve this differently.

"If I see a man as loose and pliable as Sam Snead," Clifton
says, "I'll teach him to swing that way. But, if I see somebody as
rotund as a Porky Oliver, well, then I'll let him swing in a way
that's comfortable for him."

Like all fine teachers, Clifton can get right to the heart of the
matter. "He can keynote the exact thing you need to know,"
Lightstone says. "The simplicity he teaches with is overwhelming.
You can spend three minutes with him and you feel you can go
out and shoot 65."

Some years ago, Clifton had a golf school in downtown Toronto. He also ran clinics at the Colonial Tavern and the Conroy
Hotel. Every session was an occasion. Lightstone remembers golfers such as Nick Weslock visiting regularly, wanting to listen to
the master.

Years before it was popular, Clifton pioneered the use of the
swing-sequence camera. He still has film of Mogil's swing and
believes that the camera, used properly, can aid greatly in a
golfer's understanding.

For Clifton, the camera has been another means of communication, which is the heart of effective teaching. This is not a man
who cajoles and embarrasses a student into learning; he allows
the player to see, hear and feel the swing at his own rate.

"If I have worked at anything in my career, it's to learn to
convey what I was thinking into a person's mind, even if I had
to say it four different ways," he says. "If a guy can do that, he
can teach."

Asked about the rewards of his devotion to golf and golfers,
Clifton says they are far more than turning somebody into a
champion golfer, as he very well may do with White-Brewer.

"It's also the 17-handicap who goes to a 13, the person who
starts to really enjoy golf because he can figure out what he's
doing," Clifton says.

Lightstone says he learned everything he knows about the
swing from Clifton, who will return in the spring to begin his
eighth season teaching at the Bayview Country Club in Toronto.
Mogil says he received time and patience from Clifton, that there
"was never a curt moment." White-Brewer says all she needs to

do to feel great is to be around Clifton, that he "always picks me up."

Tomorrow, at its annual meeting, the Royal Canadian Golf Association will induct George Knudson and Al Balding into its Hall of Fame. They deserve the honour, but nobody deserves it more than Clifton. He has introduced so many people to the sport.

That is the highest contribution a person can make to the game. It goes far beyond winning money and titles. While Clifton may be enjoying the Florida sunshine this weekend as he works with White-Brewer, he really should be at the RCGA's meeting — taking his rightful place in the Hall of Fame.

The Overhaul

Golf Magazine, **March 1986**
The golf swing butters the pro golfer's bread. Fills his stomach. Pays the rent. So it's not something he's likely to fool around with, right?

Not quite. When old reliable isn't doing what it's supposed to, many pro golfers head for the shop — not for minor servicing but for a complete overhaul.

In the mid-seventies, for example, Johnny Miller revamped his swing to cope with changes in his physique. Greg Norman spent half of 1978 flattening his swing before he felt confident with it. And in one of the best-documented changes of recent times, Mark O'Meara altered his entire swing plane. Those are but a few examples.

All good golfers possess a sound knowledge of their swings and know when a change is necessary. It's pro golf's version of "shape up or ship out." "When you see your ball do something funny," says Lee Trevino, "you better know exactly what you did wrong, so that you can correct it. If a player misses a shot and doesn't know why — somebody who really doesn't understand his swing — he's in trouble."

Tom Watson agrees. "You've got to know which way the ball is going. Otherwise you have no chance. You might as well just quit."

John Cook puts it more succinctly. "You can't be out there going 'Ohmigod! I snap-hooked it! What do I do?'"

What the pros do is check in the old swing and check out a new one. It's often a long and laborious process that can leave a golfer emotionally frazzled. Making the decision to change, however, can be easy.

"Real easy," says David Graham, who arrived in the United States from Australia in 1971 and spent two years transforming his wristy style into a more fluid, big-muscles swing that could handle the rigours of the PGA Tour. "It's kind of like a used car. If you get a couple of dead batteries and the engine doesn't start, well, it might be your favourite car, but it's real easy to drive into a dealership and ask for a new car. That's what golf is like. If you're out there and not playing well for a period of time, you've got to look and say, 'Well, am I not a good enough putter or what area of my game is not good enough? Is it my mechanics? My grip? My whole swing?' Then if you have the ability to seek the answer, you've got to have the patience and desire to do something about it."

Graham did something about it in 1972. Previously, his swing was typical of a player accustomed to the small ball, links courses and wind: flat, whippy and not a lot of shoulder turn to prevent being blown over. The trademark was a low hook that brought Graham little success in America. During a disappointing Colonial tournament, he sought advice from fellow countryman Bruce Devlin, who told Graham the lie of his clubs was too flat, he stood too far from the ball, his swing plane was too flat, he aimed the club left of the target at the top of the swing, his left hand was too strong on the grip and his weight was in the wrong place — lots of faults but faults that feed on one another. Graham began the overhaul by altering the loft of his clubs and standing closer to the ball. Then he toiled with his grip and, although it was some years before he achieved major success, he chalked up his first Tour win taking a playoff for the 1972 Cleveland Open. The player he beat was Bruce Devlin.

O'Meara knew for himself that drastic changes were called for; he just didn't know what they should be. His first season on Tour, 1981, he was rookie of the year. Then he slumped in '82 to 118th on the money list. Working with instructor Hank Haney, he jumped to second on the '84 list, taking his first victory. In '85, although he slipped to tenth in earnings, he won twice. If that's not testimony to the possibilities of change, nothing is.

"I'd gotten to the point where my swing would not hold up mechanically week in, week out," confesses O'Meara. When Haney emphasized mechanics over pure timing and told O'Meara he had to concentrate on what he was doing, O'Meara was shocked: "You mean I have to *think* while I'm swinging?"

Now O'Meara realizes that, at least for him, "you don't want to depend only on timing, because your hands are moving so fast through impact that you can't say, 'Okay, now release the clubhead.' What you want to do is give yourself the best opportunity to let it happen naturally." With the help of videotape, Haney taught O'Meara to swing much flatter, giving him a more effective angle of attack.

"At first it was very difficult," O'Meara remembers, "because any time you make a change, it's going to feel unnatural, uncomfortable. But all you have to ask yourself is 'How well am I doing with what's natural?' If not very well, then maybe you ought to try unnatural for a while because, sooner or later, unnatural becomes natural."

Miller had to change his swing because he changed — physically. After his searing play of the early seventies, Miller woke up one morning and found himself 20 pounds heavier, at 195 instead of 175. "Everybody thought I'd been lifting weights," he chuckles, "which I suppose I was. I was working on my land, lifting rocks, using chainsaws, digging. But I didn't realize it could affect my golf swing. I thought, if anything, it might be positive, that I'd be stronger. But in Tucson in 1976 I found my clubs felt so light. I felt I was gripping the head end and swinging the handle."

In his pre-muscle days, Miller took the club back a little outside "like Tony Lema and Hubert Green," he says. "Then I just dropped it into the slot and gave it a good hard rip once I got halfway down. I'd pause at the top, drop it in and nail it. But now I had so much tension in my muscles, I couldn't even make the pause. I couldn't drop into the slot. I'd go over the top of the slot and cut the ball to the right or if I went ahead and released, I pulled it."

Miller tried heavier clubs. He moved the ball back in his stance. He worked on his weight shift, switching from his long reverse-C action to a more straight-back position through the ball. But the toughest part was in his head.

"Quite honestly, I never did make the total adjustment," Miller admits. "My brain was saying to my body, 'Hey, your old swing is here. Go ahead and do it.' And my body was saying, 'I can't do it.' I never could get back to the old swing."

Wayne Levi is a slightly different case. If he ever reverts to his old swing, he'll never see the right side of the fairway again. As Levi moved up through the golfing ranks, he was used to addressing the ball with his hands far behind it, leaving the clubface open. He compensated on the downswing by closing the blade. But when he reached the Florida mini-tours in 1972 and moved into contention, he fell afoul of a big, sweeping hook. He sought help from Rick Christie, pro at the University of South Florida course in Tampa.

"Rick showed me how to set up," Levi says. "We looked at better swings and nobody set up the way I did. But when I made the change by pushing my hands out, I didn't think I had a chance. The blade seemed closed. 'You gotta be kidding,' I thought."

Eventually Levi won the New Hampshire Open, proof that he was on the right path. "I started winning when I went out there and trusted what I was doing. I was hitting good shots under pressure and was confident of what I did."

Levi put the overhaul to its ultimate test: He took the changes to the golf course, subjecting them to tournament pressure. Because when you come down to it, the practice range tells you nothing.

"You can hit 50 perfect shots on the range and then hit a terrible shot on the first tee," says Miller. "The hardest part of overhauling your swing is that what you do successfully on the practice tee has almost nothing to do with what you do on the first tee of a tournament. For when the going gets tough, your subconscious takes over and you get back to what you were doing originally."

It's a scary thought, having to stand up with the best in the world and subject something totally new to such pressure. But the time comes when a player — amateur or pro — feels more sure of himself. He might let himself release the club. The ball may not finish near the hole after a perfect flight pattern, but there may be just that touch of draw he's been working on. "The best results you can see," Graham is careful to say, "are the types of shots you are hitting. Are you hitting it farther? Are you doing with the ball what you're trying to do? If so, then you keep working on it."

And if it doesn't happen? A few years ago, Hubert Green got it into his head that he needed more distance. He tried to change his highly idiosyncratic, fast-action swing into something more mechanical, full of shoulder turns, hip swivels and leg drives. It was like trying to change a Ferrari into a truck, and Green couldn't do it. Eventually he returned to his old swing — a double overhaul, if you will — and last year he won the PGA Championship.

What Green reverted to was not just the swing, but the *security* that comes with it. For those who undergo the overhaul seek not perfection but an action they can bank on.

School Is Never Out for the Touring Pros

Golf Monthly, **December 1988**

Visitors to the Open Championship at Royal Lytham & St. Annes in July might have noticed the four-ball of Nick Faldo, Nick Price, David Frost and Mark McNulty during an early practice round. Their attention, no doubt, would have been on the talented players. Nevertheless, a fellow walked along who warranted the spectators' attention. During the Open Championship, in fact, Price, who went on to finish second to Seve Ballesteros, credited this man, David Leadbetter, with teaching him the golf game that would enable him to compete so successfully in an Open Championship.

"I really owe a lot to my teacher and good friend, David Leadbetter," Price said during the Open. "I didn't understand that much about the golf swing when I came over (to the U.S. Tour in the early 1980s). I've worked with him for six years and he's really helped me."

Leadbetter, a boyhood acquaintance of Price's, was watching not only Price during the Open practice round. He also watched the other golfers in the group, for he works with them as well. And no doubt other teachers were out and about at Lytham. For a fact of life at golf's highest levels — in America and in Britain, in Europe, Australia and Japan — is that almost every golfer has his own teacher: Leadbetter with Price et al.; Jack Nicklaus with Jack Grout; Bernhard Langer with Willi Hoffmann; Tom Kite, Corey Pavin and Mark Calcavecchia with Peter Kostis; Greg Norman with Charlie Earp; Curtis Strange and Peter Jacobsen with Jimmy Ballard; Sandy Lyle with his dad; Sam Torrance and Ian Woosnam with Bob Torrance, and so on.

Calcavecchia, in fact, went so far as to call Kostis prior to the third round of this year's Masters on a cellular phone that his teacher keeps on the practice tee at the St. Andrews Club in Boca Raton, Florida. He told Kostis he was feeling uncomfortable over the ball. Kostis watched him on television that round, noticed something amiss in his address position and told his pupil how to correct the flaw. Calcavecchia then played a very good final round and would have tied for the lead, but for Lyle's remarkable shot from the sand at the last hole and his subsequent winning birdie.

The examples of Price and Calcavecchia indicate how important a personal instructor is to today's touring pros. Talk to a touring pro about his swing and you will surely hear not only his words, but his teacher's. Most touring pros have troubles at least some of the time, and nearly all of them consult their teachers regularly.

It's amazing, really, when you think about it. One might think the world's finest golfers could diagnose their own problems and come up with remedies. Surely it's the average club golfer who needs a personal teacher. Oddly enough, the club golfer generally goes blithely on his way, swinging to and fro from tip to tip, rarely working at close hand over a long period of time with one teacher. Meantime, the most gifted golfers are never more than a phone call away from their advisers. Every touring pro is still learning the game. Golf does not differ from other crafts such as acting or singing, or writing for that matter, in this regard.

Consider the case of Nicklaus, who needs no introduction to golfers anywhere but who has often needed yet another introduction to his own swing, so frequently has it gone awry. Jack Grout has worked with Nicklaus since the two met at the Scioto Country Club in Columbus, Ohio, when the Golden Bear was but a lad of ten. Now 77 and, it's sad to report, suffering from cancer, Grout has been Nicklaus's main man through the years, notwithstanding Nicklaus's studies on the short game with former PGA Tour player Phil Rodgers. Nicklaus has also willingly exposed himself to other folks' ideas, but he always returns to Grout, the man who best knows his game.

"I've got some points from a few others," Nicklaus says, "but as far as actual technique goes, Grout has been my teacher since day one."

Grout has provided for Nicklaus what every golfer needs: another set of eyes. During the 1974 United States Open at the Winged Foot Golf Club in Mamaroneck, New York, for instance, Nicklaus was hitting the ball miserably. He couldn't figure out why, although it seemed evident to Grout when Nicklaus called him in. Nicklaus was lining up with shoulders closed, but had been doing so for so long that he didn't know it. He had become comfortable with the position — awkward as it appeared — and had simply compensated for his sloppy alignment by rerouting his swing. Having done so subconsciously, he could not correct himself. Nicklaus thought he was aiming down the centre of the fairway, but he was aiming out-of-bounds to the right.

When Grout saw Nicklaus, he suggested that he turn himself round, even to the point where his shoulders were slightly open. Perversely, Nicklaus felt uncomfortable in this correct position, but he was willing to stick with it — the main requirement in the golfer-teacher relationship — and soon he was launching every ball down the middle of the fairway. He had required that other set of eyes to right himself.

Something similar happened in early 1985 after Nicklaus had contracted tendinitis. He returned from a tournament in Palm Springs, California, sure that his injury had developed because he was getting into bad swing positions. But he couldn't make his own corrections, so he called his golf doctor in for a consultation.

"I told Jack that we had to do some work," Nicklaus recalls. "I felt I either had to change my swing or not play that year. Otherwise I'd tear my arm up. So we changed a lot of things, got me into the right position and, by the time I was through, my arm hurt was gone and I could swing properly." Thank you, Jack Grout.

David Graham, the fine Australian-born regular on the PGA Tour, who won the 1979 PGA Championship and the 1981 U.S. Open Championship, also feels strongly about the need for a teacher who is always on call. Graham says, "A player has an obligation to his own game to find out how and why it works, and what happens under pressure. A player will usually find one person he's got some confidence in and who has a good knowledge of the game. You always get back to that old saying." What old saying, David? "A player cannot see himself."

But should the teacher be a successful player? Or is it more important that he be able to communicate, and never mind his competitive record? Graham is of the opinion, not widely held, that golfers at his level should seek the counsel of teachers who have competed successfully.

"If anything really goes wrong with my game," he has said, "I'll go with an Ed Sneed, a Tom Weiskopf or a Bruce Devlin, someone who understands the very, very fine details. He'll be able to say, 'You're playing the ball an inch too far forward, or an eighth of an inch too far back.'"

American J.C. Snead has for years had as a teacher one of the game's best players ever, his uncle Sam Snead. Snead, J.C. that is, did not start golf until he was 22, and didn't reach the Tour until he was in his mid-twenties. When he did, there was 56-year-old Sam, ready to help.

"When I came on Tour," J.C. says, "Sam gave me all the help I wanted and needed. I still don't think I've seen anyone who can swing a golf club like he can. He told me that a golfer can't swing the way he wants every day and that he should go with what he has. If you can't draw the ball one day, well, don't try to."

Snead the elder must have been dispensing sound advice through the years. His nephew has won eight PGA Tour events, and in 1987 had his best money-winning season ever, while capturing the Manufacturers Hanover-Westchester Classic in Rye, New York.

The importance of finding someone trustworthy cannot be overestimated. Most golfers find it essential if they are to reach their potential. This is particularly true if a golfer wants to make major changes, having decided that the form he has been using is not good enough to perform the function it is meant to, namely to strike the ball accurately, time after time, no matter how severe the pressure.

Greg Norman, for one, made a big change in the late 1970s when he decided, on the advice of an Australian doctor friend, to alter his swing plane from very upright to moderately upright.

"As high as I hit the ball now," Norman points out, "I used to hit it a lot higher. I had just one shot. I'd drop the club underneath coming down and hook it back. But then I started getting some back pain and the doctor told me that, if I wanted to stop the pain, I would have to swing flatter to take the tension off the lower part of my back. I worked on that with the fellow who became my teacher back home, Charlie Earp. To learn to swing flat, I used to hit balls off sidehill, uphill lies. Gradually I moved the ball lower and lower and then my swing was flat with normal lie shots. It took me about six months to make the change."

Price, as mentioned, went through major changes in his swing. He started to work with Leadbetter in 1982, after playing poorly during the previous season in Europe.

"I didn't know what I was doing with my swing," Price said in the autumn of 1988. "I'd read hundreds of books on the swing before I saw David. But nothing helped until I went to him. I was playing from sheer natural talent. I didn't understand the physics or the dynamics of the swing. It's like an equation. You can get the result — call it 'D' — just with skill. But you have to know 'A,' 'B,' 'C,' the reasons for 'D.' That's what David taught me."

Frost also credits Leadbetter with much of his improvement in recent years. He points out that the primary ingredient in their relationship — as it is in any golfer-teacher meeting, which is after all a healing and rejuvenation process — is that Leadbetter can communicate with him. "That's the main thing."

The importance of communication has been demonstrated over the course of Leadbetter's relationship with 1987 Open Champion Nick Faldo. Faldo, in 1983, had led the European Order of Merit, but then decided his swing was simply not sound enough to bring him consistently into the top ranks. He began to work with Leadbetter, but the immediate results were hardly impressive. Faldo, in truth, nearly dropped from sight for a couple of years and was subject to intense scrutiny and criticism from golf journalists, many of whom felt he was demonstrating nothing short of idiocy in his desire to make changes in his game.

But Faldo persevered and in 1987 finished third on the Order of Merit, while winning the Open at Muirfield. He has continued to play beautifully, even if he did lose the playoff for the 1988 U.S. Open to Curtis Strange at the Country Club in Brookline, Massachusetts. Faldo also finished third behind Ballesteros and Price at the Lytham Open. He seems to have proved his detractors wrong, although it's true that the golf swing can quickly become a mysterious enterprise to anybody and deteriorate almost overnight. Still, Faldo's transformation is wonderful testimony to the results that can accrue from a productive relationship between teacher and golfer.

"I worked with Faldo for two years," Leadbetter says. "He had the strength of his convictions. It was quite amazing to see the difference before and after, all through his conceptualizing the correct aspects of the swing and being patient. That's always the problem, the patience factor. These golfers are playing tournaments while they are learning. They have to earn a living. Faldo was down in the dumps anyway when he first saw me. He had only one way to go, up. It's tough when you get a player in that situation, because you can help make or break his career. Nick is now at the point where the changes are part of him. Now it's only maintenance. He had a goal of winning a British Open. The problem now is what's next? His question is 'Where am I going from here?'"

That, of course, is a pleasant question to contemplate. Golfers so often arrive on the world's Tours with the gifts of instinct for the game, but soon find, as did Price and Faldo, that what they have isn't enough. They then set out on an ambiguous course. Only the determined survive.

Such was the case with U.S. Open title-holder Strange. He wasn't happy with what he thought was a faulty swing that he had used in his amateur days, even if he did have great success. There was simply too much hand action in his swing to give him the consistency he wanted. And so he went to see Jimmy Ballard, a swing guru who teaches at the Doral Country Club in Miami. Ballard showed Strange that he could develop a more consistent swing by utilizing the bigger muscles of his back, shoulders and legs. Soon the violent hand action was silenced, and a new Curtis Strange emerged, one whose swing was characterized by a body move away from and through the ball. The results since are indisputable, as Strange has gone on to become a most formidable player.

The very successful U.S. player Paul Azinger has also been renewed since working with John Redman. Azinger met Redman while attending Brevard Junior College in Florida, in 1979. Azinger might shoot 65 one day, but he could also come up with a 78 the next day. He didn't know how he was supposed to swing. It was as if he had a thesaurus of swing ideas in his mind; one thought would pop into his mind, but would soon be replaced by another. How is a golfer supposed to play with such confusion?

Redman has made all the difference to Azinger, who was the U.S. PGA Player of the Year in 1987 and who continued to play very well in 1988. As he says now, "It's been a long time since I went to the course with two or three different ways of swinging the golf club."

Successful as these teacher-player relationships have been, it's also important to point out that not every one is a success. Perhaps the most obvious breakdown in recent years occurred between Bobby Clampett and Ben Doyle, he of that complex system of instruction known as The Golfing Machine. Doyle worked very closely with Clampett through the early 1980s, a period in which Clampett played some superb golf. He finished fourteenth and seventeenth on the PGA. Tour's money list in 1981 and 1982, respectively, but then faltered. The mid-1980s were hard years for both Clampett and Doyle. They effectively stopped working together, although Clampett still retains some basic ideas he gained from Doyle. In recent years, Clampett has turned to Hank Haney, a U.S. teacher who became well-known for his work with Mark O'Meara, and more recently, with little-known Dave Rasmussen. Rasmussen teaches at Storm's Driving Range in Milwaukee, Wisconsin, and has worked with Clampett for more than two years. He travels much of the Tour with him. Clampett has made steady improvement, although he has not yet attained the level he once had.

"Dave and I are on the same wavelength," Clampett points out. "I'm still a long way from playing my best. I've gone through so much trial and error the last two years, but now I'm seeing some breakthroughs."

In the end, all golfers seek these breakthroughs. Whether or not they achieve them sometimes seems a matter of not only hard work, but good fortune and self-awareness. Lanny Wadkins, for one, chooses to remain with his own swing rather than seek an instructor. Lee Trevino, as natural and intuitive a swinger as there is, doesn't get into the mechanics of the swing at all, and certainly doesn't consult teachers. "I don't get into all that," says the Merry Mex. "I hit it and I cuss it if it doesn't go towards the flag. Then I hit it again."

As Leadbetter says, "Can you imagine trying to change Lanny into a one-piece, long, wide swing? What success are you going to have? And over what period of time?" Ditto for Trevino, or Ballesteros for that matter. He *feels* the swing. He doesn't want anybody else telling him what to do.

But Wadkins, Trevino and Ballesteros are the exceptions. The majority of pros do commit themselves to working closely with a teacher. They hand over something very precious — their golf swings — and say, "Help me, please." Happily, there are enough sensitive instructors to guide them in their quest for a swing that works.

Langer's Newest and Unsightly Cure for His Putting Yips Apparently Works

The Globe and Mail, February 23, 1989

The common reaction these days to watching Bernhard Langer putt is "Oh, no!" Afflicted with putting paralysis, the talented

West German golfer has come up with yet another unsightly stroke to cure his woes — and horror of horrors, it seems to be working.

Langer's history on the greens has been enough to make golfers wince. Here's a fine tee-to-green player who suffers periodically from the yips.

The yips defy clinical description. Suffice to say that the malady has something to do with fear. A golfer misses a few short putts. Then he begins to steer the ball towards the hole instead of making a free stroke through the ball. Next thing you know his action is an uncertain twitch. Soon he's terrified over every putt. His wrists break down; his head comes up. He's in agony and ready to try anything.

Langer, poor Langer, has suffered the yips for years. Now 31, he first contracted the illness as a teenager in Anhausen, West Germany. He even four-putted from six feet during the 1977 German Close championship, when he averaged 40 putts a round.

Nick Price, now a top golfer, played many rounds with Langer in the late 1970s in Europe. Asked about Langer's putting during the Canadian Open last September, Price registered a visible shudder.

"I'm not joking," he said. "I thought he should have turned in his clubs. He used to have 44 putts a round and sometimes still make the cut. A good round for him was 35 putts."

But Langer persisted.

Agonizing experimentation led to a complicated, if slightly deranged system that eventually brought him 30 tournament wins, including the 1985 Masters. He got down to 28.80 putts a round. People spoke of him in the same breath as Seve Ballesteros and Greg Norman.

Langer's method involved putting conventionally on efforts longer than 15 feet or so, and cross-handed on shorter putts. The system worked for a few years. Golfers marvelled at his ability to recover from the yips, something many considered incurable.

Inexorably, though, his symptoms reappeared.

Langer's stroke got shorter and quicker, his wrists broke down through impact and the ball jumped off the blade at bizarre angles.

Last year was terrible. Langer was not a pretty picture.

"Once you've had 'em, you've got 'em," British writer Henry Longhurst said of the yips, and Langer was proving this true.

His worst session occurred during the British Open at Royal Lytham and St. Annes, where Langer five-putted the 17th green on his way to an 80.

"I'm as depressed now as I could be after playing bad golf for three months," Langer told Glasgow's *Golf Monthly* editor Colin Callander late last fall. "It follows the classic pattern. I can putt pretty decently on the practice putting green, but when I'm on the golf course it's completely different. It's like the difference between a practice swing and a regular swing."

But Langer didn't work his way out of the yips the first time without trying. And so he showed up on the U.S. PGA Tour a few weeks ago with a style so unorthodox it made his other system look normal.

Langer now holds on to his left forearm with his right thumb while putting cross-handed. The fingers of his right hand curl under the forearm and putter. The method locks his right wrist in place. He's putting more smoothly. The ball is rolling to the hole, not sputtering and bouncing.

John Huggan is an instruction editor with *Golf Digest* in Norwalk, Connecticut. Langer is on the magazine staff, and Huggan watched him at the PGA Tour stop in Pebble Beach, California, four weeks ago. He was impressed — sort of, anyway.

"His stroke looked slower," Huggan said. "If he can hole a few putts when he needs to, then he won't look back."

Sure, John. But what if he misses a few putts that he needs to make?

"That's it, isn't it? Speaking as a golfer, I hope he can maintain his new stroke. To see somebody like him, as good as he is, putting as he has . . . "

Huggan's voice trailed off. That's what voices do when the subject is the yips.

Still, who knows? Maybe Langer has found a winner. He's finished in the money four times in four starts on the PGA Tour this year; he's twenty-third on the money list and forty-third in putting. Not bad, considering that he finished eleventh on the money list in 1988, and was sixty-fifth in putting.

Yet Langer has had the yips. Therefore he might get them again. We should say a little prayer for him. Nobody, but nobody, deserves the disease.

Golf Teacher Leaves a Graceful Tribute

The Globe and Mail, June 3, 1989

In his 40 years of golf Jack Nicklaus has had but one teacher. That man, Jack Grout, died on May 13 at the age of 78 from cancer.

Nicklaus was only 10 when he met Grout in 1950 at the Scioto Country Club in Columbus, Ohio. Grout, an Oklahoman, had become the club's head pro that year. He'd turned pro at 15, in 1925, and in 1930 accompanied his brother Dick to the Glen Garden Country Club in Dallas. Ben Hogan, then 17, and Bryon Nelson, then 18, were junior members. The threesome practised mornings and played three or four times a week in the afternoon.

Grout, Hogan and Nelson took to the road to follow the tour. They drove a roadster from tournament to tournament, tying their clubs on the side of the car. Up and down the west coast they went. Grout lasted until 1957 on the tour, the last seven while working at Scioto, where Nicklaus's father Charlie belonged.

The elder Nicklaus asked if he could enrol his 10-year-old son in Grout's two-hour Friday junior clinic. Young Jackie enrolled all right; he was the first to register and was always the first youngster on the tee. Soon Grout was asking his young protégé to demonstrate certain points about the swing.

The rest, as they say, is history, where Nicklaus is concerned. He went on to become probably the best golfer ever. And Grout was always at his side. Grout and Nicklaus went over the swing from A to Z at the start of every season. Meanwhile, they became close friends.

Grout, though, was available for anybody. Three years ago, I spent a couple of hours with him at the Frenchman's Creek Golf Club in North Palm Beach, Florida. He was clear and concise. As always, he stressed fundamentals.

"You can't overcome a poor grip," Grout told me. "A bad grip disrupts a poor swing." So we worked on situating my hands properly on the club.

Later Grout talked about alignment, pointing out that only 5% of golfers aim correctly. He said that it was important to keep the head steady during the swing, because "the head is the centre of your balance."

In the way of the world, Grout died precisely at 7:45 a.m., on Saturday, May 13. That was Nicklaus's scheduled starting time — prior to a rain delay — in the third round of his own Memorial Tournament at his own Muirfield Village Golf Club near Columbus, where Grout was also the professional emeritus. "J. Grout," Nicklaus always called him, and now J. Grout was gone.

Said Nicklaus: "Jack was like a second father to me. He was part of our family . . . He taught me how to play the game and he's been at my side whenever I needed him."

Grout also had something to say. Item 6 of his Last Will and Testament was handed to Nicklaus soon after Grout died. The document tells it all.

"Having heretofore disposed of all my worldly goods, I have just one final bequest I should like to make. If there is anytime at all in the life of a man when he should make an extra effort to be truthful, and at the same time sincere, I think it must be while he is preparing his Last Will and Testament. What I have to say in the next few words comes straight from my heart.

"Over the course of the past 30 years or so, from time to time I have read in various books and magazines about the contributions I have made to the career of Jack Nicklaus. Since this may be my last opportunity to do so, I thought maybe it would be well to set the record straight.

"In all honesty I don't think I ever hurt Jack's golf game in any way. To put it another way, if he had not come under my tutelage in the early 1950s I don't see how he could have turned out much better than he did. From the outset of our relationship I recognized that the thunder in his stroke and the courage in his heart were gifts that clearly had been bestowed upon him; and that there was very little I could do to take them away from him.

"I do not mean to suggest that I made no contribution whatsoever to his game. For one thing, I worked him hard (and he seemed to enjoy every minute of it). I made him stand away from the ball with his arms fully extended, and I insisted that he swing hard. Within a few months you could hear the swish of his clubhead all over the practice range when he took one of his legendary cuts at the ball. I made sure that his posture was correct; I fitted him correctly with equipment; from time to time I would check his grip, or maybe the rhythm of his swing. I always tried to encourage him; and in the very early days of his development I made a special effort to explain to him and interpret for him how extraordinary I thought his talents were, and for that matter still are.

"If I made any other worthwhile contributions, which I can't think of now, or if I made any of which I may be unaware, I am grateful that I had the opportunity to do so. There is not the slightest doubt in my mind that Jack Nicklaus is the finest golfer ever to swing a club in the entire history of the game. It has been a distinct honour and great pleasure for me to have played some part in his career. And that brings me to my final bequest.

"To you, Jack Nicklaus, I give my thanks."

Coach Given Task of Teaching Quayle How to Swing

The Globe and Mail, **December 7, 1991**
David Leadbetter transformed Nick Faldo into a golfer who has won four major championships since 1987. He helped Seve Ballesteros to a magnificent season this year. And now Leadbetter faces another challenge: Today he's giving his first lesson to U.S. vice-president Dan Quayle.

"Quayle's people called my office and told me he'd like to come down [today]," Leadbetter said the other day at the sumptuous Lake Nona club, where he teaches. "I told them I could fit him in with two others. They said that wouldn't do for security reasons."

Leadbetter changed his plans, as instructors are wont to do when the White House calls. The schedule now calls for Leadbetter to work with Quayle this morning, then play 18 holes with him and a friend this afternoon. Leadbetter, an Englishman who grew up in Zimbabwe (then called Rhodesia) and who was more intrigued by understanding the swing than competing, is looking forward to the game. He's so busy that he doesn't get a round much any more.

Quayle is not the first person from the current White House to profit from Leadbetter's coaching. President George Bush apparently found his book *The Golf Swing* useful; too useful, perhaps, according to political observers, who have criticized Bush for spending too much time on the golf course.

Nonetheless, a framed letter from the White House dated September 6, 1990, hangs modestly in a corner of Leadbetter's studio, which itself is in a pleasantly rambunctious structure that resembles an oversized African hut, surrounded by vegetation. The letter isn't far from swing-sequence photos of Faldo, Ballesteros and Greg Norman, not to mention an instructive 1958 photo of Ben Hogan at impact. That's exalted company for all concerned.

"Thanks for the copy of your book," Bush's letter reads. "Anything that will help my game is greatly appreciated." Bush's signature follows.

Now comes Quayle, carrying his six handicap to Leadbetter. He has come to the teacher many golfers are talking about.

Leadbetter must be listened to. He is bringing teaching to the forefront of the game and hopes to establish schools around the world. He's not yet 40, fairly young for a teacher of his reputation. But Leadbetter is so popular that as of the new year he will retain the International Management Group to handle his affairs.

IMG works with Norman, for one. Then there's British Open champion Ian Baker-Finch, who refined his skills under Leadbetter; so has Canadian Open champion Nick Price. It's an index of Leadbetter's success that he finds himself as much in demand as the players he instructs.

His popularity is no surprise once you watch him work. He and a couple of his staff members were on the lesson tee earlier this week with a father and his two sons, 12 and 14. The family had come from Indonesia for Leadbetter's teaching. It was their third visit, and by now the father had reduced his handicap to 4 from 14.

"The golf swing is all about learning to co-ordinate your arm swing with your body swing," Leadbetter told Wilson, the 12-year-old, as he helped him feel the right positions. "That will lead to control of the golf ball."

Leadbetter wasn't spouting off a theory without regard to the individual. The well-respected BBC analyst Peter Alliss has accused Leadbetter of being no more than a passing fancy who got lucky when Faldo started winning majors. Leadbetter is not lucky. He's good, plain and simple.

Leadbetter enjoys teaching, and he may well be capable of bringing to the masses what the late Jack Grout did with Jack Nicklaus and local players in Columbus, Ohio, or Harvey Penick accomplished with Tom Kite, Ben Crenshaw and amateurs around Austin, Texas. His global village is a global golf course.

"The standard of golf could be so much better," Leadbetter said on the range. "Most people don't have a concept of how to swing the golf club, and it's not their fault. The teaching isn't available on a wide scale. We try to provide a concept so that people can work on their swings at home and learn to use the proper muscles to hit the golf ball."

Quayle will make a start this morning. Leadbetter will chat with the vice-president in order to understand his goals. He'll watch him hit a few balls, then give him images and drills to work on. Before long Bush and Quayle may turn the Oval Office into an indoor range.

"The most important thing is that by doing the drills you start to feel the right things, to train your body to move properly," Leadbetter said.

Quayle will surely return to the White House a more knowledgeable golfer than when he left. Maybe he too will write to Leadbetter and thank him for helping him reach his potential as a golfer. That's Leadbetter's passion. To spend time with him is to be convinced of his sincerity.

Book Learning Doesn't Always Pay Off

The Globe and Mail, **February 5, 1992**
Golf instruction takes many forms, of which the instruction book is one. Publishers like the genre because the books sell. Whether they help golfers is another matter.

"Golf has been played since the fifteenth century," Michael Hebron, 1991 PGA of America Teacher of the Year, said yesterday from Florida, his winter base from where he travels to clinics. "Golfers have made trillions of swings, and no two have been alike. Instruction must provide information designed for a person's body type, his interest in the game, the time he has available, all sorts of factors."

Golf books can't do that, or else every player would have his own manual. That's not to say some instruction books aren't helpful. The better books provide a comprehensive theory of the swing rather than tips that usually fail.

Bobby Jones's collection *Bobby Jones on Golf* (1930) and Percy Boomer's *On Learning Golf* (1942) have stayed the course. Ben Hogan's *Five Lessons: The Modern Fundamentals of Golf* (1957) and David Leadbetter's *The Golf Swing* (1990) are standards because they provide theory, not tips. This foursome of books could represent the cornerstone of a well-considered instruction library.

Now comes news of another book that many golfers will no doubt purchase when it's published next fall. The book is *The Killer Swing*, 1991 PGA champion John Daly's look at how he hits the ball so far. *Golf Magazine* senior editor John Andrisani is a low-handicap player who wrote *Natural Golf* with Seve Ballesteros. He's co-writing Daly's book. It will be subtitled *John Daly's Guide to Hitting the Ball Farther than You Ever Have Before*.

Daly, of course, captured the golf world's interest with his massive drives and carefree manner while winning the PGA in August. That was a real-life movie, since it played on television everywhere. Now comes the book. The reversal could occur only in a culture that feeds on celebrity and the high moment.

But a fair hearing must include the possibility that there's more to the book. Daly's unique swing challenges conventional theory. He lifts his left heel off the ground and nearly touches the ground with the clubhead on his backswing. He's so relaxed that his right thumb comes off the club at the top of his backswing, then he applies severe pressure with his right forefinger coming down to the ball. Still, can he teach others to copy his swing?

Andrisani said yesterday from his home in Orlando that the book won't advise golfers to copy Daly's swing. He said the book will be honest, and is not meant only to capitalize on Daly's sudden fame.

"We'll suggest that people experiment with some of Daly's techniques," Andrisani said. "What can help the average golfer? What are the things Daly wouldn't tell anybody in a million years because they couldn't do them?"

Daly has often said he just steps up to the ball and smashes it. What does he have to tell golfers, then? Andrisani said that Daly does think about his swing, but doesn't overthink. The danger is that Daly could affect his natural moves by analyzing them for print. He'll be telling the reader how to make it happen, when he's been letting it happen.

But never mind. The publisher, HarperCollins, will have a field day. The publicity writers are already hard at work.

A January 22 release informs us that Daly "ran away with the most high-powered tournament in golf." But the PGA Championship is not that at all. Most golfers rank the PGA behind the Masters, U.S. and British Opens in importance.

Nor does Daly have "the most envied swing in golf," as the release proclaims. PGA Tour players recently voted Tom Purtzer as having the best swing. Daly does, however, have an exciting swing that many youngsters are emulating.

What does Hebron think of Daly's foray into literature? Suffice it to say that he almost choked on the phone when he heard about the book. Then he calmed down.

"Amateur golfers wouldn't be able to copy the distance that Daly's right arm travels in his backswing," Hebron said. "It's way past where any handicap golfer should allow it to go."

Hebron wanted to wait and see what Daly would say. He did observe that golfers who examine a pro's instructional book learn about the player's experience. It's personal material, rarely transferable, more "entertainment value" than instructional value, Hebron said.

"I think the most editorial comment I could make regarding instructional books," Hebron said, "is 'buyer beware.'"

Smart words, those. But golfers buy into the fantasy of instant improvement and publishers play into that fantasy. Daly's "killer swing" is intriguing, so it's no surprise that publishers wanted a book. It may help only a few golfers, but it will surely be entertaining. Maybe that's all one should expect of instruction books.

Chapter Five

ISSUES

THE WORLD of golf usually seems peaceful, a retreat where the only noise sometimes seems to be the word "fore." It's also been a world that has seemed insulated from the problems that people live with daily. Enter a golf club and you enter a separate reality. Visit a professional golf tournament and you find a sunny world where players compete for large purses, work in the best of offices — outdoors, green and always slick and clean. The competitors, male and female, get along with their parent organizations. All is well, unlike other sports. Hockey players in the National Hockey League went on strike in 1992 for the first time in the league's 75-year history. There was mistrust between the players' association and the team owners. That hasn't happened in professional golf, and when disputes have arisen, they have quickly been solved. The players like the life that their professional organizations have created for them. And they haven't exactly been involved in a sport where labour disputes are common.

The game, then, has maintained a clean image. Few if any substance-abuse problems exist because a player simply couldn't compete at the highest levels while using drugs. Golf is self-regulating that way, as it requires power on one shot, then a delicate touch around the green. Steroids, to mention one drug that is popular in certain sports, would be of no help in golf.

But this isn't to say that golf is free of problems. Indeed, some disturbing signs have come to the surface in recent years, and the game has been sent reeling from time to time. One of the main issues is that of discrimination at private clubs on the basis of sex, race and religion. Women have always been the underclass in golf, and even now few private clubs allow them to join as full members with full playing and voting privileges. Black golfers have always been few and far between in the professional ranks, for the obvious reason that they have not had access to clubs and teaching. The issue came to world-wide attention during the now infamous 1990 PGA Championship at Shoal Creek in Birmingham, Alabama. Club president Hall Thompson said that the club didn't allow blacks as members. That set all clubs to examining their policies and consciences and also compelled the various associations to insist that private clubs not discriminate in their membership criteria. Cypress Point in Monterey, California, for one, dropped out of the AT & T National Pro-Am because it would not allow the PGA Tour to dictate its policies.

Clubs have also been examining their policies towards women and many are finally seeing that there is no reason women should not be admitted as full members. This is not exactly enlightened thinking, but that it comes so late in the day indicates that golf has been rather backward in certain important areas. It's also the case that the PGA Tour itself, long a model of sports and administration, has increasingly been coming under the spotlight of investigative journalism. Marcia Chambers, a writer for *The National Law Review*, wrote a series of distinguished articles for *Golf Digest* after the Shoal Creek affair, and in 1992 she wrote a three-part series on the PGA Tour. The first was entitled "Can Beman Survive?" It was the first lengthy examination of Commissioner Deane Beman's office and opened up the entire area of PGA Tour dealings with charities, and its relationships with players and sponsors. Meanwhile, PGA Tour officials had formed a union called PAGO, the Professional Association of Golf Officials. The union asked the PGA Tour for better salaries, more reasonable working hours and an acceptable pension plan. They held out the possibility of a strike, something that would have been unheard of in professional golf just a few years ago.

As much as these issues were swirling around golf, and as much as any thinking person would have been disturbed by them, nothing hits home until it hits one personally. My awakening came in February 1989, when I was present at a gathering at a well-known private Toronto club and witnessed what I had to conclude was an undercurrent of anti-Semitism. I wrote a column in *The Globe and Mail* about the circumstances; the day the column appeared I had more calls on it than anything I had written until then or have written since. I include the piece here. I have also written elsewhere about Tom Watson's stance at the Kansas City Country Club, his home course. Watson withdrew from the club after learning it would not admit a Jew as a member. (That column appears in this book in Chapter Seven, in a section about Watson.)

Is golf as squeaky-clean a sport as it appears? It's apparent that it is not, and that problems have always existed just under the surface. I don't think these problems are inherent in the game, but that the private sector has too often turned it into a diversion for the wealthy and privileged, for the favoured groups in our society. Golf is in danger of becoming too expensive for juniors and anybody not making a substantial income. At the same time I think it is important to remember that one can play the game with inexpensive equipment and that golf courses don't need to be perfectly maintained. The game's virtues as a lifelong sport for all people need to be reaffirmed, and one can only hope that golf associations and interested people will take up the cause and give golf to the people, to whom it belongs. One can only hope that the current troubling issues will be dealt with and that the game will return to what it has been and ought to be: a meeting ground for the pursuit of an uncomplicated sport, where all people can enjoy each other's company.

Some Disturbing Signs for Golf

The Globe and Mail, **January 7, 1988**
Though professional golf tournaments are still peaceful events
when compared with other sports, there are reasons to believe
they may no longer be as immune to fan disturbances as they
have been in the past.

There were four riots at golf tournaments between 1960 and
1972, according to a study on fan violence in the United States.
A riot was defined as an incident in which people were arrested.

The study, published in 1982 as part of a book on U.S. social
problems, noted that baseball had 97 riots in the same period, basketball, 64 and hockey, 39. World-wide, soccer had — and continues to have — the most frequent occurrences of fan violence.

Golf's historical immunity to outbreaks of violence is rooted in
the nature of the game. As Allan Guttman, professor of American studies at Amherst College in Amherst, Massachusetts, explained in an interview this week, the primary reason is that golf
is an individual sport.

Guttman, the author of a recent book called *Watching Sports,*
argued that it is much easier for fans to identify with a team
than with an individual. It is no surprise, then, to see the often
excited, sometimes feverish crowds that attend team sporting
events.

Golf does not often offer a context for such behaviour. Fans
who attend next week's PGA Tour opener, the Tournament of
Champions in Carlsbad, California, will be watching the golf. Not
many will feel a need to identify with the players.

Golf has traditionally encouraged rather decorous, calm
behaviour from its fans. Spectators generally walk at least a few
holes with the golfers and sometimes an entire round. Guttman
said the very fact that a fan is not stuck in one place in the
stands might inhibit any build-up of tension that he might need
to dissipate.

The Masters, that most élite of golf tournaments, reminds its
patrons, as they are known, that it is their duty to behave. All
patrons are given a sheet that, by complimenting them, instils a
purpose to their visit.

"The Masters Tournament's patrons," the handout reads, "know their golf and they respect golf gallery etiquette. They expect to see the game at its best and regularly show every courtesy to the players and one another."

Most tournaments would like to emulate the Masters, but it's an original. Many patrons are golf-smart. They are also from the upper social classes — a factor that Guttman says has everything to do with exemplary behaviour.

"The basic fact to remember is that in all periods of history, social class is the key to behaviour," he said. "Less privileged groups are rowdy and sometimes violent."

If this in fact is the case, the PGA Tour has something about which to worry. Less privileged people, as Guttman called them, are attending events as the PGA Tour tries to attract more fans. Many are not golfers; they are party types.

In recent years, the Greater Greensboro Open in North Carolina has become known for a number of outbreaks of fan rowdiness. Tournament sponsors even encouraged such behaviour by adopting as the event's motto the offensive slogan "Party Till Ya Puke."

The par-three 17th hole at the Forest Oaks Country Club in Greensboro is the main place of action. The noisemakers gather there to drink beer and wager on players making putts. Many howl with delight when players fail.

Canadian Richard Zokol once told some yahoos at the 17th that if they thought it was so easy, they should come down from the stands and putt. His comments settled him down, but they did not stop the fans from acting as if they were at a rock concert.

"Greensboro," Guttman noted, "is a violent area. It has one of the highest rates of gun possession in the U.S., and it also doesn't have much in the way of pro sports."

However, Greensboro isn't the only place where fans have gotten out of hand in recent years. Two summers ago, Greg Norman went into the crowd to stop a fellow from baiting him at the U.S. Open. And this happened at the upper-class Shinnecock Hills Golf Club in fashionable Southampton, Long Island, where golf has been played for a century and where many of Manhattan's wealthy spend their summers.

"You are in Noo Yawk now," a youngster bellowed to Norman, "and you can expect to be heckled."

Norman walked over to the fellow and suggested that the two of them meet after the round if he had something he wanted to say. The fellow calmed down, but it was news that the incident even took place.

Neither the Greater Greensboro crowds nor the Norman incident are enough to suggest that golf is about to forfeit its identity as a genteel sport conducted under pleasant circumstances. However, as Guttman noted, the higher the purses get in golf — and $1 million is becoming commonplace — the more golfers should expect to be hassled.

The fans, after all, expect terrific golf from big money earners. Non-golfers think they should hit every shot beside the pin. They like to make noise more than they like to watch golf.

Meanwhile, stadium golf courses, where fans congregate in one place for hours, encourage a party atmosphere. PGA Tour commissioner Deane Beman has supported such facilities because they offer good viewing sites. In his fervour to imitate other sports, though, he may also be setting the stage for disturbances.

Said Guttman: "You could turn almost any sport into an attraction for a rowdy group if you wanted to." He cited Australian cricket, which used to be quiet. But sponsors in the 1970s encouraged fans to drink beer and enjoy themselves. Fan disturbances have steadily increased since.

The greater number of international golf events is also a worrisome factor. British spectators have been notorious for intentionally upsetting U.S. golfers in Ryder Cup matches. U.S. fans were demonstrative, though not abusive, at last fall's Ryder Cup in Dublin, Ohio.

Such occurrences prompted Guttman to issue a word of caution. International events enable spectators to identify passionately with their countries. This could lead to an increase in golf disturbances.

Golf tournaments remain relatively quiet affairs. Golf fans are mostly seen and not heard. But tournament sponsors and professional tour organizers might want to re-think their directions. It is difficult to imagine riots at golf tournaments, but disturbances could well lead to more serious outbursts.

Poor Taste Was Displayed during Club "Roast"

The Globe and Mail, February 16, 1989
I had hoped I wouldn't need to address the issue of racial or religious prejudices in this column. I've seen very little in the golf world. But on Tuesday night at the Scarboro Golf and Country Club, I witnessed a series of disturbing events that must be commented upon.

The occasion was meant to honour Ken Fulton, Scarboro's head professional since 1976. Fulton, 45, has left Scarboro for a new position at Toronto's Oakdale Golf and Country Club.

Oakdale is one of two Jewish clubs in Toronto — Maple Downs is the other. Both clubs have few, if any, non-Jewish members. Scarboro has few, if any, Jewish members.

At the same time, anybody can apply for membership. But few Jews apply to Scarboro and few members of other religions apply to Oakdale or Maple Downs. It's a case of people going where they feel most comfortable. And it should be pointed out that the majority of Toronto-area clubs are mixed.

Having played and visited Scarboro many times, and having felt welcomed, I was shocked at what I saw and heard Tuesday night, notwithstanding the composition of the club's membership. Jack Graham, a member of the captain's committee, had called last week to invite me to what promised to be a celebration of Fulton's years at Scarboro, or, perhaps, a roast. I have known Fulton, a fine player and teacher, for years and looked forward to the evening.

The first hint that the evening was going to be unpleasant occurred when a speaker wore a yarmulka, or ritual Jewish skullcap. Somebody then complimented Fulton on his suit, saying he must have gotten it wholesale. The reference was to the notion that Jews are always making deals, and that since Fulton was now going to a Jewish club, he would never pay retail prices again.

Fulton was standing on a platform while the proceedings unfolded. I didn't think he felt comfortable with the stereotyping. And in what way was this a celebration of his years at Scarboro?

A member then read a poem in which the word "youse" or something like that was inserted at the end of a line, so that it could rhyme with what came next, "because you'll now be dealing with the Jews."

A video was also presented, much of which was funny. But the producer, Jim French, a Scarboro member, also included a hospital surgery scene. Here was Fulton, the voice-over suggested, undergoing the ritual Jewish circumcision, standard fare, the idea was, for a pro going to a Jewish club.

Another speaker said Fulton, who is not Jewish, was now going to the "wolves" at Oakdale. The implication was that he had better be careful.

By now, the evening was well into its second hour. Graham had told me earlier that he and member Pat Bingham were going to do a skit in Yiddish. Bingham works with a Jewish woman whose grandfather speaks Yiddish. He had translated phrases such as "Keep your head down" and "Follow through" into Yiddish. Bingham would read these in Yiddish, while Graham interpreted.

I didn't stay for the skit. The evening had degenerated. It had gone far beyond good taste.

Was I being too sensitive? After all, I'm Jewish. But I don't think so. Such behaviour is improper. It speaks of hostile feelings that lie just under the veneer of civilized behaviour.

Apparently, I hadn't over-reacted. Fulton called me early yesterday morning from his office at Oakdale to apologize. He said he was embarrassed and that he had no idea the evening would become offensive.

"I'm upset by what happened," Fulton said. "It leaves people open to all sorts of criticism."

The phone rang a few minutes later. It was Graham.

"I owe you an abject apology," he said. "I felt the evening was in such poor taste. I just apologize for myself and Scarboro."

Graham said the speeches were not planned. That they weren't makes them that much more disturbing. Speakers instinctively chose not so much to honour Fulton as to discuss his move to a Jewish club. Had he moved to, oh, Lambton, surely the members would have concentrated on his contribution to Scarboro, and that's all.

French, meanwhile, said yesterday that he had been concerned that the hospital scene in his video might have been in
poor taste, but in the end, he chose to include it.

"If it was in poor taste," he said, "I apologize. People are so
sensitive today that you can't say anything."

Fulton, for his part, wanted to thank Scarboro's members for
having a party for him. But he's on a new road now.

"I'm looking forward to my career here," he said. "I don't
want to burn bridges, but I certainly don't condone an evening
like that."

Members of the organizing committee might not have allowed
such a program to take place had they considered the program in
advance. I'd like to think so anyway. However, the events took
place. There's a thin line between satire and bigotry. Some members of the Scarboro Golf and Country Club crossed it Tuesday
evening.

Discrimination Links
Finally Exposed

The Globe and Mail, **August 2, 1990**
Anybody who believed golf was innocent of discrimination on
the basis of race has had his or her illusions forever shattered. It's
about time too.

The issue that has brought the festering sore to the forefront
concerns the Shoal Creek Club in Birmingham, Alabama, site of
next week's PGA Championship. Shoal Creek founder Hall
Thompson said on June 20 that the private club excludes blacks
from its membership. His comment has touched off a wave of
protest that could peak at the club next week.

Reverend Abraham Woods, the Birmingham president of the
Southern Christian Leadership Conference who exposed the
club's policy, called for a massive protest at Shoal Creek. The
groups involved include the SCLC, the NAACP (National Association for the Advancement of Colored People) and ARISE (Against
Racism in Sports Events). The protest, however, was called off
after Shoal Creek accepted its first black member.

ARISE, for one, demonstrated at the U.S. Women's Open held two weeks ago at the all-white Atlanta Athletic Club in Georgia. The United States Golf Association, which runs the event, has said since that it will discuss its policy of site selection at its November meeting.

The Shoal Creek situation is the most significant development in golf in years. Money always talks and tells a tale, and ABC will lose at least $2 million (U.S.) now that such companies as IBM, Toyota, Honda, Ford and Spalding have pulled their advertising from the PGA telecast.

But the impact of Thompson's comments must be measured in more than monetary terms. For this is a story about how private-club golf has often supported racism, and how organizations that represent the game have all but ignored the truth.

The reaction of the PGA of America itself is enough to give one pause. When the story first came to light, the association announced that it vigorously opposes discrimination. But president Pat Reilly's original statement contained nothing to indicate the PGA would take into account a club's membership policies when selecting sites for its championship.

"The PGA," Reilly said, "recognizes that private clubs have the legal right to determine their own membership policies. Should the law change, the PGA would take into account (membership) policies in selecting future championship sites."

But look at what the PGA is saying now, weeks into a controversy that is shaking the game. The PGA said on July 14 that it is formulating new site-selection criteria that will consider the membership policies of host sites. Why didn't the PGA do so or say so before Thompson's comments?

There's also the Augusta National Golf Club, site of the annual Masters. The club has no black members, but tournament chairman Hord Hardin said recently the club is taking steps to have its first black members. He said that the decision has nothing to do with Shoal Creek.

The PGA Tour is also reacting, having not acted earlier. A recent survey by the *Charlotte Observer* discovered at least 17 clubs that hold PGA Tour events exclude blacks from membership.

The PGA Tour, in a July 27 statement, said that historically, its policy for site selection has focused on competitive and marketing aspects of the club. Exclusionary membership policies were not considered part of the equation.

The release also pointed out that the PGA Tour will soon propose a new policy to its Tournament Policy Board. This policy will demand that potential host clubs meet additional criteria, which include non-exclusionary policies for membership.

All this delayed reaction is a response in the right direction. But it points out that discrimination at private clubs on the basis of race still exists and is entrenched at certain clubs.

Many members consider it their fundamental right to invite members of their choosing, and those people only. This issue is now front and centre and will have repercussions not only at all-white clubs, but at clubs that admit men only, or clubs that effectively discriminate on the basis of religion.

The PGA Championship will go on next week as scheduled in Birmingham. Masters and British Open champion Nick Faldo was advised recently to spend some time in a sauna to prepare for the heat at Shoal Creek. But he might also want to prepare for a different sort of heat.

Things could get very warm indeed at Shoal Creek, a club that has assured itself of a place in golfing history. Let this be the beginning of the end to discrimination on the basis of race in golf, and perhaps some good will yet come out of the situation.

Black Members Rare at Canadian Clubs

The Globe and Mail, **August 11, 1990**
Shoal Creek's refusal to admit blacks to its club in Birmingham, Alabama, until recently raises the question of the membership policies at Canadian clubs. And that question leads to other questions.

Some of Canada's most élite golf clubs do not include blacks as members. That does not mean that the clubs discriminate, as their bylaws do not prohibit blacks from joining. But the absence of blacks suggests that they are not comfortable in joining the clubs, and/or that members are not likely to invite them to do so.

Consider the London Hunt Club in London, Ontario, site of the 1970 Canadian Open and host annually to a 36-hole event for Ontario's top amateurs to which blacks are welcome. But blacks have not belonged to the club for years, if ever, and none belong now.

"I was there for 32 years," Alec Walker, general manager of Toronto's Oakdale, the most prominent Jewish club in Canada, said this week. "No black ever applied. It's a case of people going where they feel most comfortable."

"We certainly don't hold prejudices against anybody," Hunt Club manager John Frantz said yesterday. "We don't have black members, nor do I know of any who have applied. But I think it depends on the population base. We have very few blacks in southwestern Ontario. And our club is also pretty expensive to belong to."

Oakdale also has no black members. Walker has worked at the club since 1982 and said that no black has applied. The club does have non-Jewish members. Anybody can apply for membership if he or she is proposed by two members. The club is full, though, and is not taking applications.

"It (the subject of discrimination at golf clubs) is a very delicate area," Walker said. "I wouldn't want to comment further on it."

The subject is indeed delicate, as becomes apparent the more one examines membership policies. The Mississaugua Golf and Country Club, for one, does not have black members. But the club's bylaws, like those of all Canadian clubs surveyed for this story, do not exclude blacks.

"We have no restrictions," club manager Walter Haselsteiner said of Mississaugua, which hosted the 1965 and 1974 Canadian Opens. "We have members from many ethnic minorities."

But why doesn't Mississaugua have black members? Metropolitan Toronto has a large population base, and surely many blacks have the means to apply. They are free to apply, but they don't. Mississaugua, to be sure, is a most friendly club that has a reputation of receiving guests warmly. The club played host to the recent Ontario Amateur. Still, blacks don't apply.

This is the case across Canada, and not only regarding blacks. Jews can apply to join the Toronto Golf Club, but few do so.

Non-Jews can apply to join Oakdale, or Elm Ridge in Montreal, but few have. Blacks can apply to Mississaugua or London Hunt, but few if any have elected to do so.

So do Canadian clubs have exclusionary policies, or don't they? Clubs don't exclude people via their bylaws or policies, but clubs do become havens for certain groups. "Other" people don't apply, policy or not policy.

"Policy is the wrong term," Canadian Open director Richard Grimm said this week upon his return from Shoal Creek, where the PGA Championship is underway and where the club is under scrutiny. "It's a fact of life that if you want to join a private club, then somebody has to propose you and then you must have the application approved."

Grimm's point was that the membership procedure can work against open membership and is tantamount to policy. The members must sponsor a nominee to Vancouver's Capilano. The application then goes to the membership for a vote.

"We have no discrimination here at all," manager Greg Hartigan said. "It's a democratic process of a ballot. We have a mixed bag of membership, every denomination and every type of individual you can think of."

So joining a private club in Canada is hardly a matter of showing up with the initiation fee, getting a locker and going out for a game as a member. The club must want you. And so other forces operate.

Those forces have created today's situation, where London Hunt and Mississaugua — to cite just two clubs — do not have black members. Some club members and managers point out, at the risk of sounding apologetic, that blacks are not the only visible minority in Canada. Club bylaws do not exclude members of minorities from applying, although one would not have to go far to find clubs where they don't belong.

Canadian Open director Grimm has a strong view on the matter of private clubs with exclusionary membership policies holding outside events.

"If the PGA and the USGA (United States Golf Association) want to go to exclusive clubs, fine. But they can't hold events at these clubs where John Q. Public will attend. You want to become part of the world, you had better be liberal. The PGA and the USGA are in trouble."

The subject of membership at private golf clubs in Canada comes down to this: Clubs do not exclude by policy. But a club's history, reputation and procedures can separate people.

There may not be a Shoal Creek in Canada, but there are important questions that deserve examination. Golf-club members shouldn't be smug. Exclusion is exclusion, be it according to bylaw, practice or reputation.

Disregard for Kids an Ominous Mistake

The Globe and Mail, **August 4, 1990**

Most kids don't have a chance to get into golf these days. That's the only conclusion one can draw on the basis of current costs and a lack of sites for learning.

Consider the experience of Ann Pion, a Toronto woman whose teenage son is a keen, talented golfer. The Pions can't afford to join a private club, and the son has been unable to find a course or good practice area to work on his game at a reasonable expense.

"We've called all over," his mother said recently. "We've tried private courses. They say they understand the problem, but that they don't let non-members on their practice ranges. In the end, they say it's an issue of money. People who can afford to belong to clubs can find places for their kids to practise and play."

She was more than a little angry, although she knows members of private clubs expect what they pay for: privacy. But what about the organizations that talk from time to time about the importance of introducing youngsters to golf?

"Why doesn't the RCGA (Royal Canadian Golf Association) do anything?" she asked. "We've called them, but they can't provide a place for practice."

The RCGA owns Glen Abbey in Oakville, Ontario. The course runs free clinics in the spring, but this major money-maker doesn't let anybody practise unless he or she has paid the heavy green fee.

Maybe a golf club supposedly built for the people should find a way for youngsters to use it without breaking their bank accounts or their parents'.

And how about city sites, such as parks? Forget it. They don't allow golf. Kids can throw a baseball around, play soccer and tennis, swim and, in the winter, skate or play hockey. But kids who want to golf are out of luck, except for the overcrowded public courses. And they're no place to learn the game.

There's an argument against kids hitting golf balls in parks. Detractors cite the possibility of injury. They also claim there's not enough space for golf.

Injuries are always possible, of course. But a properly supervised area that would allow kids to chip and putt and even hit the ball 50 yards or so would go a long way towards ensuring safety. And you wouldn't need a lot of space for such a program.

But nothing will happen because golf has no effective lobby. The associations aren't in there with the politicians, extolling some of golf's benefits for kids: It keeps them occupied in healthy surroundings; it's a lifelong game; it can teach concentration and discipline, while introducing them to new friends.

No, golf associations are too busy making money from amateur or professional tournaments to bother with kids. Oh, there's the odd junior camp, and older kids might be brought to the Canadian Open to meet the pros. And the Canadian Golf Foundation has a fine scholarship program for students entering college.

But where's the initiative that will get kids 12 or so and under on to the course? One looks to the private sector.

The other evening, for instance, a place called the Golf Ranch, in the northeast sector of Metropolitan Toronto, was full of kids of all ages. They were hitting balls off artificial turf mats at $5 a bucket, $6 if they hit from the real stuff. Other ranges in and around the city were also busy, but there simply aren't enough, and what is there might not be around very long.

"Driving ranges are becoming obsolete because of land values," Golf Ranch co-owner Jack Widdis said. "We lease 40 acres here, worth about $30 million. The land is being held for Highway 407. So this isn't a forever thing."

For forever things, one can travel to Scotland, where kids are encouraged to golf.

There's a short course just for children in North Berwick, not far from Muirfield, a British Open course. Boys and girls as young as three hit shots around the minimally tended layout a couple of Sundays ago as their parents or older siblings watched. The kids' course is free.

The King James VI course in Perth has a small patch of rough ground near the clubhouse. A week ago Tuesday, a lad was chipping balls there. He wasn't a member, but he was welcome. No wonder more and more fine golfers are coming from Britain and Europe.

So what can a Canadian kid do? Not much, it seems. Golf is in danger of becoming an old man's game in the not-too-distant future. In addition, the way the game is keeping away kids whose families can't belong to private clubs is escalating the concept that the game belongs to the rich.

Have you heard the one about the junior club champion at a certain course? He's 61, the youngest golfer the club could find for the competition.

Don't laugh. It might happen if ways aren't found to get kids on courses.

Teed Off: Tradition Meets Discrimination

The Globe and Mail, **December 14, 1991**
Golf has long prided itself on being a sport that provides recreation for boys and girls, men and women.

But a tradition that is increasingly perceived as discrimination has long existed at private clubs: Women have not been able to join most as full members, or enjoy privileges that men take for granted.

Access to tee times during weekend and holiday mornings is one of those privileges. Women at older private clubs are barred from playing at these times. The issue has become a flashpoint as women seek equal rights at such clubs. More women are contesting the inequity, but the policy is deeply rooted within the fabric of how golf clubs are structured. Access to the tee is power, and men have it.

Meanwhile, women's interest in golf is at a high. According to the Canadian Golf Foundation, 52% of new Canadian golfers are women (the figure is 40% in the United States). About 1.1 million or 28% of all golfers in Canada are female.

As a rule, older clubs that were founded by men for their recreation resist granting women equal access to starting times. Clubs that maintain this policy point to the lower fees that women pay as one justification for the regulations that restrict access.

Newer clubs, though, such as King Valley in King City, Ontario, Devil's Pulpit in Caledon, Ontario, Glencoe and Bearspaw in Calgary, Alberta, are structured so that all golfers have equal access. One member generally buys one share, same price for all. Where a family membership is available, as at King Valley, both husband and wife have full use of the course at all times. New clubs could not survive any other way.

Forty-seven women have purchased shares in the Devil's Pulpit, out of a total of 465 memberships. They can play whenever they want. A new member at the Devil's Pulpit must pay $55,500 to join. Annual fees were $3,500 in 1991. A woman who joins Mississaugua Golf and Country Club near Toronto, an older club, would pay $17,500, half the entrance fee for a man. Her annual fees would also be half those for men. A woman at Mississaugua, like her counterpart at the Richmond club near Vancouver, Mayfair in Edmonton and Ashburn in Halifax, *cannot* purchase a full share. That option is not available at the vast majority of older clubs. The London Hunt Club in London, Ontario, is an interesting exception. A woman shareholder can pay the same entrance fee and annual dues as a male shareholder. She is then eligible to be on the board of directors. But her access to the tee is still restricted.

"It's such a delicate issue," club manager John Frantz said. He pointed out that all clubs are different in how they govern themselves. But access for women on weekends is a critical issue at all older clubs.

That central issue is a problem for the clubs. They are confronted with an area that is at the intersection of what private clubs construe as their right to make their own rules, and what society is beginning to define as discrimination. The older clubs are saddled by regulations their founders formed decades ago, when fewer women worked outside the home and so were able to go during the week. The men who ran the private clubs, and who still do in the vast majority of cases, kept weekend and holiday mornings for themselves.

"Our policy is still like most clubs," Mayfair's general manager Joe Coleman said this week. "Ladies have limited access. But at the same time we have been slowly moving to a gender-neutral section [that is, a policy whereby women would have equal access to the tee]. This has become quite an issue at our club. We partially addressed it at a meeting last week and decided to study the question during the next year. The initial discussion will be whether we should provide the option to women of paying the full fee."

Mayfair does have 45 female shareholders who pay the same entrance fee as men, but a smaller annual fee. The female shareholders have voting rights in the club, whereas the 200 women who are spouses of male shareholders cannot vote. And Mayfair, like most older clubs, has never had a female president. Of the clubs that were surveyed, only Oakdale in Toronto has had a female president. Mechanisms for a woman to become president do exist at Richmond, London Hunt and Ashburn in Halifax. A woman will be Ashburn's president in 1992. And women are board members at some clubs in a fairly recent development.

What is being done about the limitations imposed upon women at conventional private clubs? How are clubs responding to the perception that they are maintaining discriminatory policies? Does a private club have the right to conduct itself as it sees fit, or is it subject to governmental regulation? These are some of the questions that the issue raises.

Capilano in West Vancouver and Earl Grey in Calgary refused to talk to *The Globe and Mail* about women's access to tee times. A representative at each club said that the club is private and likes to keep its policies to itself. The majority of clubs, however, realize they cannot shirk the issue.

"I don't know why people are not willing to talk," Dave Esplen, head pro at the Richmond Golf and Country Club in Richmond, British Columbia, said of the two western clubs. "Everybody is going to have to come to grips with it. Are women willing to pay the full fee? At some point I'm sure they will be, and they will have the right to do so."

Esplen's point about whether women want to pay the full fee given the option of doing so, and thereby gain full and equal access to the course, is an important one. The Board of Trade of Metropolitan Toronto's country club in 1990 instituted its gender-neutral golf section. The Woodbridge, Ontario, club offered the option to women who were spousal members and to its business-women's section. One hundred and twenty-five women in the club are now full golf-section members, having paid a varying amount to join depending upon when they first became members of the club.

"It went off without a hitch," club general manager Dave Fairley said. By no means did every woman choose the full option, but significantly, the Board of Trade did offer the full-payment option, which would lead to freedom of the course. The Board of Trade is essentially a business professional's club; its enlightened position is a bellwether of how things may go in Canada.

The situation is only slightly better in the United States. There was much talk after Hall Thompson, the president of Shoal Creek in Birmingham, Alabama, admitted before the 1990 PGA Championship that his club did not allow blacks as members. That led to an examination of discrimination at U.S. clubs. Many have admitted their first black members and claim to be in the process of admitting more. But most clubs have only flirted with the issue of tee times.

"There has certainly been movement at many of the private clubs," Marcia Chambers said this week; she's a columnist for the *National Law Journal*, who has written widely on the problem. "The key to the issue is that the male traditionally holds the share in the club. A female spouse can perhaps petition to become part of the share membership, and while she may enjoy many of the same privileges at the club, the major issue is still tee times. They seem to remain inviolate."

Limited access for women is often a man's way of controlling his use of the course.

"If women are asking for starting times on the weekends in the morning, then I'm not into it," said one accomplished amateur golfer in Toronto. "To me it's something in the tradition of golf that men have the course to themselves on weekends at private clubs. I don't see it as discriminatory. If clubs don't let blacks or Jews into a club, then yes, it is. It's discriminatory if they don't let women into a club. But I think the matter of women on the course on weekend mornings is different. A lot of things go with the tradition of golf. That's one of them. Guys like to get together early for breakfast. They tell jokes, go out on the course and who knows, maybe they're firing clubs. Who needs women around for that?"

Women are not around at all at one club, the men-only National in Woodbridge. The National's counterpart is the Ladies' Golf Club of Toronto in Thornhill, Ontario, a women-only club. Both clubs set aside times for the opposite sex, and women at the Ladies' Club may sponsor a man to pay an annual fee that will allow him playing privileges each time for a greens fee. But men may not join the club as members.

Many male golfers support the position of restricting women's tee times, though few speak of it publicly. Clubs point out that men are also kept away from the tee at certain times during the week, so that women can play on their own. The men claim the first tee for their own on weekends and holidays. But the crucial point is that women generally have fewer hours in which they can play than do men.

A conflict at the Beach Grove club in Windsor gained national attention. Tamra Tobin has been in a protracted struggle with the club to receive equal access to the tee. Tobin, a lawyer, has argued that women cannot play during nine and a half hours weekly, when men have exclusive access. Men must stay away for five and a half hours, when only women have access. Women cannot play until 11:30 a.m. weekends and holidays.

"I've made no headway, not really," Tobin said.

Tobin appeared on the CBC television show "Marketplace" in November. The Windsor chapter of the Canadian Federation of University Women planned its annual dinner at Beach Grove for February, but cancelled after the show was aired. Tobin's case sits with the Human Rights Commission. So does the case of Islington Golf and Country Club member Linda Tickins. She has asked that the club grant her the right to purchase a share of the same value that men hold after a restructuring of the club's finances.

But Tobin and Tickins are facing a section of the Ontario Human Rights Code whose wording seems hostile to their quest for equal rights. Section 19, subsection three, reads: "The rights under section one to equal treatment with respect to services and facilities is not infringed where a recreational club restricts or qualifies access to its services or facilities or gives preference, with respect to its membership dues and other fees, because of age, sex, marital status or family status."

A private golf club qualifies as a recreational club, and so the Code as worded does grant a private golf club the right to conduct its affairs as it chooses. But the subsection might not be the final word.

"If a situation like that [the Tickins case] would go to a Board of Inquiry, then it could come under the matter of whether it is constitutional," said Peggy Molloy, a human-rights officer with the Human Rights Commission in Toronto. Molloy is working on the Tickins case.

So are golf clubs that limit access to starting times acting against the Charter of Rights?

Neither Tickins nor Molloy would speak about the Islington case, under instructions from Tickins's lawyer, who is in negotiation with Islington. Tobin said that her case is caught in a backlog of human-rights cases.

In any case, women seeking equal access to their courses are not pleased that these cases are having to be dealt with by human-rights officers and lawyers. Neither are the clubs pleased. Tickins could reach a settlement, or even win her case, but still find herself effectively ostracized at her club.

"I'm paying a lot of money to enjoy the club," Tickins said, "and nobody has said anything bad to me at the club about what I am doing. But will it help other clubs if we work things out through negotiations with the Human Rights Commission? I don't know."

Marcia Chambers, the *National Law Journal* columnist, expressed her view based upon her extensive research into the issue. Hers is a voice of reason and hope tempered by experience.

"Human-rights cases often languish, or there might be a settlement," she said. "But women might leave the club after the issue is settled. Golf is a social game. You have to play with other members. Very few women will take their clubs on."

Change will come, slowly and inevitably. Chambers is in touch with some 100 U.S. clubs that are dealing with the issue. Some are acting out of fear of litigation. That's one way changes occur. A Women in Golf summit took place recently in Orlando, where the issue of access was discussed. And a two-year-old magazine called *Golf for Women*, has become the third-biggest golf publication in the United States. It's providing a voice for women, something they have not had. These are positive steps.

But the real and lasting changes are likely to occur in another way.

"It will happen generationally," said Chambers, who has a master's degree in law and whose husband teaches law at Yale. "We are teaching women differently today than before. The women who are coming out of college will not abide what is going on at the clubs. And the younger men in college are as appalled as the women."

The changes could take 10 to 15 years, Chambers says. Clubs know the changes are coming, though many of the men who run the clubs still believe in the old ways. Thus a shameful underside of the game persists, a shame deriving from the fact that the male policy-makers have been loath to realize that tradition can be just another word for discrimination.

Chapter Six

MUSINGS

ANYBODY DRAWN to contemplation could find the golf course a companionable place for his mode of thinking. It seems possible to come up with a solution to the world's problems while going around the course, or at least to figure out what to do for dinner that night. The reason is clear, and I've stated it before: Golf gives us time to think, and when that happy situation presents itself in our overstimulated life, good things can happen. One's mind often becomes an open book on the course. Fantasies soon fill the space.

The selections in this chapter are drawn from flights of fancy I have taken while on the course, or later, as I transported myself easily back to the game, perhaps to a favourite course. Sometimes I took notes while playing, curiously observing my thought patterns. At other times I sat down after playing and reflected on something that presented itself during the round. In the early spring of 1992, I went off on another mental journey. A *Globe and Mail* reader had written to tell me that the pars of the holes on the back nine of the Augusta National Golf Club read the same backward and forward; that is, they formed a palindrome, as such a sequence is called. I wondered — were there more palindromes? The column that resulted is included in this section.

Palindromes are one thing, but real golf is another. I wanted to make pars, not only discover whether they formed unusual patterns. Golf at its best is a sensual affair, one in which many disparate images connect. And autumn golf when the day is a gift is a time when the imagination can run free. It's a glorious time for musing. I write here of such a day in November at Glen Abbey in Oakville, Ontario. That day I felt Glen Abbey was the best course in the world, but on other days I felt similarly about other courses. Once I even felt that a group of us were playing real golf way up north in Yellowknife in the Northwest Territories on a frozen lake. Surely that was golf, and so I wrote of the day there. The round was full of good cheer, something that Canadian humorist Stephen Leacock understood is at the heart of golf. He wrote brilliant and pithy pieces about the game, poking fun at it and its adherents, the golf-obsessed.

But not all is pure fun along the course. I played the century-old Homestead course in Virginia and wondered what happened to all the caddies. It's still the best way to golf, with a caddy at your side. But if there were few caddies left at the Homestead, where they had thrived for years, how likely was it that we would see many of the dying breed again? That led to a column, as did the statistics sheet that the PGA Tour sends out weekly. The statistics as provided emphasize only the good shots that the players hit. What about the miscues? I had seen Fred Couples and Payne Stewart miss shots. But they never registered on the stats sheet. It was all grist for the mill, subjects for musings.

Questions led to many of the pieces here. Why has the hobby of golf memorabilia collecting turned into a business for many people, and what has that done to the simple joys of collecting, of rummaging in antique stores for a club, a board game about golf, a well-preserved book? What's behind the resurgence of miniature golf? What is the Golf Nut Society of America all about, and why do people use golf as a theme for their vanity licence plates? And how do people get their golf-related nicknames, Bad Luck Chuck, for one?

What's behind it all anyway? I address this question throughout this chapter. Musing about the game, rambling and walking
along the course and meandering in the arcana of the game are
some of the pleasures, I think. There's no end to the "stuff" of
golf out there. Here's a short walk on the wilder side of the
game. There's no telling where it will lead, which to me is really
one of the primary pleasures of starting out on a round.

Golfers Get into the Swing
of Autumn Play

The Globe and Mail, **November 11, 1983**
If golf is a good walk spoiled, as some wag once said, you wouldn't
have known it by the activity around Toronto golf courses during
this week's mild weather. Enthusiasts rescheduled business meetings in favour of a round over their favourite courses. Many caught
the 24-hour flu, otherwise known as the golf bug.

At the Glen Abbey Golf Club one player found himself con-
tentedly alone on 238 acres still as midnight in Algonquin Park.
The only sounds were the swish of the clubshaft through the air;
here and there a bird whistled in the trees. Once there was the
whoosh of an airplane, but it seemed far away.

Down in the valley holes of Jack Nicklaus's spectacular creation — referred to by course superintendent Don McFaul as "a
microclimate all its own" — mallards glided over the clear waters
of Sixteen Mile Creek. Green-necked and yellow-billed, they attracted the golfer's attention as much as the shots he had to play.

In these same waters where dreams of birdies — and golf
balls — had been lost for such professionals as Nicklaus and Lee
Trevino, different dreams had recently come true. Anglers cast
their lines into the streams and came up with three large salmon.
Running downstream with their catch to shallower waters, the
fishermen reined in their prizes.

It was a naturalist's delight and reminded the golfer of all that
is best about the game and all that can come too infrequently: an
open course, and a championship course at that, nobody ahead

and nobody behind. Only 18 holes to play, and the sunlight flickering through the trees and across the greens. And all around the course, there were groupings of golden maple leaves that crackled under the golfer's spikes.

On this day at Glen Abbey there was no sense at all of a good walk spoiled, only a lovely walk enhanced. The clubs on the golfer's shoulders weighed nothing at all; the fairways had what British golf writer Bernard Darwin called "lovely turf that can put a little spring into the most leaden and depressed foot."

For this was autumn golf in Canada at its finest, and one wished the golfers who missed last summer's Canadian Open could have ranged over this sequestered park. Golf was stripped to its essential elements: a player, clubs, a ball and the course. The pace was brisk, the senses awakened.

Things not normally noticed captured the attention. As the golfer ascended the hill to the 15th green, a yellow-and-black butterfly fluttered in front of him. On this day golf seemed a marvellous balm. It was easy to understand why, in the 1955 movie "A Star Is Born," James Mason, playing Norman Main, a successful actor on his way down, told Judy Garland, on her way to becoming the star Vicki Lester, "If I'm happy or if I'm miserable, I putt golf balls around the living room."

Norman Main knew that golf had the capacity to take him away from whatever emotion preoccupied him. On a fall day at Glen Abbey the atmosphere drained away all cares until, by the time the last few holes came round, it seemed the golfer had been there for hours and hours, so much had he absorbed.

Yet through the 15th hole the round had taken only two hours and 18 minutes. The golfer had decided when he set out on his cross-country hike that he would play but one ball a hole, and play it seriously. Could the game be enjoyed, he wondered, without agonizing over each shot?

As he holed out on the final green in two hours and 48 minutes he realized, yes, of course it could. This was the way to play golf, moving quickly, the senses alive, each shot a challenge. When he was through, he longed for more autumn golf and was left with nothing more than an agreeable sense of fatigue. He had confirmed again, as another wag once said, that golf is indeed the best game in the world at which to be bad.

Humour a Link That Binds
Those That Tee Off

The Globe and Mail, **March 23, 1984**

One of the delightful aspects of golf is that it can't be taken too seriously. After all, what can you say about a game in which participants often wear slacks that look more like shower curtains, gaily decorated with smiling golfers swinging every which way?

But there it is. Golfers are a strange breed and thankfully, golf humorists during the years have celebrated their foibles. Some of the best of the genre include P.G. Wodehouse, Ring Lardner and George Houghton. Those who have meant to write seriously about the game — Bernard Darwin, Henry Longhurst, Paul Gallico and Herbert Warren Wind — also have been unable from time to time to keep out of their prose a lively wit, say every second sentence or so. It goes with the territory.

Some of the richest humour, however, comes from people who really didn't write much about golf. There was, for example, John Hulteng's hilarious piece written in 1953 in the *Providence Journal-Bulletin* in which he described his sweaty misadventures while watching his wife compete in the national amateur.

"Things aren't looking too bright," it was suggested to him after his wife lost the first two holes. "Oh," he answered, "it's nothing to be upset about. After all, it's only a molf gatch."

But one of the greatest golf humorists — though it was hardly his specialty — was Canadian writer Stephen Leacock, who died nearly 40 years ago, on March 28, 1944. In two pieces called "The Golfomaniac" and "A Lesson on the Links: The Application of Mathematics to Golf," Leacock very nearly defined the genus Mr. Average Golfer.

The golfomaniac turned every conversation towards golf. Told by a companion on a suburban train that the U.S. Navy was ordered again to Nicaragua, he mentioned how progressive it was that the Navy had recently made golf compulsory at the training school at Annapolis.

The golfomaniac also had an endearing and rarely seen quality that belongs to at least 300 members of every golf club: He believed he knew what the game was all about, though the only progress he ever made in golf was to the bar.

"He explained to me," Leacock wrote, "how you can do practically anything you want with a golf ball, provided that you keep your mind absolutely poised and your eye in shape, and your body a trained machine. It appears that even Bobby Jones of Atlanta and people like that fall short very often from the high standard set up by my golfing friend in the suburban car."

That high standard was, of course, a fiction in the golfer's mind, which Leacock exploited beautifully, mostly by exaggeration.

In his story applying mathematics to golf, Leacock addressed the feeling of every golfer that he rarely plays to his potential.

"How often," Leacock asked, "does a man really play his game?" First, Leacock pointed out the many things that can put a player off his game, taking his friend Amphibius Jones as an example.

On some days, "the light puts him off his game; at other times the dark; so, too, the heat; or again, the cold. He is often put off his game because he has been up too late the night before; or similarly because he has been to bed too early the night before."

Leacock suggested that there were 50 disturbances that could make a hash of Jones's game, each occurring once every 10 days. He then asked: "What chance is there that a day will come when not a single one of them occurs?"

The formula as expected, by which Leacock answered the question, is simple: x over 1 plus x squared over 1 . . . plus x to the nth power over 1 "worked out in time and reckoning four games to the week and allowing for leap years and solar eclipses equals once in 2,930,000 years," which is when Jones can expect to play his game.

It's not clear whether Leacock actually played golf, never mind playing his game. His golf pieces, as minuscule a fraction of his 35 books of humour as they are, do suggest a familiarity with the game that could only have come from playing it.

In 1941 Yousuf Karsh photographed Leacock in his study at his summer home on Lake Couchiching, Ontario, which he called Old Brewery Bay. On a wall rack to one side of a clock hang two tennis rackets, and to the other side hangs what looks like a golf club.

We do know that Leacock's wife, Beatrix, played golf. It's nice to think that he too sometimes thrashed around a course; if not, it's equally as pleasant to read his work today, and to thank him posthumously for knocking a bit of the stuffiness out of a game that is sometimes a bit too "royal," a bit too "ancient" for most of us.

Golf Caddies Are Vanishing

The Globe and Mail, **October 18, 1985**
Hot Springs, Virginia — Let us now lament the passing of the caddy at golf courses in Canada and the United States. What was once a respected profession is a thing of the past as golf carts now ride where caddies walked.

The departure of the caddy has meant the disappearance of a noble golfing tradition, and along with it, one of the most pleasant ways to play. A golfer could form a relationship with a regular caddy. Young men were introduced to the game. Students worked the courses after school and during summers. Others were permanently employed.

Nowhere in North America was the caddy more a part of the scene than at the Homestead, a resort that includes three courses in the Alleghany Mountains in Virginia. One can almost accept the demise of the caddy at modern resorts and private clubs, but at the Homestead, where golf has been played for nearly a century, the sense of loss somehow is more deeply felt.

After all, this is where Sam Snead, born, raised and still living in Hot Springs, caddied as a youngster. There are 26 club professionals who have come out of Hot Springs — from a total population of 5,000. All began as caddies.

Caddying also provided a place for the permanent part-time worker who had a distaste for regular employment. Herman Peery, the pro at the Cascades course, one of the three owned by the Homestead, knew a few rogues who fit into this category.

"At one time, we had 200 caddies at our courses," Peery recalled yesterday. "And about 75 to 100 were real good. A bunch of them would get drunk for two or three days, but when they came back to caddy, they would do real good jobs."

The 200 caddies of which Peery spoke have now dwindled to a handful. There aren't even enough to work for the 16 golfers in the championship flight at the Virginia Women's Amateur, held annually at the Cascades. The state golf association has ruled that the players must use carts.

The Homestead caddies used to wear uniforms and were also given badge numbers. If a fellow held No. 20 but No. 19 was the last to get out on a given day, he would be first up the next day. On a good day, a caddy might get out for two rounds — or loops, as they were called.

As a caddy improved, he would carry double — two bags. Don Ryder, now the head pro at the Homestead course, used to get $6 for his labours.

Ryder, 38, is a perfect example of what caddying could do for a young man. Not only did he develop an appreciation for the game, but he became a fine player. He once shot 29 over the back nine at his course. But more important, he absorbed the golf course atmosphere by caddying.

Peery, 59, began as a ball-chaser when he was 10. He graduated to carrying single when he was 12 and soon moved up to two bags.

"You had caddies and you had guys who just carried the bag," Peery said. "A good caddy was worth a lot to a player. He knew the distances, he could read the greens and a good caddy didn't run his mouth on down. He'd just watch."

Sometimes a caddy had to be a sphinx. "Speak only when spoken to" was the golden rule. That couldn't have been easy — caddies have always been rather gregarious sorts.

Johnny Gazzola, a spokesman for the hotel, once caddied for Robert Stranahan, the founder of Champion Spark Plugs. This was what was known as a "good bag." Do the right job and you might find steady work and a good tip. But Stranahan first put Gazzola in his place.

"I went up to Stranahan," Gazzola recalled, "and said, 'Sir, I'm Johnny Gazzola. I'll be caddying for you today.'

"He came right back at me and said, 'All right, Johnny Gazzola, you've told me your name and that's all I want to hear from you. When I hit that ball, I want you to go get it and lay my golf sack down beside it. Remember, I'll do the talking around here.'"

These stories are now folklore since caddies are as rare as vaudevillians. George Carpenter caddied at the Homestead for 45 years and still works in the pastry shop at the hotel. He gets out on occasion — but those times are further and further apart.

Today, young executives who wouldn't know a good caddy if they saw one await their turn on the first tee at the Homestead, from where they take off on their carts. The tee is the oldest in continual use in the United States, having been first put into play in 1892. The site of the old caddyshack is just a few yards away, behind and out of the golfer's view — gone forever, as are its residents.

Tales of the Golden Fleece

Golf Digest, **December 1988**

After each weekly event, the PGA Tour sends me a list of player statistics. I learn who the scoring leader is, who's driving the ball the farthest, who's hitting the most greens in regulation. It's all upbeat, positive stuff. You'd think that Strange, Azinger and company never dunk a ball into water, or miss a straight uphill three-footer.

I want negative stats. I want categories for bogeys, double bogeys and drives hit out-of-bounds. I want to know about skulled wedges, bunker shots left in the sand, missed greens from 150 yards in, three-putts, four-putts. Being human and therefore subject to all the frailties of our species, the pros make these errors. You've seen them. I've seen them. Players talk about them, and sometimes they even laugh about them. But the PGA Tour ignores them.

An example. Jack Nicklaus was tied with Curtis Strange when they walked onto the 16th green the last day of the 1985 Canadian Open at the Glen Abbey Golf Club near Toronto. Nicklaus had hit the green on the par-five in two. He putted from 25 feet to within three feet of the hole, but missed his birdie putt. Yes,

Jack Nicklaus missed from three feet. The great man attributed his error to the sun, saying that it cast a glint over his putter. Creative excuse that, but the fact is Nicklaus missed the knee-knocker. Strange saved par on the hole and went on to win.

Nicklaus's mistake didn't show up in the tour stats. There's no such category as missed birdie putts, a birdie putt being, say, anything inside 10 feet. There's something wrong when stats only show us what's right.

Look, I know how good the pros are. But I'm tired of reading about their successes, not only in the weekly releases, but in that major source of information for the golf writer, the *PGA Tour Book*, as it's known, or the media guide, as we call it. Golf fans can also buy it, but they won't find any stats about guys who can't finish an event well when they're in or near the lead after three rounds.

Check the 1988 *PGA Tour Book*, which tells us about the 1987 season. Whereas the weekly stats tell me the top-10 leaders in a variety of categories, the book shows me the top 50 in each area. So I know that Howard Twitty made 317 birdies in 1987, and that Fred Couples, though sixth in driving distance, wasn't in the top 50 in driving accuracy. But I need details as to errors, not hints.

And what about the time Curtis Strange threw a Masters tournament into Rae's Creek? Now there's a stat for you. Number of times a major was dumped into the water. And, of course, Seve Ballesteros gets one of those as well. And I'd like to know how many bogeys Twitty made all year. I hope the 1989 *Tour Book* will inform me that Couples drove into the lake on the last hole at the 1988 Phoenix Open when all he needed to do was par the hole to win and that he did the same thing on the hole in a playoff with Sandy Lyle. Lyle himself won with a bogey. Sure, would require plenty of work to compile such negative stats, but are we after fiction or truth?

The tour's release on the Phoenix tournament read as follows: "Lyle earned his third tour victory by defeating Fred Couples in a three-hole playoff."

Earned the victory? Come on. And did he really *defeat* Couples? He was given the victory. Couples lost it. Lyle didn't win it. Not the way I see it anyway.

Neither the LPGA tour nor the PGA European Tour do any better when it comes to letting us in on the gloomy side of performance. The LPGA gives us birdies, eagles and rounds under par, etc., but nothing Frankensteinish. The European stats gatherers are an equally cheerful lot. If weathermen did the same, every day would be sunny. Maybe you live in such a climate. I don't.

The PGA Tour should issue stats that indicate a player's fumbles. Basketball gives us freethrow percentages, fouls, turnovers. Tennis the number of unforced errors. Baseball has passed balls, wild pitches, errors, left on base, balks. Football has fumbles, interceptions, penalties, missed field goals. Hockey has penalties in minutes.

The pros say that golf at their level is 80 to 90% mental. Wouldn't it tell us something about their mental states if we knew what kinds of shots they come up with under duress?

Evidently, the PGA Tour doesn't think so. Its statisticians live in the myopic world of public relations, where all is well and things are getting even better. Maybe I'm a sourpuss, but that ain't reality, folks, and neither are the PGA Tour's saccharine stats.

Costly Memorabilia Newest Bogey

The Globe and Mail, **October 4, 1989**
Once upon a time in a land where golf was a game and not a big business, a group of people got together for the purpose of collecting books, clubs, artwork and the like. The hobby became so popular that people more interested in investing than collecting soon got involved, and lo and behold, the fun went out of it all.

True story No. 1: Christie's auction house sold a rake iron for $89,000 (U.S.) at a July 20 auction in Glasgow. This club from the early 1900s was designed to slice through casual water. The club is now illegal, and the particular iron in question wasn't even in great shape.

True story No. 2: Philadelphian Joseph Murdoch put together a bibliography of golf books in 1968. Murdoch was a co-founder of the Golf Collectors' Society around that time. A copy of his book sold for $600 at the GCS's annual meeting that was held recently at the Doral Country Club in Miami. Murdoch told Kansan Charlie Yaws, the buyer, that the first thing he should do on his return home was see a psychiatrist.

True story No. 3: Mort Olman, a collector from the days when it was fun and the founder of the Old Golf Shop in Cincinnati, is holding an auction this Saturday. An all-day seminar will be held tomorrow. One fellow is in from Helsinki, Finland. *Sports Illustrated* will be there. Phillips auctioneer Robert Gowland, from Chester, England, will be knocking down the bids. The catalogue alone is $15 and sure to become a collectors' item. It's all big-time stuff.

True story No. 4: Janet Seagle, the respected curator of the United States Golf Association's museum and library, said yesterday that new dealers, many of whom know very little, have shown her key rings and ash trays with golf motifs the likes of which she won at local golf tournaments. And they've been asking and will likely get upwards of $100 each.

Finally, true story No. 5: The USGA, on its application for championships, points out that entrants give the USGA the right to sell their scorecards to the public as a donation to the museum. Each golfer signs his scorecard, so anybody can pick up, say, Jack Nicklaus's autograph. Some people have bought up to $300 worth of cards. Seagle had a call recently from an autograph dealer who wanted to know what they were worth, or perhaps to sell them to the USGA. They were bought from the USGA in the first place.

Times have indeed changed. Major houses conduct auctions regularly. Dealers have entered the field solely because they see it as a way to make money. Some, Seagle said, are so woefully lacking in knowledge that they can't identify such things as patent markings on clubs.

But the public is even less discerning. Do they know the background of the writer in a U.S. golf newspaper who recently described the Christie's auction as a "buyer's market"? He's a dealer. Of course he'd say that. The onus is on the collector, then. He should do his research.

"This guy came in," Olman said yesterday from Cincinnati, "and he wanted artwork for his house. He asked me what he should buy. I told him he should study the area first and make up his own mind. These people get burned, but they're still doing it."

People are getting so burned, in fact, that there is now some question as to the validity of the $89,000 purchase of that rake iron. A rumour suggests that a couple of Englishmen drove the price up to teach Christie's a lesson about the marketplace in antique clubs. Olman was in Glasgow during the auction and offered the underbidder a similar club for $3,000. The fellow didn't take the club.

What happened? Why would a fellow bid a club up near $90,000 and then refuse a similar club for $3,000? Nobody knows, but Christie's claims the club did sell. The point is that this craziness is becoming the usual thing. Three auctions were held in Glasgow in July during the British Open. Olman said they were a joke.

A joke they may have been, but so many people are taking golf memorabilia seriously now that it's difficult for the beginning collector. Seagle pointed out that prices have escalated tenfold in a short period. First it was antique clubs, then feather balls and gutta-percha balls. Next came books, some of which are selling for nearly $30,000. And then it was ceramic pieces and artwork.

About all that's left are the ephemera — advertising pages out of magazines, tournament brochures, scorecards, etc. Who knows, somebody still might uncover a rare item in an attic, but he'll learn what it's worth and feel compelled to sell it to a dealer. That's not collecting, that's number-crunching. As Seagle said before heading for Cincinnati to learn more about what's going on, "It's a shame, and people should be warned."

Ice Tee Time a Cool Effort in the Snowy North

The Globe and Mail, **April 12, 1990**
The celebration of golf known as the Masters ended on Sunday in the deep south even as another celebration of the game was set to go on a frozen lake north of the 60th parallel. The event

unintentionally paid homage to the possible origins of golf in the Netherlands, on ice. Quite intentionally, it raised $110,000 for the Northwest Territories Literacy Council.

The first Peter Gzowski snow tournament would take place across a nine-holer on the frozen lake, probably the first course designed by telephone. Danielle Nadon, the professional at the Chaudière Club near Ottawa, had consulted with Yellowknifers. The course included an elevated third tee accessible only by steps sculpted out of snow, fairways framed by snowbanks, and 40-foot square greens of sheer ice, protected by fringes of stippled, hard snow.

The golfers first saw the makeshift links at midnight Saturday. Former Montreal Canadiens goalie and author Ken Dryden accompanied the group on a walk from the centre of town to Frame Lake. The night skies offered a mild but still vivid rendering of the Northern Lights; enough light, to be sure, and accompanied by a full moon, to enable the visitors to loft orange balls into the starry darkness.

So it was that golfers from southern Canada were introduced to northern golf. Gzowski, the host of the CBC radio show "Morningside," who also leads a now Canada-wide series of tournaments for literacy, must have known this would be special when he and his assistant, Shelley Ambrose, scheduled the event around the Masters. Call the tourney on Frame Lake the northern Masters.

The event, a scramble for twosomes, occurred on Monday, midday. My partner was Cynthia Dale, the actress who plays lawyer Olivia on the Canadian television show "Street Legal." She and folksinger Valdy had joined Gzowski earlier Monday as they read a Robert Munsch story to local schoolchildren. Cynthia sang, and very well, too, and later she played the part of a golfer on ice. She caught on quickly in her first game of golf and said she would take to a grass course come summer.

Winter rules were in effect on Frame Lake, but not off the fairways. The golfers scattered around the lake were a visual reminder that golf may have started on ice in the Netherlands. The late historian Stephen van Hengel wrote in his book *Early Golf* (1972) that a game like golf was visible in thirteenth century paintings. One such painting was displayed recently at the Art Gallery of Ontario in Toronto.

These paintings depict people on frozen lakes holding what may be golf clubs or field-hockey sticks, while hitting an object towards a target on the ice. Seven centuries later, Gzowski and friends did the same in Canada, and there was no doubt it was golf.

Unusual things happened. One golfer marked his ball on the ice green with a penny, then found it stuck to the ice. This was the other side of the coin, so to speak. The late George Knudson had told of a similar experience while playing with the notoriously slow Cary Middlecoff at the southern Masters.

"It was hot," Knudson had said. "Middlecoff marked his ball on one green, then took so long to line up his putt that when he went to put his ball down he couldn't pick up the marker, it was so hot."

The heat on Frame Lake came from the warmth the event generated. The sun was high, there was no wind, and golfers were treated to crystal-like formations under the surface of the ice as they putted. The greens were faster than those at Augusta, fast as ice, excuse the phrase, and so four putts were common.

Still, a northern twosome shot a course record 33 to win, a record that may never be broken because the course may never be set up again. The golfers then gathered for tea and bannock, a local bread, and listened as the Gumboots sang its newly composed song "The Ballad of Gzowski's Golfers."

Lorna Crozier, two times a nominee for a Governor General's award in poetry, then read two poems she had written only an hour before. (That's pressure.) She called one of the poems "What Is Worth Knowing in the World of Golf," and she said it better than Masters tournament chairman Hord Hardin could have.

We know, she read, that the Canadian Open is not the wilderness that some might have thought it was, and that it is also a golf tournament. (She read much more effectively than cold type can suggest.) Lorna spoke of the tricky meanings of golf words, in an area where there are eight official languages and a dozen words for snow. Her message was that words are important and that to be without them is to be lost.

But nobody was lost at the northern Masters on Frame Lake. Here, golf could well have been an acronym for give our languages freedom, freedom so that all Canadians can read, whether or not they ever hit a golf ball.

Depression Game Makes Comeback

The Globe and Mail, **October 31, 1990**
Golf associations and club professionals like to pride themselves on introducing youngsters to the game. But many kids first try miniature golf, a game that has often been associated with hard economic times and that is now making a modest comeback.

The summer just past indicated the resurgence of the sport, a sort of folk art where people putt balls in jungles, through the mouths of dragons and along the corridors of castles. It was possible to stop in Toronto, Edmonton, Chicago, Myrtle Beach and elsewhere and see kids and their parents engaged in the sport.

That was the outdoor version, or more accurately, a fantasy-like diversion that became popular 60 years ago during the Depression. Money was short, and people looked to a cheap pastime. Miniature golf filled the bill and became so widespread that the movie industry lost 25% of its business to the new rage. Never mind; some theatres that were short at the box office were converted into miniature courses.

It was quite a time, as John Margulies wrote in 1987 in *Miniature Golf,* his fascinating book on the subject. Fred Astaire played, as did Fay Wray and Mary Pickford, who built her own, surreal layout. President Herbert Hoover's son Allan fell for the game, and the Marines put in a course at the presidential summer camp in Maryland.

By 1930 there were up to 50,000 miniature golf courses in the United States — on deserted corner lots, rooftops and hotel grounds; and in ballrooms, where couples danced the waltz and then golfed the ball. The game had gone indoors, even into bowling alleys, where miniature-golf layouts replaced the lanes.

Inevitably, however, the craze ended. The sport was blamed for taking people away from the serious business of reviving the economy. Legislators fretted over the fact that the 4 million U.S.

players were spending all night on the miniature links, and many communities banned Sunday play.

Miniature golf was on its way out as a big-time hobby as quickly as it had taken off. The ranks of miniature golf players dwindled by 1931, though the number of courses eventually stabilized.

Anybody who grew up in the 1950s probably recalls with fondness visits to the local miniature-golf centre. It was still a cheap way to spend time with parents and friends, if not the mania of a quarter-century before.

As times improved, though, miniature golf receded further. There wasn't much action after 1960, when authentic golf was cheap and real money was available. But now things are different; we're in a recession, and one senses that the sport is on its way back.

Evidence of this was found on the weekend in a strip plaza in Thornhill, Ontario, where a place called Tropi-Golf opened. Stan Afriat and James Hal, marketing and finance graduates in their twenties, had seen the future, and it was miniature golf. It's called niche marketing, and the niche is kids with their families, as it was 60 years ago.

So here came Sarah Gentle and Robyn Levine, kids laughing and putting their way down an indoor Caribbean island. A local rule imposed a five-stroke limit per hole, an idea that regulation courses should incorporate; no more than a triple bogey would be permitted, say, and wouldn't that speed up play?

Sarah and Robyn needn't have worried, as they holed out more often than not in less than five strokes. One shot went under a mockup of a Canada Post box; the ball even reached its destination quickly.

"It's fun," Sarah said. "Real golfing is harder. This is smaller; it's easier."

Robyn agreed and also pointed to the theme as a source of her enjoyment.

"I like this because I've played in Florida. It's like being in a tropical forest."

Well, not quite, but the sport does offer a fantasyland. Not to play sociologist, but people want to escape when times are tough. And the courses are alluring, a small place where we are large.

Maybe that's why some 2,000 miniature layouts are open in the United States, with more starting up regularly there and in Canada. Maybe that's why miniature golf inspired the International Association of Amusement Parks and Attractions to set up a separate committee last year.

Sharpen your putters, then. Vest-pocket golf is in. Who knows what will follow? Let's see, maybe a rap version of that thirties hit "I've Gone Goofy Over Miniature Golf."

Society Gathers Golf Nuts Even in Winter

The Globe and Mail, **February 14, 1991**
Let's not be serious. That means a mid-winter, diversionary look at a wacky bunch, the Golf Nut Society of America.

The group really exists and is thriving. Computer salesman Ron Garland founded it on July 4, 1986, and now the Head Nut can speak of 1,650 members. Prospective members need to be wild about golf and to express their attachment in often outlandish ways.

There's no shortage of well-known people who do so. Bob Hope, Nut No. 25, even asked for identification as one of what he called "The Lunatic Fringe of Golf." Instead he was appointed to the Society's Board of Directors, reward (or penalty) enough, one supposes, for a lifetime of goofy golf jokes.

Then there's basketball star Michael Jordan, also a member. The Chicago Bull virtuoso has visions of playing the PGA Tour after he leaves basketball — a nutty idea, to be sure. Meanwhile, Jordan was chosen the Golf Nut of the Year in 1989.

Golf Nuts earn points via an entrance exam and bonus points that they accumulate for oddball behaviour. The award goes annually to the golfer who best exemplifies true "commitment" to the game. As the society's motto goes, "If you're not registered, how can you be committed?"

Jordan was committed. He apparently didn't show up for his 1988 National Basketball Association award as Most Valuable

Player. He was in Pinehurst, North Carolina, playing 36 holes. No doubt he was at the grand old Donald Ross designed Pinehurst No. 2.

But not every member can become Golf Nut of the Year. How about Pete Schenk, for instance? He took a camping trip to get away from the game for a while. Instead he built a makeshift nine-hole course in the woods.

Then there's Bob Ball. He was the first Nut to achieve the GNSA Slam by golfing on New Year's Day, Easter, Mother's Day, Thanksgiving and Christmas in the same year. His achievement earned him 200 bonus points.

Inevitably, the Golf Nuts like to prove their commitment by rededicating themselves to the games on their wedding days, honeymoons or anniversaries. Steve Thorwald golfed with his future father-in-law on his wedding day. Tom Jewell golfed in below-freezing temperatures and bitter wind on his honeymoon as his wife, who didn't play, accompanied him. And on and on.

But none of this is surprising, given the GNSA's entrance exam. A person who golfed on his wedding day compiles 50 bonus points. Somebody who suffered a golf-related divorce in the previous year gets 100 points. It's all in good fun, right?

Is "Caddyshack" your favourite movie? You get 25 points. Do you change your putting stroke after every putt? That's a 50-point bonus. Do you practise putting at the office? Give yourself 25 points. David Earl, the 1990 Golf Nut of the Year, is highly regarded for his ability to see breaking putts on the straightest of office floors.

Earl is also a member of another golf fraternity — the Golf Writers Association of America. He was selected Golf Nut of 1990 at the PGA of America's Merchandise Show in Orlando last month and said yesterday that his automatic appointment to the GNSA's board of directors means he will have to forgo one of his best shots — the "camel-head," where a golfer buries his clubhead in a bunker after messing up a sand shot.

"I like the society because it assumes we are willing to laugh at ourselves in front of other people," Earl said from the United States Golf Association in Far Hills, New Jersey, where he is managing editor of *Golf Journal*.

Earl is a highly qualified golf nut. He belongs to the Royal North Devon Golf Club in England and plays some events there. He's a musician who formed a rock band named Brutal Rough and particularly enjoys playing his composition "Opening Day Snowed Out Blues."

That's the way it goes for Golf Nuts. Their official handshake is the Vardon, golf's popular overlapping grip. (Try shaking hands with somebody this way.) The official bird is the Eagle, a score most Nuts rarely achieve. And their flower is Poa Annua, a weed that often gets into greens, but that can actually provide a decent putting surface.

Authentic golf nuts don't require perfectly conditioned courses anyway. They'll play anywhere. In fact, yours truly is playing a winter tournament this Saturday — the Polar Chili Open — in a park near Toronto.

It's all for charity. Then again, it will also be good for bonus points on the GNSA's entrance exam. So excuse me now. I need to hit some putts in my office. (Green rug, of course.)

What's in a Name? Ask Bad Luck Chuck, or Check the Plates

The Globe and Mail, **October 26, 1991**

It's the time of the season when analysts of the golfing psyche can find plenty of material to examine. Golfers freeze while playing in damp cold. They lose golf ball after golf ball but don't mind. Having fallen for the game, they play the leaf rule whereby a ball lost in the ground cover can be replaced at no penalty.

But the truly golf-obsessed go further. The game for them is a year-round sacrament. These golfers are doctoral dissertation material, and no doubt you have met them. They identify themselves by golfing nicknames, and some use vanity licence plates to better indicate the extent of their madness. Spare me, you say, but they don't.

Consider current U.S. Amateur champion Mitch Voges. His licence plate reads Lip-Out, which tells you what he thinks about his putting.

Then there's Gary McCord, CBS's irreverent colour analyst. McCord, 40, has played the PGA Tour since 1973 without winning. His California licence plate reads No Wins. But he won a Ben Hogan Tour event in March. Now there's an asterisk on his plate. Food for thought, that.

Vanity plates run the gamut of feelings that golf nuts hold about the game. Former U.S. and British Amateur champion Bob Dickson's Oklahoma plate once showed the word Birdie. A plate spotted at the King Valley course in King, Ontario, this year read Pynn Hi. Another at Glen Abbey during the Canadian Open featured Hi Fade.

Some golfers flagellate themselves in public with their licence plates. The BBC's Peter Alliss is golf's most astute analyst, and he also represented Britain in the Ryder Cup. His swing sang, but his stroke stunk. When last seen, the plate on his Rolls-Royce read 3-Putt. Truer words, he said, were never written.

Alliss wrote the words himself. But nicknames are different. They're often the snickering creations of outside agencies. That can lead to curiosities. Ask Hal Sutton.

Sutton, the 1983 PGA Championship winner, has had his share of marriages. Some people enjoy reminding him of the costs of his settlements and call him Halimony. Fuzzy Zoeller (for Frank Urban Zoeller) called him Halimony during an exhibition in Memphis. Sutton did not see the humour.

Speaking of humour, or a lack of it, there's Canadian Dave Barr. He has a couple of nicknames. First came Hands, an honorific, shall we say, to mark Barr's wristy, yet elegant, swing. And Ed Fiori has recently taken to calling Barr Smiley. Barr is good-natured off the course, but he's not known for ear-to-ear smiles on the course.

Hardly any pro escapes a nickname. Greg Twiggs is rather large, so he's Twiggy. Billy Ray Brown is Billy Ray Jim Bob. Steve Jones is religious. Tour players call him Reverend Jones because, they say, he preaches.

If the pros have colourful nicknames, their caddies are given some bizarre designations. Reptile worked for PGA Champion John Daly earlier this year. Jazzman did some noted work for Bobby Clampett. When finished, he went off to see his girlfriend, Jazz Lady.

Daly's caddy at the PGA Championship was called Squeaky for his high-pitched voice. English golfer Martin Gates, who also holds Canadian citizenship, had Two-Shot carrying his bag at the Irish Open in June. The fellow was so named because he cost another player two shots at an Australian tournament.

And who can forget Bad Luck Chuck? Not Billy Mayfair, for whom the sombrely named fellow worked. And not Vancouver's Dick Zokol, who also had the misfortune of hiring Bad Luck Chuck.

"He's a two-stroke penalty," Zokol said recently. "I wanted to hit him, he says such dumb things."

Zokol also told about a caddy called Snake who worked for Mike Nicolette. Zokol was at a tournament in Hawaii and had yet to hire a caddy for the week. A caddy called him in search of gainful employment.

"It's Worm," said the fellow. "You know, Snake's brother."

"I just about died," Zokol recalled. Then he mentioned Silly Billy, who has worked for Paul Azinger, Canadian Bob, a caddy from Toronto, and Bullet Bob, Steve Elkington's caddy. He's called that because he's always asking for a cigarette.

Zokol didn't mention Phil Mickelson's new nickname, Fickle-son. Actually, only a few people in Ireland call him that. Mickel-son got their Irish up by making some offhanded remarks during the recent Walker Cup matches at Portmarnock near Dublin.

But Mickelson needn't worry. He's a smoothie on the greens. PGA Tour players could be calling him One-Putt soon.

One-Putt. Now there's a nickname you can live with. That can't be said for some of the goofier vanity plates and nicknames that the golf-obsessed give themselves or are given. A South Carolina plate that reads E Tee? Or Greg Norman, the Great White Shark? Get serious.

"Madam, I'm Adam" on the Fairways

The Globe and Mail, April 1, 1992

Back in November 1986, it was proposed here that an organization called SAGES be formed — the Society for the Analysis of

Golf as an Exact Science. The tongue-in-cheek proposal met with some enthusiasm but soon slipped into the oblivion it warranted.

Now, however, a reader's interest in golf numerology has revived the idea. Duncan Bath of Peterborough, Ontario, noted in a recent letter that the pars for the holes on the back nine at Augusta National, site of next week's Masters, read the same backward as forward. It's also the case for the front nine; each nine, therefore, forms a (numerical) palindrome.

Then there's the Old Course. If any course is mystical, this is the one. And what do you know? Bath will be happy to learn that the Old Course's sequence of pars form a palindrome over the entire layout. The par at the first matches the 18th, the second the 17th, and so on.

Some background is needed. The word palindrome is from the Greek *palindromos* — running back again. It refers to a word, phrase, etc., that reads the same backward and forward. "Madam, I'm Adam" is a palindrome.

Bill Bryson, in his amusing book *The Mother Tongue: English and How It Got That Way*, mentions an inspired palindrome that tells a story: "A man, a plan, a canal, Panama."

Palindromes are rare, in English and on golf scorecards. A search of the 188 highly regarded courses in *The World Atlas of Golf* reveals only Yomiuri in Tokyo, Winged Foot in Mamaroneck, New York, and Lagunita in Caracas as having palindromes, and then only for the front nine. The Old Course's 18 holes show the only complete palindrome. Rare? You bet.

Augusta National was the only course in the book where both nines formed palindromes within themselves. As Bath, a retired engineer, said in a phone call the other day, it's all quite something.

Truly, it's a job for a SAGES expert. But first comes the question: Might not more palindromes lurk in the golf landscape?

A personal random walk through memory did turn up one complete palindrome. The Weston Golf and Country Club in Toronto, where Arnold Palmer won the 1955 Canadian Open, offers an 18-hole palindrome. The scorecard reads the same back to front as front to back. None other such sequence turned up in the not-at-all-exhaustive course ramble.

Strange, isn't it? Is there something hidden in palindromic courses? After all, Augusta National and the Old Course are authentic classics. They feel right. And golf connoisseurs know that Weston is as fine a place to play day in and day out as one could want.

Yet one demurs. Surely the architects could not have planned the numerical sequences. That would be forcing a pattern on the land. And Augusta National, the Old Course and Weston feel as if their routes are gentle. The holes fit; they mesh.

So it was on the phone, then, in search of Tom Fazio. His peers voted the North Carolina architect the top designer last year. He designed the National in Woodbridge; a wonderful course in the North Carolina mountains called Wadehampton; an amazing, flamboyant new course in Las Vegas called Shadow Creek for Mirage casino owner Steve Wynn; and, recently, two new courses at Disney World in Orlando, Florida. What did he make of golfing palindromes?

"My first reaction is that it's just a chance happening," Fazio said yesterday from his office. "If anybody asked me to design a course with that numerical sequence, I don't think I could do it. Other considerations would be more important."

Fazio had not been aware of the curious numbers at the above-mentioned courses. At first, he didn't think the sequences meant much. But he soon became intrigued.

"I wouldn't mind checking it out to see if there's some phenomenon related to the sequence that works on a mystical plane," Fazio said. "And I'll tell you, you could do it on flat terrain, where you in effect create your own topography by moving earth. It could have been done at Shadow Creek, where we created something from nothing."

The talk led to an examination of the meaning of par and the way holes are put together. Fazio's mind was turning. It wouldn't be surprising to find him sitting on the lawn under the oak tree in front of the Augusta National clubhouse next week discussing palindromes.

"I'm curious with it," Fazio said. "Maybe I'd have it in my mind now."

Those are words spoken by a true prospective member of SAGES. Now a question as we move to Augusta and the Masters: Do you know of any course palindromes? The as-yet-to-be-formed SAGES awaits your reply.

Chapter Seven

TOURING PROS

IN THE YEARS that I have been writing about golf, since 1976, PGA Tour purses have increased from just over $9 million to just under $50 million. Jack Nicklaus led the Tour in earnings in 1976 with $266,438, while Corey Pavin won $979,430 to lead in 1991, that after three consecutive seasons in which the money leader won more than $1 million. Purses have increased dramatically on the PGA European Tour as well; during the period in question, the percentage increase was higher than on the PGA Tour, and so it was that Seve Ballesteros, Nick Faldo and Ian Woosnam were winning as much as $1 million on the European Tour. Bernhard Langer led the world money list in 1991 with earnings of more than $2 million. Fred Couples, meanwhile, picked up a cheque for $525,000 when he won the Johnnie Walker World Championship in Jamaica to close out his season. A few months later Davis Love III won the Players Championship in Ponte Vedra, Florida, and the $324,000 that went along with the victory.

The money available to the professionals on the course through their individual enterprise is something to behold; it's important to realize, as well, that professional golfers are not paid a salary. They don't make anything when they miss a cut, and their annual expenses come close to $100,000. Professional golf is free enterprise, all right. The golfer who posts the lowest number at the end of the week gets the biggest cheque; that's all there is to it.

Those golfers who do become regular winners can multiply their earnings dramatically off the course. Norman earns $10 million annually from a myriad of contracts and appearance fees. Arnold Palmer is still the most highly paid golfer and still has the power to draw fans in to his electricity generating station. Palmer — Arnie to everybody — is still the king of the game. He's in his early sixties, but he plays with the enthusiasm of a youngster belting the ball miles down the fairway.

Norman, Palmer and Nicklaus are compelling figures to watch. What sustains them? What keeps them at the game? Surely they have done it all before. Doesn't the same reasoning apply for Ballesteros, Nick Faldo, Curtis Strange and Tom Watson, all of whom are included in the series of sketches in this chapter? And what kept the Canadian artist of the swing, George Knudson, going, even as he was dealing every day with lung cancer? Knudson died in January of 1989, but something kept him moving forward even while he was so very ill.

The short answer is that the older superstars of the game have had a handle on the swing for longer than most. They also feel that the game is understandable at some basic level, and they believe that they can always find their game again. Hence the spectacle of Jack Nicklaus winning the Masters at 46; hence the drama of Palmer leading the Los Angeles Open after three rounds, when he was 53 years old. Hence the shivers that ran through the back nine at the 1991 Masters when Watson was coming back from a double-bogey at the 12th to eagle the 13th and 15th and get into a tie for the lead as he stood on the last tee. It's true: We always expect one more major, one more big win, from the giants of the game. Nicklaus himself says that Watson will win again, that he is too good a player not to. Watson may not have won on the PGA Tour since 1987, but no matter. He has something in him that is different; that's why he's Watson and that's why he won eight major championships through the 1991 season.

And what of the younger stars? Ballesteros is all instinct and passion, as is Norman. I have often thought that these fellows would be as happy beating balls at a banged-up range at the end of town as they are playing major championships. The best golfers, I think, share a quality of having a deep interest in the task at hand. They are rarely bored by golf. Faldo, for one, is driven to comprehend every nuance of the swing along with his instructor, David Leadbetter. Strange, having won the 1988 and 1989 U.S. Opens, is and has been driven by some combination of mechanical aptitude and feel for the game. He and Faldo seem placid on the surface of their personalities; but be assured that they are the epitomes of the phrase "still waters run deep."

And I include a couple of pieces on Vancouver touring pro Richard Zokol. He's one of the brightest young golfers one could encounter, and I believe he may well live up to 1992 U.S. Open champion Tom Kite's idea that golfers don't mature until they are in their thirties. Zokol turned 34 in August of this year, and contended for the U.S. Open that Kite won at Pebble Beach in June. He was four shots out of the lead before shooting a final round 80 in the almost imaginably difficult conditions at Pebble Beach the last day. Still, Zokol said he felt he would learn and grow from that experience. To spend time with him is to sense that he will do just that.

Then there was Knudson. He won eight PGA Tour events during his career while fashioning a technically efficient swing. His goal later was to explain and communicate to others how they could build a swing that was reliable and effective. He died young, at 51, but he did leave behind his book, *The Natural Golf Swing*. We worked on that book together, and I learned as much about taking joy in life as I did about the golf swing from George. I think about him often and hope that those who knew him are living life to the fullest as he would have wanted them to. It's pleasing to picture the flight of his golf ball as it penetrated the air. George had control of that flight, and that's the ultimate.

I have enjoyed watching the top players in the game and have wondered what makes them special. It's impossible to reach any conclusions, but the intrigue is in the attempt. These players last, and I am confident I will still be writing about them a decade from now.

Seve Ballesteros

The Globe and Mail, **September 26, 1987**

Dublin, Ohio — Put these shots in the Museum of Modern Golf. Let the Prado Museum in Madrid commission some oils for all Spaniards to see. Seve Ballesteros played a series of shots yesterday during Ryder Cup competition that were meant for history. Who is this guy anyway — golf's Houdini?

Yes, he is. Look at him yesterday, in the closing match of the first day's foursomes. Ballesteros and partner José-Maria Olazabal are tied after two holes of the alternate-shot competition against U.S. players Larry Nelson and Payne Stewart. It's early in the match, but not too early for magic.

Ballesteros must play from a bunker short of the green. The hole is some 35 feet away, but Seve has to aim, oh, 15 feet to the left and let the ball roll to the top of a hump. He hopes then to see the ball turn around and roll back towards the hole. That's *back* to the hole, as in reverse gear.

Into the bunker, then. Seve plants his feet, signalling seven or eight thousand people to go silent as if on cue. Seve's club comes back, the sand splashes, and the ball lands *exactly* where Seve had pointed to and rolls *exactly* as Seve imagined. Olazabal makes the short par putt for the half.

Four holes later the Spaniards are one hole down. Seve the wizard is 20 yards short of the green on the par-five. So what if there's a bunker between Seve and the hole? So what if the green tilts more than a sailboat in a gale? This is Seve. He can get up-and-down from anywhere.

Ballesteros feels the shot in his fingers and pictures it in his mind's eye. His ball hits the hole and rolls a foot or two away. Routine. You begin to expect this. But what's his next act, and when?

Showtime, folks, come right up.

Olazabal plays his tee ball at the eighth 25 feet past the hole. Ballesteros stalks the green. He points to a spot over which he would like to roll the ball. Olazabal agrees. Seve taps the ball; it curls over the spot and disappears into the hole. All square.

The teams are still tied after 14 holes. Olazabal puts Ballesteros into heavy rough on a hill beside the green at the par-five 15th. Nelson fades a wood that finishes just through the green. Both teams have played two shots. Advantage United States, given the relative ball positions.

Never mind. Ballesteros plunges into his alpha-wave state. He envisions his ball popping out of the rough and dropping on the crest of the hump on the green and sliding near the hole. Which it does. Advantage Europe.

Poor Payne Stewart. He doesn't even look like Payne Stewart, wearing regular slacks instead of his knickers. Captain Jack Nicklaus is leaning on the stars-and-stripes of a U.S. golf bag as Stewart chips and chops. The ball collapses miles from the hole. Nelson misses the putt and Nicklaus walks away. Europe, one up.

Up ahead, the United States has won the first two matches. Welshman Ian Woosnam and British Open champion Nick Faldo are coming back in the third match against Lanny Wadkins and Larry Mize and will go on to win after being four down after nine holes. So Seve knows that a win in his match will keep Europe even after the foursomes matches. He also knows the confidence it will bring to his teammates.

To the 17th, then. Olazabal hits two poor shots and leaves Ballesteros with a 15-foot bogey putt. Nelson has three feet for par. The bet is that the teams will head to the 18th tee even.

Seve has other ideas. He visualizes. He shoots. He scores. Right into the middle of the hole. Nelson follows with a half-Nelson that misses the target. Europe is still one up, one to play, the rest of the matches in.

Magic realist that he is, Ballesteros hits a 6-iron from an awkward lie in a fairway bunker onto the 18th green. Olazabal putts along a ridge and down a hill five feet past the hole. Ballesteros sets up over the ball, this par putt for the match.

Captains Nicklaus and Tony Jacklin watch. Wadkins and his teammates watch. The Europeans watch, except for Olazabal. He turns away.

So what did you expect? Houdini putts his ball into the middle of the hole to win the match. He hugs his partner. Jacklin hugs him. And on the first hole of his better-ball match in the afternoon, Seve chips in from 40 feet for a winning birdie. Then he makes seven more birdies to win the afternoon match and lead Europe to a clean sweep in the afternoon. See you at the Prado.

The Globe and Mail, **September 22, 1988**
Seve Ballesteros is winning a lot of golf tournaments this year — six European Tour events, including the British Open, and the Westchester Classic on the PGA Tour. He's 125 under par for his past 10 events. Is this the dawning of a new age, with Ballesteros alone at the top?

It could be. Sure, Curtis Strange won the U.S. Open and has been making oodles of money. Greg Norman often shreds courses with his powerful game. And Sandy Lyle won the Masters and a couple of other events. But nobody can touch Ballesteros's accomplishments.

Consider his history. In 1976, when he was only 19, he won two European Tour events and nearly stole the British Open from Johnny Miller, finishing second. Through 1987, he had won 47 tournaments around the world, including two British Opens and two Masters. And now this season.

Ballesteros's golfing contemporaries are in awe of him. Lee Trevino said at the Canadian Open that there's Ballesteros and then the others. Nick Price, having gone head-to-head with Ballesteros in the final round of the British Open, only to shoot a 69 to Ballesteros's 65, predicted the Spanish golfer will take over the game.

These are reasons enough to suggest a Ballesteros era is beginning. But there's more. He's been charismatic and brilliant and petulant and moody and witty — and many other adjectives — for years, but now he's touched. People are drawn to him.

Cut to Act 1, Scene 1. Ballesteros is hitting 2-iron shots from a practice bunker at the Tournament Players Club in Ponte Vedra, Florida. The thing is that he's hitting them from a greenside bunker, lofting shots near the hole as if he were using a sand iron. Touring pros gather around, amazed he can hit these shots.

Okay, the guy can play. We know that. But it takes personality if you want to start your own era. How does Ballesteros stack up here?

Well, there's nobody funnier in the game, not even Trevino. Cut then, to Act 2, Scene 1 at the 1983 Masters.

Ballesteros had to get up very early on the Sunday that year to complete a rain-delayed third round. He did so, went back to his room and then returned in the afternoon to play the final round. And he won.

A journalist looking for the real scoop asked Ballesteros what he did so early that final morning. Surely he had some extraordinary routine to prepare him for the unusual day ahead.

Ballesteros thought for a moment.

"Well, the alarm goes off at six. I get out of bed. I go to the bathroom. I come back to the room and take off my pajamas. I put on my clothes. I have breakfast. I come to the course."

That's his dry wit. But Ballesteros also has a dark side.

There was the time Ballesteros was practising his putting at a Florida tournament. A kid said, "Steve, can I have your autograph?"

Seve glared at the teenager. His eyes narrowed. He took a step towards the inquisitor.

"No Steve," he said. "Seve." Then he signed the youth's program.

But back to his golf. Last week, Ballesteros won the Lancôme Trophy in Paris in a walkover. A month ago, he closed with a 62 at the Frankfurter Golf Club in Frankfurt to win the German Open. At the British Open, he was a genius. Price called his play "sheer class" and said it was the thrill of a lifetime to play one-on-one against Ballesteros.

Price touched on something there. It's a main ingredient that goes into the making of an era player. That's the interest his contemporaries have in playing with and observing him.

Golfers watched Bobby Jones for the elegance of his swing. They gathered around the practice tee to study Ben Hogan's technique. They studied Arnold Palmer for his belief in himself despite a less-than-ideal swing. They watched Mickey Wright for the rhythm of her swing and caught Jack Nicklaus's act because he is, well, Jack Nicklaus. And they studied Watson for the one-two simplicity of his swing and the wizardry of his short game.

When we look back, we might see that the Ballesteros era began last September when he led the European team to victory

at the Ryder Cup in Columbus, Ohio. It was the first time the
Europeans had won on U.S. soil. And much of the credit for the
win had to go to Ballesteros, a golfer now on a high peak indeed.

Maclean's, April 10, 1989

The world's most gifted golfer is a Spaniard with *manos de plata*
(hands of silver) and more than a touch of the conquistador. As
handsome as Louis Jourdan and as moody as Marlon Brando,
Seve Ballesteros is also a perpetual outsider, a farmer's son
born in a northern village in Spain who learned his golf on a
nearby beach. Now he is playing a game populated by golfers
reared on the manicured U.S. country club scene, who attended sunny college golf factories on scholarships. Ballesteros,
who turns 32 on April 9 — the last scheduled day of the Masters — is the best of them all. He still makes his home in the
village of Pedrena, where he grew up. He has just married a
Spanish woman and refuses to play the 15 tournaments a year
in the United States that are mandatory for remaining in good
standing with the PGA Tour. Ballesteros is to Europe born, and
there he wants to remain, even if the price he must pay is his
outsider status on the PGA Tour, if not in the hearts of golf fans
around the world.

Ballesteros (pronounced bai-ES-tare-OS) is the most appealing
golfer to come along since Arnold Palmer first hitched up his
pants in front of his army in the 1950s and attacked every golf
shot. Young Seve was an infant then, the fourth son, who at the
age of six was inventing golf shots on the beach with a hand-
made 3-iron that he fashioned from wooden sticks and discarded
metal golf clubheads. He practised so diligently that the club
often splintered; the youngster simply made another, first putting
the wooden shaft in hot water for a couple of hours so that it
would fit into the iron head.

It was on the beach that Ballesteros developed his hands of
silver, improvising shots that he still uses and that still astound
observers. The golf world first became aware of his touch when
he played a brilliant pitch shot into a hill between two sand traps
on the last hole of the 1976 British Open at the Royal Birkdale
club near Southport, England. The ball finished four feet from

the hole, Ballesteros made the putt for birdie — and finished tied for second in the Open. He was only 19.

Since 1976, Ballesteros has hit many such shots. He won the British Open in 1979 and again in 1984 and 1988. He also won the 1980 and 1983 Masters and will be favoured to win the glamour event at the Augusta National course in Georgia this week. Two-time British Open winner Lee Trevino says that Ballesteros is the finest golfer in the world. Not many golf watchers would disagree. Last year, he won seven tournaments in seven countries and more than $1 million in prizes. He led the European Tour, his home tour, in money winnings with $900,000, and also won $200,000 in just seven appearances on the U.S. Tour. In 1988, Ballesteros finished No. 1 in the Sony Rankings, which rates golfers according to their performance around the world.

Despite Ballesteros's crowd-appealing style and looks, PGA Tour commissioner Deane Beman refuses to allow him to enter Tour events whenever he wants. In 1984, Ballesteros played the minimum 15 events in the 10-month PGA Tour season starting in January. But he decided that he could not play that many U.S. tournaments in 1985, and Beman suspended him from the lucrative PGA Tour for the 1986 season. The Spaniard has never been a big fan of American food or hotels and concentrates on his international appearances, many of which provide lucrative appearance fees. Indeed, Ballesteros has not applied for PGA Tour membership — nor does he intend to unless the Tour reduces its requirements.

Beman wants Ballesteros on the PGA Tour, but only under the rules that apply to others. He has said that anybody who is going to reap the benefits of the PGA Tour, the best organized and richest in the world, should play the 15 events, as do Australian Greg Norman and South African David Frost. Says Norman: "Fifteen is not that many to play. You should never make an exception for one person."

Ballesteros will play eight tournaments in the United States this year: the five PGA Tour events that he can compete in on sponsors' exemptions as a non-PGA Tour member, plus the Masters, the U.S. Open and the PGA Championship, over which the PGA Tour has no jurisdiction. One tournament Ballesteros definitely will not enter is the Canadian Open in June at Glen Abbey in Oakville, Ontario, one week after the U.S. Open in nearby Rochester, New York. The Canadian Open might have attracted Ballesteros had it taken place the week before the U.S. Open, enabling him to use it as a tune-up for the American title quest. But that spot is taken up by the Manufacturers' Hanover Westchester Classic in Rye, New York, where Ballesteros is the defending champion.

Ballesteros is disappointed that the PGA Tour insists that he play 15 tournaments. He says that 12 is the most his schedule will permit: "I feel any player who is good for golf and who can bring people to the gate should be able to play anywhere in the world. I think it is unfair to the game of golf that this cannot be. The game loses, people who come to watch lose and I lose. Everybody loses." Jack Nicklaus, for one, agrees with Ballesteros. "I am very much against restricting someone like Seve Ballesteros, or Sandy Lyle, if he were not a member of our Tour. They should be allowed to play if a sponsor wants them. The current restrictions are too severe."

Severe as the restrictions might be, they have not hindered Ballesteros's earning power. He commands up to $100,000 simply to appear in some tournaments. Jerry Tarde, the editor of the U.S. magazine *Golf Digest*, which recently hired Ballesteros away from its rival, *Golf*, to contribute instructional articles, estimates that Ballesteros's annual earnings are at least $5 million.

Ballesteros recently consolidated his wealth while enriching his life. In November, he married Carmen Botín, 24, his steady girlfriend for years, in a private ceremony in Spain. His wife, a 1987 Ivy League graduate from Rhode Island's Brown University, where she earned a degree in organizational behaviour, is the daughter of Emilio Botín Jr., president of the Bank of Santander and one of the wealthiest men in Spain. Botín now takes care of his son-in-law's finances, but in the beginning Ballesteros was not accepted by the family. His mother-in-law expressed concern about his farm background and whether he could fit into the aristocratic Botín family.

Ballesteros is unlikely to worry about whether he fits in. He is more concerned with those hands of silver and displaying his flair. Few of those who watched his win at the British Open at

Royal Lytham and St. Annes last year will forget the tricky pitch and run he played from thick rough behind the final green. The ball finished right beside the hole. Ballesteros exploded with excitement as he saw the result. It was a conquistadorian gesture, reminiscent of Arnold Palmer in his prime. Said Ballesteros about the entire last round: "It was the best of my life. I have never been so much in control. I was 100% in charge."

South African-born Nick Price, who finished second at Lytham, says that he saw something in Ballesteros that convinces him that he can do even better. "I think we'll see a change in Seve. He's matured that little more," says Price.

That "little more" could elevate Ballesteros to the category of Bobby Jones, Ben Hogan and Jack Nicklaus as one of the best ever. Price says that Ballesteros lives to play golf. Nobody plays it better.

Fred Couples

The Globe and Mail, **March 4, 1992**
Fred Couples's win in the Los Angeles Open on Sunday shows again that there's no justification for branding any professional golfer a choker. A player's career is so long that his later play often renders that harsh judgement premature.

Check the data. Tom Watson was called a choker when he shot in the high 70s in the last round of the 1974 U.S. Open after starting the day as leader. Nick Faldo was maliciously called El-Foldo after playing his way out of a Masters a few years ago. Curtis Strange was ridiculed after shooting 39 on the last nine of the 1985 Masters and losing to Bernhard Langer.

Watson has won five British Opens, two Masters and a U.S. Open since his 1974 U.S. Open experience. Faldo has won two British Opens and two Masters titles. Strange won the 1988 and 1989 U.S. Opens. Chokers all, right?

Then there's Dawn Coe, the Lake Cowichan, British Columbia, golfer who had come close to winning many times on the LPGA Tour before this season. Critics said she was getting too used to losing in her nine-year career.

But Coe won the Women's Kemper Open last weekend in Hawaii. She birdied two of the last four holes to do so. Maybe her first LPGA Tour win will silence those who behind her back called her a loser, a choker. They should have kept quiet and given her career a chance. Coe is 31, an age when careers are just starting in golf.

Now comes Couples, the prime target in recent years for those who deem golfers chokers. These 19th-hole experts take an incident or two as ultimate evidence. And Couples gave these people fuel for their tanks, unreliable though it has proved to be.

Couples missed a series of short putts to let the 1988 PGA Championship slip away. Then his errant 9-iron on the final hole of his match against Christy O'Connor Jr. in the 1989 Ryder Cup cost him the match and was instrumental in allowing the European side to retain the Ryder Cup. Did Couples choke? That was the word.

Couples took it all in, and every snide comment hurt. But none cut so deeply as the one Tom Weiskopf uttered in a *Golf Digest* interview. Weiskopf claimed Couples didn't want to win badly enough. That was enough for the usually mild-mannered golfer. Wrongly accused, he spoke up.

Couples responded that Weiskopf could question his swing, but had no right to judge his desire. He also was upset because he said Weiskopf had never talked to him about his desire, or alleged lack of same.

Maybe his PGA Championship and Ryder Cup experiences represented the truth about him. Weiskopf's comments were blunt, but maybe they also held a grain of truth.

Couples decided to act. He was aware of the knocks against his friend Watson, and his subsequent successes. Couples visited Watson last season. Maybe he could learn that something extra he needed.

Couples spent a few days in Kansas City, Watson's hometown. They went to baseball games and talked golf. Watson told Couples to think only of the flagstick the last nine holes of a tournament. That's how small the target is, Watson said. He told Couples he was talented enough to focus so narrowly.

Boom-Boom, as Couples is known, finished in the top six of almost every tournament during the remainder of the 1991 season. He was the leading point-getter while helping the United States to its Ryder Cup win in September. And he walked away with the $525,000 first prize at the Johnnie Walker World Championship in Jamaica to close the season.

But guess what? Some fool told Couples before Sunday's last round of the L.A. Open that he was going to choke. The two fellows had words. Couples then hit the first shot out-of-bounds. He was choking. Had to be.

But Couples birdied the hole with his second ball and went on to play excellent shots the last few holes to get into a playoff with Davis Love III. Then he flagged his approach on the second playoff hole to set up a winning birdie.

Couples is not a choker. He's now the best player not to have won a major. Fate as much as skill and heart will decide whether he will win one. But dissenters can be confident he won't beat himself.

Beating oneself is one definition of a choker. The label also happens to be an unctuous assessment that should be made during the course of a career, if ever. Couples's real career is just beginning. He's learned, and he's no choker. Weiskopf ought to believe that now, and so should all other people whose snorts only betray their shortage of smarts.

The Globe and Mail, March 25, 1992

The hottest golfer on the planet has the coolest style. Fred Couples is as laid-back as the kids rollerblading along the boardwalk at South Beach, Miami's popular art-deco historical area. He's the hippest golfer going.

Cool Couples has won twice in the past month and finished second twice. He's made $704,412 (U.S.) this year to lead the PGA Tour, and it's only March. But soft-spoken Freddie would rather talk about his wife, Deborah, a polo player as adept at her sport, it seems, as her sweet-swinging husband is at golf.

There was last weekend, for instance. Fred was shooting 63 at the Bay Hill club in Orlando on Saturday — a "fun day," he calls such rounds — while Deborah followed. Meanwhile, the folks down at the Palm Beach Polo club, where the pair golfs and plays polo, were preparing the field for a big match Sunday.

Your faithful correspondent happened to visit Palm Beach Polo last Saturday, checking out the scene. Long-time Canadian amateur wizard Marlene Streit is a member at the chic club, and the 11-time national amateur champion played beautifully. The show was something to see, yet one couldn't help but hear people talking. Members were chatting about the next day's polo match and the golf at Bay Hill.

People expected both Fred and Deborah to win. After all, the golden pair is on top of the world. Fred swings like a baby and the ball goes eight miles. Deborah, whom *Sports Illustrated* wag Rick Reilly referred to as Fred's "killer wife" in a recent story, climbs on her horse and wins on the polo fields. Regularly.

And so, one begins to wonder. Why take life seriously? Why not just get up in the morning and whistle through the day? Why not stand up to the golf ball and hit the damn thing, as Couples does? Why worry about the science of the swing?

Let's face it. Nick Faldo worked 10-hour days with his teacher, David Leadbetter, in Orlando before the Honda Classic two weeks ago, then played indifferently there and missed the cut at Bay Hill. Science, schmience.

None of the technical stuff for free-swinging Freddie. He nearly canned his wedge shot on the last hole of the Honda at Weston Hills two Sundays ago. That got him into a playoff with Corey Pavin, who had slam-dunked a 135-yard 8-iron moments before. This was Florida — fantasyland, sunshine and miracles. An assistant pro at a club in Vero Beach recently had shared a $50-million lottery ticket with four friends.

Couples didn't win the playoff with Pavin. He was bothered, but only just. He now had finished second in consecutive weeks after winning in Los Angeles. One would think Couples then might have worked on his game to get ready for Bay Hill.

But no. Couples wanted to rest. His game was wicked. Why worry?

"I'll go to Bay Hill Thursday morning," Couples said after the Honda playoff. "I'm tired, and I'm ready for a few days off. I think I can play Bay Hill that way."

Now there's a laid-back guy. He wasn't even going to practise at Bay Hill. Instead, Couples and his wife would spend a few days at their home on the edge of the Everglades.

It's a sure bet that Couples didn't think about his golf swing at home. He probably watched lots of television, maybe cleaned the grooves on his Lynx irons, which he's paid a million a year to use. Worldly thoughts were far away.

Here's Freddie, friends, responding to an innocent question Jim Nelford once asked him.

"Hey, Freddie, what do you know?" Nelford asked Couples in passing one fine day.

"I don't know," Couples answered, "and I wish I knew less."

There you have the measure of the dude. He's nobody's fool, but he just ambles along, launching 3-woods off the tee nearly 300 yards. He did that at Bay Hill on Sunday as he cruised to a nine-shot win over Gene Sauers. Couples made it look so easy that it was scary.

And Deborah. She won her polo match Sunday, naturally. Then Greg Norman flew her to Bay Hill on his plane so that she could watch South Beach Freddie romp. It was art-deco golf all the way — breezy, as easy on the eye as the pastel buildings down on Ocean Drive.

It's amazing — what's going on down there in Florida, that is. Couples's swing is slow and his walk is slower. You could read a chapter of *A Round of Golf with Tommy Armour* as he makes the transition from the top of his swing to his downswing.

But why would you want to? Just watch Couples and inhale the air. It's fresh; it's cool. Like Freddie says, "Great fun." That makes one think about what's next on Couples's funmeter. His first major, maybe? The Masters in two weeks?

Torrid Couples Dominates Masters

The Globe and Mail, **April 13, 1992**

Augusta, Georgia — Away out in the corner of the Augusta National Golf Club a concerned woman was trying to contain her emotions as a golf ball flew over the fifth green. The ball belonged to Fred Couples and the emotions belonged to Deborah, his wife. The ball settled in a tough spot behind the green, which did nothing to soothe Deborah Couples.

"Oh, I hate this hole," she said. "He's been hitting good drives here, but his second, I don't know."

Mrs. Couples needn't have worried. Her husband played his third some 25 feet from the hole, then nudged that downhiller near the hole. He got his bogey and he got out of there, still in contention for the Masters, still in the hunt for his first major.

"I'm not really worried," Deborah said, having calmed down quickly after seeing Freddie slide his tricky long putt for par near the hole. Freddie: That's what golfers have been calling him since he began a torrid streak last summer that has led to four PGA Tour wins, victory in the Johnnie Walker World Championship, and a leadership role in the U.S. win over Europe last September at the Ryder Cup.

Now the people can call him champion. Couples won the Masters yesterday, and how. He prevailed over his buddy, 49-year-old Ray Floyd, a man who influenced his younger friend in all the best ways. They were paired during matches at the Ryder Cup, and Floyd helped Couples believe in himself.

That Ryder Cup showed Couples he had what it takes to win a major. He got more points in the matches than any of his 11 teammates. Moreover, captain Dave Stockton had something in mind when he teamed Couples with Floyd, whose experience could only help. How ironic and yet how fitting that when it came down to the back nine yesterday Couples and Floyd were the two golfers with the best chance to win.

It was storybook stuff, to be sure. Corey Pavin got to 10-under par, but that wasn't enough. Third-round leader Craig Parry three-putted the third, fourth and fifth holes to take himself out. And one by one, all the others with any chance slipped away.

But not Floyd, a "hard case from North Carolina," to slightly alter a writer's comment about Ben Hogan some years ago, "a hard case from Texas." Floyd, 49, had been woken from a deep sleep in Los Angeles in March to learn his home in Miami Beach had burned to the ground. He won the Doral Ryder Open the next week.

Floyd was playing like a man touched. His colleagues have known him for the 30 years he has played the PGA Tour — yes, 30 years — as a man with a powerful mind, a fellow who when in the lead almost never gets caught. That's also the way Couples saw him. That's one reason Couples has always looked up to him.

Strange, these alliances between golfers. Floyd saw something in Couples, and to a certain extent took him in hand. He encouraged him, and played practice rounds with him at Augusta. The two golfers were paired in the tournament as well. Couples said he couldn't hope for a better pairing.

But still, who would have thought the two would be the only golfers left at the end yesterday? Floyd was one group ahead of Couples, who was in the last twosome with Parry. He was seeking to be the oldest golfer to win the Masters, but he didn't look old. He only seemed an inspiration to all.

Down the stretch they came, and one might be forgiven for falling prey to hyperbole here. Floyd got within a shot when he nearly eagled the par-five 15th after a heroic approach over the water. But then Couples essentially shut the door when he birdied the 14th with a 10-foot putt. That gave him a two-shot lead. It also brought to mind Couples's words a few days ago in a quiet moment.

"I want to win the Masters so bad," Couples had said, this from a golfer who rarely bares his soul.

And one thought of something his wife had said back at that fifth green yesterday, when the result was still in doubt, very much in doubt.

"Wherever we've gone, everyone says, 'Win the green, win the green.' Not too many people have had everybody telling them to win it and then gone ahead and done it. But you know, whatever he does, I'll be proud of him."

Those were thoughtful words, but somehow it was apparent in Deborah Couples's tone that she wanted this Masters win as much as did her enormously talented husband. He had been showing the golf world this past year just how exceptional a golfer he is. And yesterday, as he snap-hooked a 7-iron around a tree at the par-five 15th that ended just left of the green, you knew he was truly a wonder.

The crowd knew it, too, and so did Couples's colleagues. Some wanted for him as he walked up the hill to the 18th green, there to be feted by Floyd, by everybody. The evening sun was shining brightly through the tall pines left of the fairway. It shone above Couples, above all, and it was right that this should be so.

Couples had won the green, the green jacket that is symbolic of a win in this first major championship of the season, this first major win by a player who now should be recognized as magnificent, nothing less.

Nick Faldo

The Globe and Mail, **July 31, 1982**

Oakville, Ontario — Far from his home in London, England, Nick Faldo swings his way elegantly through the valleys and flatlands of the Glen Abbey Golf Club. A first-round 68 brings him within one shot of the low shooters. A second-round 70 keeps him in touch with the leaders.

Two weeks ago, Faldo finished fourth in the British Open at Troon, Scotland. Peter Oosterhuis, also London born, but now living in Santa Barbara, California, tied for second. Last year, Oosterhuis made the Canadian Open his first win on tour, and if Faldo keeps playing as he has, he could do the same.

From January through April, Faldo played in 13 tournaments on the PGA Tour. His best finish was a tie for seventh at the Hawaiian Open in February. So far, he has won $37,000 on tour.

But that success has not yet brought Faldo on tour full-time. He is a self-proclaimed "trans-Atlantic hopper," dividing his time between the European Tour, the PGA Tour and Japan.

"A golden year for me," Faldo said, "would be to win the European Order of Merit (by leading the money list on the European Tour) as well as doing well on the PGA Tour."

Faldo is well on his way. His winnings on the PGA Tour in the first four months guaranteed him an exemption to next year's tournaments. And through the British Open two weeks ago, Faldo stood eighth in the Order of Merit.

"The position I'm in is great," Faldo said. "I've got the best of both worlds, and I've got a beautiful place in the country near London to go home to."

Faldo's fourth-place finish at Troon wasn't surprising. He had already finished seventh, and eleventh twice in the British Open.

"At the British Open," Faldo said, "you don't have to force yourself. You don't need to get fired up. And this year was particularly good. I went into the Open quietly. I knew when I got to the course, I would be excited."

The British Open offers historical flavour and depth of competition to golfers such as Faldo. The courses, too, are usually in first-class condition. Such factors also make the PGA Tour enticing to Faldo. While the history isn't always there, the strong fields, good courses and large purses force a player to find out what he's made of.

"At home, there is more chance involved," Faldo said. "This is true especially on inland courses. We get many poor lies, usually play in strong winds and find ourselves on greens that are sometimes receptive to good shots, and sometimes not.

"Conditions here breed confidence. A player knows what a ball is going to do."

The result is that the best players rise to the top on the PGA Tour. Take a look at the winners of the Canadian Open over the years: Walter Hagen, Sam Snead, Arnold Palmer, Lee Trevino, Tom Weiskopf and Bruce Lietzke. Players learn to trust themselves, sure that good swings will bring good results where the conditions are favourable.

"I think I'm fortunate in coming from Britain and playing here, rather than the other way around. Players who go the other way can become frustrated. But I'm keyed up when I play here," Faldo says.

Faldo's game is well-suited to golf on tour. He hits the ball high with the upright swing common to players of his and Oosterhuis's height.

It is a swing that Faldo refers to as American rather than British. By that, he means that he has learned to swing in balance, and with a swing-plane appropriate to height.

But there is more to Faldo's game. His deft touch around the greens, so necessary for success on tour, has been impressive at Glen Abbey. Yesterday, he holed chip shots on the 12th and 16th holes for birdies when bogeys were possible.

It is that ability to turn his game around that suggests Faldo has what it takes to do well on tour. Ben Crenshaw, for one, thinks he does have the game, and Oosterhuis said he would not be surprised if Faldo plays on the PGA Tour full-time next year.

"I've been shocked by the scoring ability of these guys on tour," Faldo says. "You know the cuts will be low. Sixty guys are always playing well." Including Faldo, one might add, one of the international golfers capable of breaking through anytime.

The Globe and Mail, July 23, 1990

St. Andrews, Scotland — It's premature to make a final reckoning, but Nick Faldo's victory in the Open championship yesterday suggests he may well be modern golf's equivalent to Ben Hogan. Faldo was relentless while dismantling the Old Course, shooting 270, 18 under par.

Accounts of Hogan's 1958 Open victory at Carnoustie across the Tay River from the Old Course suggest a similar virtuosity. Hole by hole, stroke by masterly stroke, Hogan found the exact lines of play with which to conquer Carnoustie, always a dreaded course.

Faldo did the same at the Old Course. The English golfer hit but one bunker all week, drove cleanly to the preferred spots and approached the immense greens without confusion. The putts went down. He had no problems.

"My iron play was really good," Faldo said minutes after walking off the final green. "I hit only two, maybe three iron shots off line all week."

That is as near to perfection as a golfer is likely to get. But Faldo has said his goal is to hit shots of more than 200 yards not more than a few inches from one another. So there is more to come.

What Faldo has already done is remarkable. To be sure, he showed his exquisite form most emphatically during Saturday's third round, when his expected duel with Greg Norman did not develop.

Faldo, a master of the scientific approach to golf, and Norman, full of flair and always exciting, had begun the penultimate round four shots clear of the field at 12-under-par 132. Faldo shot a flawless 67, but the Australian putted poorly from the start, and slipped sadly away to 76. This was a Faldo solo, not a duel, never a duet.

Faldo's ability to manoeuvre the golf ball stood out. It has often been said that the Old Course will expose whatever flaws lurk in a golfer's game. It revealed none in Faldo's, for none are apparent.

In that way he resembles Hogan, the most technically accomplished player of his day, probably ever. Unlike twice U.S. Open champion Curtis Strange, who plays his best golf on watered courses that demand high shots to the greens, Faldo can play any course, any shot.

So it was that Faldo won the 1987 Open at Muirfield near Edinburgh with 18 straight pars that last day. He then lost a playoff for the 1988 U.S. Open to Strange at The Country Club in Brookline, Massachusetts. Faldo knew there was still work to do if he was going to win majors in America, and so he continued to refine his game with instructor David Leadbetter.

Faldo then won the 1989 and 1990 Masters, both in playoffs on the strength of high irons into the heart of the 11th green at the Augusta National Golf Club, where water protected the flagsticks. Links golf and parkland golf: Faldo could do it all.

Next came the 1990 U.S. Open in June near Chicago. Faldo needed to birdie the last hole to get into a playoff with Mike Donald and eventual winner Hale Irwin. Not many golfers would have had the confidence to hit a 3-iron from the tee, then to be left with a long iron to the green. Faldo did, then just missed the birdie putt from 15 feet away.

That one putt kept Faldo from possibly coming to the Old Course with a chance at golf's Grand Slam — wins in the Masters, U.S. and British Opens and the U.S. PGA Championship that takes place next month. The closest a golfer has come to that most improbable collection was in 1953, when Hogan won the first three. He did not play the PGA.

But there is more than their swings to the Faldo-Hogan comparison. Faldo, like Hogan, is devoted to his craft. He allows no intrusions. Golf is first.

Faldo and his wife, Gillian, have two children, and a big home in Ascot. But Faldo has delegated all domestic and business duties to an entourage whose sole purpose is to allow him to focus on his golf. He had no idea how much he paid for his new Mercedes and said he couldn't care less.

Faldo works with an exercise physiologist, a former judo player who represented Britain in two Olympics. His wife has said he doesn't tolerate people who are not near the top of what they do. Failure to Faldo means weakness.

And so he changes whatever needs changing in order to enhance his chances for success. He rebuilt his swing starting in late 1984; it is now a machine. He changed caddies recently, to Fanny Sunesson, a Swedish woman who is the only full-time female caddie on the European Tour.

All week at the Old Course he asked her, "How far is it to that bunker, what is the wind doing, what did I do here yesterday?"

In such ways has Faldo organized himself to become a complete golfer.

As did Hogan before him, he is showing how well golf can be played. Faldo knows exactly what he is doing. Nobody came close to him at the Old Course, because day in and day out, nobody is as consistently on form.

The Globe and Mail, **April 11, 1991**

The Augusta National course is treacherous, its problems inevitably betraying any deficiencies in a player's game. But the course won't be the focus of talk when the Masters begins today; that's because Nick Faldo's quest for his third Masters win in a row is capturing everybody's attention.

Faldo's intense pursuit of an unprecedented three consecutive Masters isn't a surprise to those who have followed his career. He points to the major championships more than any golfer in the game and says that other events serve only as preparation for the big events — the Masters, U.S. and British Opens and the PGA Championship. He thinks he can win them all in one year; never mind that nobody has done so.

"I want to do the Grand Slam at least once before I retire," Faldo, 33, has said. "I reckon I have another 10 years before I think about that. Winning all four would be the ultimate."

Ultimate concerns require a long-range view, and Faldo has that. It's not difficult to recall Faldo on the practice green at Glen Abbey nearly a decade ago, before he had accomplished much. Yet Faldo seemed driven even that evening during the only Canadian Open he has played. Alone on the green that late hour, Faldo putted and putted.

Faldo's focus has only become more precise. He seemed almost in a trance as he practised this week with Welsh star Ian Woosnam. He glared at putts as they rolled across the slick greens. He chipped balls to specific spots on the greens, then analyzed the twisting paths the shots took. Faldo seeks perfect control over the golf ball.

Faldo has driven himself in that direction for years, but his search for his best golfing self really began with his successful effort in the mid-1980s to revamp his swing under the guidance of instructor David Leadbetter. He showed what was possible when, last July, he played 72 of the finest holes imaginable in winning the British Open over the Old Course in St. Andrews, Scotland.

That was Faldo's fourth major championship since 1987 — the consecutive Masters wins and a couple of British Opens. But he believed he was only scratching the surface of the attainable and after last season decided to strengthen his body. The changes might lead to a shot saved, and that could make all the difference.

Faldo set to work with Paul Ankers, a former European Games silver medallist in judo. He worked on weights to strengthen his upper body, but not too much, since the golf swing requires flexibility. He also built up his legs, because the golf swing requires leg speed to create accuracy and distance.

Faldo gained 20 pounds of muscle while losing 3% body fat, and he was lean before. At 6-foot-3 and 210 pounds, Faldo looks formidable now. He's an athlete, as opposed to some of his colleagues who have as much body fat as beer-guzzling, cart-riding amateurs.

"I'm generating more speed in my shoulders and more resistance in my legs," Faldo said. "I feel as though I'm hitting the ball farther, maybe 10 yards. I've been waiting 20 years for that."

Today Faldo will begin to learn if his most recent attempt at self-development will work. There is no reason to doubt that it will; Faldo is, after all, the same person who, as Rick Reilly has written in *Sports Illustrated*, took his bicycle apart when he was 12 years old, then put it together again. He wanted to see how it worked.

That desire for technical mastery has fed Faldo since. Reilly called Faldo Robo-Par for his ability to make par after par. But Faldo understands his golf swing the way nobody since Ben Hogan knew his 40 years ago. It is no small feat to make 18 consecutive pars to win a major, as Faldo did the final day of the 1987 British Open at Muirfield near Edinburgh.

And so Faldo will play away today in a featured group with brilliant amateur Phil Mickelson. He will attempt to manoeuvre the golf ball around Augusta National at will, leaving nothing to chance. Only a fool would argue that he seeks the impossible.

"I see Nick trying to master the course," two-time Masters winner Tom Watson said, having played a practice round earlier in the week with Faldo. "He has the swing, so he's just been hitting the ball to various parts of the greens. He's playing awfully well."

Watson's comments may prove prophetic. One thing is certain: It is impossible to think that a golfer could prepare himself better for a major than has Faldo for this.

Faldo may not win his third Masters in a row, but that will be because he is human and therefore frail. It is a frailty he acknowledges but seeks to subdue, even crush. He has done quite a good job of it so far.

The Globe and Mail, June 28, 1991
Nick Faldo is an iron man who swings a golf club as if he were deciphering a long-lost code. From time to time, he breaks the code, and then, as at the Carroll's Irish Open he won on Sunday, he is almost a perfect golfer.

That perfection has not come easily to Faldo in much of the past year. Indeed, it can be argued that he reached a pinnacle last July while winning the British Open at the Old Course in St. Andrews, and that he had not been himself until winning the Irish Open.

Faldo's performance bodes well for next month's British Open at Royal Birkdale in Southport, England. He has declared that the majors are the only important tournaments for him. He said at Killarney that he would gladly sacrifice a quick fix and even a win in a particular tournament. Faldo is after long-term success, golf for the ages.

That is why Faldo sought the help of now world-famous teacher David Leadbetter at the end of 1984. The two fellows found they had something in common. Faldo believed the swing could be broken down and understood — and that he had the will to make whatever changes Leadbetter deemed necessary. Leadbetter felt he could spot Faldo's problems and teach him how to swing like a champion.

"I took to David right away," Faldo reflected during a chat at the Irish Open. "Others had told me that they thought I was doing wrong, but nobody had said this is how I could cure my faults. I thought about it and decided to work with David when I saw him at Muirfield Village (in Dublin, Ohio) in '85. I couldn't hit a green with a 9-iron then."

Faldo's rise to prominence while working with Leadbetter has been well-documented. But perhaps not as well-known is how obsessive has Faldo's search for the perfect swing been, and how it continues to be so. There is a quality of severity to Faldo's quest. He cannot tolerate less than total commitment to a cause, not in himself and not in others.

There was a revealing moment during the Irish Open. Faldo waited on a tee and took the driver from its head cover. He examined the cover and noticed some lint and loose threads. Then he picked the offending materials away until it was to his liking.

That intense focus on minor details has made Faldo seem as single-minded a golfer as ever there has been. He eschews the idea of playing by feel, as Payne Stewart, for one, plays. They are opposites when it comes to the golf swing, yet both are major championship winners.

"It just did not work for me to play only with feel and flair," Faldo said. "I get totally bogged down that way. I would look at videos of my swing and see so many faults, then take my checklist out of things to do while on the tour. Straighten this, don't bend this. After three holes I could see it was impossible."

That's why Faldo drove himself to learn a scientific swing. And he didn't care how long it would take. He needed only to see some improvement, slow improvement, if need be.

"It's the going backward to go forward that is tough, the time you put in until you turn a move into muscle memory. But teaching has advanced so much the last five years. You don't have to beat balls to improve. You can do it with stretching, with resistance exercises. That's how you create the feeling you want. I can do more in an hour of stretching and drills than by beating 1,500 balls."

There is no point in questioning the validity of Faldo's approach, no point in judging whether his and Leadbetter's way is the best way. The result of their success is that Leadbetter is now teaching an enormous number of pros, that you see his videos and books and drills and teaching aids everywhere. Golfers believe in the Holy Grail, that's all there is to it.

"I've had periods that were incredible," Faldo noted. "Every day I would have at least a dozen putts inside 15 feet, no matter what club I was using. My iron shots at the Masters in 1989 were spot-on. It felt like 90% started where I intended them to."

So what's the secret? One cannot talk to Faldo without asking him for at least a few ideas. Never mind the years of work it takes to make changes.

"When it's going well, your legs resist the top half of your body going back and through," he said. "Your arms feel like they're just going along."

Right. That's the golf swing according to Nick Faldo, current British Open champion. And it can only get better, says the new Irish Open champion.

George Knudson

The Globe and Mail, **October 24, 1986**
Who'd have thought it? George Knudson, 49, has decided to play the Senior PGA Tour next year. He turns 50 in June and there's big money where Gene Littler and company are playing.

But Knudson won't be playing only for the money. He wants folks in the United States to know he's a teacher and that he's done a concise and smart instructional tape called "The Swing Motion." What better way to do so than by playing the tour and, presumably, covering the flags as he did in the past?

The key to Knudson's return to competition is that he'll need to play only six tournaments a year to keep his playing card. Knudson will be able to start in October, after his golf school near Toronto closes.

Most of Knudson's heart, not to mention his head, is in his golf school these days. He's spent the past decade thinking about golf — the swing, life and how they're related. And boy, has he learned.

Knudson now understands, as he said yesterday while relaxing at the Oakdale Golf and Country Club in Toronto, that good golf, and life itself, "is all to do with being natural, doing things in a natural way. The bottom line is that you have to give up control to gain control."

Now this is a very subtle concept — like the psychologist Fritz Perls's idea of losing your mind and coming to your senses — and Knudson has yet to convey it as well as he'd like. But he was impressive yesterday as he demonstrated his ideas.

"Look," Knudson said, assuming an address position without holding a club, "the golf swing is all based on centrifugal force. That means letting the club flow as it may. We've all been taught to control the club, to get it in this or that position."

Knudson seemed loose all right. He wasn't the stiff golfer who won eight PGA Tour events while making himself into a machine. Now he just swings. That's what he'd like all golfers to do.

But how, a tense gentleman golfer of the press asked, is one to get so relaxed? How is one to feel natural, when every muscle, every memory, screams, "Careful, you don't want to hit it in that bunker and make a triple-bogey"?

The idea, Dr. George elucidated, is to feel the clubhead and let it go. The club pulls itself. Knudson often gives his students a 45-ounce 5-iron, three times normal weight, and tells them that they'll be on their way once they can also feel the clubhead with the 15-ounce variety. He can feel the clubhead in his hands even when he doesn't have a club in his hands. Anybody can, he said.

"Take this business of keeping the left arm straight. I can do chin-ups on people's left arms at the top of their swings, their arms are so straight and so tense. Tense is short. Soft is better. It only gives you two things; you can hit the ball farther and straighter."

A fellow wondered. Does the same idea apply to putting? He knew that Knudson looked frozen in place on the greens, and that he'd need to putt well to win on the senior tour. But could he enjoy putting? Could he put a little rhythm in his stroke?

The line of thinking went further. Knudson was getting older, and just yesterday morning, his inquisitor had read the words of Peter Gzowski, quick-minded host of "Morningside" on CBC radio, and a senior golfer himself. Gzowski knew that older putters are often poor putters. Could Knudson help him?

Knudson might have something for Gzowski. He's discovered what he calls a "passion for putting," having found a putter he likes and, more important, having learned to simply swing the blade.

The news from Knudson, then, is all upbeat. He's feeling the putter; he's also watching what he eats and he'll be working out in the gym to prepare for the tour. This time, he said, he wants to do it right. Who can argue with him, freedom fighter that he is?

The Globe and Mail, July 1, 1987
Golfers practising yesterday for the Canadian Open at Glen Abbey Golf Club concerned themselves with the nuances of their swings and the speed of the greens. But they also asked, "How's George?"

They were asking about George Knudson, still recognized as one of the finest ball-strikers in the game. Knudson turned 50 last Sunday, a few days after he learned that doctors had found a cancerous spot on his lung.

"I'm ready to face the battle," Knudson said from his hospital bed Monday.

Knudson woke up with severe chest pains a couple of weeks ago — "a little pull on my chest and groin." When the pain didn't go away, Knudson checked into the hospital.

Tests revealed the spot on his lung. Knudson was kept in hospital until last weekend for more tests and returned Monday for a chest scan and bone marrow analysis. He expects to return home today or tomorrow and to begin chemotherapy next week.

Knudson has responded courageously to the news of his illness. Said Gary Alles, who had written a tune to celebrate Knudson's fiftieth birthday: "He's playing this typically George — straight from the deck. His attitude is, 'Okay, I've got it under the trees, but I'm gonna get it out and make par.'"

Knudson doesn't back away from a challenge. He won eight PGA Tour events in a 20-year career, more than any Canadian. His success was due in large part to his persistence and innate optimism. In the past decade, he has brought those qualities to his teaching at his golf school near Toronto.

Not that his teaching or his learning have come easily. "People used to say I was a natural," Knudson said recently. "But I said, 'No, I had to learn what was natural.'"

Knudson took 15 years to learn his swing. In the past 10 years, he has been learning how to communicate what he finally understood. The dining-room and kitchen tables in his home often resemble a writer's study — notes strewn all over and thesaurus at hand.

"To this day," Knudson said, "I'll get up in the middle of the night and go to the kitchen and leave a note for myself. I'm not saying I have all the answers, but not a day goes by that I don't find a better means of expression. That's stimulating, a relentless source of energy for me."

Knudson's instruction book is scheduled for publication next spring and he means to get it out. Also, he still plans to play the Senior PGA Tour in the fall. He means it when he says his current setback won't change anything.

Knudson has done plenty of good for Canadian golf. He has worked on an instruction manual for Canadian pros, given seminars throughout the country and donated a percentage of the proceeds from a video to junior development.

Dedication and vision? Knudson is an inspiration in these areas. He believes in the power of the individual to remake himself.

Though he spent last week in the hospital, Knudson didn't mope around his home on the weekend. Instead, he and his wife, Shirley, visited St. Andrew's and Beacon Hall, two new courses in the Toronto area.

"I think they'll be sensational," Knudson said from the hospital. "We're so lucky to have both of them. When they open in a year, we'll have a bunch of great courses in Toronto where guys can test their artillery and mettle at the same time."

Knudson's comment wasn't surprising. He has always seen life as a test. He might have come out of Winnipeg as a talented teenager, but he cashed only one cheque on tour his first three years. Today, he says he was more interested in studying the greats of golf, particularly Ben Hogan.

Knudson saw Hogan some years after Hogan had recovered from extensive injuries suffered when his car crashed into a bus in a Texas fog. But Hogan came back to win major championships and swing better than ever. The lesson wasn't lost on Knudson. He reconstructed his swing and has since encouraged many struggling golfers.

Let's hope his strong mind carries him through and that we'll see him back on the lesson tee and the golf course before long.

The Globe and Mail, **April 27, 1988**
George Knudson, one of Canada's most successful golfers, is returning to the pro tour tomorrow, almost 10 years after he gave it up and a year after a battle with lung cancer.

The Toronto pro, now 50, is to play in the Legends of Golf Tournament in Austin, Texas. It's a competition on the Senior PGA Tour, the sports world's success story of the 1980s.

Knudson gave up full-time regular tour play in 1979, deciding he no longer enjoyed the travelling. He had won eight PGA Tour events — more than any Canadian — and was then one of the top 50 lifetime money-winners. He won the 1968 Phoenix and Tucson Opens in consecutive weeks. His last tour win came in the 1972 Kaiser Invitational in Napa, California.

Regarded as having one of the game's classic swings, Knudson modelled himself after Ben Hogan. The Winnipeg native caddied on the tour before he played and that was where he learned the fundamentals of his swing.

"I spent more hours sitting on the range watching the fellows than I did caddying," Knudson said. "Hogan, Snead, Jackie Burke, Lionel and Jay Hebert, Billy Maxwell, Julius Boros — they were my teachers."

His return to the tour was delayed a year or so because of his bout with lung cancer. The cancer is in remission and he follows a strict nutritional and vitamin regimen. He also is conditioning himself physically.

Knudson is scheduled to play the Legends in a twosome with Johnny Pott, one of 30 pairs in the 72-hole, better-ball competition with a $650,000 purse.

"I hit some balls on Friday," Knudson said yesterday from Austin, "and then hit balls and played nine holes on Saturday. On Sunday I hit balls and played 18. For me, conditioning is going to be the biggest thing."

Since arriving in Austin last Thursday, Knudson has run into some of his old cronies, including Maxwell, Snead, Art Wall and Australian Kel Nagle. His wife, Shirley, spent the day yesterday with Wall's wife, Jean.

Knudson rode a cart during his first couple of trips around the Onion Creek course. But he walked 18 holes with Pott on Monday and planned to walk again yesterday. He'll ride in today's pro-am and during the tournament itself. Carts are allowed on the senior tour.

"My feet and hands hurt," Knudson said, "which they normally would if I hadn't played for a while. But I hope that by Thursday (tomorrow) my hands will be good and firm and my legs will be willing to carry me. My swing depends on proper use of my legs."

He isn't worried about his swing, but admits his game needs plenty of refining.

"We're not going in as contenders," Knudson said with a laugh. "Johnny just plays this one tournament a year — and this is my debut. So we can't expect much. We're just here to have fun."

The Legends got the senior tour off the ground. It began in 1978, when a full-time tour for professional golfers aged 50 and over was only a dream. But golf fans enjoyed watching players such as Sam Snead and Gardner Dickinson, who won the first Legends, and on January 22, 1979, the PGA Tour's policy board approved a full-fledged senior tour.

Only two official events were held in 1980. By 1983 there were 18, with purses totalling $3 million, and this year there are 37, with total prize money of $10.5 million.

After the Legends, Knudson plans to return home to Toronto for a few days. Then he's off to Bermuda to film his second instructional video. His book, *The Natural Golf Swing*, will be published May 21, after which he'll do a cross-country promotional tour for the book.

Of further Senior PGA Tour action Knudson said: "I'm not making any commitments as to how much I'll play. If I'm satisfied with my progress, I plan to come out around mid-July. We'll see."

For now, he's taking it slowly. The good news is that Knudson is back on his turf.

The Globe and Mail, January 25, 1989

George Knudson, Canada's pre-eminent golfer, who died yesterday, never gave up and he never stopped giving. He never complained, either, though he was in great pain in his final days. His family and friends will remember him as a fellow who gave his best.

Still, he never claimed perfection. He smoked heavily for 30 years, calling it a stinking habit that he wished he could quit. In June 1987, when he found out he had lung cancer, he didn't say he should have known better and he didn't feel sorry for himself.

"Hey, I smoked those things," he said. "Who was I to think that cancer wouldn't get me?"

Knudson was relaxing at home beside the pool as he spoke. The woods and ravines of Toronto's Don Valley provided the backdrop. There was space, wind in the trees and fog some mornings. Knudson spoke of his favourite place in golf, the Cypress Point Club in Pebble Beach, California, sometimes serene, sometimes vulnerable to a howling wind off the sea. He wanted to return some day.

But the man Lee Trevino ranked with Ben Hogan as one of golf's purest swingers didn't get back to Cypress Point. The cancer that doctors found after Knudson complained of chest pains didn't go away. Chemotherapy and radiation sent the disease into remission at first, but, when it spread last summer, there was no stopping it. He entered hospital for the final time November 27, after completing a short videotape to send to a conference in Dallas on teaching.

Knudson worked hard on that tape. He wanted to present his ideas to the group of top instructors, even if he couldn't attend. He sat on a couch at home the day before he had to go back to the hospital, and he gave some last-minute instructions for the people producing the tape. He was in pain, but he had something to say and was determined to say it.

He knew his prognosis but didn't dwell on it. He lived each day as hard as he could and often got up in the middle of the night to jot down a thought or some new insight into the swing. He'd be on the phone the next morning to pass on his wisdom.

During Knudson's illness, we did a book together, *The Natural Golf Swing*. It was his way of helping people learn to enjoy golf. He wrote that it can be a relaxing game, but that people tie themselves up with theory. His pet phrase was "Never do anything at the expense of balance."

Some people might say that Knudson didn't live up to that ideal himself. There was his smoking, for one thing. And why didn't he pay more attention to putting?

Trevino said Knudson could have won many more PGA Tour events than the eight he did capture — more than any other Canadian — if only he could have putted decently.

But Knudson didn't enjoy putting, and so he didn't practise. He got his kicks from knocking the flag down from 180 yards. He liked to play call-shots — predicting that he would hit a slight draw, 30 feet off the ground and that the ball would land 10 yards short of the green and would scurry on up to the hole. Then he would do it.

Knudson did things his way, and his way of swinging a club was close to ideal. His legacy is the message that the swing can be understood and mastered. Jack Nicklaus once said that the

Canadian had a million-dollar swing. Those who watched Knudson agreed. He made the ball dance.

He was passionate about the swing, but he also loved people. He and his wife encouraged their sons — Kevin, Paul and Dean — to do whatever they wanted and to do it with gusto. He had received similar advice from his own father and said it was the second-best thing that happened to him. Meeting Shirley was the best.

Knudson's feeling for people went far beyond his own family. To come into his orbit was to become part of a closely knit community. Once, battered by chemotherapy, he still found time to encourage a friend whose business had fallen on hard times. Knudson's words helped the fellow get back on his feet.

Knudson also contributed to my career. We had known each other for a couple of years when I had my first article published. Knudson called me right away.

"You've got your foot in the door. Just keep writing. Good things will happen."

He always was positive that good things would happen. That's why he played the Legends of Golf Tournament in Austin, Texas, last spring. Never mind that he hadn't practised much and wasn't strong enough. He wanted to see his pals: Tommy Bolt, Johnny Pott, Sam Snead. Hogan told him his swing looked as good as ever. Knudson birdied the first hole he played.

Things seemed promising. He started to hit balls and visit his health club most mornings. Our book was published, after which Knudson went on an exhausting but exhilarating cross-country tour. He rested as much as he could, watched over by his family. And he looked forward to a full-time return to the senior tour.

Return he did, but not full-time. He flew to a tournament in Newport, Rhode Island, in July but was too weak and had to return home.

In his final few months, Knudson rested between sessions of chemotherapy and radiation. One afternoon, he said he was spending a lot of time in bed, thinking of the sweet places he had visited, the people he had met, the life he had led while mastering the art of hitting a golf ball. Again his mind went to Cypress Point.

"I played 18 holes there in my mind this morning. It was just like I imagined it: the fog heavy, that big lone cypress down on the first fairway, the view of the water from the green. My favourite spot."

That's one way to remember him, by the places he cherished. It was just like him to appreciate a public course such as Keltic Lodge in Nova Scotia. Knudson thought the best courses were like parks, there to be enjoyed by everyone. He enjoyed them and he enjoyed people. It was good to know him.

The Globe and Mail, January 26, 1989

George Knudson's all-too-brief life touched many people and it's appropriate that he's being appointed a member of the Order of Canada.

The governor general recommended Knudson for the appointment December 16 and he accepted the honour soon after in his room at the Princess Margaret Hospital in Toronto. The appointment is to be announced today.

It's unfortunate, of course, that the government had to wait so long to make public the appointment — the date was decided long ago — but this shouldn't detract from its significance. It may help the public realize what Knudson meant to golf and to people who knew him.

Knudson was unquestionably Canada's finest golfer. His accomplishments speak for themselves — eight PGA Tour wins, five Canadian PGA victories, World Cup triumphs, victory after victory on the once-significant Caribbean Tour. But when people remember Knudson, they don't think as much about his performance as the way he went about it, along with his style on and off the course.

Art Wall, for one, played many rounds in the 1960s with Knudson on the PGA and Caribbean Tours. They became good friends, as did their wives. The foursome reunited last April at the Legends of Golf Tournament in Austin, Texas.

Knudson and Wall, the 1959 Masters and 1960 Canadian Open champion, played a practice round together in Austin. Reached at his home in Sonoita, Arizona, yesterday, Wall remembered his friend with affection.

"I'll never forget one time when George and I were chatting in Mexico City," Wall said. "George told me he thought it was possible to make 18 birdies in one round. That's how positive he was."

Wall also remembered Knudson's competitive spirit and confidence in his swing. Some of the fairways on Caribbean courses were particularly narrow, but that didn't matter to Knudson. He still pulled the driver from his bag.

"I don't recall George ever backing off," Wall said. "I'd have a 2-iron out, but he'd take the driver. He just put it there and turned it loose."

That's how sure Knudson was of his swing. It was lean, stripped of any excess. He once sat with a friend, Gary Alles, in a restaurant, drew a few lines on a napkin, added a few words and handed over his work.

"That's everything I know about the swing, Gary," Knudson said. "And it's all you need to know."

Anybody who met Knudson was taken by how straightforward he was. He didn't wear fancy clothes and he didn't seek attention. Said Wall: "He had class."

The world's pros were aware of his class, even if the golfing public was less informed. No matter. Knudson sought the highest levels of the game, not the tops of the front pages.

"The players respected George," Wall said. "They knew how great he was. That's not a word we use too much, but it applies in his case. I'm sure that Canadians realize how talented he was, but I don't think people in the U.S. knew what kind of player he was. But the players on tour knew. That's what counts."

Dale Douglass, a five-time winner on the Senior PGA Tour, which Knudson had looked forward to joining, was very aware of Knudson.

"Everybody still comments on what a fine player George was and how many shots he could hit that the rest of us couldn't," Douglass said from his home in Phoenix.

Alles told a story about one such shot. Knudson was playing the par-four 11th hole at the National Golf Club in Woodbridge, Ontario, one day when he hooked his tee shot near a tree. His only route to the green was on a path roughly akin to getting from Toronto to Winnipeg via Chicago. That's how much he had to fade the ball.

At the same time, though, Knudson couldn't swing through the ball for fear of smashing the club and his hands against the tree. No problem, he told Alles.

"I'll just let go of the club after I hit the ball," Knudson said.

And that's what he did. The ball flew along its own channel in the sky — Knudson had his own channel, as did Hogan — curved way to the right and hit the narrow entrance to the green. From there, it toddled up near the hole. Alles applauded.

That's the kind of golf Knudson could play. He put on a show, as Toronto writer David Cobb remembered yesterday.

"I watched him at the 1970 Masters," Cobb said. "He wasn't a flamboyant guy at all. Just unloaded his clubs from the car and started hitting some shots on the practice tee. There were a lot of guys there chatting, but when George began to hit balls, a hush came over the range. Players started stealing glances at George. I thought that was remarkable."

The admiration to which Cobb referred showed up in many small ways. Knudson once walked on to a practice tee where Hogan, his model when he was younger, was practising. The fellow beside Hogan withdrew so that Knudson could practise beside Bantam Ben. The two masters lit up the sky with marvellous golf shots. Such brilliance always made watching Knudson special.

That brilliance sprang from his passion for the game. Jim Nelford worked with Knudson a few years ago. He feels he has lost a kindred spirit.

"I think of his passion," Nelford said yesterday from Pebble Beach, California, where he was practising for his week's PGA Tour event. "He was consumed with the game. He wanted to be more and more concise in his thinking. It's a great thing to have that passion in life. That's what we would all like to have. It makes life worthwhile."

Knudson had that passion, all right, and his intensity sometimes got the better of him. He was often hard on himself, but maybe that goes with the passion. Knudson didn't always do the things that were good for him. Who does? But he lived a full life. He did what he wanted to do. And he was respected.

"George's death is a tragic loss to us all," Jack Nicklaus said in a statement released yesterday through Larry O'Brien, his right-hand man in North Palm Beach, Florida. "He was a good guy and a good friend. I'm sure he'll leave us all with a lot of good memories."

That he has. As O'Brien said — and he has known Knudson since his days as a sports writer in Montreal — "George was the best-liked Canadian we ever had on tour. He never hurt anybody, never spoke a bad word about anybody. A class guy."

Score, **May 1989**

Soon after George Knudson died in late January, I received a letter from J.S. Vanderploeg, a 91-year-old man living in Toronto. He had a story to tell about George that indicates how deeply George touched people in his all-too-short life.

Mr. Vanderploeg wrote: "Starting about 1926 I used to visit Winnipeg (George's birthplace) on business once or twice a year. My host at St. Charles (the course where George learned the game) would provide me with a caddy. In 1952 or so, that caddy was none other than George Knudson, and a damn good caddy he was. He could find my wild shots, and if I could use it right, would hand me the right club without being asked. He certainly was a bright perceptive youngster. And courteous. In another year or two he was caddy master, so no more caddy for me. I would drop in the shop to say hello and he usually remembered my name. I followed his budding career with interest but didn't see him again until 1962 when he was playing in the Venezuelan Open. I got invited to a reception by the Seagram people in the Caracas hotel where I was staying. George was among the guests and when I greeted him, he called me by name. I was flattered."

Those of us who knew George well wouldn't be surprised to learn of this incident. After all, George caddied for the fellow, right? And caddying is a job he'd take seriously, a one-on-one, personal relationship demanding that the caddy concentrate even when his golfer's mind wanders, and that he help the golfer move round the course without undue difficulty. These requirements appealed to George.

There's no way that George's mind would wander on the course. He lived in the present, all his life. He was able to savour the moment, which is why so many moments stayed with him.

Maybe that's why when I think of George I picture him standing still. It's as if he doesn't care at what pace the world moves; he's going to find his own, slower pace. He lived in his own time, George Knudson Central.

I think of George now and I see him on the tee of the 16th hole at Cypress Point, his favourite hole on his favourite course. The tee and the green sit above the Pacific, separated by 233 yards of ocean and rock and sand. The hole is dangerous, but awesome in its beauty.

As I envisage the scene, the wind is howling every which way, and the waves are crashing against the rocks. The sun and scudding black clouds are playing tag with one another. George is standing on the tee, coolly assessing the situation. One hand is on his golf bag. He knows he's got the swing — was there ever any question? — and he knows the shot he wants to play. Why, then, is he standing there? Why doesn't he pick the club and hit the shot?

I think it's because George wants to savour the moment. He likes the feel of the wind slapping his shirt collar against the back of his neck. He's enjoying the action of the water spraying against the rocks, and he's visualizing his ball soaring over the ocean and settling on the green. He's in paradise.

George carried paradise with him wherever he went, all the way, in fact, into his room at Toronto's Princess Margaret Hospital. It was engraved on his mind's eye and visible to the nurses, doctors and friends who visited him. He studied art for a short time in Winnipeg and enjoyed painting. That visual sense was strong even as his body was ravaged by cancer. He lay there and he saw something beautiful.

One evening at the hospital George whispered, "You've just got to play Cypress during the Crosby. It's heaven."

George was in rough shape that night. But he still brought joy to others. Nurses no longer on duty visited. Friends came and went, uplifted by a man who knew that he didn't have much time. He tried to find something good in every moment.

That's how he lived, as Colin Brown, one of George's students at his golf school, knew. He wrote to me after George died.

"If George sensed you were half as enthusiastic about the game as he was, there was no limit on the time he would give you. I remember one busy day at the school last summer, and how George came out of the shack where he was resting and stood with me for 90 minutes working in the rain."

Brown played a round soon after that he described as an absolute disaster. "I don't know what you've done to my swing," he told George, "but that was the first time I've shot 102 and enjoyed it." "George gave me a big smile and said, 'Well, we've accomplished the most important thing.'" Brown went on to tell me that as a result of working with George, he now understands and appreciates the game more than he thought possible.

George accomplished a lot in his life, but I think he would have liked to hear Brown's latest words. He wanted people to understand and appreciate golf. "It's not what you do that counts," he said, "but what you attempt to do." He knew that change was difficult, but that long-term improvement was possible.

George wanted us to enjoy golf, "a physical game played for relaxation," he said. That's why he devoted so much energy to the school that he started in the late 1970s. And when we wrote our book *The Natural Golf Swing* in mid-1987, soon after he was diagnosed as having lung cancer, he gave everything he had to the project. He wanted to get his message across, and he would have been pleased to learn that the Canadian PGA has adopted his teachings and will be implementing them with its young professionals. It's one step at a time, one improvement at a time. Savour the moment. Swing the club to the target. Practise a drill. Enjoy your surroundings.

George taught many of us to do our best and never to feel sorry for ourselves. He wanted to help us ignite the spark he felt each of us has.

George had that spark. It lives on in his teachings, and for those of us who knew him, in our memories of his fearlessness. He died a harsh death, and he fought until the end. I miss him, but more important, I remember, and I'll always remember, what he stood for.

Jack Nicklaus

The Globe and Mail, **June 17, 1982**
If Jack Nicklaus is not the best golfer in history, he is at least the golfer who has played the best golf over the longest period of time. Twenty years ago, at the Oakmont Country Club in Oakmont, Pennsylvania, he won the U.S. Open for his first victory as a professional. Ten years ago, at Pebble Beach, California, he won the U.S. Open for his eleventh major championship.

Today, Nicklaus again plays in the U.S. Open, again at Pebble Beach. Should he win it, it will be his twentieth major championship.

There has been an inevitability about Nicklaus's success since he first played golf in 1950 as a 10-year-old. His instructor then and now — Jack Grout — noticed the youngster's strength and co-ordination.

Sensing he had somebody special, Grout called Paul Hornung, long-time sports editor of the *Columbus (Ohio) Dispatch.*

"I'll never forget that day," Hornung said recently. "Grout told me to get over to Scioto (Nicklaus's home course) and take some pictures of this little fellow in his golf class. Little did I know then how far he would go."

Nicklaus has won five Masters, three British Opens, five Professional Golfers' Association Championships, four U.S. Opens and two U.S. Amateurs. In 81 majors as a professional, he has also finished second 16 times and third 9 times. When he is not in contention, something is missing. He is as conspicuous by his absence as by his presence.

But the absences have been infrequent. In the late sixties, Nicklaus went a couple of years without winning a major. Stories were headlined "What's wrong with Jack?"

Nicklaus responded by winning six majors from 1970 to 1973. Now the headlines were "Jack is back."

But from 1976 to 1979, his only win in a major was the 1978 British Open. In 1979, he finished seventy-first on the money list with $59,434. His scoring average went over 72 for the first time in his career.

To Nicklaus, though, 1979 was just a bad year, a signal, certainly, that changes were called for. Piqued by endless questions about his commitment to competitive golf, he went to work.

"You have to change," Nicklaus said last month, a week before winning the Colonial National Invitation for his sixty-ninth tour victory. "I change the answers I give the press as I get older, the way I handle my kids. If my golf game doesn't change as I get older, I'm going to fall behind.

"I was 40 years old and I went ahead and changed my whole swing plane. I then changed my whole chipping game."

For the first three months of 1980, Nicklaus was awkward and uncomfortable. But then the changes rooted in as a new swing pattern. He won the U.S. Open and PGA Championship that summer.

Soon, though, his putting stroke deteriorated. Through 1981 and the first months of 1982, he didn't win: not until the Colonial. In the meantime, he had altered his putting stroke. If the most delicate manoeuvre in golf had to be changed, so be it.

It is not only Nicklaus's ability to make physical changes that is so impressive. Nicklaus's swing may be the weakest part of his game. It doesn't repeat time after time as did Ben Hogan's, hardly looks elegant as does Tom Weiskopf's.

Not until Nicklaus takes the club back, having stood over the ball longer than seems possible without fraying one's nerves, is there the sense of something good about to happen. Looked at more closely, it is evident the real measure of Nicklaus is in that space of time he spends over the ball.

Nicklaus seems to defy basic physics principles that only mass and velocity are involved in the flight of the golf ball. When he stands rigid over the ball, grafting imagination, visualization and will to his knowledge of the golf swing, he is waiting for a clear picture: that the ball will fly this way, and that it will land there.

On the greens, Nicklaus stands over the ball from 17 to 19 seconds. It is as if that period represents his personal, biological clock working well. It used to be said that Hogan had his own exclusive channel in the sky that his ball flew in. Nicklaus has an internal channel, a pathway from mind to muscle to the hands that trigger the golf swing. No golfer on tour stands over the ball as long, and no golfer on tour has been as successful a putter as

Nicklaus over the years, particularly on the critical putts inside 10 feet.

It is Nicklaus's mind, finally, that one turns to when trying to understand his achievements. Sports writer Hornung said Nicklaus "has total concentration on one thing, and is then able to focus his attention on another. His mind works in sequence."

Weiskopf, once asked to explain what set Nicklaus apart, referred to a "presence of mind that allows him to stand in the middle of a fairway in contention, make up his mind to hit a particular shot, and go ahead and hit that shot."

Nicklaus says: "Golf is a challenge with myself. I am stimulated every time I play. When I play poorly, it puts me to work. As long as I'm playing golf and as long as I can make myself work at it, I'll be a serious competitor. When I play badly and all I can say is the heck with it and just go on and wait for the next tournament, I will probably cease to be a serious competitor."

Score, July/August 1986

Pictures of Jack Nicklaus at the Augusta National Golf Club remain vivid in my mind's eye though it is more than two months since he won the Masters. I see him on the hill in the 15th fairway looking down to the green, a 4-iron away. "Dead the right club," he said hours after he made his eagle there. I see him on the 16th, bending to pick up his tee as his ball arches over the pond within three feet of the hole, so certain he's hit a perfect shot that he doesn't need to watch it. And then I see him in the interview room, sitting magisterially in his green jacket, winner of his sixth Masters, his twentieth major championship, responding to the affection and admiration of anybody who cares about golf and golfers and doing the best one can.

It wasn't easy. Nicklaus's swing, after all, deteriorated through the late 1970s and bottomed out in 1979, when he won less than $60,000 on the PGA Tour to finish seventy-first on the money list. Nicklaus went back to first principles with his lifelong teacher Jack Grout and won the 1980 U.S. Open and PGA Championship. But last summer he missed the cut in the U.S. and British Opens, his swing having sputtered again. It was time for more changes.

After Nicklaus successfully made three major swing changes beginning at the start of 1980, he won the aforementioned U.S. Open and PGA Championship. He's called his last nine holes at Oak Hill in Rochester during the PGA the best he's ever played. That was true, presumably, until the last nine at Augusta, when he was in another world. He took the rest of us there on a journey we won't forget.

Nicklaus took us on that trip because it hurt him so much when he was playing poorly. Nicklaus grimaced inwardly every time he made a bad swing. There were many of those affronts to his dignity and his belief he could play the game exceedingly well.

Grout felt Nicklaus's pain as a father feels his son's. "Jack's swing was dying out here back then," he recalls. "I talked to him and said, 'You're a young guy still.' People get despondent when things aren't going well and they want to chuck everything. But I knew he could come back and succeed."

Nicklaus put great faith in Grout. He worked extremely hard, though it didn't always go well. Maybe some observers felt he was trying something that was inherently impossible — like altering one's signature or personality — but those who knew Nicklaus well thought otherwise.

Last year I visited the Frenchman's Creek Golf Club near Palm Beach. Grout and Nicklaus often worked there. Some members remembered when Nicklaus hit balls for two hours in a downpour. Grout and Gardner Dickinson watched from under an umbrella as Nicklaus, soaked and uncomfortable but oblivious to the circumstances, gave all his considerable attention to the matter of hitting the golf ball properly.

His attention to that matter has never wavered, though he has often been criticized for spending too much time on his business affairs. But that is like chastising a classical musician for studying jazz. Nicklaus's way has been to feed his appetite for knowledge and experience. His interests are not "outside" interests at all; they give his life balance. "The fault, dear friends," he might have said, "lies not in my other interests but in myself, to wit, my swing."

Last year Nicklaus had more trouble with his swing. One late afternoon at the Loxahatchee Golf Club in Jupiter, Florida, he tore his swing to pieces in front of a few friends. He spoke with the candour of a person free-associating in psychoanalysis; he said that when he feels as though he has snapped his lower body out of the way, then he can play; he used to feel he had all the time in the world to swing the club, but that he was too quick now; his golf swing requires more work now than it ever did; he knew what he wanted to do and wondered why he couldn't do it.

Nicklaus also showed a wry sense of humour. When pro Ed Dougherty came by to wish him luck in a coming event, Nicklaus smiled and said, "Yeah, I got a tough guy I'm playing against tomorrow; myself. That's why I'm out here tonight."

Nicklaus stayed *out there*. His confidence — but not his determination — was dented when he missed the cut in both the U.S. and British Opens last summer. After the Doral Open last March, he told Grout he was "hitting the ball awful." He took a week off and Grout helped him quiet his hands at the top of his swing. He also improved his chipping game and bunker play. Meanwhile, he'd started to putt better with his new, outsize blade.

Then it all came together at the Masters. In one mad, furious burst of seven-under-par golf in 10 holes, Nicklaus was more himself than he had been in years. He showed us the rewards inherent in taking risks. If it is exciting to go to the practice tee day in and day out, he showed us why. We might find out that we can improve. If not, at least we tried.

Ben Hogan once wrote, and Nicklaus would agree: "Whether my schedule for the following day called for a tournament round or merely a trip to the practice tee, the prospect that there was going to be golf in it made me feel privileged and extremely happy, and I couldn't wait for the sun to come up the next morning so I could get out on the course again."

Nicklaus at Augusta made us feel privileged to be a part of golf and eager, so eager, to get out on the course again. He warmed our hearts and helped us believe in ourselves a bit more. How nice that golf — which is only a game — and a golfer — who is, after all, only a human being, even if he is extraordinary and his name is Nicklaus — can do that for us.

The Globe and Mail, **March 3, 1988**
Jack Nicklaus is teeing it up today in the opening round of the Doral Ryder Open in Miami. That's Jack Nicklaus the ceremonial

golfer, not Jack Nicklaus the competitive, hungry-for-a-win golfer.

Anybody who saw him win the 1986 Masters knows the second Nicklaus. He's the guy who stuck his tongue out at the 71st hole as his winning birdie putt dropped. Hungry? Nicklaus was starving, after six years of not winning a major, and showed it.

The win was Nicklaus's twentieth major. It electrified the golf world and thrilled Nicklaus. But he knew that it also ended his career as a serious competitor.

Last year, Nicklaus played in only 11 tournaments, the fewest in his career. He finished 127th on the money list, by far his worst performance. As the year wore on, he acknowledged that he simply wasn't playing enough to be competitive.

The year proved to Nicklaus that even he needs practice and competition to win. But he had no interest in putting in the time. How could he? What else was there for him to accomplish? What had he to prove, to himself or anybody?

There was also another factor. Nicklaus has become the most active course designer in the world. He had 18 courses under construction at the beginning of 1988, 12 of which were scheduled to open this year. He has another 18 under contract. Forty-eight, including Glen Abbey in Oakville, Ontario, the home of the Canadian Open, are already in play.

"Ninety per cent of all the good golf course projects in the world come across our desk," Nicklaus said recently at his annual "state-of-the-Golden-Bear" session in North Palm Beach. "We don't do them all, of course. We couldn't do all of them."

Nicklaus's efforts in course design are more than a hobby. He visits each project at least a few times and plays exhibitions to open the courses. Tournament golf is the sideline these days. He's a businessman.

It was at the session in North Palm Beach that Nicklaus, 48, first referred to himself in his new capacity as a golfer to be seen, not worried about. He's still a presence when he does play, but he no longer sends waves of fear through the field.

"I didn't play enough golf in 1987 to fill a thimble," Nicklaus said, "and what little I did play wasn't very good. Obviously, it's not my No. 1 priority any more, and probably hasn't been since I won the Masters in 1986."

Then came the pronouncement.

"I've been sort of a ceremonial golfer since then, sort of passing out of the game."

Nicklaus played in the AT & T National Pro-Am in Pebble Beach, California, a month ago, but only because he and his son, Gary, were partners in the pro-am segment. He's at Doral because it's convenient — besides, he needs to play a bit before the Masters next month.

Nicklaus fans can expect to see less of him at tournaments. But they can expect to see more of him as an architect.

"The sense of satisfaction, the great sense of pride, is the same when I finish a project as it was when I prepared for a tournament, executed the proper shots at the right time and won the title."

Meanwhile, the ceremonial Nicklaus will be visible on television and in other media.

The public will see the new, ceremonial Nicklaus — less intense, more accessible. Toronto commercial artist Neil Harris has learned that's what Nicklaus's people want. Harris has been working with Dick Grimm of the Royal Canadian Golf Association to produce a poster of Nicklaus. The golfer has approved the project, which is meant to raise $75,000 for the Canadian Golf Foundation, an arm of the RCGA.

Ken Bowden, who works with Nicklaus on special projects, rejected as too serious the first sketch that Harris sent along. He wanted fewer wrinkles on Nicklaus's face, less determination in the look.

"I'm working on something more lighthearted now," Harris said. "That's what they want."

He hopes to have the poster out well before the Canadian Open in late August. In the meantime, Nicklaus the ceremonial golfer will continue to follow in the footsteps of legendary amateur Bobby Jones, who gave up competition in 1930 after winning the British Open and Amateur in the same year.

"With dignity," an unprecedented editorial in *The New York Times* read then, "he quits the memorable scene on which he nothing common did, or mean."

The same might be said of Nicklaus, if and when he does totally retire. As it is, golf fans still will be happy to have him around when he does play, his self-proclaimed "ceremonial" status notwithstanding.

The Globe and Mail, **March 24, 1990**

Lee Trevino has been sending Jack Nicklaus's wife, Barbara, a dozen roses from time to time this year. It's his way to thank her for every week that Nicklaus doesn't play on the Senior PGA Tour. Nicklaus's absence, the message suggests, has helped Trevino win three of the four senior events he has played.

But Trevino won't be sending roses next week. Nicklaus, the Golden Bear, will be playing his first Senior PGA Tour event since he turned 50 in January.

Nicklaus's debut, and widely assumed two-man contest with Trevino, will occur in the Tradition, a new, $800,000 event that begins Thursday at the Desert Mountain course in Scottsdale, Arizona.

The tournament has been billed as golf's biggest story so far this year because Nicklaus should be a thorn in Trevino's side.

"I'm really charged up," Trevino said recently. "I'm looking forward to seeing the Bear out there.

"But, hey, I'm not coming out to play one man. I'm coming out to play the course."

But there's no getting around what is sure to be a rivalry between the two superstars. There's more pressure on Nicklaus because everyone thinks he should win.

"Jack is the first guy to come out on the senior tour to be in a losing situation," Chi-Chi Rodriguez said recently. "If he wins, it was expected. If he loses, people will ask what's wrong with him."

Any expectations of Nicklaus on the senior circuit may be too many. After all, golf is a game in which a player who wins once or twice a year out of 25 or so tournaments is deemed to have had a successful season. Mark Calcavecchia is the season's leading money-winner on the PGA Tour, but he has yet to win.

But there's a more important reason why observers ought to temper their hopes for Nicklaus. He differs from Trevino, and indeed from nearly all the older golfers, in that the Senior PGA

Tour is to him a thing apart. To the others, it is their life. He plans to play only occasionally, whereas Trevino, for one, will play the full schedule.

In fact, Nicklaus may be competing next week in Arizona for reasons not related to the Senior PGA Tour. He's using the tournament as preparation for the Masters the following week. And he's also designed the tournament course at Desert Mountain.

But he also has something to prove: He needs to make peace with some of the seniors.

Nicklaus was quoted recently as saying he felt that the majority of the senior competitors had been marginal players before and that he had defeated them. He also suggested that he isn't interested in playing short courses that have little rough.

"I'm a little disappointed that the comments came out as they did," Nicklaus said. "I can't fault the writer, since I did say those things.

"But I also said a lot more. The tone of my comments was that the players who weren't doing all that well before are making a good living now. I meant that as a compliment."

Nicklaus, no doubt, will be able to pacify his fellow senior players, but he may have trouble with someone else — himself. For the salient fact of Nicklaus's life at 50 is that he is suffering from an identity crisis.

"I'm having a hard time being 50," Nicklaus said candidly during the Doral Ryder Open three weeks ago at an extended, and rather personal, news conference.

"I still feel competitive on the regular tour. I'm still excited about it. Does being 50 mean I have to turn my back on the regular tour? Until I'm convinced that I can't do well on it, I'll have trouble getting excited about the senior tour."

There is more to it than that, though, as Nicklaus knows all too well. There is something of the lost soul in him. He has accomplished so much in golf — 20 major championships, courses designed all over the world and a reputation for excellence. But now he is finding there may be a cost to his commitment. It is almost as if he has excelled in too many areas.

"I'm in a quandary about what to do," he said. "Should I play the senior tour? Should I play the regular tour? Should I play at all?

"I have a darn good business that's far more important to me than playing, with 130 employees in Palm Beach (Florida) and 600, 700 world-wide. I can't turn my back on them.

"So my days of being competitive all the time are over. I know that because I can't practise or play enough. But I hate to play poorly."

There's also Nicklaus's family. His wife still joins him at many tournaments and worries over every shot. He has five children and his first grandchild.

Nicklaus has always been a family man first. He has flown home between rounds of tournaments to see his children play football or basketball games or for the simple reason of being with them.

"I love to play golf," Nicklaus said, "but I don't want it to dominate my life.

"At the same time, I don't want to turn my back on golf, the regular or the senior tour. But I've juggled a lot of balls before. I'll figure out a way to do it again."

The Globe and Mail, **April 13, 1991**

More than a little magic was made at the Augusta National Golf Club yesterday afternoon, and more than a couple of merely talented golfers put on the show. Jack Nicklaus and Tom Watson played together in the third last group of the day, and the joint was jumpin' something fierce.

This was a dream pairing, and all because six-time Masters winner Nicklaus and two-time champion Watson had opened the Masters with four-under-par 68s, a shot out of the lead. It was only the second round yesterday, but everybody knew this was something special, maybe spectacular.

The show was that, all right. Watson and Nicklaus shot even-par 36 the front nine, and then the wild and crazy stuff started happening on Augusta's fabled back nine.

Here came Watson first, holing a mid-size birdie putt on the 10th to get it to five under for the tournament. He'd been hitting the ball majestically for weeks, but had admitted to a case of the near yips with the putter. Now he was using a heavy putter called the Zebra for the first time, and he had changed his shoulder alignment at address. Maybe the alterations would help.

Nicklaus, meanwhile, had won the Tradition, a senior tour event last week in Arizona. He had hit the shots under pressure when he needed to. How else do you win 20 majors as he has?

But now Nicklaus was on the tee of the short par-three 12th. He'd been there for 30 years and had done everything possible, or so you would think. Now he plunked his ball into Rae's Creek in front of the green. Then he took his penalty drop in front of the green and found the water again. The result was a quadruple-bogey seven. Surely it was all over for Nicklaus.

Not so, not at all. Nicklaus birdied the 13th, the 14th, the 15th. The game's greatest player was showing why his colleagues feel he has the strongest mind in the game. Give up? Forget it.

Watson caught the spirit. He'd missed a short birdie putt on the 12th. But then he hit a gorgeous, high 4-iron within 18 feet of the hole on the par-five 15th. The putt went in the heart for an eagle. Watson had taken the lead at seven-under par. The crowd down in the pines of Augusta National was vibrating.

But this was nothing compared with what would happen at the 16th, a sweetheart of a par-three, where the green may be the trickiest in the game. Seve Ballesteros, for one, four-putted it during the first round. There's no such thing as a straight putt here. The green is a hall of mirrors.

So there was Nicklaus, some 30 feet from the hole. Watson was just inside him. If ever there were unplayable lies on a green they had them. Two putts would be wonderful, three more likely, four possible.

Nicklaus settled over the ball and stared at his target. The ball was soon on its way, up and over a crest in the green, turning and twisting. And then it fell in on its last breath for Nicklaus's fourth consecutive birdie after his quadruple-bogey.

Nicklaus was stunned. He hunched over in amazement, then raised his hands in thanks to the golfing gods. He was back, all the way back after his apparent Waterloo at Rae's Creek.

Now Watson, on the same line, same curves, same hopes. And unbelievably, his ball also dropped, and in the same way, on its last right-angled roll.

"I played 20 feet of break on the putt," Nicklaus said after his round. "The putt started looping around, dying, then fell in the hole. It was a 30-foot putt that travelled 50 feet."

Watson also had something to say about the double play at the 16th.

"You practise those putts for just such an occasion," he said, a big smile on his face.

An occasion it was, but still there was more. Nicklaus and Watson approached the last green, and as they walked up the hill, Nicklaus first, the crowd gave him a standing ovation. Nicklaus, class act that he is, waited for Watson and invited him to walk on the green alongside. The crowd loved it and knew the gesture was appropriate.

Then the twosome putted out for par, Nicklaus doing so after his approach shot had ricocheted off a lady's foot back on the green. They walked off the green to another standing ovation.

"I enjoy playing with Tom," Nicklaus said. "He's a great competitor. He loves to win and loves to play hard."

That's the bottom line for each golfer. Together they have won 28 majors and now Watson leads the Masters while Nicklaus is right there. Sure, so are former champions Ray Floyd and Bernhard Langer, along with European star José-Maria Olazabal and Welshman Ian Woosnam.

But this moment was for Watson and Nicklaus, and now the golfing world waits to see if tomorrow's last moments will be for one of them as well. That, too, would be magic. Whether it can match yesterday's show is another question.

The Globe and Mail, **June 17, 1992**

It seems ridiculous to use the word "desperate" in conjunction with Jack Nicklaus. But that's one way to describe his mood as he prepares to play his thirty-first consecutive United States Open. The Open begins tomorrow at Pebble Beach, which is second only to the Old Course in St. Andrews as Nicklaus's favourite course.

Nicklaus, 52, isn't doing well in tournaments. It's been ages since he really contended in a PGA Tour event. And make no mistake; Nicklaus cares much more about winning on the regular Tour than on the Senior PGA Tour. He longs to be in at the end with a chance. But he's rarely there.

One reason is that Nicklaus isn't completing his rounds well. Earlier this year at the Doral event in Miami he was three-under par after 12 holes in one round, one-under after 12 in another.

"I didn't finish either day," Nicklaus said in a recent interview, "and I don't know why."

Nicklaus was admitting his frailty. Here's a fellow who has won 20 major championships, including four U.S. Opens. In the past when he had a swing problem he saw Jack Grout, his mentor since childhood. But Grout died three years ago, and Nicklaus has since struggled.

That struggle is particularly nettling to Nicklaus as he sets out at Pebble Beach. He won the United States Amateur there in 1961, and the 1972 U.S. Open when he rapped a 1-iron off the flagstick on the 17th the final day to ensure a birdie. He contended in the 1982 Open at Pebble until Tom Watson claimed the championship with a deft pitch into the 17th hole for a birdie the last day.

Pebble, then, is special to Nicklaus, who has also reconditioned the course for this year's Open. Muirfield in Gullane, Scotland, is also special to him. The British Open will be played there next month. Nicklaus won the 1966 British Open at Muirfield to complete his first modern Grand Slam-wins in the Masters, the U.S. and British Opens and the PGA Championship.

"The U.S. and British Opens are on courses I have done well on," Nicklaus said in an understatement. "I'm looking forward to them and to having my game in shape."

But Nicklaus's game is not in shape. He has not won on the regular tour since the 1986 Masters. Sure, he has won often on the Senior PGA Tour, but he shrugs off those wins. He's after a U.S. Open at Pebble Beach, a British Open at Muirfield.

"I still feel that I have a major championship left in me," Nicklaus said.

Perhaps that's possible. After all, Nicklaus was written off prior to the 1986 Masters. Somebody took an article from an Atlanta paper that suggested Nicklaus had no chance and taped it to the refrigerator of the home in which he was staying. Nicklaus hated every word. Then he won the Masters.

If Nicklaus's win in the 1986 Masters declared that he was far from finished, what would a win at Pebble or Muirfield be?

It would be an amazing feat. It would be a shock. One hesitates to make these statements, because Nicklaus has always had that "one more major" in him. That's how he reached 20 majors. It's an astounding number.

And yet even Nicklaus cannot compete forever against younger players. He feels he is hitting the ball as solidly as ever, but said that when he reaches his drives they're 20 yards behind the other golfers. And he is dumbfounded. To what should Nicklaus assign his diminution of skill? He doesn't know.

Age is the obvious reason. But golf plays jokes on all players, even Nicklaus. A 66 in the evening can make a golfer think his day has arrived, again.

Nicklaus is susceptible to that notion, as are all players. But he must be the finest golfer of all time, and he is also one who has conducted himself impeccably. His father taught him how to behave.

"Dad always said to me that when I got beat I had better have a smile on my face. You may not want to inside, but you should give the winner a good firm handshake and say, 'Well done.'"

Nicklaus has been saying "Well done" too frequently for his liking. He needs to contend at Pebble or Muirfield to feel he has a legitimate place in tournaments. Hence the desperation one senses in this man who has towered over the game for 30 years.

"I don't think I'll enjoy the day when I can't come to the 18th tee without a chance to win," Nicklaus said, his voice rising.

The 18th tee at Pebble Beach sits on a promontory on the edge of cliffs above the coastline. It's an ultimate destination in golf. It is that way for Nicklaus, who has crested at Pebble like no other golfer. It has been a place where he has renewed himself.

Will Nicklaus be in the hunt this week at Pebble? He needs an answer in the affirmative. And he needs it badly.

Greg Norman

The Globe and Mail, June 21, 1987
"That wasn't the real Greg Norman you saw this week," Pete Bender said yesterday as the player many people consider the world's finest golfer came off the final green at the U.S. Open. Bender should know; he's Norman's caddy and had watched him shoot a 12-over-par 292 to finish way back in the field.

Norman wasn't himself all week. He hasn't been himself all year, though he'd won $276,655 on the PGA Tour before the U.S. Open. "The whole year hasn't been flowing," he said while packing his bags yesterday for a quick exit from the Olympic Club. "I haven't been able to get any momentum going."

Momentum to Norman is like fuel to a car. He needs it to get moving. But just when it appeared he was about to become supercharged at the Masters in April, his tank ran dry.

Norman thought he had holed a 20-foot putt to win the Masters on the last green. But it hung on the left lip. Then he watched as Larry Mize pitched in from 140 feet on the second playoff hole to win. Norman hasn't been the same since.

Norman won the British Open last year. He led going into the last round in the three other majors. And he was excited when he got to Olympic. "I was pretty keen on doing well, all right," he said, but then nothing happened.

To watch Norman yesterday was to watch a golfer in a position he's not used to. As he triple-bogied the par-five 16th hole from the trees and deep rough, the leaders were teeing off. Norman was in a world he doesn't like and from which he means to escape.

Canadian Open officials may not like the strategy he's considering. "I'm contemplating taking three weeks off," he said, which would mean he would miss the Canadian Open in two weeks. "I haven't taken that kind of time off since November." (Jack Nicklaus, however, said after his round yesterday that he will play the Canadian Open.)

Norman acknowledged that things could change. He's got a business outing today and another tomorrow, "which doesn't help," he said. But when he gets home to Orlando tomorrow night, he'll think about his schedule.

"I say that about the Canadian Open walking off the course after what I shot," Norman explained. "Maybe by Saturday night I'll feel differently. I like Glen Abbey, so maybe this will all change."

Maybe. Maybe not. Norman isn't enjoying golf any more. And he certainly doesn't want to be in his current funk when he defends his British Open title at Muirfield in Scotland in four weeks. He'd also like to spend some time with his wife, Laura, and their two young children, an understandable sentiment that he expressed yesterday, Father's Day.

"When we left home," Norman said, with more than a trace of unhappiness, "Morgan (his four-year-old daughter) didn't want us to go. And when I go practise eight hours a day, as I did before the U.S. Open, she doesn't like it that I won't be back until late."

Will a rest be the answer for Norman? One hopes so. Along with Seve Ballesteros, he's the most exciting golfer in the world when he's on his game. He shot 62 in the second round of the Canadian Open last year and 63 in the second round on his way to winning the British Open at Turnberry last July.

The real question is whether Norman has been adversely affected by his experiences since Bob Tway holed from a sand trap on the 72nd hole to beat him in the PGA Championship last August. Mize followed with his shot to the heart at Augusta, and now Norman has played a poor U.S. Open.

Sports Illustrated writer Rick Reilly thinks Norman might be more affected by his experiences than he lets on. Reilly recently spent some time with Norman at his home in Orlando for a story in the current issue of the magazine.

"Outwardly," Reilly said at Olympic, "Norman sheds the past. He keeps himself busy. He seems to crave speed and action to get away from yesterday. After the Mize thing, he got right on a plane and had a good time."

Norman, for his part, said yesterday that there's no need to worry. "There's always another tournament."

True enough, but surely Norman isn't impervious to what's happened to him in majors. Said Reilly, "Maybe he's acting. He says the past doesn't affect him, but the night I spent with him at his home he talked a long time about history and his place in it. I think he loves the game too much for things not to affect him."

The Globe and Mail, May 12, 1990

Of all the ways to become a golfing legend — making pots of money or winning multiple major championships, for instance — Greg Norman has had thrust upon him a method he finds repugnant and refuses to acknowledge, let alone accept: that of a celebrated victim.

Norman's unwanted place in contemporary golf is the result of having stood by as four golfers holed out four shots on the last holes of tournaments to take what looked like sure victory away from him. The shots that everybody remembers, and which Norman is trying to forget, make up a genuine Grand Slam — Norman being the one who has been slammed.

First came the 1986 PGA Championship at the Inverness Club in Toledo, Ohio, where Bob Tway holed out from a greenside sand trap on the final hole to take the title by a shot over Norman. That led Norman to make one of the great understatements in the game's history, considering what was yet to come.

"You always have to expect the unexpected," he said.

Larry Mize delivered the next knockout punch. He sank a 140-foot pitch and run on the second hole of a sudden-death playoff to beat Norman at the 1987 Masters. Norman had now been twice stripped of what looked like certain wins in majors.

"That was an impossible shot Larry made," Norman said after Mize's miracle. "When it went in, I couldn't believe it. Tway's shot was much the easier."

Nobody would have believed that anything similar to what Norman had experienced could happen again. And it didn't, not for a while anyway. But rookie Tour sensation Robert Gamez holed a 7-iron shot from 176 yards on the final hole last March in the Nestlé Invitational at Bay Hill in Orlando. Norman was leading at the time and playing behind Gamez as he heard the noise up ahead. Now he was suddenly a shot back. He parred the final two holes and lost by the one shot.

"I knew exactly what happened," Norman said. "A roar like that, you figure somebody holed out. At least the shots are getting longer."

Norman was philosophical, as he had been after the first two knockout punches had been administered.

"I'm fine," he said. "I know I'm playing well . . . What can you say? If a guy holes a shot, God bless him."

But there was more. Two weeks ago, Norman had finished the USF & G Classic in New Orleans with a flourish, smiting a 2-iron across a lake to within six inches of the hole for an apparent winning birdie. He needed only to wait for David Frost to finish. Frost was tied with Norman and in the bunker in front of the green. He holed the shot to win.

"What can you do?" Norman asked. "Good on Frost for making the shot."

Norman then started to think about what exactly was going on. He began to reel from the accumulated impact of the four shots.

Norman betrayed his sensitivity on Wednesday when a *Golf Magazine* writer approached him at the Memorial Tournament in Dublin, Ohio, to discuss the series of shots. The writer didn't have much luck with Norman, who is a playing editor at the magazine.

"I blew *Golf Magazine* out of the water," Norman said in a phone interview yesterday from Memorial. "It amazes me, all these people who think I should be falling apart because of the four shots."

Notwithstanding his client's stoical stance, Norman's manager Hughes Norton of the International Management Group in Cleveland said this week that the shots may be affecting his No. 1 golfer.

"The coincidence of the four shots is so profound," Norton said from Dublin. "It's like Zeus or God is up there saying, 'I've given Greg Norman so much — looks, charisma, wealth, talent, a loving family. Let's see how much he can take.'"

Norman has taken it well thus far and has often played remarkable golf. He won two PGA Tour events last year and won the Doral Ryder Open earlier this year when he chipped in for an eagle on the first playoff hole against three golfers. Norman has also contended in most tournaments.

Nevertheless, Norton feels that Norman may now be losing patience with the gods of golf.

"He's mystified by it all," Norton said. "On the other hand, he doesn't want to talk about it, to rehash the disappointment. I've tried to console him. I told him after New Orleans that with all due respect to that tournament and Bay Hill, the only tournaments that matter are the majors."

Not everybody agrees with Norton's view that eerie things have been happening to Norman. Vancouver touring pro Richard Zokol feels that Norman has designed his own destiny, rather than being a victim of fate.

"I'm a Greg Norman fan," Zokol said this week from Vancouver. "He has more ability than anybody, and he's a pure gentleman. But he beats himself. What's happened isn't eerie at all. He should be tied for the lead going into the last round instead of having to shoot 65 to get near the lead or on top. He's that far superior to everybody else."

Zokol was referring to Norman's penchant for shooting low final rounds. Norman does have the lowest last-round average on Tour and wonders why he puts himself in arrears with mediocre early rounds. But does that account for the shots that Tway et al. have pulled off?

Norman, meanwhile, has his own views.

"What keeps me going," he said, "is that I love the game with a passion. One time this year, I walked on to the course early in the morning and told Bruce (Edwards, his caddy) that I really do love the game. I simply enjoy playing.

"My first objective," Norman went on, "is to give myself pleasure, and then to give other people pleasure. I have made a commitment to myself to play at this level for the next 10 years. My attitude is that every shot I hit will be the best shot I can hit."

One problem, of course, is that his four opponents have hit their best shots just when they needed them most, and when they would hurt Norman most. But Norman disagrees with the theory that the hurt will accumulate and affect his play in the long run, or that the game has mystically chosen him as its victim.

"My love of the game is going to last a lot longer than any shots that go in," Norman said. He sounded as if he meant exactly what he said, never mind what others believe.

The Globe and Mail, July 28, 1990

Bewildered, surely, Greg Norman left the Old Course at St. Andrew's, Scotland, last Sunday after the biggest disappointment of his unusual career. Was he beaten? Would he recover from his self-inflicted but inexplicable blows? No one knows, least of all this fascinating, now dismayed golfer.

He has lost before, of course. Golfers have holed full shots on him to win major tournaments and lesser events. The world has heard that Norman is a victim of cruel golfing fates. But each time he said not to worry, that he could do nothing about what others do, that he didn't take personally sand shots or chip shots holed on the final holes of major tournaments to beat him.

Norman was convincing, too, and this year came to the British Open at the Old Course as the top money-winner on the PGA Tour. He was relaxed and said after his opening rounds of 66-66 that he looked forward to a weekend of more of the same sensation, or lack of it. His opponent would be Nick Faldo, or so many thought. But more than a few observers suggested Norman might need to overcome an occasional tendency to falter when on or near the lead in major tournaments.

There is evidence of this, should one choose to examine Norman's failures rather than analyze his many successes. He won the 1986 British Open at Turnberry, but detractors have said he won because he shot 63 in the third round and was not challenged in the final round. The point was that it's one thing to win a major tournament when well ahead and unchallenged, another to win when up against top players.

This argument can be extended to Norman's experience at the 1986 Masters, when he misplayed his 4-iron shot to the final green and missed a playoff with Jack Nicklaus. Norman said later that he should have hit a hard 5-iron, rather than trying to fade a 4-iron near the hole. Why did he make that error?

This wasn't the first time Norman had come up empty, or at least wrong. He wasn't a factor in a playoff for the 1984 U.S.

Open against Fuzzy Zoeller, though he did hole a big putt on the 72nd green to reach the playoff. Norman hardly seemed a part of the proceedings that day, though he had played gallantly to get there.

More curious, perhaps, was Norman's experience as leader heading into the final round of the 1986 U.S. Open at Shinnecock Hills on Long Island in New York. He came out flat, as he volunteered after Ray Floyd had won. Something was missing, some energy or even excitement that golfers require to play their best. Norman didn't know why it happened, but he noticed that he played differently in the final round than in earlier rounds.

One worried that this might happen again at the Old Course after Norman's breathtaking opening rounds. On the one hand, here he was speaking about how calm he felt. But such placidity can bespeak a lack of vitality. It's not that a player intends this, but that his constitution can produce the suppressed emotional state. Norman's play in the third round of the British Open suggested this might have happened.

Norman is exuberant and friendly, a favourite of golf fans. But his game showed doubt and darkness in the sunshine last Saturday, after two exemplary rounds. He followed his 76 with a closing 69, but by then he had no chance of winning.

"Four holes got me yesterday," Norman said after the final round. "Two three-putts and a couple of good drives that ended in the bunkers."

One had to sympathize with Norman, golf's mysterious almost-best golfer. But one also had to think there was something in Norman with which he must come to grips, else he might continue to come to grief in major championships

Curtis Strange

Golf Monthly, **September 1988**
A professional golfer must know how to think. And when to think. And what to think. In other sports he can react to the ball in motion, give his mind over to reflex. The successful golfer is the one who can stand in the middle of the last fairway with a

chance to win and demonstrate what Tom Weiskopf once said Jack Nicklaus had so much of: presence of mind.

"Jack has the ability to stand in the fairway," Weiskopf said, "knowing he has to hit the shot to win and still keep calm while everybody else is nervous. He keeps his head."

This brings us to Curtis Strange, the new U.S. Open champion now reaching the highest levels of the game. As we observe him, he's standing on the 72nd green during the U.S. Open at The Country Club in Brookline, Massachusetts. He's waiting to descend into the sand trap in front of the green, where he must get his ball up and down for par to have a chance to get into an 18-hole playoff with Nick Faldo. Faldo is on the fringe of the green some 25 feet from the hole, with two putts for his par.

The supposedly proper Bostonians gathered in the stands around the green are in a frenzy. They can't keep quiet. A few reporters are at the edge of the green, kneeling as if in prayer, figuring Strange will walk into the trap as soon as things settle down. If they settle down. They imagine that's what Strange is waiting for, the noise outside himself to stop.

But there's more to it. Strange is waiting for the noise *inside* himself to quit. All during the last round, for instance, he's shut out thoughts of his father, who gave him so much encouragement until he died of cancer when his son was a teenager. During the 1987 U.S. Open at the Olympic Club in San Francisco, a friend of Strange's approached him on his way to the 10th tee while he was in contention to tell him to win the tournament for his dad. It was Father's Day, the last round.

"I went to the 10th with tears in my eyes," Strange would say a year later. This time he didn't want that to happen. So he kept himself from thinking about his dad, how much he did want to honour his memory by winning his first major. He thought he might be able to thank him for all he did after the 1985 Masters, which he was on his way to winning until he hit two balls in the water at the par-five 13th and 15th holes.

"Losing that Masters hurt so much," Strange says. "I wasn't able to thank my dad, and everybody else who has helped me. I didn't get the chance."

So Strange wasn't about to let any internal voices interfere with his chances of winning this time, even if the sounds were personal and intimate. He could thank everybody after the U.S. Open, if he won. Now he had to silence the tape in his head. He had to go into the bunker on the 72nd hole and forget he was playing to get into a playoff for the U.S. Open. He had to forget he may never again have the opportunity to win a major, to thank his dad. A few weeks before, he'd won the prestigious Memorial Tournament in Dublin, Ohio, at Nicklaus's Muirfield Village course. That's about as close to a major without being one as there is. Strange thought of thanking his dad then. He silenced that thought as well. He'd wait for a major. He believed he'd win one yet.

"The noise of the crowd there on the 18th on Sunday didn't hurt me at all," Strange says. (And we thought he was waiting for *them* to get quiet.) "It gave me the extra 30 seconds to think about the shot. You can't go into the trap and think how important the shot is. That's when you choke. The crowd gave me the time to realize I had hit this shot many times, that it didn't have to be a great bunker shot, just a good one, and then make the putt. So I went in there not nearly as nervous as I might have been."

Strange walked into that bunker a calm, rational man. He hit the shot he'd hit thousands of times before, and it popped out a foot short of the hole. Faldo two-putted, Strange holed his putt, and the next day Strange shot 71 to Faldo's 75 to win the U.S. Open Championship.

"This is the greatest thing I've ever done, the greatest feeling I've ever had," Strange said to the world's press immediately after his win. He spoke emotionally during a moving soliloquy that lasted 15 minutes. The room was absolutely silent. We were listening to a man who was in the right place as he sat at the head of the room, a 33-year-old man who had incubated so much hurt until this moment.

So much hurt. So much hurt. This is what we need to know about Curtis Strange to appreciate how far he has come. The deepest hurt came when his father died. Strange was just 14; his dad was a golf pro, who was diagnosed as having lung cancer while in the process of buying a course in Virginia Beach. He'd taken his son golfing since the lad was nine years old, and every day the boy would play and practise from morning till night, always encouraged by his father. He taught his son the basics of the golf swing, and more, "a lot of intangible things I think about nearly every day," Strange would say after winning the U.S. Open.

When Thomas Wright Strange died, Curtis Strange began to nurture a dream: to win a major championship and to thank his dad. He could have given up — many talented youngsters might have, without the support of their father — but Curtis already had what he calls "the fire in my belly," a quality that he believes is part of his nature.

But more hurts would come. This was not to be a Jack Nicklaus story — ever onward and upward. There was a day in New Orleans early in his career, when Strange led going into the last round and walked into the press room, only to be ignored by writers who had just interviewed Lee Trevino. Trevino was second, but he was somebody. Strange was then the golfer nobody knew. "I wanted to cry," he says, "but everybody is an unknown sometime. You've got to start somewhere."

Strange's start was not always pleasant. Invited to Arnold Palmer's Bay Hill Classic in Orlando, Florida, Strange wanted so badly to do well that he chastised a female volunteer for an incident that had more to do with an intrusive photographer than with her. But Strange reacted and was soon the recipient of some unfavourable press, not to mention that he had upset Palmer. Still, he handled it gracefully, for two weeks later he sought out the great man to apologize.

"I was scared to death," Strange explains, and you can still hear the misery that he felt then. "I was shaking, but I had to apologize. 'Mr. Palmer,' I said, and it was *Mr.* Palmer then, 'I lost my cool. I'm sorry. It won't happen again.'"

Palmer accepted Strange's apology, especially as he was the only one of the three golfers who were involved in the incident to come forward. "Arnie and I have been a lot closer since then," Strange points out now. In fact, when Strange came to Toronto a week after his win in the U.S. Open to play in a skins game with Palmer, Lee Trevino and Canadian Dave Barr, he and Palmer went out to dinner. "We talked about my win," Strange says, "and about Arnie's win in the 1960 Open. He was tickled to death that I'd won. It was really a lot of fun to see how excited he was."

That was hurt number three that Strange absorbed in his golfing apprenticeship. Later came his now well-known experiences
on the par-five 13th and 15th holes during that last round of the
1985 Masters. Strange was on his way to completing what would
have been a storybook comeback after starting the Masters with
an 80, and following with 65-68. His four-under-par 32 on the
front nine on Masters Sunday put him in the lead. And then it
was over. Bernhard Langer, who shot 32 on the back nine, won.

Why did Strange sometimes seem to pull the wrong shot out
of the bag and the wrong response from his heart? Would this
young man reach his potential? Yes, he had won eight tournaments in a little over six years on the PGA Tour, heading into the
1985 Masters. But he seemed to be missing something. What
was it? He tried so hard, and every emotion he felt was written
on his face. Asked about his play in his first half-dozen years,
Strange will answer that he was having some success, but that
he had a long way to go.

Cut, then, to Sunday, July 7, 1985, at the Glen Abbey Golf
Club. Strange leads by two shots over Greg Norman and three
over Jack Nicklaus as he tees it up in the last round of the Canadian Open. It's two and a half months since the Masters débâcle.
He's said so many times that he would go for the 13th and 15th
greens in two again if he were in the same spot. He's tired of the
question, though he's answered it thoughtfully each time. More
important, he accepted the blame for his misplays. That kind of
responsibility can be painful; the next question one might ask
oneself is "Why? Why did I come up with the poor swings just
when it counted?"

"There was one player out there in the fairway in my shoes,"
Strange says, "and that was me; one person who was going to
live with the defeat if he failed, and that was me. I'll be damned
if anybody could help me with that. To me there wasn't any
decision to make on each hole. I would have had to lay up with
some kind of short iron on both. I would definitely make the
same decisions to go for the green if I had to do it over again."

Three weeks after that Masters, Strange had a chat with Jack
Nicklaus, who told him that his Masters experience would either
make him a better player or hinder his career. Now, in the last
round of the Canadian Open, we would see if Strange had "it,"

whatever "it" is. Or had his two swings at Augusta exposed flaws that would keep Strange from ever playing as observers thought he could?

By the last few holes at Glen Abbey, Norman had slipped and was too far back. Nicklaus missed a three-foot birdie putt on the 16th that he needed to tie Strange, who went on to a two-shot win. All along he had been aware that the crowd's cheers were mostly for Norman, the defending champion, and Nicklaus, the perennial favourite who had already finished second six times in the Canadian Open. Norman and Nicklaus were the golden boys, Strange the interloper come to ruin the party.

Never mind. Strange simply did what was required. He got stronger as he went along, though, paradoxically, he was physically drained from five hours on the course. But he had the ingredients, especially when the momentum suddenly shifted his way when Nicklaus unexpectedly missed that short birdie putt.

"You dig a little deeper at times like that," Strange says. "You've gone 70 holes and now you're in the lead. I'll be damned if I want to go that far and then lose in the last two holes. Nobody wants to. I think you find out who really wants to win the most when you come to a position like that, and who is playing the best, first of all, because that's when your game can fall apart. The question is, who's playing the best? Who really wants to win the most?"

Strange was the one that day. He showed a fierce commitment to winning when in or near the lead. At other times he's demonstrated a nearly equivalent commitment to finishing as high as he can. Strange hates to miss cuts, as he displayed at this year's British Open when he started with a 79 but clawed his way back to finish thirteenth. And he'd rather finish fifty-second than fifty-third. Maybe this is as much a measure of the man as is his ability to win. He doesn't quit.

Asked where his tenacity comes from, that a man can hit two balls in the soup while leading at Augusta and gain strength rather than come apart and slide into oblivion, fearful of a repeat performance, Strange says simply, "A lot of it is natural." He also says he always had it. No fooling around. No equivocating. Just the straight goods.

That's what you get when you talk with or watch Strange. Honesty. Sincerity. Directness. Sharpness. These qualities led to his ripping into the volunteer at the Bay Hill Classic. Not that his reaction was acceptable; not at all. He knew he had been wrong. But it was just unbridled desire, and anger when he felt thwarted. He'll still get angry, pitches a club lightly at the bag when he's missed a shot, but it's a fine-tuned anger now. As he says, "Sometimes you need to slap yourself in the face or kick yourself in the rear end to get going. It happens to everybody. Some people just show it more than others. But I've learned to control more of it because I realize it just doesn't look so good."

Strange not only won that 1985 Canadian Open, he showed all year that he had the goods to be one of the finest players in the world, if not the best. He won three tournaments and led the PGA Tour money list. He proved Nicklaus right. He *did* learn from the Masters. There wasn't much he couldn't survive as far as the vicissitudes of the game go, if he could survive the back nine that year at Augusta. And so what if he had a relatively lacklustre 1986 season, in which he won but one tournament and finished thirty-second on the money list? That was only a let-down. The tournament he won was the Houston Open, in which he whacked his putter on the ground in anger and putted with a wedge for a few holes.

Last year Strange won four times. He set a new record for earnings with $925,941. His play during the Canadian Open, particularly during the last round, indicated just how consummate a golfer he had become. His 69 was a portrayal of how the game should be played, down the middle, on the greens, and in the hole in one with the makeable putts, around the hole for gimmes with longer approach putts.

"I made no mistakes that day," Strange explains. "I was very confident, not necessarily outwardly, but in my shots, my swing."

And what a swing it is. Many astute observers feel Strange has the most effective swing in the game. Yet it did not come naturally. Before the spring of 1980 Strange played inconsistently due to excessive hand action in his swing. "I knew I had to make changes, and so I went to see Jimmy Ballard."

Ballard teaches at the Doral Country Club in Miami. He advocates what he calls "connection," the use of the bigger muscles of the shoulders, back and legs to convey the clubhead back from and through the ball. Strange understood Ballard's suggestions immediately. They made sense, and he saw good results right away, winning the Houston Open just a few weeks later.

Even here Strange showed a fierce determination. He felt uncomfortable with his new swing, precisely because he soon found that by using the bigger muscles he was losing much of his hand action. "I felt like I was moving a foot behind the ball and two feet forward of it," he now says. "It felt awful. But I was getting the results, and I believed what Jimmy was telling me. So I stayed with it."

That's the fire in his belly.

Augusta National Golf Club, the Masters, 1988. Strange is not a happy man. He's played poorly for much of the season, having won but $40,000 for seventieth place on the money list. Settled in for lunch in a dining room at the club, he tries to adopt a philosophical perspective on the nature of golf.

Strange is hurting. His swing is off. Typically, he's hard on himself.

"The way I look at it, you're only as good as your last round. My play hasn't been very good this year. A certain part of me stands here and questions. It's a circle. You're always working, always fighting to get out of a bad spell. Then you can get to playing good and win three or four. After you finish fifth, you're mad. Your confidence is so high. You think you can win every week. But you can't."

As Strange talks, it's clear how deeply he feels about the game, and his place in it. Still fairly young as golfers go at 33, he's learned from all his experiences and plans to continue doing so. Not much escapes him. He's also not afraid of the slump he's now in and figures it won't be long until he works his way out of it.

"I've moved too far away from the ball at address," Strange explains. "That's thrown me out of whack. The club has been coming up too abruptly, for one thing, and I've gotten into all sorts of bad habits. So I'm working on getting closer to the ball. It feels awful, but I'm starting to hit the ball well."

Anybody who has tried to change his or her position at the ball knows how uncomfortable it can feel. Imagine trying to do so while competing. Yet Strange knows that all it might take is a few good shots at the beginning of a round, and he'll start feeling better right away.

Still, he's troubled. He'd like to talk about 1988, but he hasn't done much, and so his great 1987 season is still the main subject of conversation; at least for a while anyway, because before long Strange is off on 1988. He's eager to get the new season rolling, his way. Trouble is, there really isn't much to talk about yet, so Strange chats about golf-related matters.

"I'm introspective," he says, "and I do think a lot about the life I lead. It's not always easy, because I've got a family growing up at home, but so much of my life is on the road." (He and his wife Sarah's sons are aged six and three.)

"But I'm fortunate. Sarah understands the demands of the game. She understands completely what I'm all about, and what it takes to play well. She knows what it means to me. It means a lot, and that's why I get disappointed when I'm playing poorly."

Strange's poor play doesn't last long. Three weeks after the Masters, he wins the Independent Insurance Agent Open in Houston, formerly known as the Houston Open. There he defeats Greg Norman after hitting a 192-yard 3-iron within four feet of the final hole of regulation play to force a playoff. Then he birdies the 18th hole again to win on the third extra hole of sudden-death. Four weeks later Strange takes Nicklaus's Memorial Tournament in Dublin, Ohio, with a stunning display of controlled, nerveless golf over the last few holes.

Following the Memorial, Hale Irwin commented that Strange was playing the best golf of anybody in the world just then. Irwin played with Strange the last round, so he should know. The Memorial was further proof of Strange's ability to win, as was Houston. He gets better and better and tougher and tougher as he gets closer to winning. By the time the U.S. Open came round, he was a man at the top of his form. He was ready to reach the next level, air breathed by those who win the majors.

Like Norman, like Nicklaus, like Arnold Palmer and Ben Hogan before them, Strange is still wrapped up in the quest for titles.

Indeed, he might have been so wrapped up in it that he could not see what was good for him in the world of golf. Today Strange admits that he might have erred in not playing year after year in the British Open Championship. He received rather poor press — "rightfully so," he now feels — after not going to Royal St. George's for the 1985 Open, that in a year during which he was playing very well. But he claims he has nothing against British courses, that he rather enjoys them.

"The conditions aren't always to my liking," he explains, "I just don't like the cold. Still, I have always had a great time when I've gone over. I look forward to going over regularly now."

Strange can also look forward to at least a year of carrying the title of the champion of his country. Yet with all his will to win, his intense desire to continue improving, we don't have to worry about his personality changing. Strange, one expects, will always present a touch of class. He has done so for years, but never more than after his win at The Country Club.

The new champion was asked the evening before the playoff with Faldo if he thought this was a battle between the U.S. and Britain. Perhaps it might be his chance to atone for the American side's loss in the Ryder Cup last autumn. "Nonsense," Strange answered. "We're all golfers. We aren't fighting a war. I'll be damned if I'll be drawn into that discussion. It's just plain silly."

Having won the U.S. Open, Strange was asked if he had received any messages of goodwill from players before the playoff round. "I did," he said, "but I won't tell you who they were from." Another touch of class, as Strange later said that to do so would have been to indicate partisanship on the part of his fellow golfers. That would have been a slap against Faldo.

Strange will also not be drawn into a discussion of who is the best player in the world. He knows how quickly one can fall down the list. He will admit to being one of the best players right now, but no more. He would rather let the record speak.

That record speaks clearly. It tells the story of a still young man with the memory of his dad in his heart and the fire in his belly. Curtis Strange is not the next Jack Nicklaus or the man who will make us forget Greg Norman, Seve Ballesteros, Sandy Lyle or Faldo himself. But he has become one of the most interesting golfers in the game. He has won one major in glorious fashion, with the kind of swing and character that belong to the best that golf has had to offer through the years. In doing so, he has achieved the appropriate level in the game for a golfer of his vast ability and deeply felt commitment to doing the best he can.

The Globe and Mail, June 18, 1990

Medinah, Illinois — The applause for Curtis Strange began after he hit his approach to the 18th green yesterday at the U.S. Open. It was one standing ovation after another.

Strange was not going to win his third consecutive Open, but he had moved into position to do so and then conducted himself graciously in failure.

It didn't appear that he had much of a chance as the rounds unfolded at Medinah, Illinois, a course softened by rain and thereby rendered breakable. But on Saturday he shot four-under-par 68 to move from eight shots behind leader Tim Simpson to within two shots.

And so Strange went out for his Open weekend, a man closed to all thoughts except preparing properly. His wife was worried about the weight her husband had been losing, and he, too, was concerned. "Yes, I've lost some weight," he told his questioners during the week, "and no, it's not on purpose." That was all he would say on the matter.

Strange was more concerned with a different sort of wait, the kind that is measured in days and hours and minutes and seconds rather than pounds. He and his wife had gone out for dinner Friday night with Billy Ray Brown — who tied for the lead after three rounds — and his wife, Cindy. Brown had asked Strange many times about how to play an Open — this was his first — and Strange told him to hit the ball in the centre of the fairway and the middle of the greens. Let the putts fall and be patient.

Strange did that Saturday during his flawlessly played round. His drives were arrows, his irons bull's-eyes and his putts started falling, finally.

Now he was back in it. He couldn't wait for Sunday.

"I am in the position of having everything in the world to gain and nothing to lose," Strange said before heading off to two hours of solitary practice Saturday evening. "I have changed drastically in two days and am ready to go now."

And so he struck his opening tee shot just after high noon and headed out to whatever fate awaited him. He thought only about himself then, 30 minutes before Mike Donald and Brown teed off. He had one target: Do what is necessary to win the Open for the third consecutive time.

But this time the fates didn't co-operate. Strange barely got over the water on the par-three second hole, then hit a poor chip and made bogey. He seemed lacking in energy, as if he had nothing left. On one hole he hit a poor drive, lost another shot and walked off the green, his head down.

Soon he was out of it and long before he finished, Hale Irwin, his counterpart in hitting the ball straight down the middle, began knocking the flags down on the back nine. Irwin holed a startling putt on the last hole to reach eight-under-par, then danced around the perimeter of the green, high-fiving the fans, blowing kisses all round, one happy man at eight-under-par, a score good enough to tie Donald and head into today's 18-hole playoff.

Strange was finished and off the premises by the time Donald came through in the last group. One had to admire him, even if he did refuse all interviews. He said he had a plane to catch, but it was a reservation made in case of loss. Strange was disappointed, no doubt as saddened in his moment of loss as Irwin was happy after holing his mammoth putt on the 72nd hole.

"I think it would have been wonderful for golf had Curtis won three in a row," Irwin said as he waited to see what was in store for him. "It would have been unbelievably remarkable."

Yes, it would have been, because Strange wanted the U.S. Open trophy badly. He said he had walked with this fellow beside him for two years, a friend he didn't want to lose. He meant the once fictional but now real person: Curtis Strange, the twice-in-a-row U.S. Open champion.

"You just don't want to let go," Strange had said. There was talk, though, that perhaps he had crossed the threshold. Maybe he was coveting the trophy too much. There was something almost agitated about him as he made his first few swings yesterday.

He could not get himself back on track, not this time anyway. He had chased a magnificent, improbable vision, and now he was gone, so quickly it all seemed like a dream.

But that's what it was. Strange had come close and in the process given golf back to dreamers, all of whom understand that disappointment is often the other side of a dream, yet well worth whatever price there is to pay. Ask the two golfers in today's playoff, chasing something Irwin calls "indescribably delicious," a feeling Strange knew intimately, and now relinquishes.

Tom Watson

The Globe and Mail, **April 11, 1987**

Augusta, Georgia — Out on the 12th tee at the Augusta National Golf Club during Thursday's first round of the Masters, Tom Watson lofted an 8-iron over Rae's Creek to within three feet of the hole. Then he made the birdie putt, and one couldn't help but wonder: where has this Watson been for so long?

This Watson is the fellow who has won one U.S. Open, two Masters and five British Opens. He hasn't won a tournament since the June 1984 Western Open in Chicago and, as he said this week, "he's had enough of answering questions about what's wrong with Tom Watson."

Watson is tired of the questions because even he can't supply the answers. But there was a clue to his problems yesterday, when Watson came to the green at the par-five, 535-yard eighth hole at one under par and just three shots out of the lead. Having reached the front of the green in two mighty wallops, Watson went from birdie to bogey in four distressing putts. The birdie putt was from 10 feet and the par putt from 3 feet, the lengths Watson used to hole from with relative ease.

Fair enough, but why can't Watson putt as well any more? And for that matter, why isn't he swinging sweetly, like the Watson of old? Is it his tempo, or his long swing, or his discomfort while putting? "You tell me," a mystified Watson might answer when asked, before heading for the practice tee.

It's not that the cerebral Watson hasn't thought it out. "It's like ironing a shirt," he's said. "When you smooth out one wrinkle, another wrinkle shows up somewhere else. That's been my swing," a swing, he can remember, that was once wrinkle-free. And what a different, and unhappy, golfer he has become.

Five years ago, to recall the way it was, Watson holed out a chip shot on the 71st hole to win the U.S. Open at Pebble Beach. Four years ago he hit a 213-yard 2-iron over the flag at the final hole of the Royal Birkdale Golf Club in Sandwich, England, to win his fifth British Open. He was golf's best then: Watson, not Nicklaus, not Seve Ballesteros, not Greg Norman.

At the 1984 British Open, however, Watson pushed a 2-iron on to the road on the 71st hole at St. Andrews, Scotland, to lose to Ballesteros. He had wanted this Open so badly; it would mean he'd won a British Open on every Scottish course used for the championship. He would also have won at the Old Course, where Bobby Jones and Nicklaus had won.

Watson has always claimed that the 2-iron he missed at St. Andrews didn't bother him, and that the dozen makeable putts he missed the last round didn't agitate him. But if a chip-in to win a U.S. Open gives self-assurance, might not miscues to lose a British Open instil self-doubt? Watson hasn't been the same since St. Andrews.

This week at the Masters, Watson decided, as he put it, "to be quiet, to let others do the talking." Sam Snead, a man Watson watches for the tempo of his swing, worked with him a bit on the range and spoke later.

"I think Tom's timing is off," Snead said. "That's what he needs to work on. And maybe he shouldn't be as hard on himself. In golf, if you don't have more than seven shots after a round that you want to take over, you've done awfully well."

Earlier this week, Watson said he was swinging better, that he "has the clubhead on the path I want it, which for me means better timing." He also said he felt more at ease over short putts. "At least when I set up for the putt I feel I'm going to make it. That's half the battle."

The other half is good results. Watson has holed some very tricky putts and hit a number of good iron shots during the first 36 holes at the Masters. Every shot that turns out as he planned it helps to cancel the frustrations of the past few years.

"I'm not close to the level I was when I was playing my best," Watson said. "But I am hitting enough good shots to make me believe I can win the golf tournament."

The Globe and Mail, July 22, 1989

What a pleasure it would be to see Tom Watson win the British Open this weekend. His opening rounds of 69-68, seven-under-par, have put him two shots from Wayne Grady's lead and set up what could be golf's most exciting finale since Jack Nicklaus won the 1986 Masters.

Scores of 69 and 68 are what Watson was shooting in his heyday, when he won five British Opens, two Masters, and one U.S. Open. His last British Open win was at Royal Birkdale in 1983, the year after he won at Troon. He has good memories heading into the weekend, and he may have some exceptional ones after it's over.

Troon has brought out the Watson of old. He's holed shots from off the greens and made pars from perilous lies. And he's been emotional, even nervous — feelings he hasn't often experienced since 1985, a period during which he's won only one tournament on the PGA Tour. He hasn't won a major since 1983 at Birkdale. The game has been beside him, not part of him. He's searched for it, and now, maybe, he's found it.

"I felt very much in command and control," Watson said after his round yesterday. There was a smile on his face. He had a look Watson observers have seen before — at Turnberry down the road from Troon, where he shot 65-66 to take Nicklaus by a shot in their famous Open duel in 1977; at Pebble Beach in 1982, where he advanced to the scrubby rough left of the 17th green in the final round and then holed a pitch shot to wrest the lead from Nicklaus, and go on to win. He relished each shot, felt nothing was impossible.

That's been his mood at Troon. There's an appealing reckless-
ness about the way he's approached the ball. He said his golf has
been exciting. He's involved.

Should Watson win, golf intellectuals will say that the few
miracles he's performed the first two rounds by holing pitch
shots and bunker shots were omens, and that's what happens to
people meant to win majors. Should he lose, the same Ph.D.s of
golfdom will say a man can't expect to go on holing shots from
off the green for four rounds.

Watson's task this weekend will be to hole the crucial short
putts. He'll need the tunnel vision he had for so many years,
years when he could miss a green by 30 yards and still make par.

Watson will also need to rebound from the inevitable adversity
that he'll face as the weekend unfolds. He's admitted many times
in recent years that he's come unravelled on the weekends. The
sureness of stroke hasn't been there.

But it may be a revitalized Watson at Troon. Recently he saw
David Leadbetter, guru to such golfers as Nick Faldo, Nick Price
and David Frost. His swing mildly adjusted, he has been more at
ease. A complex man who thinks deeply — not always a good
thing in a slow game like golf, where there is too much time to
think — Watson seems to be playing unconsciously at Troon.
That's the way winners play; they subdue the buzzing interrup-
tion of the conscious mind, and let the game play through them.

Thus far at Troon, Watson hasn't even gone to the practice
tee — not since Monday evening. Why work when you're performing magic? Let it happen. Let things be.

"I haven't found it necessary to go to the practice tee," Watson
said yesterday. "I want to keep good thoughts about the swing.
Going to the practice tee might confuse me."

Maybe Watson won't get confused this weekend. Maybe Seve
Ballesteros was right a month ago when he said at the U.S. Open
that top golfers usually have one more major left in them, at
least one more. It happened when Nicklaus won the 1986 Masters, at age 46; when Ray Floyd won the U.S. Open the same
year, at 43. Watson turns 40 in September.

Should Watson win, he'll join Englishman Harry Vardon as
only the second man to win six British Opens. More important, a

win would regenerate Watson; we could look forward to more crisply played golf from him.

Six years ago I watched Watson hit the finest pressure shot I've seen: a 213-yard No. 2-iron that covered the flag all the way to the last green at Royal Birkdale. Watson needed par to win that Open and got it. He didn't waste a moment to hit the shot. Step up, assess and hit.

Will he hit such a shot under similar circumstances this weekend? Will his putting hold up? Will the Scottish fans — Watson-lovers almost without exception — be able to chant "Tom Watson, Tom Watson," as they have done in the past, as they would love to do this weekend?

"You get close enough to feel you can master golf," Watson once said. "You breathe it, smell it. But you really can't master it. Ben Hogan may be the only person to have really come close to it for a long time."

Golf needs a Watson win. Watson needs to win. Let's see if he's got the magic one more time.

The Globe and Mail, **December 19, 1990**

Sometimes it hurts to have integrity. And make no mistake: Tom Watson is hurting, three weeks after he resigned from the Kansas City Country Club because it wouldn't allow Henry Bloch, a Jew, to join.

Watson acted swiftly when he learned that Bloch, co-founder and chairman of the tax preparation company H & R Block Inc., was refused admission to the club. Watson's wife, Linda, and his two children are Jewish and so there was only one decision to make: Leave the club to which he had belonged since he was a child.

No one who knows Watson could have been surprised at his move. For instance, the winner of eight major championships has turned down invitations to participate in the Sun City In-vitational in South Africa. Never mind the $1 million first prize offered to the limited field. Watson won't play.

He also hasn't turned himself into a walking billboard for commercial sponsors, unlike golfers who adorn every corner of their apparel with company names. Watson can't be bought and he will not compromise his principles.

That's why he acted when Bloch couldn't get into the club. In fact, Bloch's application never even reached the club's board, though he was properly sponsored by scions of the community. Watson was distressed, to say the least.

"This is something I personally can't live with," he said in late November, when news of his withdrawal was made public. "I wish people would get together and say that a person with different religious beliefs is okay. It's time for people to take their heads out of the sand."

He hasn't spoken publicly again on the subject, as is his way. He has never talked to the media about his reasons for not playing in Sun City. He rarely discusses his commercial associations. His actions say enough. What they don't indicate is how upset he feels.

After all, Watson grew up at the Kansas City Country Club. Some years ago, he sat in the locker room, where he was being interviewed, and pointed to an area of the course where he likes to hit balls, no matter how cold it is. This was his golfing home, where he learned the game from Stan Thirsk, still the club pro.

"Tom is terribly upset by the matter," his brother-in-law and manager, Chuck Rubin, said this week from his law office in Kansas City. "It's a deeply personal matter to him, one that is very troublesome."

Watson has taken a lot of heat from certain factions of the Kansas City community. Some people think he's out to embarrass them. But he doesn't act for those reasons.

Watson makes up his mind about acting on the issue of the day. He feels strongly about the Jewish issue, but has chosen not to act on the matter of the men-only club to which he belongs.

"Tom isn't a crusader," Rubin said. "He belongs to Butler (a club near Chicago where Watson won his first pro event and that has given up the Western Open next year because it refuses to change its men-only membership policy).

"He defends the right of private clubs to invite who they want to, even to have a bigoted club. Whether he belongs or not is his decision, a personal statement."

Watson's statement couldn't be much stronger on the matter of the Kansas City club not admitting a Jewish member. The issue obviously got to him more, it appears, than the one at Butler National.

Watson's action, however, had nothing to do with his receiving the William Richardson Award. The Golf Writers Association of America recently gave the award to him for his contribution to golf over the years, but the voting was done before anyone knew there was a problem at his club.

This is important to understand because it diminishes Watson to suggest his recent action is unusual. He has always had an instinct to act intelligently. He likes an award and a big cheque as much as the next golfer, but he plays the game for love, not money. That's a cliché, but it's true.

Watson is simply a man to whom golf isn't everything. In an interview at the 1988 U.S. Open in Brookline, Massachusetts, he asked about the condition of George Knudson, then battling the cancer from which he died. Next, Watson chatted knowledgeably about the issues in the Canadian federal election.

Now he feels called to act against discrimination on the basis of religion at the club to which he still feels so close. As it happens, the club has decided to invite Bloch to join and he has indicated he will accept.

Watson hasn't responded to the club's change of heart. Who knows whether he will apply to get back in? He doesn't have too many changes of heart.

The Kansas City Country Club has damaged its reputation forever. And Watson can never feel the same way about it. He's wounded, but that's because he cares about important issues. Maybe his balanced stance will make other people care.

Richard Zokol

Toronto Life, **June 1984**
There's a credo of golf that goes something like this: Those who mean to play the game well must be careful not to become upset by bad shots or enthralled by good shots. It is best, as British writer Bernard Darwin once said of five-time British Open winner James Braid, to be "resolute, yet tranquil and serene."

A wonderful homily to be sure, but it's a difficult state to achieve. Temperament is as often credited as the reason for victory as it is for defeat. For it's human, all too human, to react to the birdies and bogeys of an outrageous game that offers no release for elation or tension. What's a golfer supposed to do if he cares? Should he take his frustrations out on the ball, only to find it veering into the woods? Should he spike the golf ball after sinking a birdie putt across the green?

Without any place to ventilate their emotions, golfers do what comes unnaturally: they suppress them. There's a received wisdom at the heart of golf that every player takes as his own: Feelings can hurt your game, so be on the lookout lest they overwhelm you.

And yet a golfer can't turn himself into a zombie. He has to feel the blood flow. He has to be stimulated enough to concentrate on his golf, but not so overloaded that he can't swing without rhythm. He needs what Canadian professional George Knudson calls a "volcanic desire," the kind that gets him up in the morning with a hunger for competition. But he also needs, as Knudson says, "to know how to control that emotion, to let it enhance his performance rather than detract from it."

Most golfers don't know how to control their emotions. Out of fear, they try to achieve a Zen-like self-control. In his first 2 1/2 years on the Professional Golfers' Association tour, Vancouver pro Richard Zokol has gone so far as to make an art and science of the quest for the appropriate emotional state; in fact, no other golfer on the tour has made quite the effort Zokol has in this very challenging area of the game.

Cut from the same sensitive, high-strung and intelligent mold as Knudson (who has retired from the tour to teach) and U.S. pro Tom Weiskopf, the 25-year-old Zokol has come to appreciate that he cannot play his bet unless he is master of his reactions. This will be particularly evident during the Canadian Open from June 28 to July 1 at the Glen Abbey Golf Club, where Zokol, along with fellow Canadians Jim Nelford, Dave Barr and Dan Halldorson, will play in front of a home crowd for the first time this year. Pressure? There will be plenty, much of it self-imposed.

Zokol will be trying to play what he calls "cold-blooded golf." What that means, he explains, "is hitting a 1-iron two feet from the hole and not reacting. The ball doesn't care that I've hit it in that close. I've got the next shot to play. That's all that matters. Cold-blooded golf means getting the job done. Who cares about the course record I shot yesterday? Who cares if I'm not feeling well? No excuses, no rationalizations, no emotional ups and downs."

But emotional ups and downs are exactly what Zokol has been battling for the past 2 1/2 years. In 1982, his rookie year, he won $15,110; last year he improved to $38,107. This year he won $15,000 his first week out and then went into an extended tailspin. At various times he has shut himself in his room with the lights out to think his way through difficulties. He gave up friends at home in Vancouver so he wouldn't become dependent upon them for support. He fired caddies when he felt he was becoming too sensitive to their problems. At a tournament in California last year he miscalculated the yardage on one hole — an unpardonable error for a professional — and sent his ball over the green into shrubbery. When he finished the round he told me he had to stop losing his concentration. "I'm a professional golfer trying to make a living out here. But I'm losing my mind on the course. I get so I don't think right."

Zokol's bet pro finish was a tie for fifth at the 1982 Greater Milwaukee Open. It was also the tournament at which he demonstrated, in an obvious way, to what unusual lengths he would go to gain greater self-awareness and, ultimately, self-control. In the first round Zokol wore stereo headphones between shots. The soft rock he heard from a local FM station enabled him to quell the mental disturbances that, in the past, had descended into his swing. While the music played between shots, he put together a 65 to share the lead. A 69 in the second round kept him tied for the lead.

One magazine called him Walkman Zokol. Disco Dick was the name that stuck. But what counted was that the music allowed Zokol to concentrate on the shot at hand. It took care of the time between shots, surely the most invisible foe in golf. For golfers are prone, as American poet Wallace Stevens once wrote in a statement that could apply to the game, to becoming "too conscious of too many things at once."

Zokol held the lead in the tournament with four holes to play. He then faltered. "All of a sudden I felt so uncomfortable," he said after the round. "My anxiety made it hard for me to hit good shots. I was a product of the situation. It was controlling me rather than the other way around. I didn't know what to do with my excitement."

Still, Zokol had learned what anxiety could do to his game. He was one person for 68 holes, somebody else for the last four. He also learned that he could control his anxiety — but only to a point. Zokol came to realize that the music had only limited value, that it was like a drug, and thus something he didn't want to become addicted to.

About a year ago, Zokol met up with Richard Lonetto, a sports psychologist who studied at New York University and now teaches at the University of Guelph. Lonetto grew up playing stickball and basketball on the streets of Brooklyn and knew the value of controlled aggression. He also knew that emotions could savage performance when allowed to run rampant.

Lonetto had worked with Jim Nelford, Zokol's closest friend on the tour. He had shown the easily combustible golfer that anxiety and elation were quite normal and desirable emotions during a round of golf, but that he needn't be victimized by them. It was the difference between putting the lid on a pressure cooker for fear it would boil over, or simply letting the steam out. It was seeing emotions as vapours rather than vipers.

Zokol and Lonetto got together at a tournament in New Hampshire last summer. There Lonetto found a very confused golfer, who often stood over the ball without having decided what shot to play. Indecisiveness, Lonetto knew, guaranteed anxiety. So he encouraged Zokol to make his decision before stepping up to the ball. Zokol began to line up behind the ball and point his club down the fairway while doing so. He was developing a routine while maintaining his idiosyncrasies.

To further focus his attention, Zokol began to concentrate on his breathing. He developed a ritual that has since become his signature: After his practice swings, and before he sets the clubhead behind the ball, Zokol lifts his club parallel to the ground and takes a deep breath. That positive step adds further to the calmness induced by his decision about what shot to play. Without anxiety, Zokol can more easily feel the swing he wants to make, an absolutely essential element of good golf.

After Lonetto helped Zokol build his routine step-by-step, he wanted to dramatically illustrate the effects of anxiety. On the practice tee and on the course in New Hampshire, Lonetto wired Zokol to a cardiometer to measure his pulse rate. When Zokol went back to his old haphazard ways, the needle swung wildly. But when he tried his new methodical approach, there was a common pattern: As he lined up to the ball and looked down the fairway, his pulse rose steadily until he made his decision; that done, his pulse went into what Lonetto calls "a nice decline, which meant he was locking in and concentrating"; while he walked to the ball there was a rhythmic, smooth rise, and while he stood over the ball the rise continued until he took his deep breath; finally, as he swung, another rise occurred, which peaked at impact then dropped.

"It's a wave-like pattern right through," Lonetto says. "When Zokol is really into it, the pattern is almost identical from clue to club, although it is necessarily shortened for the shorter clubs and especially shortened in putting. But the pattern, the rhythm, is what we are looking for. Now Zokol knows what's going on when he's winning well, and he sees that the more focused he is, the better he plays."

What it's meant for Zokol, since he and Lonetto started working together, is that he knows he must curb outside distractions. This is a golfer who needs a quiet mind to play his best. And the quieter his mind is, the more effectively he can play "cold-blooded golf."

During the Bay Hill Classic in Orlando, Florida, this past spring, Zokol showed just how well he could now focus his attention and energies. In the last round, he played with Victor Regalado, another close friend and the person with whom he was rooming that week. He was so into his round that when Regalado talked to him he brushed him off. On one hole he saw Regalado hit his ball into the water, knew he had made a double-bogey, but still marked down a par on the card after Regalado two-putted.

"My data was all confused there," Zokol said. "I had seen every shot, but it just didn't register. If I had thought about it for a minute I would have marked the double on the card. But I felt so stimulated that round. And that stimulated my mood, got me cold and callous. I neglected my friend because my concentration was all on my golf."

Coming into the Canadian Open, Zokol says he's the same person he was when he began to work with Lonetto, but "far less confused. Lonetto kick-started the engine. He enlightened me. He opened the door. I know who I am now, how I want to feel, how to feel that way. Now it's a question of my going ahead and doing it. Those are two great words: Do it."

To which George Knudson, who has had his own battles with emotional upheavals on the course, adds: "If Zokol was so hypertense before, and still managed to stay in competition on the tour, then there's no telling what kind of talent he is — or will be — now that he's learned how to control that hypertension. We'll see what happens if he gets into contention. That's where he'll really show his goods."

The Globe and Mail, **April 15, 1992**
While Fred Couples was winning the Masters Sunday in Augusta, Georgia, Richard Zokol was winning the Deposit-Guaranty Golf Classic in Hattiesburg, Mississippi. And Zokol's win could mean as much to his progress as Couples's will to his.

For confirmation of that fact, one need only listen to Jack Nicklaus. He's won 70 PGA Tour events, as well as three British Opens. The man knows what winning can mean to a player, no matter where he wins.

Consider what happened when Nicklaus played his first Senior PGA Tour event. That was the Tradition in April 1990, a week before the Masters. Nicklaus hadn't been playing well, and needed something good to happen; a win in his senior tour debut would do the job.

Nicklaus did win. Then, asked about his chances at Augusta the following week, he had a simple answer.

"My chances are terrific," he said.

Nicklaus didn't win that Masters. But he was in contention and finished sixth. It was all because he had won the week before. His confidence was back. Never mind that his win hadn't come on the regular PGA Tour. A win is a win.

Zokol knows that. He's been on the PGA Tour since 1982, and hadn't won prior to Hattiesburg. Zokol even had to go back to qualify for his PGA Tour card the past two years. That sort of career path doesn't guarantee confidence.

But his win at the Deposit-Guaranty should help. The $54,000 first prize will also help ensure that he can play the rest of 1992 with some security. Zokol and his wife, Joanie, have 4-year-old twin boys and a daughter who's not yet 2. They can use the money.

"But the best thing about the win is that I broke the ice," Zokol said yesterday from Kelowna, British Columbia, where he was having some business meetings. "Sure, it's not the Masters, but it's a PGA Tour win."

That it is, even though it's an odd kind of PGA Tour win. The PGA Tour counts money won there as official money, so Zokol is a long way towards ensuring he will make the top 125 and retain his PGA Tour card. But the win doesn't get him into such limited field invitations as the World Series of Golf and the Memorial. And it won't qualify Zokol for the Tournament of Champions or next year's Masters. The reason is obvious. The Hattiesburg tournament didn't draw the quantity of top players that a tournament such as the Canadian Open, for one, does. It was played opposite the Masters, and so players who hadn't qualified to play in the azaleas and dogwoods were left to fend for themselves in Hattiesburg.

But let's not forget, this was a win. Zokol had to put his game together and beat, oh, Mike Donald for starters. Donald led after three rounds in Mississippi and he also did some good in the

1990 U.S. Open. He got into a playoff there with eventual winner Hale Irwin.

Donald is also Couples's closest friend in professional golf. That being the case, maybe it's not too much to think that the energy swirling around Couples could influence Zokol.

Something happened at the tournament Zokol won anyway. That was especially time during Sunday's last round, when Zokol worked hard to keep himself calm and in control.

"I'd said to my caddie at the beginning of the week that we should be sharp," Zokol said. "I'd been playing well, but I hadn't put the ball-striking and putting together in the same week. But I felt good about all parts of my game coming in. My goal was to be alert, to give myself every opportunity to win."

Zokol had been helped during the years in such matters by Dr. Richard Lonetto, a Toronto psychology professor who has worked with athletes. Zokol is hyper by nature, and needed to learn to relax on the course.

"I drifted in and out of what we were working on," Zokol said. "Recently, though, I've been focusing more on controlling my emotions."

He needed to do just that as the tournament wound down. Zokol made two mid-length birdie putts on the 15th and 16th to tie for the lead, and then a par-saving 12-foot putt the next hole after rattling his drive around in the trees. He got a good break when his ball stayed two inches in bounds.

That's the kind of break golfers often need to win. Couples got one at the 12th hole on Sunday when his tee shot on the par-three held up on a bank above Rae's Creek. He took advantage of that mind-boggling break that seemed to defy gravity.

Zokol also took advantage of his break. He went on to par the final hole and then won when Donald and Mike Nicolette couldn't tie him.

"What I like," Zokol said, "and I'm quoting Ray Floyd, is that when luck goes their way winners capitalize on it. That's what happened to me."

But more than luck got Zokol the win. His game seems more solid than ever, and his self-talk calmed him down. He let himself play well.

And now that Zokol has conquered Mississippi, can the next step be far behind? Who knows, maybe a PGA Tour event where everybody is entered is next on Zokol's agenda. He knows he can win now. Thinking it is one thing, doing it quite another.

Chapter Eight

LEGENDS

SERENDIPITY PLAYS its part in golf writing as it does in other walks of life. That was the case early one April evening in 1985 at the Augusta National when, turning a corner on the second-floor veranda overlooking the course, I nearly bumped into Gene Sarazen, winner of the 1935 Masters, the 1922 and 1932 U.S. Opens, the 1932 British Open, and the 1922, 1923 and 1933 PGA Championships. Sarazen was then 83; two days later he would play the front nine to lead off the Masters as part of the ceremonial twosome. His swing was still easy and fluid, and his memory sharp. We talked that early evening at some length, and I include in this section the column that developed from that chance encounter. I also include a section on Arnold Palmer, a golfer who needs no introduction. I particularly enjoyed a conversation we had in the parking lot of the Cherry Hills club in Denver during the 1985 PGA championship about his win in the 1955 Canadian Open.

The glimpses offered here represent some of my most cherished moments in golf. Certainly each of the golfers warrants treatment at greater length and depth. But when that wasn't possible, I was always pleased just to have a short time with a player, or, in the case of Byron Nelson, to write of him on the occasion of a celebration of an astonishing achievement. While I have yet to sit down with Nelson for any stretch of time, I do recall a brief chat with him in the clubhouse of the Tournament Players Club. His student and friend Tom Watson was having some swing difficulties then, and when I asked Nelson what he thought the problem was, he answered, "Tom's in that unfortunate position where he's trying to try." Watson, that is, wasn't at ease with his swing. I believe Nelson's comment is one of the most astute observations I have heard in the game.

Nelson's remark was brilliant in its clarity, and perhaps it was derived from his having to answer one question, and one question only, in a passing moment. His statement was so quick, so sharp, that it stands out in my mind. That's also the case with some of the wise comments Roberto De Vicenzo made when he was honoured in 1986 at Jack Nicklaus's Memorial Tournament. Then he spoke to a gathering, and we all listened as he imparted some of the ideas that he had gathered in a long golfing life.

Lee Trevino played in that tournament as well, but I did not see him there. To me, the real Trevino can best be appreciated during a major championship, when the rough is high, the fairways narrow, the requirement of accuracy into the greens at a premium. Trevino may be the most accurate ball-striker in the game, day in and day out; even today, when he plays the Senior PGA Tour exclusively but for majors, Trevino is still, along with Nick Faldo, the golfer to watch for precision. Indeed, his win in the 1984 PGA Championship at Shoal Creek in Birmingham, Alabama, was a demonstration of golf at its best. Trevino was especially sharp with his driver on the skinny fairways bordered by punishing rough. He could be counted on to find the fairways. His win was cause for celebration; I did not attend that PGA but followed on television. Images of the Trevino I had seen over the years came to mind; it was good to write about him again.

I also write about Chi-Chi Rodriguez. If you didn't know who he was you would think he had a 10 handicap. How can somebody swing so wildly, nearly fall off his feet after hitting the ball? But Chi-Chi is testimony to golf as an individual game. Moreover, he is one of the real gentlemen in golf, a joyful person who must be a wonderful guest around the dinner table. He can talk and he can talk and he can talk. Chi-Chi's rap is dimpled patter, chock-full of anecdote, busy with side trips to people and places in the game.

That's also true for the great Sam Snead. Sweet-swinging Sammy is supposed to be a curmudgeon. Maybe so, but he seemed a real softie the day I visited him at his home in the mountains outside Hot Springs, Virginia. We had a round of golf and then we talked at his home. It was certainly one of the more memorable experiences that I have had, a glimpse into the life of one of the true legends of golf. I treasure many of these experiences, but the day with Snead stands out. It was a highlight, and I'm glad I can share the day again.

Byron Nelson

The Globe and Mail, **October 17, 1990**
It all happened 45 years ago. Byron Nelson, then 33, won 11 consecutive tournaments, the finale at the Thornhill Country Club outside Toronto. His was a remarkable performance that nobody had come close to before. Nor has anybody since.

Now the Hope Valley Country Club in Durham, North Carolina, where Nelson won his fourth consecutive event in 1945, has invited representatives of the 11 clubs to honour Nelson's streak. The celebration will occur on Friday, and representatives of eight clubs, including Thornhill and Islemere, where Nelson won the Montreal Open, will attend.

Nelson will also be there. Now 78, he is one of golf's special people: one of the game's sweetest swingers, friend and mentor to Tom Watson, often a member of the honorary twosome that begins the Masters 30 minutes before the competitors play away. He lives on a ranch in Roanoke, Texas, with his wife, Peggy, and when you talk about him, you speak of one of the game's most courteous players.

Here's an example. Nelson had finished his final round at Thornhill and was the clear winner. A crowd gathered on the last green.

"If you don't mind, gentlemen," Nelson said, "let's move off the green before doing our talking. There are still some players out on the course and there's no need to spoil this green for them."

That was Nelson, or Lord Byron as he was known. His upright swing was a precursor of the modern power swing. Nelson ranks with Sam Snead, Ben Hogan and Jack Nicklaus as one of the four finest golfers of the last half-century.

Still, some people disparaged Nelson's accomplishments in 1945. They argued that he was playing against fields diluted because of golfers involved in the Second World War. Some quibbled that he played on shorter courses without much rough, and that he was sharp because he was never away from competitive golf.

Let's take the last argument first. It's true that Nelson had played through the war. He hadn't been conscripted because he was a hemophiliac. So he golfed; was he to sit at home until his colleagues returned to the course?

Anyway, the war was over by 1945 and now many golfers were back. Snead had already won three Canadian Opens when he teed it up against Nelson at Thornhill. Top golfers Toney Penna, Claude Harmon and Vic Ghezzi were in the field, as were Canadian stars Gordon Brydson, Bob Gray and Jules Huot.

As for the courses, it's true that they might have been more troublesome in times of better maintenance. Still, Nelson was well under par for every tournament in his winning stretch — every tournament but the Canadian Open, and therein lies a story that will no doubt be told many times at Hope Valley on Friday, when Thornhill member John Parkinson attends the event on behalf of his club.

Parkinson worked during the tournament as a gofer. The youngster didn't watch Nelson the last day, but he's reconstructed the events around what was then the 10th hole and is now the 11th. The par-four hole is called Nelson's Folly.

"Nelson was three up on Ed Furgol after nine holes," Parkinson said before leaving for Durham the other day. "He was two under for the day, and even par for the tournament. But he wanted to break par for the Open, as he had for the other 10 tournaments."

Nelson examined the 10th hole and realized that if he cut the corner — there weren't many trees then in the area — he could reach the green. Why not go for it, maybe make an eagle?

"I believe he went for the green," Parkinson said. "But there weren't many birdies on the hole that last day. My guess is that the pin was on the front of the green and the green was hard. Nobody could get close to the hole. Nelson made a five instead of a sure par. I've decided that this is the truth because nobody will contradict me, and neither do books or records I've consulted."

Nelson doesn't remember what transpired on the 10th hole. But Hope Valley pro Johnny Cake will take Nelson wherever he wants to go on Friday to hear whatever others remember. Nelson will then speak at dinner.

"It's like a dream come true," Hope Valley member John Moorhead and the instigator of the event said of the coming affair. "If you've ever been around Nelson, you know that there's an aura about him."

That there is. Nelson is one of the game's main gentlemen, and it is appropriate that Hope Valley has seen fit to honour him.

Arnold Palmer

The Globe and Mail, **January 22, 1983**
Palmer, 66; Palmer, 69; Palmer, 68. The three-round scores came from the Rancho Park Municipal Golf Course, scene of last week's Los Angeles Open. Arnold Palmer was one stroke from the lead, and it was 10 years since he had won on the PGA Tour. Now, in the final round, Palmer was birdieing three of the first five holes to take the lead and people who hadn't uttered the word "charisma" in years were garnishing every sentence with it. A short distance from the ecstatic fans, Tim Pierce, an assistant professional, looked out from his shop's window.

"Arnie's hot," Pierce said. "I've been watching him, and I think he's going to win. People haven't been as excited around here in years."

But Arnie (imagine fans calling Jack Nicklaus "Jackie") did not win. Victory had been but an idea for too long and now, over the final holes at Rancho, he could not make it happen. Eventually, he finished 10th, a model of persistence, an illustration that one can play golf until later in life, but also a dramatic example of the costs of the game, and of aging.

For Palmer's thrust was not only the wild call of a 53-year-old man whistling through 18 flagsticks at one of golf's graveyards. Neither should it be exaggerated as more than one week where experience and talent fused. But it is a reminder that golfers can, and do, go on and on, and that there are limitations to their performance.

When Palmer's swing shortened noticeably on the 10th tee and his drive skulked down the fairway and finished near a fence not far away, golfers watching him recognized a truth sometimes hidden: Flexibility and power decline with age, even with professional golfers.

Throughout a golfer's earlier years, maximum power and maximum accuracy are geometrically and physically compatible. Swing the club with maximum extension and there are no breaks in the arc. It is as if a car were being accelerated over three blocks rather than one. Clubhead speed is generated. Shots run long and straight, far and sure.

But then comes constriction. Muscles tighten, the sense of balance deteriorates with age, and, although golfers can remember and can feel a correct swing, they cannot produce it repeatedly.

Perhaps this is the price of aging. Byron Nelson was once asked how he knew it was time to leave golf. "When I found myself trying to try," said the man who won 11 professional tournaments in a row in 1945.

The belief that golf should be a game for all ages sometimes seems a curse. The golf swing is nothing but a motor skill. Once learned and grooved, for better or worse, it tends to remain. Quit the game for years and then come back. You still can be identified as easily by your swing as by your fingerprints. The memory of the good shots is visceral. Age does not diminish it; if anything, it makes acceptance of the changes more difficult.

It appears golf can be played forever. Once, on the Bruntsfield Links on a hilltop overlooking Edinburgh, four males played. A visitor walking the course noticed similarities in bearing and car-

riage in the members of the group. Upon questioning them, he
learned that four generations made up this foursome: a great-
grandfather in his nineties, the grandfather, father and son.

Because there are competitions for all ages, the golfer might
not notice the impositions of time. It is as if a group of teenagers
play hockey once a week into their mid-thirties and never realize
they are all slowing down at the same rate. But when a player in
his early twenties plays with the aging gang, the frame of reference is altered.

Similarly in golf. Palmer does not as readily notice his inevitable erosion when he plays on the Senior PGA Tour. He takes as
long as others to defrost on the practice tee. And so, hope is
generated. Last year, Palmer won $73,848 on the senior tour,
fourth behind Miller Barber, Don January and Bob Goalby. But
on the regular tour, he won only $6,621. That was good for
190th place.

The burgeoning of the senior tour combines with the nature of
the game — slow and methodical — to breed a brave arrogance
in the face of time on the part of the seniors. It is at once attractive and saddening.

Consider the Los Angeles Open again. There was Palmer, challenging the fates. There was Gene Littler, at 52, tied for the lead
after 54 holes. And Gay Brewer, 51 this March, tying for twelfth.
Here were golfers who will play the senior tour regularly when it
begins March 17 in Daytona Beach, but now they were contending with golfers half their age.

Could it be that the senior tour is not only acting as a forum
for competition, but as a kind of fountain of youth? There, golfers slake a universal thirst for rhythm, form, ease of motion and
grace, not to mention money. Revitalized, they then shuttle over
to the main tour to test the always false hypothesis that the wisdom and heart of the older man can beat the nervelessness and
sinews of the younger.

Golf might be the only game in which every player has a chance
to be a Gordie Howe. Julius Boros, now 61, had quintuple-bypass
surgery little more than a year ago and within 12 months shared
the lead, with Palmer, after three rounds of the PGA Seniors Championship. And how about Sam Snead? At 70, he still attracts a
following of golfers 50 years younger whenever he competes.

Of course, there are the distressing aspects of extended careers. Doug Floyd and Jim Ferrier have lifetime exemptions on the regular tour from their wins in the 1955 and 1947 PGA Championships. In past years, there has been no small resentment from younger players when Ford or Ferrier have taken their place on tour. And, in last year's Masters, Herman Keiser, the 1946 winner but now nearly 70, played in the tournament, only to shoot two very high scores. One wondered why he bothered.

Last year, Jack Nicklaus, J.C. Snead and George Archer were the only golfers over 40 to finish in the top 60 money-winners. Nicklaus, making his first start of 1983 in this week's Bob Hope Desert Classic, turned 42 yesterday.

On a spring day last year at the Muirfield Village Golf Club in Dublin, Ohio, Nicklaus extinguished one of the cigarettes he smokes away from the course and reflected on the changes he sees in his own body.

"There is nothing now, as far as ability goes," Nicklaus said, "that could keep me from playing well. Health, though, could, and that is something I had not considered until recently. I have been fortunate in that I have had very few injuries that have amounted to anything.

"But, in the last 18 months, I have had some back problems that have been lasting longer than they should. They don't keep me from playing, but they are annoying in that they are more frequent than they used to be. As you get older, those things happen more often, and I wonder whether these problems will get me before my desire to play good golf leaves me."

If Nicklaus is like others — a debatable point — his body will continue to change. And yet, he will still want to be on the course having to birdie the final hole to win. For that is the fun of the game, and Nicklaus, moderating a view he once held, understands that is a desire that bubbles forth even when the body is rejecting it.

"I think it's difficult for anybody to know when enough's enough," he said. "I once thought Arnold should give up competitive golf, maybe not play as much. But then I thought, Why? Arnold loves to play golf. It would be a shame for him to quit. Why in the world shouldn't he give pleasure to himself and others who watch him?"

The Globe and Mail, **April 13, 1985**

Augusta, Georgia — The word on the back of his irons was Peerless. The name on the golf bag was Palmer. Put them together and you had Peerless Palmer, Peerless Arnold Palmer, a man who shot 83 in the first round of the Masters on Thursday but still had more fans following him yesterday than did Curtis Strange, who was shooting a seven-under-par 65 right behind him.

The fans were talking about Strange's round as he brought his score down from an opening eight-over-par 80. He birdied the second, holed out an 8-iron on the third for an eagle and birdied the 11th, 12th, 13th and 14th. But they were watching Palmer, still the king of Augusta National, as he shot 72.

Palmer wasn't even playing with another Masters competitor. Since he had shot the highest round of the 77 competitors on Thursday, he was the odd man out and had to play in the first group.

Charlie Coe, an Augusta National member who tied for second with Palmer behind Gary Player in the 1961 Masters as an amateur, played along as a non-competing marker. But after nine holes, Coe left because of a knee problem. Palmer played alone from then on, accompanied by a tournament official who marked his card. It was the first time that he's played a tournament round alone.

But Palmer didn't really play by himself. He had friends everywhere. He was part of a love triangle that has included the Masters and its fans since he won the first of his four titles in 1958.

There was no sadness in a round that might have been an indignity for others not gifted with Palmer's ability to enjoy people. He looked at them. He made them feel they were important. It started when he arrived on the practice tee after 8 a.m. and it continued until he left the course.

"I want to make eye contact with the people," Palmer said after his round. "I want to say hello. I've done that all my life from the time I was a little boy. My dad taught me that."

Palmer never has wanted the gallery to think he wasn't noticing it. Some golfers, such as Gary Hallberg in his Indiana Jones hat, prefer to avoid eye contact, thinking it helps their concentration. That's one reason Hallberg wears the hat, in addition to thinking it gives him an identity on the course.

Palmer never has needed such assistance. They would have been encumbrances. His personal magnetism has made anything else unnecessary. He has thrived on eye contact, surely the most elementary way to relate to somebody. He may not be a social anthropologist, but he instinctively has understood what happens when eyes meet.

When Palmer left the practice green before his round, he was surrounded by teenagers, young men and women and people who must have been more than 80. They smiled and he returned their smiles, looking directly at those who spoke to him. They knew they meant as much to him as he does to them.

"The people understand when you enjoy them," he said, "and then they have a reason to follow and enjoy you. I feel they are really friends, though I might not know their names. But I recognize faces. Some people have been coming here for the 31 years I've been playing the Masters."

Throughout his round, it was apparent that Palmer doesn't take his friends for granted. He joked with them, though he didn't like the reason he was teeing off first.

When the starter introduced Coe as his playing partner, Palmer cast his first spell. "If he beats me," he said, "I'll kill him."

A couple of middle-aged men named Harlan Milstead and Leward Gainey walked along as Palmer played. They have had business dealings with him in Charlotte, North Carolina, where Palmer has one of his Cadillac dealerships, as well as an office building. Though Palmer doesn't get there much, they feel close to him.

Gainey spoke first. "That man, he's super. He's still the king, even if he shoots 100."

Then came Milstead. "After shooting that 83, Arnie didn't tuck his tail and run now, did he?"

No, he didn't. But he ran around the golf course yesterday. He played 18 holes in 2 hours 45 minutes, the final nine in an hour. He walked so briskly that you would have thought he was 25, not 55.

The gallery didn't care how he hit the ball. He was vigorous and youthful. He waved to his fans every time they applauded, acknowledging sections of the crowds like a symphony conductor bows to his audience around the concert hall.

By simply being himself, Palmer made an early-morning round at Augusta a celebration of affection between an athlete and his people. He was giving back to the game that has given him so much, because he wanted to, not because he had to. He won't be here on the weekend, but he has given his friends a Masters to remember.

The Globe and Mail, August 17, 1985

The king is now 55, and sometimes his game is tired. But 30 years ago this week, he made a mockery of the Weston Golf and Country Club and the Canadian Open, winning his first tournament as a professional. Pro golf hasn't been the same since.

Arnold Palmer was a strong young man who had won the U.S. Amateur the previous August. He had turned pro in November 1954, but had been able to accept money only since May. In those days, a new pro had to wait six months before cashing his cheques. It wouldn't have mattered to Palmer, though. As he recalled last week at the Professional Golfers' Association Championship in Denver, "I hadn't really had a lot of strong finishes, though I felt I was playing pretty well — hitting it long and fairly straight."

But then as now, long and fairly straight didn't necessarily mean low scores. Pro golf seemed foreign to the man who was to become the most popular figure in the game. He had some help on the pro caravan — Tommy (Thunder) Bolt as his mentor. But the kid who wasn't yet the king was still wet behind the irons — the pro nobody knew.

Palmer wasn't even mentioned in pre-tournament reports. Bolt and Slammin' Sammy Snead were favoured, along with Jackie Burke Jr., Dick Mayer and Porky Oliver.

Weston historian Claude Hergott wrote in a recent club newsletter that although a group of caddies had their pick of players — Snead and Burke excepted — Palmer's bag was one of the last chosen. "Among the caddies," Hergott wrote, "it was strictly a case of 'Arnold who?'"

Stan Leonard, meanwhile, was the Canadian choice. At 40, Leonard had just retired after 13 years as head pro at Vancouver's Marine Drive Golf Club to concentrate on competitive golf.

Palmer never had to make this decision. His every instinct pointed him towards pro golf. And so he arrived at Weston in quest of the $2,400 first prize in the Canadian Open.

At the time, an article in *The Globe* speculated on the Coca-Colonization of the world, a process whereby U.S. culture was filtering into foreign societies. This had already happened in golf, where nobody really felt a Canadian could win against the U.S. players, and where the Royal Canadian Golf Association had even put up a separate trophy and extra money for the low Canadian in the Open, as if to say the leader in that category would not be the winner in the tournament.

Weston was in top shape for the tournament, having survived the ravages of Hurricane Hazel in October 1954. At 6,408 yards, it was shorter than many tournament courses and the pros were predicting that 16 to 20 under par would win.

In the end, Palmer won with a 23-under 265 after rounds of 64-67-64-70. Burke was second with 269, while Leonard shot 272 to finish as low Canadian. Some 15,000 fans attended the tournament, including 6,000 on the final day. They walked right along with the players and Palmer had them in his overlapping and charming grip.

"The crowds were tremendous," Palmer said, "and they were very supportive." He also didn't mind admitting that, more than once, his ball hit a member of the gallery and rebounded into play. But those things happen when a golfer is winning.

As much as Palmer might have been assisted by lucky bounces, however, he also made his own breaks. Though it was another five years before he became known in the United States as the most aggressive player in golf because of his tendency to go for broke, he readily showed this style at Weston.

"I was playing with Bolt the last round and hooked a drive off the sixth tee." Palmer, still able to remember nearly every shot at Weston, said, "I had a six- or seven-shot lead at the time, and I remember Tommy indicating to me that I should pitch it out into the fairway. I sort of laughed at him, took a 6-iron and knocked it up through the trees on the green.

"Tommy wouldn't speak to me the rest of the round," Palmer continued, "because I took that shot through the trees. But that was my way. My father taught me to go get it. If you're shooting between two trees with a 10-foot opening, and you try to calculate the percentages, you'd be there forever."

But Palmer has never been a calculator. He's been the quintessential gambling golfer. Thirty years after Weston, he remembered the Canadian Open with a fondness reserved for life's special moments.

"It was the kicking-off point for me. It got me started on the winning trail and smoothed things out for me. The next year, I won a couple of tournaments and felt much more comfortable about what I was doing. The Canadian Open started all that."

The Globe and Mail, July 21, 1990

St. Andrews, Scotland — The crowds were applauding Arnold Palmer's every charismatic move during the second round of the Open Championship at the Old Course yesterday. That's because Palmer, the man who helped make the Open what it is, had announced that this was his last Open. An era that Palmer began in 1960 at St. Andrews ended yesterday in St. Andrews, when he missed the halfway cut despite playing as well as he thought was required.

Palmer was a wonder the first two rounds, shooting 73-71, even par. He came here playing poorly and even practice did not help. But something happened, and Palmer played inspired golf, especially over the last holes in the middle of the day. That was long before Greg Norman and Nick Faldo shot the lights out to push Palmer out; it had seemed that even par would make the cut, since all golfers within 10 shots of the lead get in. The low score was only seven-under par when Palmer finished.

Still, Palmer was impressive, especially after he stood on the 13th tee at one-over par for the tournament. He figured he needed to play the last five holes in level fours, or one under over that stretch. Palmer wanted to make the cut partly because he had missed it last year at Royal Troon with a pair of 82s, and

also because he had decided this would be his last Open, and
that the appropriate place to bow out would be at the Old
Course.

And so Palmer set himself a task that once he would not have
found onerous. But he has been shooting over 80 in some Senior
PGA Tour events. His swing was awry, his concentration gone.

But never mind, Palmer went to work and parred 13 and 14.
He made a 10-foot birdie putt on the 15th, then parred the 16th.
Next came a par on the frightening 17th Road Hole, when
Palmer ran his approach putt dead to the hole from 80 feet.

But there was still more to do, because Palmer hit too little
club into the shortish 18th and left himself in the Valley of Sin,
that depression at the front of the green that swallows golf balls.
Palmer hit a majestic approach putt from there, the ball running
all the way to the front lip of the hole before stopping. He
thought he had made the cut.

"It had been an ambition of mine to play the Open from the
day I could read newspapers and watch what was happening in
this Open championship," Palmer said earlier this week. "I also
never felt you could be the complete professional without having
won the Open. I felt that was something you had to do to complete your professionalism in the game of golf."

Palmer's presence has made people feel at home in the world
of golf, and in a large measure he contributed to the creation of
a world of golf. He wouldn't say so himself, but his first visit to
the Open in 1960 at the Old Course — the centenary year of the
championship — encouraged golfers from around the world, especially the United States, to play the Open. He finished second
to Australian Kel Nagle, and the era of the world Open began.

"As for the Americans coming over after I did," Palmer said in
his genuinely humble way, "I don't think the fact that I came
meant they were going to come, because I feel very strongly this
championship would have eventually become the championship
it has been."

That may be true, but still we must listen to others who willingly speak of what Palmer has done for the Open, and for golf.
We can listen, for instance, to Greg Norman, the man who, along
with Nick Faldo, has been shredding the Old Course in atypically
benign conditions.

"We owe everything to this man," Norman said this week. "He shaped the boundaries of modern golf. Whatever we achieve now is only because Arnie was out there to make it happen. I think he's a little sad, this being his last Open. But when you have set the highest standards, you must do what you think is right."

"We all have to be realistic," Palmer said after his round yesterday. "I'm chasing 61 years old, and if I could play good golf and know that I could, I would not be stopping. There would be no reason to stop. I love to play golf. But I don't like shooting 81 and 82 and will not do that."

And so Palmer took his last competitive journey round the Old Course yesterday. Nobody at midday felt that would be the case, least of all Palmer. In the end, Palmer walked proudly, as always. He never won at St. Andrews, but he did win the 1961 and 1962 Opens at Royal Birkdale and Troon. This Open is his twenty-second. His walk along the last fairway was memorable, though the people gathered all round would not have believed that his 36-hole score would not be good enough to grant him weekend play one more time.

Chi-Chi Rodriguez

The Globe and Mail, **April 17, 1987**
Montego Bay, Jamaica — Holding court on the practice range between the Tryall golf course and the deep blue sea, Chi-Chi Rodriguez, the world's kindest professional golfer, dispenses his usual brand of sunniness: a smile and a laugh here, a handshake there, and then a crisp, low-flying shot down the middle. If this is work, Chi-Chi implies, let's have more of it.

Rodriguez, a 52-year-old Puerto Rican, is here along with 11 colleagues from the Senior PGA Tour and 12 LPGA golfers. They're playing the $850,000 Mazda Champions, a team event that pairs the No. 1 Senior Tour player with the No. 1 LPGA player, and so on, for a first prize of $500,000. The 54-hole best-ball tourney begins tomorrow at Tryall, Jamaica's finest course. Chi-Chi's partner is Ayako Okamoto, as quiet as Chi-Chi is loquacious.

The money is nice, Chi-Chi acknowledges, but he's got other things on his mind. Though he's the top money-winner on the senior tour this year with more than $500,000, he hasn't forgotten his roots, the desperation that lurks off the course. Whack, another straight shot, and whack, another comment that shows this man isn't just another pro stashing dollars away.

But Chi-Chi doesn't have to talk about doing good for other people. He's shown his concern via the Chi-Chi Rodriguez Junior Golf Foundation, a program in Clearwater, Florida, that has been introducing troubled kids to golf for nine years and that has 18 of them in college. Chi-Chi says this means more to him than winning 10 U.S. Opens. His actions signify he isn't speaking falsely.

Chi-Chi started the Clearwater program to get kids off the street and into a healthy environment. Girls who have been raped, boys on their way to lives in and out of jail cells, kids without homes: these are the people Chi-Chi works with, former captives of a world far removed from the country clubs he's privileged to play, and from which he often calls them, friend that he is.

"I've never thought that kids have a problem," Chi-Chi explains as yet another shot soars towards a stand of palm trees. "To me, society has the problem. The kid is a version of what society creates."

It doesn't matter whether this stands up as accurate social theory. The point is that Chi-Chi and his volunteers at the foundation have provided a place for kids without any place. In the process, Chi-Chi himself has become a role model, not only for the kids but for his fellow golfers, if only they would pay attention.

Watch Chi-Chi on the course. He makes a birdie putt and dances to the hole, all the while flashing his putter like a sword, twisting and turning it in the sky and above the hole. This is golf as sport and entertainment, break-dancing on the links. No wonder he's been invited to the 1988 Seniors' Skins Game.

Chi-Chi's attitude derives from his own difficult circumstances years ago. He didn't have much while growing up in Puerto Rico. A smooth golf stroke led him to the pro golf scene and a world of friends, all of whom call him by his first name, just as they do Arnie, Jack and Fuzzy, themselves ambassadors of golf.

Chi-Chi won the first Ambassador of Golf Award in 1983 at the World Series of Golf. Here at Tryall he's shown why: At home on the range, happily grazing at pro-am cocktail parties or sitting at a seaside bar, he's a contented man.

But never complacent. Not the King of the Clinics, as the U.S. magazine *Golf Digest* will title a February piece about the golfer who can turn an instructional session into a party. Not Chi-Chi, who has plenty of work to do, even if he is wealthy.

"What does it mean to be rich?" Chi-Chi asks towards the end of his practice session. "Mother Teresa is the richest person on the earth, but she doesn't have a penny. A person is successful when he helps the needy, when he's learned the art of sharing."

And so go Chi-Chi's thoughts. His foundation has been leasing a course from Clearwater for a dollar, but is now building its own course. The program has taken some kids from a 0.60 grade-point average to 4.0.

Chi-Chi has one more thought, this time for George Knudson back in Toronto. Chi-Chi knows that Knudson has cancer, states flatly that he is one of the finest golfers ever — "George always had the club in the same slot" — and is aware that Knudson, 50, is eligible for the senior tour.

"I hope George gets out and plays here," golf's No. 1 ambassador says. "Tell him we want him out here. Tell him we need him."

Gene Sarazen

The Globe and Mail, **April 11, 1985**
Augusta, Georgia — On Tuesday evening, a man in a green jacket lingered on the clubhouse veranda at the Augusta National Golf Club. His name was Gene Sarazen, formerly Saraceni, winner of the 1935 Masters. He looked out in the direction of the 15th hole and remembered a shot he hit that called the world's attention to the Masters.

The shot was a 230-yard 4-wood that Sarazen, then 33, hit to the green on the par-five, 485-yarder in the final round. When he stood over the ball in the fairway, he was three strokes behind Craig Wood, who had finished with a six-under-par 282. Sarazen holed his shot for a double eagle, making up the three shots in one hole. He won the 36-hole playoff the next day by five strokes.

"Fifty years since the double eagle," Sarazen said, "I hate to think of it. It was great for the tournament, started it off."

A cool breeze blew across the veranda as Sarazen gazed over the course. He folded his arms across his chest to warm himself. In a few minutes, he would attend the Masters Club dinner for former champions, with 22 other winners.

The champions would remember the shot, although few, if any, saw it. The double eagle has become the golf shot heard around the world. It carried the pond in front of the green and rolled into the hole like a putt.

Sarazen's swing for that shot was smooth and effortless. If ever the swing is the reflection of the man, it has been, and still is, with Sarazen.

Could he possibly be 83? He spoke so clearly, and he laughed when reminded of a phrase that has been used to describe his swing rhythm.

"Sarazen just takes that club," somebody once said, "and rides through the ball."

British golf writer Henry Longhurst once marvelled at the ease with which Sarazen swung the golf club. "Whenever I get fouled up in the mechanics of the game," he wrote, "I just think of Sarazen."

Longhurst meant that Sarazen's swing was simple. It was simple in the way Sarazen is simple: unforced, relaxed, delightful to watch, easy to be around, pleasing to the eye and ear.

There is a touch of George Burns in Sarazen. He spoke with feeling when asked about anything to do with golf, always droll, always smiling.

On Arnold Palmer: "He's the most remarkable player this century, to have lasted with his swing. The same thing with Cal Peete and Miller Barber. There's no such thing as a good swing any more."

On golf balls: "People don't realize that the more dimples there are in a ball, the easier they are to putt. The ball doesn't slide off line as easily."

On aging: "I still enjoy golf. And I still play quite a bit. But when I was younger, I could get lots of stiff games. Now, nobody wants to play with an 83-year-old."

That's not quite true. Sarazen can get a game with anybody. Golfers everywhere would feel privileged to spend a few minutes with him.

Last night, at a dinner held by the PGA of America, Sarazen was given the Charlie Bartlett Award for service to golf. (Bartlett was a golf writer for the *Chicago Tribune* who once made a 22 on the par-five 13th hole at the Dunes club in Myrtle Beach, South Carolina, during the Golf Writers Association of America tournament.) The award should have been given at last year's U.S. Open, but Sarazen couldn't attend. It's more appropriate, anyway, that he received it at Augusta, 50 years after the big shot.

Today, at 8:45 a.m., Sarazen will lead the Masters field as it begins the tournament. He and Sam Snead, a mere 72, will form the ceremonial opening group.

Sarazen and Snead will play only nine holes. Around the sixth green, Sarazen might be able to catch a glimpse of the 15th green. He won't have to remember very hard to see his ball rolling into the hole again.

"My mind goes back to (Bobby) Jones when I'm here," Sarazen said the other night. "After a round, I'd go over to his cottage by the 10th tee for a drink. He'd ask me how I played, but, before I answered, he'd say, 'I know, if you didn't shoot a good score, you wouldn't be here today.'"

Sarazen shot a good score, all right, in that closing round in 1935. He and Jones must have enjoyed at least one good shot of bourbon, and maybe a couple of more the next day after Sarazen won the playoff. Fifty years later, on a night in Augusta, Sarazen's eyes twinkled when he remembered the way it was.

Lee Trevino

***The Globe and Mail,* August 24, 1984**
Lee Trevino's win in the PGA Championship last Sunday was an encouragement for every golfer who believes there's more than one way to swing a golf club. It was also a victory for golf watchers who feel the name of the game is accuracy, that tournament

courses should reward those who keep the ball in the fairway and punish the player who strays.

Shoal Creek in Birmingham, Alabama, was the perfect place for Trevino to show his class as one of the game's great shotmakers. The fairways of the Jack Nicklaus-designed course are 27 to 30 yards wide in the landing areas. Then there is an intermediate area of one-and-a-quarter-inch deep rough that extends seven feet off the fairways. Beyond that is the three-inch deep, Bermuda-type rough that keeps golfers from advancing the ball more than about 125 yards with even a full swing.

Trevino, 44, has long been able to shape his shots to the demands of a course. His quick mind calculates the flight the ball should take and, like a chess master playing an amateur, he makes his moves without hesitation.

Nobody would teach a beginner to swing like Trevino. He lines up far left of his target and sometimes seems to be aiming out of bounds. From the top of his swing, he makes a strong lower body move towards his target, drops the clubhead down with its face dead square, and comes through the ball with the face of the club on line longer than anybody, except perhaps Canada's Moe Norman. His patented left-to-right shot results, although he can draw the shot if the need arises. He's an individual who has always done things his own way, and not always the easy way.

Trevino came up the hard way. He lived in a four-room shack in Dallas without plumbing, electricity or windows. The kitchen had a dirt floor. He never knew who his father was.

But Trevino knew he belonged in the pro ranks. He knew his game, which was ball control. And he had the desire. Dirt floors and childhood without candy can do that to a person.

From there to Merion Golf Club for the U.S. Open against the finest golfer in the world was some kind of journey.

Trevino won that 1971 U.S. Open against Nicklaus. It was his second such victory, having taken the 1968 Open. He also won the British Open and Canadian Open that season during a five-week spurt and went on to win a total of 26 PGA tour events plus two British Opens through 1981.

That was it, or so it seemed. Trevino suffered through 1982 with serious back problems. Observers felt his problems began when he was hit by lightning during the 1975 Western Open near Chicago. Others felt his swing stressed his back. Trevino didn't know whether to buy the first opinion, but he certainly didn't agree with the second. How could he injure his back with a swing that was so much his own?

During the 1982 Canadian Open at Glen Abbey, there was a sad moment when Trevino couldn't get his tee shot across the water on the par-three, 12th hole, a distance of about 140 yards. He withdrew from the tournament. Shortly thereafter, he entered hospital to have a nerve deadened. That substantially reduced his back difficulties. However, during the past two years, he has only come close to winning.

At last March's Tournament Players Championship in Ponte Vedra, Florida, Trevino finished second to Fred Couples. He played the final 54 holes in 14 under par. He said that, because he no longer felt he was the player he once was, he could compete without expecting a lot of himself.

Trevino was putting his listeners on. He knew what kind of golf he was capable of, and his new wife, Claudia, was also telling him he could still win.

Last week, Trevino followed his usual practice routine since hurting his back. He hit only 25 to 30 balls before playing. His feel for the game is so acute that, instead of banging balls, he is able to relax in the locker room and visualize the shots he will need on the course.

At Shoal Creek last week, where the rough proved a psychological hazard equally as harsh as the island green on the 17th at the Tournament Players Club in Ponte Vedra, Trevino was the complete golfer. He was fifth in driving accuracy, second in hitting greens in regulation and ninth in putting. The combination brought him his sixth major championship and showed there's still plenty of jalapeno-hot spirit left in Supermex.

Sam Snead

The Globe and Mail, May 7, 1991

Hot Springs, Virginia — A person's life includes sadness and joy, not always in equal measures. The other day, while privileged to play golf with the legendary Sam Snead, I learned that the person who spends time in his natural habitat might be better able to cope with life's ups and downs.

There is no questioning Snead's status as a living legend and as a man of many parts — man of Virginia's Alleghany Mountains, man of golf's most elegant swing, man of regrets and still a few dreams. He gradually revealed these parts while we played the Cascades course, and later at his home high on a hill with views all round of the mountains, the wild country he grew up in and where he has always lived. It was a memorable experience.

Just short of his seventy-ninth birthday, Snead retains the balance that won some 135 pro tournaments, including three Canadian Opens, three PGA Championships, three Masters and a British Open. He never won a U.S. Open, and it still grates.

Sweet-swinging Sammy hit many fine shots during our round, but cussed every time he missed a shot. He sets up to the ball beautifully, and though his hands quiver momentarily, he is all smoothness and grace once he takes the club back. After his muscles loosened, he hit some long drives and irons that were right on the money.

Speaking of money, Snead likes to play for some and was holding court on that subject and others when I drove up. He said that he would rather watch squirrels than play for no money. Still, we decided to play for fun only and set off accompanied by Meister, Snead's golden retriever.

"You don't lose a ball with him," Snead said. Later Meister proved himself as he plucked an errant shot of mine from a stream on the fifth hole.

By then Snead had played some arresting shots. He'd missed the first four greens, but had saved par on three of the holes. And soon he favoured me with a tip.

"I'm gonna tell you something that'll help you stop hitting left, stop you from coming over the top," Snead said after I pulled a tee ball at the sixth. "Hit that ball with the club coming in at the same angle you set it at address. You can get it if you keep your right elbow tucked in to your side."

It doesn't matter how many lessons you've taken — Sam Snead talks, you listen. I did and played the sixth through the 16th holes as well as I could; then I succumbed to the golfer's disease of thinking about the good score that was possible. A couple of closing double bogeys and I was suitably chastened.

"Listen," Snead said, chuckling. "I wouldn't have given you the tip if we were playing for money. But stick with it."

Aside from the instruction, there was story after story. Slammin' Sammy has a million.

Snead spoke of how Ben Hogan was supposed to be so accurate that during a 36-hole day he had to play his shots in the afternoon round from his divots in the morning round.

"I told people that if Hogan was so good he could have put his ball a little right or a little left of the divot," Snead said.

The round soon ended, and Snead drove his Jeep at a fast clip to Chestnut Rail Farm, where he lives on 200 acres. A wall in his impressive trophy room holds a framed photo from a 1940 edition of *The Globe and Mail*, after Snead shot 67 in the first round of a Canadian Open that he would win. The picture is of Snead and his bride, Audrey. They were celebrating their honeymoon at the Open.

"I always thought the Canadian Open should be a major," Snead said.

The talk continued for a couple of hours. Snead spoke fondly of his wife, who died two years ago. He spoke quietly of his sons, one retarded since birth. The other hasn't found his place in life, and Snead has gone into golf course design in hopes they'll work together.

There was sorrow in Snead's voice and then a minute later there was a twinkle in his eyes. He had done what he had loved for 70 years, and exceedingly well, too.

"I thought if I was on I could beat anybody in the game," Snead said. "You got to think you can kill the cats. If you don't think that, you can't do it."

Then the visit ended. Snead walked past the Masters plates in a dining-room hutch before showing me to my car.

"Nice view here, isn't it?" he said. "You look down into the valley and up to the mountains when the leaves turn, there's no place prettier. My dad and his dad were born here, in a log cabin."

And so there was continuity at Chestnut Rail Farm. Golf had taken Snead far from his birthplace in Hot Springs, but he had really never left his home. Nor had the powerful swing he'd developed in these mountains left him. I can vouch for that.

Roberto De Vicenzo

***The Globe and Mail,* May 23, 1986**

"I tell you a secret about life and health," says Roberto De Vicenzo, winner of 240 golf tournaments around the world and honoree at the 1986 Memorial golf tournament. "Good teeth and a slow pace at all times. If you hurry then nothing seems to go right."

These words came to mind the other day as De Vicenzo sat beside Jack Nicklaus behind the 18th green at the Muirfield Village Golf Club and heard some of golf's elder statesmen speak of him. Invariably they turned to the famous incident in the 1968 Masters when De Vicenzo lost a chance to go into a playoff with Bob Goalby because he signed an incorrect scorecard.

That was the one time, perhaps, that De Vicenzo, 63, hurried. Disappointed after bogeying the 18th hole, he didn't notice that Tommy Aaron had given him a par-four on the 17th rather than the birdie three he'd made. Since a golfer is responsible for the score on each hole, when he signed the card he had to accept the higher score. That put De Vicenzo a shot behind Goalby, and, one would think, set the stage for a major depression.

The depression never came as De Vicenzo reacted to his misfortune in a way that won and continues to win friends for him everywhere. "I am a stupeed," he told the world, and that Sunday evening in Augusta at dinner with rules official Ike Grainger he said, "I'm sorry I cause you trouble."

Of course he didn't cause Grainger any trouble, just heartache. Nobody likes a rule to take a victory away from a golfer, particularly when everybody knew that De Vicenzo had birdied the 17th. But De Vicenzo believed then and believes now that "the rule is very good, very clear. I feel sorry after the Masters, but that is the rule."

Although the rule may have cost De Vicenzo the Masters, it has also in the intervening years made the golf world aware of

the gentleman that he is. In a game in which players become
consumed with their worries about swinging the club — sometimes their very identities seem to hang on whether they can hit
a high 6-iron to a pin hidden behind a bunker — De Vicenzo has
focused outside himself.

This week has been full of examples of De Vicenzo's gracious-
ness. Maybe it's the way he speaks — some people call it PGA
English — but he has charmed all who have met him. "I feeling
fantastic," he said when Nicklaus honoured him at the ceremony.
"This be nice for me, my family, friends and my country."

His country is Argentina, and it was at his home in Buenos
Aires a year ago that he received a call from Nicklaus asking if he
would accept being the honoree this week. He did accept, of
course, but when he got off the phone he said to his wife,
"Maybe Jack, he got a wrong number."

Nicklaus doesn't come up with many wrong numbers — as
evidenced by his final-round 65 to win the Masters last
month — and he certainly didn't come up with one when he
called Buenos Aires. A year after the call, De Vicenzo flew to
Columbus, to join such figures as Bob Jones, Walter Hagen, Gene
Sarazen and Byron Nelson as an honoree. Sarazen and Nelson
have been at Muirfield Village this week; it's part of Nicklaus's
stature in golf that he can invite such people to his tournament,
and that they attend.

De Vicenzo is doing more, however, than accepting an award.
He is the first honoree to play in the Memorial; though he
knows he has little or no chance of winning, he still can play the
kind of golf that makes watching him a lesson in how simple the
golf swing can be, and how rhythm and tempo are necessary in
golf no less than they are in music. De Vicenzo is a sweet
swinger who never is out of balance. No hurry, as he says.

His style allows De Vicenzo to sometimes hit the ball tremendous distances. In a practice round the other day, Nicklaus hit
two long balls off one tee. De Vicenzo turned to Nicklaus and
said, "I knock it 100 yards by you." Then he drove past both of
Nicklaus's shots.

De Vicenzo still hits 400 balls daily in Buenos Aires. He took
up golf more than half a century ago when he caddied at a
course a couple of blocks from his home. He turned pro at 15,

won the 1967 British Open, nine events on the PGA Tour and the national championships of 15 countries.

With a record like that, and given his character, it's appropriate that De Vicenzo was elected a Memorial honoree. Through today, at least, he will compete in the Memorial "to make my appreciation to all the people who make me feel so good." No doubt he will also apply another aspect of his philosophy: "Play it with your heart, pick up the club and hit."

Chapter Nine

TOURNAMENTS

A SORT of manic quality overtakes golf writers as a tournament draws to a close. We scramble around the course, particularly at majors, trying to figure out where we should be. It's a guessing game, because the appeal of the majors in particular is that anything can happen over the closing holes. It's often said of the Masters, for one, that the tournament really doesn't start until the last nine holes on Sunday. That's borne out most years, and it's not surprising: The back nine at Augusta National can cause more swings in fortune than the failure of a bank.

Consider 1986, the year that Jack Nicklaus holed a birdie putt of modest length on the ninth hole and then shot six-under-par 30 to win his sixth Masters. This was an emotional day for everybody privileged to see the event, and no doubt even for viewers watching on television. Events were unfolding so rapidly and in such astonishing ways that it was hard to keep up. I remember feeling swept along a current the likes of which I could not control nor wished to. This was the thrill of watching a major at the end, and I suppose it may be a double thrill for a golf writer. We are caught up in the maze, and while we hope things will soon clear up so that we can write our stories, we also want the tournament to come down to the final putt. It's amazing how often majors do just that.

During the last day of the 1986 Masters, I felt as if I had run a race. Nicklaus was playing golf that was jumping off the skin of the course, while Seve Ballesteros, Greg Norman and Tom Kite were also in it. I took up a position to the left of the 15th green on the top row of a spectator stand. It was possible from there to watch second shots into the par-five 15th from the crest of the hill, and to follow the play all along the par-three 16th to the left. First came Nicklaus, holing his eagle putt at the 15th, and then soon after Ballesteros was slumped over in the 15th fairway. I remember so vividly the arc of his shot from the fairway; it barely rose off the ground, like an airplane that had lost power and couldn't take off. The ball then swung left in a sickening hook flight and never looked as if it had a chance of carrying the water in front of the green. That was it for Ballesteros. Meanwhile, just before that, Nicklaus struck a perfect 6-iron across the water to within three feet of the hole at the par-three 16th. He bent down to pick up his tee before he even saw the ball land; Nicklaus has trouble seeing his shots land, anyway, but in this case he knew he had hit the required shot. Next came his birdie putt at the 17th, his tongue hanging out of his mouth as the ball headed straight for the hole. This was the greatest golfer in the game, and here he was, hungry as ever for another major, his twentieth. He got it, too, as neither Norman nor Kite could stay with him.

But that Masters was not the only memorable major that comes to mind. There was the 1984 British Open, when Tom Watson hit a 2-iron over the green at the Road Hole, the 17th, when tied with Seve Ballesteros at the Old Course. Ballesteros a moment later holed a birdie putt at the last hole to secure the championship. I was back with Watson at the 17th green as he tried to save his par from the road, but couldn't. The roar from the 18th when Ballesteros's putt fell rings in my ears.

Then there was the 1986 PGA Championship at Inverness in Toledo, Ohio, when Bob Tway holed from a greenside bunker at the last hole to defeat Greg Norman, who was playing with him. A year later, Larry Mize pitched in from 140 feet away on the second playoff hole at Augusta, and again it was Norman who felt the decisive blow. But the picture I most remember is of Ballesteros trudging back up the hill from the 10th green towards the clubhouse, having missed a five-foot par putt that would have kept him in the playoff. There were tears in Ballesteros's eyes as he made the long walk up the hill.

Majors are full of such moments: Curtis Strange parring his way along the back nine the last day of the 1989 U.S. Open at Oak Hill in Rochester, biding his time until, as he felt, a birdie putt would fall. It did at the 16th, and a few minutes later Strange had won his second consecutive U.S. Open. A year later it was Hale Irwin on the last green at Medinah No. 3 outside Chicago, holing a 45-foot birdie putt on the last hole that would get him into a playoff for the U.S. Open with Mike Donald; Irwin went into an antic dance around the green, high-fiving fans who reached to touch his hand. Irwin won the playoff the next day, thereby taking his third U.S. Open.

Soon came the British Open, just a month after Irwin's victory. The grand old championship was back at the Old Course, and Nick Faldo played the most discriminating golf one could hope to see. Tactfully, he placed his drives and approaches in the right spots and didn't three-putt once in 72 holes over the massive, undulating greens at the Old Course. His was a Hoganesque performance.

As precise and perhaps expected as was Faldo's play at the 1990 British Open, John Daly's assault on the course during the 1991 PGA Championship at Crooked Stick in Indianapolis was as unexpected, although as precise in its own aggressive way. Daly was the golfer nobody knew; then he drove the ball miles down the fairway and came into the greens with short irons and holed putts for birdies to walk away with the PGA Championship. Crooked Stick was one wild and woolly place that August week, and Daly was the whole story almost right from the opening round. His was a story that writers enjoyed telling.

And then there was the 1991 Ryder Cup at the Ocean Course on Kiawah Island. Having attended the 1987 Ryder Cup at Muirfield Village, and having felt the passion that this international event generates, I looked forward to the renewal at the Ocean Course like no other event I had seen. As Mark Calcavecchia would learn when he found the water at the 17th hole the last day of singles matches that nearly cost his team the victory, there's nothing quite so intense and pressure-filled in golf as playing the Ryder Cup. It's team golf; a player is responsible for more, much more, than his own welfare. Bernhard Langer also found that out when he missed the final putt that allowed the U.S. the win; but in truth Langer had holed difficult short putts over the closing holes to stay in his match against Hale Irwin. His was a performance to respect, as the Ryder Cup was an event to celebrate.

But there are also other events in golf, and I begin this chapter with some reflections on some not-so-well-known tournaments, such as the ever-appealing President's Putter at the Rye Golf Club on the English Channel. I also consider the possibility of a world tour, where the top players in the game would compete with each other on a regular basis. There's a peek at the Walker Cup, golf's major event for male amateurs, and an examination of the many ways golfers can find to lose a tournament. Of course it's never easy to win any tournament, let alone a major. I think that one can have only the utmost respect for the golfers who find the right stuff to play into the last holes of a tournament; and in addition to that respect, wonder and amazement at the ability of the best players in the game to hit just the shot required of them, just when they need to, when a major championship is on the line at one of golf's hallowed courses.

The President's Putter

The Globe and Mail, January 14, 1989
Some people believe that the 1989 golf season began last week with the PGA Tour's Tournament of Champions in Carlsbad, California, won by Steve Jones. Well, the real golf season began last week all right, but the venue was the Rye Golf Club in England, where amateur Mark Froggatt won the President's Putter.

The Putter is _the_ tournament on the calendar at Rye, an old club on the English Channel. It's also an important event on the international golf calendar. The annual tourney for members of the Oxford and Cambridge Golfing Society is always held the first week of January, no matter the weather. The worse the weather, the more the golfers enjoy themselves.

The President's Putter began in 1920 as a gathering for former students from Oxford and Cambridge. The Society wanted to make the match-play competition special, and so the members chose January. Golfers have played in frost and snow and gale-force winds, but only once, in 1979, has the Putter been cancelled.

Not surprisingly, the Society includes some eccentric members. H.D. Gilles, a noted English surgeon who won the 1925 Putter, was rather analytical when it came to the golf swing. He decided at one time that a flat swing would most likely produce consistency. So he invented a contraption that encouraged such a swing.

The good doctor came up with an extremely deep-faced driver, which he used to hit shots from a tee that was a foot high. His tee consisted of rubber tubing inserted into the neck of a glass bottle. It appears that he didn't have much success with the equipment, as he soon discarded his invention. Still, he did win that one Putter. British writers attended the Putter that year as they do every January. If the Masters is a rite of spring, the Putter is a rite of winter.

Arthur Croome, long the secretary of the Society, was also quite a fellow. Crumbo, as he was known, taught classics. He believed that a golf swing depended on a dance-like tempo. "One, two, deliver the cue," he would say to himself as he played a shot.

Eccentric as these golfers seem, they were also upstanding British citizens. Indeed, anybody who hopes to be elected to the Oxford and Cambridge Golfing Society must prove himself worthy. Membership is not conferred automatically upon Oxford and Cambridge golfers, though 98% of applicants get in, Society president Peter Gracey said.

Last fall, Gracey sat in the dining room at Rye and explained the nuances of the Society.

"You must at least have been an undergraduate at Oxford or Cambridge," he advised. "And I might add that membership is not standard, and that everybody knows it."

Gracey pointed out that prospective members must be put up for election by the outgoing captain of the university team, and that Gracey and his committee then look at their suitability. Such examination presumably helps produce gentlemen of high character, if not always of low handicap.

"The method of selection has a wonderful effect on behaviour," Gracey said. "We ask that prospective members not upset people, or that they not turn up punchily. These are reasons why they should not be elected."

Froggatt, the latest Putter champion, was, of course, elected. The 27-year-old native of Belfast graduated from Clare College, Cambridge. He defeated Jamie Warman, Selwyn College, Cambridge, 3 and 2 in Sunday's final match. The weather was cool, but not chilling, and the winner was a character, in true Putter style. He wore a baseball cap, swung in a loopy swaying manner and walked off with his first Putter.

Froggatt, like all previous winners, donated to the club the ball with which he holed out on the final green. By now it's hanging in the clubhouse from the third President's Putter, the first two having been weighed down to capacity by 1986. The first putter belong to Hugh Kirkcaldy, a Scot who used it to win the 1891 British Open.

All of this means that the President's Putter at Rye has class. The event is just as writer and former Putter winner Bernard Darwin described it long ago, "a little red glowing jewel set in the cold waste of winter." Here's one vote, then, for the Putter as the tournament that raises the curtain on another season.

The World Tour

The Globe and Mail, July 6, 1991
This is a Ryder Cup year, which means there are five rather than four major championships. But why shouldn't golf have 20 to 25 important tournaments, though all would hardly be majors? Maybe a world tour is called for in which each event would include the game's top players.

There are good reasons for this, not the least of which is that events on each separate tour are diminished by the absence of significant players. Seve Ballesteros and Payne Stewart are playing in the Torras Monte Carlo Open this week, which means they aren't in the Centel Western Open. Ray Floyd is in the latter, which means he can't play the former.

A world tour would ensure a first-rate field each week. The ingredients are there already in the various tournaments themselves. The idea needs the will of a few major corporations. The International Management Group could probably create a world tour on its own.

IMG is the Cleveland-based organization that according to *Sports Illustrated* employs more than 1,000 people in 43 offices in 20 countries. IMG dominates world golf, having started such tournaments as the Suntory World Match Play Championship and the Lancôme Trophy outside Paris. Its clients include Greg Norman, Curtis Strange and Nick Faldo.

"A world tour could happen in one week with IMG," Faldo says. "In some ways it's already here, since IMG runs about 20 tournaments in the world."

But a true world tour would include events other than those IMG runs. The collective will of the world's finest golfers to break away from their respective tours would therefore be needed. Tom Watson, Seve Ballesteros, José-Maria Olazabal and Payne Stewart aren't IMG clients, to cite one impressive foursome.

This point is important, since a world tour would mean the end of the PGA Tour and European Tour as now constituted, and perhaps the Japanese and Australian Tours as well. Many players are understandably reluctant to endanger a circuit that has made them wealthy. Others want a world tour.

Ballesteros and Norman regularly say a world tour is a distinct and appealing possibility. They do point to the fact that they and all other golfers require releases from their respective tours to play elsewhere. Still, the best players aren't worried about this roadblock.

Stewart's appearance in the Monte Carlo Open this weeks tells you all you need to know about releases from the PGA Tour. He applied to the PGA Tour for his 1991 releases some time ago, but as of two weeks ago hadn't received clearance for the Monte Carlo Open.

"I'll get it," Stewart said during the Carroll's Irish Open, "and if I don't, I'll still be there."

That's the point. Nobody can stop the game's élite players from going where they want, and so conflicting event releases wouldn't be an obstacle to the formation of a world tour. Besides, the top golfers get excited about playing in the best tournaments, no matter where they are. They'll be there.

Here's a possible schedule, then a rudimentary proposal for a world tour.

The Masters, U.S. and British Opens and PGA Championship are at the head of the list; they're the majors. Important national opens also would be on the world tour: the European, Japanese, Australian, Canadian, Irish, Scottish and English Opens. That's 11 events.

Six significant PGA Tour events would make the world list: the Los Angeles Open, the Players Championship, the Memorial, Colonial, Western and World Series. Some events would require modification; the World Series, for instance, would include winners of the World Tour events. That's 17 tournaments so far.

Certain special events would be included: the Volvo Masters in Spain, the Lancôme Trophy, the Australian Masters and Japan's Suntory Open. That makes 21 World Tour events.

Then there are the team events: the Dunhill Cup for teams of three pros from qualifying countries, played at the Old Course in St. Andrews; the World Cup for two-man teams from many more countries, a sort of festival of world golf; and the capper, the Ryder Cup, still held every two years so as to be a much-anticipated highlight.

The package includes 23 tournaments in non-Ryder Cup years, 24 otherwise. Make every purse minimum $2.5 million, allow no appearance money but ensure last place each week is a minimum $30,000, pay the golfers' expenses and watch the excitement build in the game.

"You'd be guaranteed the top 60 players in the game," Faldo said. "It would be fantastic for golf and an absolute disaster for the tours as they are now. That's the problem."

Indeed it is, but problems can lead to creative solutions. Golf is an international sport that demands and needs a world tour.

The Walker Cup

The Globe and Mail, **August 31, 1991**
Many eyes in the professional golf world will be on next week's Canadian Open at Glen Abbey in Oakville, Ontario. But all sharp eyes on the amateur side will shift towards Portmarnock near Dublin. Come Thursday and Friday, two 10-man teams will compete in the Walker Cup, as special in its way as the Ryder Cup for professionals at the end of September is in its.

The Walker Cup has been played since 1922 between teams from the United States and Britain/Ireland. The matches take place every other year. Venues have included the Old Course in St. Andrews, Scotland; Sunningdale in Berkshire, England; Pine Valley in Clementon, New Jersey; Cypress Point in Pebble Beach, California; and other historic courses.

Such courses are granted for wonderful occasions, and the Walker Cup is that. It doesn't yet have the stature in North America that it has in Britain, but Portmarnock will play host to 10,000 spectators a day, a sellout. English writer Bernard Darwin observed in 1945 that "we cannot have a great occasion without a great crowd." Portmarnock will have both.

The Walker Cup deserves to catch on in the United States. Like the Ryder Cup, it was once dominated by the U.S. team. Now things may be different, as with the Ryder Cup, which the British/European side has held since 1985.

Consider what happened during the last Walker Cup, at the Peachtree Golf Club in Atlanta. Britain/Ireland held a one-point advantage over the United States with one match to go. (Each match is worth a point.) Scotland's Jim Milligan was two holes down against two-time U.S. Amateur winner Jay Sigel with three holes to play. It seemed that the United States would win the match and halve the competition.

But Milligan won the 16th with a birdie and Sigel flubbed chip shots the last two holes. Milligan chipped in on the 17th for par to win that hole. The players tied the last hole. Britain/Ireland had won the Walker Cup for only the third time in 32 matches.

"I feel like I let down the whole team," Sigel said after the final match. "I just feel awful."

Those are hurting words, but that's because the Walker Cup is *the* international team event for male amateurs. Oddly, Canada had something to do with the origins of the competition, though a Canadian team has never participated.

In 1919, the Royal Canadian Golf Association invited the United States Golf Association to send a team north for a competition. The USGA accepted and sent a formidable team that included U.S. Open and Amateur winners Chick Evans, Jerome Travers and Francis Ouimet. Bobby Jones, then 17, also was part of the team and he became the champion of the game until he retired at 28.

The United States won that first match 12-3 at the Hamilton Golf and Country Club in Ancaster, Ontario, then and now one of the country's classic courses. The United States defeated Canada 10-4 the next year on Long Island.

The two matches between friendly neighbours sparked the idea of an international match between teams appointed by the USGA and the Royal and Ancient Golf Club of St. Andrews. George Herbert Walker, USGA president in 1920, liked the idea and donated a trophy for the competition. (Two years later his daughter gave birth to a boy named George. That infant, George Bush, grew into the man who is the U.S. president.)

Meanwhile, the Walker Cup became important. USGA *Golf Journal's* managing editor David Earl said this week that an amateur knows no higher honour than being appointed to a Walker Cup team. It's one reason among others that Phil Mickelson, who has already won a PGA Tour event, has remained amateur.

Mickelson and his teammates won't have it easy at Portmarnock. The U.S. side will have more experience, led by Sigel in his eighth consecutive Walker Cup. Britain/Ireland's ace at Portmarnock could be 21-year-old Englishman Jim Payne. He was the low amateur in the recent British Open, beating out Mickelson. Jack Nicklaus played with Payne and liked what he saw.

The crowds at Portmarnock will also like what they see. The teams play four 18-hole alternate shot matches each morning and eight 18-hole singles matches each afternoon. Portmarnock is a robust links that sought the Ryder Cup and didn't get it. So what? The Walker Cup is a grand old event, and a true golfer's competition.

THE MASTERS

The Globe and Mail, **April 9, 1982**
Augusta, Georgia — So this is the Masters, as much a ritual for visitors as a golf tournament. A first-timer, enamoured of the romance of the game, observes the rituals with the same enthusiasm he watches shots at other tournaments. And here, at the Augusta National Golf Club, there are many worth observing.

Veterans tell newcomers they must "do a deal" under the oak tree on the clubhouse lawn. That deal, whatever it may be, is best arranged while one drinks a mint julep, preferably on the final day as golfers battle the course.

Inside the dining room, it is mandatory that the rookie eat a peach cobbler. He must also go for corned beef and hash. If he is smart, he should have at least one lunch of the cottage cheese, strawberry, apple and orange fruit salad.

Then, of course, he must wash it down with brandy before wandering into the players' locker room, where he might hear Sam Snead regaling everyone with stories of Bobby Locke, Jug McSpaden and Wild Bill Mehlhorn.

Absolutely obligatory is a visit to the Trophy Room for a private consultation with Bobby Jones's clubs. One must also say, quietly but firmly, to anybody within hearing range, "My God, all of Jones's clubs have different swing weights. What remarkable feel the man must have had."

Filled with food and history, the Augusta newcomer must saunter on to the veranda well above the clubhouse lawn. He must watch the golfers practising their putting below. He must say, brilliantly, "The greens are at speed again. Finally they are as they were in the 1940s and 1950s. The winner will be of championship stuff this week."

All this, of course, can be done early in the week. It is also a good idea to do one's shopping then. Friends, envious of what they imagine to be a visitor's week-long exposure to the sun at this event, have asked for shirts, head covers, ashtrays and mugs — anything with an Augusta National emblem.

That's done by Wednesday. The next ritual is to walk the par-three course. Nine tiny holes surround a pretty pond. Golfers play casually. The observer, strolling the grounds, must remark on what a lovely touch this is. Of course, it's better if a Masters committee member hears the comment.

The loveliest, classiest, sweetest ritual comes Thursday morning at 9:15 a.m. Then, two legends of golf — Gene Sarazen and Byron Nelson — begin the Masters with the ceremonial nine holes, and a visitor prepares to walk the course with them.

As if by design, he finds himself next to another legend — a wonderful kind man — Herbert Warren Wind, golf writer for *The New Yorker* magazine.

The rookie has journeyed to the Links of Dornoch (in Scotland) through Wind's writings; he has sat by the fireplace during a Toronto winter and read *Thirty Years of Championship Golf*, Wind's book about Sarazen.

The rookie introduces himself and is honoured to walk with Wind for the nine holes. Sarazen, 80, approaches the first tee with the impish look of a young boy. Nelson follows, nearly 70 years old, as erect and dignified as Tom Weiskopf or Tom Watson.

No quarter is given. The greats play from the same tees as Watson. Wind mentions that Nelson is looking "chirpy" and that when he visited Sarazen in February at Naples, Florida, he was told the Squire had shot a 75 on a 6,400-yard course.

Dressed in blue knickers and playing an orange golf ball, Sarazen swings easily. There is a "spank" when he contacts the ball. On the fourth hole, a par-three of 205 yards, he hits his ball between the traps on to the green, exactly on the line he had planned.

It is a marvellous stroke, and the observer understands what Sarazen meant with his phrase "I rode into the shot." That he did, in perfect balance. "If you see nothing else all week," Wind says, "you've seen something beautiful."

Nelson, meanwhile, plays a shot from 90 feet to the right of the hole. Below the fourth green, he closes the blade on a pitching wedge and chips the ball across a flat section, over the crest of an undulation and down into the hole.

Across the fairway, the tournament has begun, but the observer is absorbed by his visits with the past. "There's a different mood in this crowd," Wind says. "It's an *esprit*. The people seem lost in the game. I don't think we'll have a more pleasant walk all week."

After their nine holes — played in 85 minutes — Sarazen and Nelson give way to the contestants. The crowd disperses. Wind spots a crony, and the observer heads for the pro shop. He remembers one more visor that he must purchase for a friend.

The Globe and Mail, **April 10, 1982**

Augusta, Georgia — Serena Stoney doesn't know the difference between a birdie and a bogey. To her, a drive is something people take on Sundays, an iron an instrument used to press shirts. There's no way she could talk golf to Hord W. Hardin, tournament chairman at the Masters. She's 20 and has never seen a golf tournament, but this night, drinking margaritas at Annie's 16th, a local watering hole, she's an expert on the scene in her town.

"Man, I wanna tell you this town is dead 51 weeks of the year. I mean, there's no action. But this week everything goes crazy."

Stoney is surrounded by a mob of golf nuts, with a drink to their lips and an opinion in their mouths. A golf club representative from Chicago is in town because of the tournament's tradition. A marketing man for a U.S. golf magazine is here because, well, everybody else is here. And Serena? She's here because they're here.

"If you're from Augusta," she says, "you've got no chance for a ticket unless you know somebody. Everybody here is from somewhere else, and this bar is the place to be."

A mile and a half down the road, behind an enormous hedge and across from a Piggly Wiggly grocery store, Azalea Hairstyles and a restaurant called the Green Jacket, there's another place to visit — the Augusta National Golf Club. For the rest of the year, the club is absolutely private. Today's equivalents of yesterday's Rockefellers and Whitneys come up for some golf on the course that was once a nursery. While they play, they are reminded of former members by cabins alongside the 10th tee and fairway, those belonging to course founder Bobby Jones and former U.S. President Dwight Eisenhower.

But this week the course is open to anybody lucky enough to have a ticket. Fans arrived to find a course that sweeps away from the clubhouse like a park.

The golf course could be Toronto's Edwards Gardens or Vancouver's Stanley Park. It takes a few minutes to forget the beauty of the surroundings and realize this is a championship golf course.

For many of the fans, though, the course is the main attraction. "It's the only place I will drive five hours to see the golf course rather than the players," says one fan from Rutherfordton, North Carolina.

Bill Thames, a Pinkerton security guard for the week, normally works as a systems technician in Atlanta. "But I take this week off," Thames says, "and I'd be here if I didn't get paid. It's just a good feeling to be here around the flowers and the superior golfers."

Serena Stoney may like the noise and the action at Annie's 16th, but the real golf fans like to be at the golf course. The colour here may be in the pink and white dogwoods, the azaleas and the rust-like pine needles that give the course a burnished antique look, but there's something more, a quality that was visualized when Jones founded the course 50 years ago and that is somehow more than the sum of its parts.

Maybe it's that an observer can stand on the clubhouse lawn behind the 18th green and look down to the course knowing that out there Jack Nicklaus and Tom Watson and the rest are fighting the same elements that Walter Hagen and Ben Hogan did years ago.

Or maybe it's the little things. The pairing sheets with starting times are free here. Sandwiches cost only 75 cents. Concessionaires sell headache powder, although it's hard to believe anybody could get a headache in this garden.

Everything is understated. On the first tee, golfers are merely told to play away. There is no exaggerated blaring of a player's accomplishments and, conversely, fans do not have to know that some amateurs may not have accomplished all that much to be here.

The game is the main thing. Golfers simply tee off and head out onto the course. There are no standard-bearers walking the fairways with the group, and there are no scorers either. Players keep their own scores as they do at other tournaments. But elsewhere, women scorers embellish the scene, more to get people involved than out of any real need.

Leader boards are everywhere. They tell the fans how a player stands in relation to par on an accumulative basis. At a glance, a fan knows exactly what's going on.

The ambience is as important to the golfers as it is to the fans. "I love coming here," said four-time Masters champion Arnold Palmer yesterday. A large crowd had followed Palmer during the second round. It could have been 1958 or 1962, years that Palmer won. There were fans in the gallery who had seen Palmer then, and Palmer knew it.

"There's no other tournament in the world like this," Palmer said. "I don't know if there ever can be. I see people out here from years ago. They get me going. Everybody who comes to Augusta is golf-oriented. Even people who don't play understand the game. The tradition of Jones, Hogan and (Gene) Sarazen, it all rubs off on the players."

Somehow the cream comes to the top at the Masters. The amateurs have their day early in the week and sometimes continue on to finish well. In 1961, amateur Charlie Coe finished second to Gary Player by one stroke. This year, Coe is here as a committee member.

Amateurs are truly favoured by the Masters' organizers. They are welcome to stay in the Crow's Nest, a dormitory-like area on the second floor of the clubhouse. By tomorrow, most will be out of contention and playing only for the honour of low amateur, but they will have honoured the tradition of amateur golf that was so important to Bobby Jones, a lifelong amateur. Come tomorrow afternoon, names such as Watson, Nicklaus and Seve Ballesteros will probably be at the top of the leader board. They, too, feel privileged to receive a Masters invitation in the early winter, and when they get here are only too happy to accede to various Masters conventions.

In practice rounds, golfers are instructed to play only one ball, and most times, they do. On the driving range, golfers hit their own balls to their own caddies, a practice long since gone on the regular PGA Tour.

PGA Tour representatives are in the background at Augusta. This is very much an invitational tournament run by the Augusta National Golf Club. Perhaps Nicklaus said it best in a letter to Jones and the late tournament chairman, Clifford Roberts, in 1965. After winning, he wrote: "As usual, the tournament was run with the dignity and perfection that will never be topped in the game of golf. I want to thank you both very much for allowing me to compete in this tournament. As I have said, Augusta National is my favourite course and the Masters my favourite golf tournament. I feel the Masters is a monument to everything great in golf."

The Globe and Mail, April 9, 1983

Augusta, Georgia — On a sticky evening at the Augusta National Golf Club, the 19th annual Tacky Tailgate Party is moving right along.

The accoutrements include automobiles with trunks open to serve as bars, and a bright red carpet, spread decorously in the mud of a parking lot 100 yards from the National's clubhouse. On the carpet sits a bridge table painted with flowers. A chandelier hangs from the roof of a car belonging to one Judge Hill of Atlanta.

"I'm going to crank the car up," the retired federal circuit court judge says, "and see that the battery ain't dead." The chandelier is made of Swedish crystal — imitation crystal, naturally — and operates off the car's cigarette lighter.

The Tacky Tailgate Party is a revelry begun by the Hills, the Battles, the Keeses, and the Fricks, Atlantans all, and the Ballantines from Wilmington, Delaware.

Bob Battle serves bourbon and doesn't seem to know about traditional one-ounce alcohol limitations. He wears an orange-

and-white checked bib that reads "Who invited all these tacky people?"

This is at the home of the Masters, where the officials wear green coats and long-sleeved shirts, no matter how hot it gets, and where it seems General Eisenhower and Bobby Jones could walk out at any time from their cabins beside the 10th fairway. Parvenues here have held tickets for 10 years.

There is something for everyone at the Tacky Tailgate Party, including food, drink, music and conviviality.

Newcomers don't wear the crests needlepointed by Doris Kees in Masters-green wool, but are promised evidence of their participation if they return next year. Meanwhile, they are asked to sign a guest book on the bridge table. The table is covered with a crocheted cloth that can be purchased at any variety store.

Judge Hill's chandelier, though, attracts most of the attention and a few moths. "I not only built it," he drawls, "I invented it. The crystals are made in Hong Kong and the chandelier looked real good before it fell. But that only gave it more classic lines.

"One time," he continued, "we went to Singapore and stayed at the Raffles Hotel. We had the same fake chandelier in our room, so I took a picture of it and keep it right beside a picture of ours. It's not nearly as graceful."

While Judge Hill speaks, someone named Charlie strums a banjo, and a few yards away, a fellow points to a Pennsylvania licence plate with the inscription "Giggle."

"We asked for 'Smile,'" the owner of the car says, "but that was taken."

The Tacky Tailgate Party originated when the Hills et al. noticed various elegant parties taking place all around Augusta, some in the parking lots. Says Kate Battle: "People used fancy silverware and china; it was all so ail-egant," and she stretches the first syllable of the word. "But it wasn't interesting. We decided to do a takeoff on those parties."

And take off it has. Willie Peterson, Jack Nicklaus's caddie, once stopped by for a drink.

A fellow wandered over one time and said he was from *National Geographic Magazine*. "He took his microphone," Kate Battle says, "and put it right up to our food. I didn't know what he was looking for. Then he asked a lady to take off her blouse and put a bone in her nose so he could take a picture for his publication. Turned out he wasn't from *National Geographic* at all, but from *Southern Living.*"

The Tacky Tailgate Party convenes Thursday, Friday and Saturday evenings of Masters week. Proper people walk by and wonder if it's a garage sale. A duet of pink flamingos seems to pulse on the muddy ground; pink is a proper Masters colour that does suggest the azaleas, dogwoods and magnolias on the course.

"It's so pretty, isn't it?" Kate Battle says. "Just the right, tacky touch. This party and this place spoil you for any other tournament. We have such a good time here. By Sunday, if we get a day of sun, the course will be gorgeous. A lot of the azaleas aren't open yet, so it can get even more beautiful out here."

And so the Tacky Tailgate Party ends, until it resumes tonight, after the last golfer has holed out on a quagmire of a golf course. Just come into Augusta National Golf Club through Gate 4. Listen for the banjo and look for the bright lights from the chandelier. You'll be most welcome.

The Globe and Mail, **April 9, 1987**
Break out the Jolson and Gershwin music. Ring in the old. It's Masters time, and if this isn't a rite of spring, romance is dead.

The Augusta National Golf Club is a place for sentiment. One thinks of the 11th, 12th and 13th holes, known as Amen Corner, and the par-three, nine-hole course, the sweetest nine holes anybody could want. One thinks of the influence of co-founder Bobby Jones and the continuing presence of six-time winner Jack Nicklaus. Here the past is the present, which makes for timelessness.

The Masters begins with Magnolia Lane, the entrance to the club that is flanked by a double row of magnolia trees planted before the Civil War. It will end early Sunday evening when one of 87 invitees is presented in Jones's cabin with the green jacket, symbolic of victory. In between, we can be certain of some things, all pleasant to contemplate.

Above all, we will be reminded that this is not a place for the money-hungry. The Masters fills the soul rather than the pocket. Last week, the pros played at Greensboro for a first prize of

$108,000; the Masters tournament committee won't announce its "cash prizes" until the weekend.

Here, there is hunger for something else besides money. Golfers reach deep down for courage in circumstances that can make it difficult to get beyond their throats. The best make it through and find a new dimension in themselves. Who can forget Nicklaus at last year's Masters, when he went seven-under-par the last 10 holes to win and had to fight back tears on the way?

A year later, the memories of Nicklaus winning are engraved, powerful images of a strong-willed man. A now-famous photo shows Nicklaus sticking his tongue out towards the 17th hole as his winning birdie putt fell. He appears starved, yet alive, so alive.

Lesser golfers crave what Nicklaus has known. Johnny Miller has finished second three times at the Masters but says he would trade these in for one win. This is a place for brides, not bridesmaids. The green jacket Nicklaus was given is not a gown, but it envelops a winner as completely.

Augusta, Nicklaus knows, is for the heart, not the heartless. Cynics need not apply. Nobody snickered when Nicklaus and his caddying son Jack Jr. embraced each other after the greatest golfer in history won a year ago Sunday. The twosome is back again, and everybody is urging them on.

But the Masters's flavour does not depend on a Nicklaus win or challenge. The tournament honours individual success but refuses to glorify it. There will be no fanfare when Nicklaus tees off shortly after noon in today's first round. The starter will say, "Jack Nicklaus driving, fore, please," and that is all.

This is all that is necessary because there is so much more. The golf course was once a nursery and is as enjoyable to walk as to play. Mac O'Grady calls it a "poetic corner of the world." That's close. Augusta National is rhythm and flow, like a sonnet.

If it is exaggeration to call most courses beautiful, here it is understatement. The course sweeps away from the hill where course co-founder Jones first stood in the spring of 1931. He later remarked: "It seemed that this land had been lying here for years waiting for someone to lay a golf course upon it." And what a course it is.

Yesterday, Augusta National gleamed under a warm sun that finally delivered itself to this corner of Georgia near the South

Carolina border. Some golfers, such as Hal Sutton and amateur Jay Sigel, played alone. Companionship in golf can be pleasant, but at Augusta National it is not essential.

By 1 p.m. more people than had yet attended a Wednesday practice round were gathered on the par-three course to the east of the regular course. There they saw a unique event, the "par-three contest," as Masters officials refer to it.

Players and spectators — called "patrons" at the Masters — mingled. Gene Sarazen and Sam Snead and Byron Nelson played. A few fans stood near a display case near the pro shop, where they admired crystal vases, bowls and decanters that would be given as prizes for the par-three. Money goes, but well-thought-out mementos find a home.

This was the Masters yesterday and it will be the Masters a year from now, and presumably 50 years hence. Some things never change, which makes the Masters the Masters.

The Globe and Mail, April 10, 1989

Augusta, Georgia — Years ago, while Masters tournament founder Bobby Jones was winning his 13 major championships, he said that he couldn't help but believe that destiny plays a part in major championships. Had he seen what happened yesterday as Nick Faldo won, he would have been even more convinced of its role.

For one thing, Faldo had heard a newsman say earlier in the week that he wasn't a capable enough putter to win majors, which are generally played on courses with treacherous greens. Sure, Faldo had won the 1987 British Open, but that was with his trademark methodical driving and iron play, not with an always deft putting touch.

That comment irked Faldo, probably because there was some truth to it. Aside from a monster 100-foot putt that he holed on the second hole during the third round, he had been putting only average during the Masters. The problems continued on the six greens he had still to play yesterday morning to complete the third round. He holed nothing.

Faldo was miffed. He went directly to his locker and pulled out four putters from the half-dozen or so he had brought from England, where he lives. He was looking for a feel, and he had an idea that he needed a new wand. He found what he wanted, and the stroke to go along with it, during a 45-minute putting session directly after the morning play.

Faldo then went home and rested. He returned for two 20-minute putting sessions sandwiched around hitting a few balls before his last round. Then destiny showed its hand.

Faldo's second shot on the first hole came to rest on the front of the green, 17 yards from the hole. It was not the type of putt one expects to hole. Two putts for par would have been acceptable.

But Faldo holed the putt, up and across the slopes of a green that like all Augusta National's greens offers little or no margin of error. "Perfection" is what Augusta demands, Faldo would say later, and so he came up with a perfect stroke. He thought then that something was up — call it destiny, he later agreed.

Such things happen on the way to major victories. Ben Crenshaw holed a monster putt on the 10th hole during his march to victory in the 1984 Masters, and it was at that moment he felt the golfing gods were in his favour. Jack Nicklaus stood over a 20-foot eagle putt at the 15th the last day of the 1986 Masters and suddenly recalled that he had the exact putt many years before on his way to winning; he made the putt and went on to win.

Destiny also operates in reverse, of course, and there seems no stopping it. Seve Ballesteros had a chance yesterday until his shot to the par-three 16th slammed into the bank in front of the green and trickled back into the water. It was all over for him.

Then there was Greg Norman, who may be destined never to win the Masters. He does everything to put himself into position to win, as he did yesterday with birdies down the inward nine, then bogeys the last to miss a playoff. That happened in 1986 as well.

But there was no stopping Faldo yesterday. He became the man to watch as his putter turned into a magic wand. Came the 16th, and he holed what he called "just a joke" of a putt, straight downhill for 15 feet, with eight feet of break. When he saw the putt, he thought of Scot Sandy Lyle, his good friend who holed a birdie putt there last year on his way to winning. Such things happen when a player is touched.

Jones would have known what was happening. He would have known that destiny was taking over when Scott Hoch missed that short par putt to win on the first playoff hole. He might have even surmised that Faldo would make the winning birdie putt on the second playoff hole, that he would close with a final-round 65 and then win outright with the right stroke at the right time.

"Yeah, you do believe that fate plays a part," Faldo said after it was all over. "I've seen it happen to others. I've watched Nicklaus shoot 65 to win . . . For me to hole ridiculous putts, and to be given one opportunity to win it, and to do it — it amazes me."

Amazing it was, but yesterday was Faldo's turn to win. How else does one explain Hoch missing that short par putt on the first playoff hole that would have given him the win? How else does one explain every other golfer coming so close, and then retreating?

Bobby Jones had the answer. It's destiny and, yesterday, it was in Faldo's favour.

The Globe and Mail, April 15, 1991

Augusta, Georgia — There are many ways to gauge a golf tournament, but in the end the only one that really matters is who won it. Yesterday, Welshman Ian Woosnam won the Masters, his first major, when he parred the last hole. His pluck showed that he truly deserves the world No. 1 ranking, at least for now.

Woosnam, 33, made it to the top of the Sony world rankings only the week of the Masters. He had long wanted to get there, and after winning the USF & G Classic in New Orleans and the Mediterranean Open this year, he made it. But he hadn't won a major, and that was next on the agenda of a golfer many observers, including Tom Watson and José-Maria Olazabal, think is as hard-nosed a competitor as there is in the game.

"Some people over here don't even know my name," Woosnam had said at the halfway mark of the Masters, when he was a couple of shots behind then-leader Watson. "I've been a bit overshadowed by [Nick] Faldo. But that keeps me going and makes me want to do what he's done, to win a major."

Woosnam also said something that turned out to be prophetic. He was asked if he would like to have the last shot to win the Masters.

"If I have to make a par up the last hole, I'll take it now," he said.

Woosnam set out yesterday at the Augusta National Golf Club with winning a major in mind, and it was clearly within his reach. He had shot 67 the third round to overtake Watson by a shot at 11 under par. Olazabal and Lanny Wadkins were another two shots back.

In the end, it all came down to the back nine at Augusta, as the Masters usually does. Woosnam was tied at the 18th with Watson and Olazabal, and in the end he hit the right shot off the tee and made par. Olazabal couldn't do that, nor could Watson, with whom Woosnam was playing. And that was it, as far as the score goes. Woosnam finished with 11 under 277 to win $243,000.

"I had a chance to win and I didn't," Olazabal, a 24-year-old-Spanish star, said after the round. "It's a lot of pressure, but at the same time I think it's nice. That's why I love the game of golf, the thrill. I think it's very important."

Watson also had that thrill and eagled the par-five 13th and 15th holes to get back in the hunt after double-bogeying the par-three 12th. But it was the swing that sent the ball into the water there, and the one that sent his drive into the woods on the last hole that did him in.

"It's a great disappointment not to have won today," Watson said, and you could see the hurt in his face. "I just didn't play well enough to win."

No, he didn't, but still Watson came so close to winning his third Masters. The real story, however, might well be how he conducted himself over the last holes, and also how Woosnam handled difficult conditions.

The fact was that play was very slow, and Woosnam and Watson had to endure long waits on at least half a dozen holes. Watson eagled the 13th after such a wait, and on the 14th tee showed his class by helping Woosnam in a potentially volatile situation. It was there that a fan behind the tee told Woosnam that Augusta National isn't links golf. The implication was that he couldn't win on Augusta National. It was an odious comment, and Woosnam, fiery golfer that he is, got angry.

"Ian looked back," Watson said, "and then I told him a little story that might have helped him. I said, 'Let's cool it and think about what we're doing in front of the tee, not behind.'"

Woosnam related the story Watson told him.

"He told me that Don January used to turn around to anybody who said something. He'd say, 'Thank you very much.' I hit my drive down the middle, turned around and then said, 'Thank you very much.'"

Woosnam then went on to play his way to his first Masters jacket, and after it was all over Watson and Olazabal expressed well just what kind of a player is Woosnam, or Wee Woosie, as he is known because he is only 5-foot-4.

"We're good friends," Olazabal said. "He's a real player. We always have a good time on the course. He's very competitive and aggressive."

"Ian is a winner," Watson said. "A good guy and a lot of fun to be with. He's just a tough competitor."

That was the phrase that ran through Augusta National all during the tournament. Woosnam, people said, is one strong golfer. He proved that yesterday, and looked right at home in the green jacket, size 40, small.

THE U.S. OPEN

***The Globe and Mail,* May 28, 1987**
The United States Open that will be held in San Francisco is a month away, but already people are talking it up. They remember the 1966 U.S. Open there, when Arnold Palmer blew a seven-shot lead over Billy Casper in the last nine holes and lost the next day in a playoff.

Things really changed starting on the 15th hole in the final round, when Palmer still held a five-shot lead. He bogied there and on the 16th against Casper's birdies. A few minutes later he missed a five-foot par putt at the 17th — a straight uphill putt that he left two inches short, dead centre — and he and Casper were tied.

Palmer almost lost the tournament outright on the 18th hole. Were it not for a mighty slash from the left rough with a wedge that left him 35 feet past the hole, and a great four-foot downhill putt that he made, it would have been all over. Casper then defeated Palmer in the Monday playoff, 69-73.

Palmer and Casper recently chatted about the 1966 U.S. Open while playing a seniors event in Jamaica. Palmer was reticent at first. Casper spoke freely.

"It sure was a dramatic event," Palmer said. "I do remember it and recall it from time to time. I suppose in some way I relaxed a little bit. I took my position for granted."

Casper has pleasant memories. "I remember all the shots I played. A great gallery was following Arnold, but as I started catching him in the final round many of the members of his army deserted ranks and they became Casper converts. You could really feel the momentum change."

Palmer's comment that he took his position for granted was right to the point. Figuring that he was going to win his second Open — he'd taken the 1960 championship — Palmer took aim at the record 276 that Ben Hogan set in 1948 at the Riviera Country Club in Los Angeles. A one-over-par 36 on Olympic's back nine would do it.

Hunting the record, Palmer shot for the pins. Casper planned "to try and make pars and birdies, make sure I kept second place." Little did he know what pars and birdies would do.

Palmer went for the flag on the par-three, 150-yard 15th. But he caught a trap and bogied. Casper birdied after holing a 20-foot putt. Now he was only three shots behind.

"It all started there," Casper remembered. "Arnie is the type of player who goes for the flag. If they put it in the top of a tree he'd go for it, and then he'd figure a way to keep it on a limb where he had a birdie putt. But this time the shot didn't come off."

At the 604-yard par-five 16th, Palmer pull-hooked his drive into deep rough only 150 yards away. He then ripped a 3-iron through deep rough but only advanced the ball 75 yards. Eventually he bogeyed the hole, while Casper birdied. Now Palmer was just a shot ahead.

Then came the uphill par putt on the 17th that Palmer missed. What had seemed impossible had happened. A teenager in awe of Palmer, I couldn't believe my eyes as I watched on television. Palmer and Casper were tied.

Today Palmer says it was ridiculous to try the recovery shot from the rough on the 16th hole. When he spoke of it in a sea-side tavern in Jamaica, he still got riled up.

"I didn't have to be aggressive on the back nine," Palmer exclaimed. "I could have gone along and just played and not had any serious trouble."

But Palmer was all too aware of Hogan's record, and in typical style, he went for it.

"That was the worst part. That was the part that really ate at me. I wanted to break the record. Now I think what a foolish idea it was. The record that I might have broken would one day be broken anyway."

The putt that Palmer left short on the 17th was the shocker. Short? Palmer? On an uphill putt? Unheard of. It was as if Pete Rose had decided not to slide into home plate when the World Series was on the line: a failure of nerve, a moment of vulnerability.

"That was the key putt," Palmer explained. "It was really when I felt in trouble. I was going right up the hill and I left it short."

So it happened that Casper instead of Palmer won the 1966 U.S. Open. It's tempting to argue that the events at Olympic had a long-term negative effect on Palmer — after all, he didn't win another major — but he disagrees.

"I think it probably had more of a positive effect. Things didn't turn worse, they turned better. People knew I couldn't win every time I had a chance."

Casper attributes his win to fate. "What happened at Olympic was one of those things that happens in this game. It just proves a guy can't afford to give up no matter how many shots he's behind."

"The whole combination of things," Palmer feels, "made it one of those days."

The Globe and Mail, **June 16, 1990**

Medinah, Illinois — Someone said a player must be very stupid or very smart to succeed at championship golf — stupid enough to not realize or feel the pressure and demands of an event such as the U.S. Open, or smart enough to understand them and then rise to the occasion.

This brings us to Hale Irwin, a most cerebral man, who was at five-under-par 139 at the halfway point of the U.S. Open over Medinah's No. 3 course. The skilfully achieved score placed him in contention for his third Open championship.

Irwin, 45, is a budding course architect who recently returned to serious golf. His classic form always has been suited to the U.S. Open's typically rigorous courses, but, during the late 1980s, he took time away from the game to develop other interests. Now he's back, having placed those interests in perspective, and he may be ready to play his best golf again.

"I've reached a comfort level as to what I can do on and off the course," he said after yesterday's second round over a lush course. "I feel I'm getting more into the groove of how I used to play."

Irwin isn't kidding himself. After all, he tied for third at the Kemper Open in Potomac, Maryland, two weeks ago, his best finish in more than a year. He has surpassed his 1989 earnings and could not have had a better runner-up to this event.

"The Kemper finish was a nice boost, a shot in the arm. I did not play the Western last week, and so I feel good coming in here. I have some momentum."

That momentum might have been halted had Irwin not received a notice from the USGA some time ago. It came as he was filling out a form to enter qualifying rounds for the U.S. Open. Irwin didn't have to bother: The USGA had decided to give him a special exemption.

"I would have been glad to go on and qualify. I just had not done the things to get in, and so would have had to find a different way. I would have no problem with that."

But the USGA did have a problem with forcing Irwin to qualify, realizing that, as one of the classic swingers, his presence would enhance the field.

And that's just what has happened. Irwin, in his quiet way, has insinuated himself into the tournament, missing only three fairways off the tee and controlling the ball as if by remote control. Moreover, he is thinking like the wise golfer that he usually is.

"If my thinking is right, I will play right. I've always felt that your mental game will bring the rest of your game on."

If Irwin's mental game is sharp — and who is to doubt that it is? — his main concern this weekend will be to subdue an emotional component of his personality that sometimes has hurt him.

His play in the 1984 U.S. Open comes to mind. At the Winged Foot Club in Mamaroneck, New York, Irwin led going into the final round but let his imagination run away with him, as sometimes happens to smart golfers. It happened to Bobby Jones, who was so emotional during major championships that he lost quite a bit of weight during those events.

The best golfers, at times like these, think themselves out of their predicament. But, as Irwin said yesterday, "You also have to accept that some days you are on and others you aren't."

He was not on during the last round at Winged Foot. First of all, his father was ill and died two weeks later. The New York-area crowds were also rowdy and noticeably partial to eventual winner Fuzzy Zoeller. Irwin was ill at ease.

"I did not handle it well. I just let it all get built up in my mind, wanting to play well for my dad, taking on the New York crowd."

Irwin took a lot of heat for his hang-dog look during and after the final round. Not many people expected him to return one day and challenge for another U.S. Open, but here he is. And, no, as some people argue, he does not feel he is too old to win.

"There are other guys out here who are younger than me in terms of years. But they are older in terms of how they think and what they want to do and be."

Irwin also knows what it's like to win the U.S. Open. His most recent victory in this event came 11 years ago at the Inverness Club in Toledo, Ohio, but he's beginning to remember his feelings back then.

"I have played very few U.S. Opens as well as I have played these first two rounds. I would call my style cautiously aggressive. Where must you absolutely not miss the ball? Where is the best spot to put your shot?"

So goes Irwin's thinking process. His shotmaking has measured up thus far. The weekend will tell whether he can handle whatever emotions go with contending again at the Open.

One thing is sure: He is smart enough to meet the intellectual requirements.

The Globe and Mail, **June 20, 1990**

Major championships leave major memories. Here are some, culled from the just-concluded U.S. Open at Medinah outside Chicago.

First, the course. Medinah was tough, but played easier due to rain. Worried members huddled over the matter. They felt the U.S. Golf Association had set the course up too easily.

Their sentiments were ridiculous, and their petulance unforgettable. Why do club members worry when the world's best players make birdies? The USGA didn't care, knowing that golf is an outdoor game — no Golfdome available. The golfers are talented, and so be it.

Medinah's members might have concentrated on the golf. One image is of Greg Norman in the middle of the 14th fairway in the first round. Norman had decided to go for the green, 265 yards away over a fronting bunker. The crowd roared when he pulled out his fairway wood. Norman hit the green with a José Canseco-like shot to centre field, then almost made his eagle putt.

Next came José-Maria Olazabal — the Spaniard nobody knows, compared with Seve Ballesteros. Olazabal shot 73 the first round while putting poorly. But he fired shots at the flag all day, nearly holing two full irons.

But there was more than golf during the opening days at Medinah. Much of the goings-on occurred, as usual, off the course.

USGA's director of rules and competitions, P.J. Boatright, spoke one evening at a dinner. He remembered working the 1972 Open championship at Pebble Beach in Monterey, California, where Jack Nicklaus complained that the greens were too slow. Boatright encountered Nicklaus on a par-three hole the next day.

Nicklaus, said Boatright, hit his tee shot through the green. His chip shot was straight downhill, and his ball ran on and on to the front of the green. Nicklaus two-putted for bogey, then noticed Boatright.

"You've got the greens some kind of fast today," Nicklaus said. But the USGA hadn't altered the speed of the greens. And Nicklaus ended up winning the tournament.

Another night at Medinah, the USGA played host to a small affair at the Chicago Golf Club, a historic course. Ben Crenshaw, who could lead a post-doctoral seminar in golf history, is a member, which is one of the only ways to get on the course. Anyway, the clubhouse was open this night for the party.

What was happening wasn't quite history, but it did represent the USGA's attempt to infuse the Open with art. Well-known American artist Arthur Weaver was unveiling his latest work, a portrait of former USGA presidents William Campbell and Joe Dye. Both have played important roles in the USGA's ascendancy to its prominent role.

If the event at Chicago Golf Club was worth recognizing, then it must be said that the significance of a U.S. Open also brings into focus less attractive elements of the game at large. I visited a café in downtown Chicago one day, where I met a middle-aged woman named Katherine Smith. The U.S. Open was another world to her, as was Medinah.

"I could never get on a course like that," said Smith, a 10-handicap golfer at the public Jackson Park course. "That's for people with money. But I want to tell you something. Come out to our course. I'll introduce you to good golfers, folks you'll never hear about, folks who can't afford a ticket to a U.S. Open."

It was $35 for a daily ticket. But despite the price, some 50,000 spectators followed the play during each of the final rounds.

It was late Sunday afternoon, and Hale Irwin holed his monster birdie putt on the 72nd green. I was standing behind the green when he spontaneously erupted. Irwin danced around the green in a one-time celebration. He was not celebrating a victory prematurely, as some writers said, offering opinion as fact. He was simply reacting to his feat.

And then Monday, the playoff. Mike Donald played beautifully in a rough wind, and if golfers didn't know him before, they do now. Donald made one serious error on the 18th hole, when he hooked his tee shot into the trees. His subsequent bogey combined with Irwin's birdie on the 16th hole to erase Donald's two-stroke lead and send the twosome into sudden-death.

Irwin holed his eight-foot birdie putt on the first hole to win. His wife and daughter emerged from the crowd to share the moment, but Irwin went first to console Donald. Both golfers were in tears a moment later.

In the end, the ninetieth U.S. Open will prove to be one of the more memorable in recent history. Irwin, a veteran champion — and Donald, a champion veteran — showed that Greg Norman, Seve Ballesteros and Nick Faldo aren't the only golfers.

The Globe and Mail, **June 22, 1992**

When Tom Kite won the 1989 Players Championship in Ponte Vedra, Florida, he tried to convince himself that this championship of the PGA Tour was a major. He had heard for too long that he hadn't won a major, and so wanted to invent one.

But Kite couldn't fool himself then and he has no need to now. In winning the U.S. Open yesterday with inspired shotmaking, a dreamy short game and exact putting, Kite put to rest any notion that he could not win a major.

Kite now has, and in some of the most arduous conditions imaginable. Pebble Beach was not the same course PGA Tour players see every February during the AT & T National Pro-Am. It was more akin to the 1972 U.S. Open at Pebble that Jack Nicklaus won with a two-over-par total of 290. And maybe that's why it took a player of Kite's courage to take the championship.

Here, for instance, was Kite on the par-three seventh hole, a mere slip of a thing at 112 yards, and from an elevated tee. A nothing hole, right?

Wrong. Players were hitting mid-irons into this hole that plunges to a skull of a green that hugs the ocean. The win was blowing hard here, as it was everywhere on the course. Only one of the last 16 players in yesterday's final round hit the green with his first shot. Master ball controller Nick Faldo whacked his ball to the left near the sea and double-bogeyed. Goodbye Faldo.

It seemed that might also be Kite's fate. The shot is unspeakably difficult, and Kite's 6-iron shot sailed left. Then, in one of those moments that define major championship winners, Kite lofted his ball on to the rock-hard green from the deep rough and watched as it rolled. And rolled. Off the green, he figured.

But Kite's caddy, Mike Carrick, is as experienced carrying the bag as his employer is using the clubs in it. "Hit it, hit it," Carrick shouted, his words constituting a prayer.

Kite's ball hit the flagstick, all right. Nicklaus's tee shot on the 17th during the last round of the 1972 U.S. Open slammed off the flagstick. He won. Watson's second shot from green-side rough on the same hole in 1982 hit the flagstick and fell in the hole. He won.

Now Kite's ball rattled off the flag and found the hole. Kite suddenly had a three-shot lead. At the same time, he was heading to the eighth, the hole that ABC's Open host Brent Musburger told us time and time again began a run around the "cliffs of doom."

Cliffs of doom they almost were. Kite saved a bogey with a six-footer at the ninth, got up and down from 30 or 40 yards on the 10th for par and also parred the 11th. Later he bogeyed the 16th and 17th. Kite had a two-shot lead as he went up the par-five 18th, perhaps the most famous finishing hole in golf.

This was class all the way. Kite had suffered the ignominy of not being invited to the Masters last spring because he didn't qualify by any of the club's arrogant rules. Kite kept more or less quiet on the subject, although he was bothered. Then he won the BellSouth Classic last month in Atlanta.

The win got Kite into the 1993 Masters. The money he earned qualified him for this week's U.S. Open. The confidence he got was worth more than he could measure.

Now he can measure it by the terms of the U.S. Open. Oh, how Kite must have longed for the victory walk he took up the last fairway after he hit the 18th green yesterday to win his first major, and his national Open on an extraordinary course.

But maybe there was more to it also. Kite, after all, is 42. He once said that golfers mature after they turn 30. But surely Kite didn't mean they mature in their forties. And yet there is something, because Kite seemed changed in an important way after he knew he would have to play his way back to the Masters.

Listen to something the old *New York Post* sportswriter Jimmy Cannon said in 1971 about Willie Mays, the marvellous San Francisco Giants outfielder. Mays was playing in the National League Championship Series against the Pittsburgh Pirates. He was 40. Could Cannon's words apply to Kite's feelings as the Masters to which he wasn't invited came and went last April?

"This isn't a pensioner playing out the final seasons," Cannon wrote. "The Pirates respect him. They know that there is a source of vitality within him. It bubbles up like a geyser in instances of crisis as though the force of his desire rehabilitated him."

Kite may have found that source of vitality when the Masters tournament committee didn't invite him last April. It bubbled up in the instance of crisis. And then the force of Kite's desire rehabilitated him. And he now knows why this win was worth waiting for.

THE BRITISH OPEN

The Globe and Mail, July 18, 1984

St. Andrews, Scotland — Most golf courses take an hour or so to walk without playing. The problems are obvious, the lines of play apparent. But the Old Course at St. Andrews, where the 113th British Open begins today, takes at least four hours to walk and study, and years to fathom. It is without a doubt the most mysterious course in the world.

At first glance the Old Course seems easy, a featureless plain with 11 greens, seven of which are enormous double greens used by 14 holes and eight pairs of shared fairways. The first and last tee shots appear to be the easiest shots in golf, open with no apparent trouble.

But the hazards of the Old Course are there, even if they are not always visible. The bunkers that defend the course from outright assaults are often invisible from the tee boxes or approach areas. When the wind blows, as it usually does from the River Eden and Estuary to the north-northwest and from St. Andrews Bay to the east, these bunkers are a real source of confusion to the golfers. Many are in the centre of the fairways and "gather" the ball from nearby bumps in the terrain; the player must find a way to play over, short of or around them.

Then there are the greens. These are protected in a few cases by bunkers, but, in most instances, by the uneven terrain. Given the breeze that is expected, the greens will also get firmer and faster, giving the Old Course the qualities the top golfers feel it must have to show its proper, subtle face.

The par-four 470-yard fourth hole offers a good illustration of the Old Course's devious ways. From the tee the golfer's eye is drawn to an alleyway right up the centre to the green. It is appealing precisely because it looks like a funnel. But the space is only 22 yards wide; a shot missed even a little to the right will find two tiny traps that cannot be seen from the tee. The faces of these traps are so steep that a golfer cannot reach the green from them.

At the 14th hole, called the Long Hole In, the hazards of the Old Course are further developed. An old stone wall that begins at the tee and curves with the flow of the hole for a while is out-of-bounds. The proper line from the tee is towards a church spire visible to the right of St. Andrews, which lies in the distance. A series of four bunkers called the Beardies threatens the tee shot hit left and away from the wall.

Should a golfer wish to get near the raised green on his second shot, he must carry Hell Bunker. This fearsome gash in the earth directs the prudent golfer to its left. From there the correct approach will be a running pitch through a ridge in front of the green.

The final holes on the Old Course bring with them not only the malevolence implicit in every situation, but the prospect of soon reaching what Ben Crenshaw calls "the most welcoming site in golf": the town itself.

A golfer who reaches these last holes Sunday afternoon with a chance of winning will have a real problem on his hands. The thought of capturing what is undoubtedly the most coveted title in golf must be quelled if he hopes to breathe, let alone swing the club.

The hard part is next: to just play golf as if it were nothing more than a comfortable round with friends. Greg Norman, winner of the Kemper and Canadian Opens in recent weeks and playoff loser to Fuzzy Zoeller and Tom Watson in the U.S. and Western Opens, says, "If I can crack the barrier of the final stretch when I am in contention, the toughest mental barrier of all, everything else will be like a piece of cake."

Historically, few golfers have won the Open on the Old Course who have not gotten on intimate terms with it. In 1964, the late Tony Lema did come through in his first try and with very little practice, but he had the sage advice of caddy Tip Anderson. Jack Nicklaus was second in his first appearance that year. But Nicklaus's experience and love of the Old Course have given him wins in the last two Opens held at St. Andrews.

This year, the attention has been given to a group of five golfers: Nicklaus, Norman, Crenshaw, Tom Watson and Seve Ballesteros. St. Andrews bookmakers have made Watson the favourite at 5 to 1, with Nicklaus at 9 to 1, Ballesteros and Norman at 10 to 1 and Crenshaw at 16 to 1.

Norman, of course, is the hottest and most confident golfer at the moment. Feeling he ranks better than joint fourth favourite (though his odds have been dropping), Norman has been moderately annoyed, something he has been known to use as a spur in his career.

"I have beaten the Americans, the British and the Australians," he argues, "all on their own ground. My confidence is high and my attitude is positive. I don't think this will change over the next three or four weeks."

Watson, meanwhile, is far and away the leading money-winner on the PGA Tour with $426,959. He edged Norman to win the Western Open two weeks ago. He has also won five British Opens in the past 10 years, including consecutive victories in 1982 and '83. And he is certainly well-liked in St. Andrews, if not yet well-loved, as Nicklaus is.

As high and successful as Watson is riding now, he shows a humble side when discussing the Old Course. Humility being a quality the Old Course likes in its champions, Watson is no doubt in good shape.

"The most difficult thing here," Watson says, "is to judge where I want to hit the ball, but I have gotten closer through my practice rounds. But the Old Course is difficult to understand, and I don't think anyone can get very close to it. Maybe that's why it's great."

Ballesteros, with his 1979 British Open victory and Masters wins in '80 and '83, is certainly a candidate for his first win at the Old Course. But he has not been playing well this year.

The same holds true for Crenshaw. Since his Masters win, he has played what he calls "patchy" golf. But, Crenshaw revels in the challenge of the Old Course. He tied for second with Tom Kite in 1978.

Somehow, though, one always comes back to Nicklaus in thinking about this Open. There is plenty of reason to believe he could win for the third consecutive time here, making him the only winner at the Old Course in the past 20 years. He has the experience, he has the savvy to play the course intelligently and he has been there before.

"To win a third time here would be special," Nicklaus says, "particularly at this stage in my career. The Old Course is an amazing place in that it can still challenge golfers after all these years."

The Globe and Mail, July 20, 1984

St. Andrews, Scotland — The morning of the first day of the 113th Open championship dawned, dappled in light, delicate as a French impressionist painting. The warm sun that has bathed the links of the Old Course in softness all week continued to enchant, while in the cobbled streets of the town and down by the bay gentlemen and gentlewomen took an early walk.

This was just after 6 a.m. and the Open had yet to begin. One visitor's stroll took him past the University of St. Andrews's departments of Logic and Metaphysics, and further on to a splendid structure overlooking the bay, the department of Moral Philosophy. Behind him was the cathedral at the end of North Street, where Old Tom Morris and his son Young Tom, winners of the first Open championships, were buried. At the other extreme was the clubhouse of the Royal and Ancient Golf Club of St. Andrews, standing sentinel over the hallowed links.

Though all was quiet on the Old Course, here and there was the sense of the life that had given birth to the links so many centuries ago. A hike into the dunes near the beach brought the walker in touch with nature. No rabbits were in evidence, but perhaps that was because the rabbit-catcher hired by the Royal and Ancient had been doing his job.

In any case, it was easy to recall the words of British writer Sir Guy Campbell, who said that it was the animal life around the beach and in the dunes that once fertilized the ground upon which the world's finest golfers were soon to frolic.

It was also a pleasure to think of philosopher, golfer and metaphysician Michael Murphy, who had written a book called *Golf in the Kingdom,* set on a course he called Burningbush, but which was obviously the Old Course.

Murphy detailed his meetings with a spiritually inclined Scottish golf professional named Shivas Irons. Through him, and a phantom named Seamus Macduff, whose ghost still lurked on the Old Course, Murphy was instructed on the fine art of using "true gravity" to guide his way around the links. Who would have guessed that later one of the first day's leaders would say he had read the book carefully, and indeed had learned so much from it?

A most orderly procession of golfers began at precisely 7:30 a.m. and would continue until 4:35 p.m., when the last of 52 groups would heed the starter's call to the post. In the mood for metaphysics rather than swing-physics, this visitor followed his own call to the links.

The crowds that followed the golfers included fans whose enthusiasm might have seemed a little wild and crazy to those who approach the royal and ancient game more conservatively. There was, for example, a rosy-cheeked fellow named Bill Birch from Lancashire in England, who, when he watches the Masters on the "telly," methodically surrounds himself with tournament memorabilia such as programs, books and pictures, the better to call up thoughts of Bobby Jones and Gene Sarazen.

Birch, it should be noted, was not at the Old Course this week merely to watch the Open. This was a mission: to come back with proof as to who was the taller golfer, Jack Nicklaus or Tom Watson. Apparently there was a bookmaker in Lancashire who had been giving odds that Watson was the taller. Hard to believe, but Birch was serious.

If Birch was "a bit off," then what was one to make of Archie Baird of Aberlady, near Edinburgh? Last week, Baird and a companion played six rounds of golf in one day over the three courses of Gullane near Muirfield. Then, he and his wife, Sheila, went out for dinner.

There was more to charm and delight, but perhaps most enjoyable were Peter Jacobsen's comments after his five-under-par 67 put him in a tie for the lead. A gifted golfer, Jacobsen has rarely played to his abilities, having won just two tournaments in his seven-and-a-half-year career on the PGA Tour.

But yesterday Jacobsen was on his game. A 15-foot putt went down on the first hole for a birdie and by the 16th it was obvious the Old Course was his friend. Already five under, he bounced a shot short of the Principal's Nose bunker, but somehow the ball jumped over it. He took advantage, by wedging to 10 feet from the pin, setting up a birdie putt. A bogey on the harsh Road Hole followed, and a par gave him the 67.

As well as he played, Jacobsen credited better thinking rather than better swinging. For the past two months, he has worked with Sports Enhancement Associates in Eugene, Oregon, where a series of two-hour philosophical sessions have helped him believe in himself and face up to his talent. Part of his mental training has included immersion in Murphy's book, and it just might be that Shivas Irons and Seamus Macduff were at the Old Course yesterday, pushing his ball beyond the Principal's Nose.

"I didn't see them out there," Jacobsen said, laughing, "but they're out there and I'm looking for them."

Shivas and Seamus, wherever they are, and Murphy, if he is still in California writing a book on the influence of the mind on performance in sport, would have loved to hear this.

The Globe and Mail, July 19, 1990
St. Andrews, Scotland — To North Americans, the tournament that starts today at St. Andrews is the British Open. But this

event is more than a national championship. It's a world championship, *The* Open, as it's properly called.

Everything in St. Andrews calls attention to this fact. Shops sell clothes marked Open Championship, 1990. The tournament program is about the Open golf championship. Scots and others wandering the streets never talk about a British Open; only visitors from North America use that term.

The British Open, to be sure, is a North American invention. It was only with the advent of the United States Open in 1895, and subsequent national championships, that observers began to use the term British Open. But this is as much a British Open as Wimbledon is a British tennis championship.

Consider the venue first. St. Andrews is the acknowledged home of golf, from where the game spread around the world. Many golfers make pilgrimages here, not only to watch the Open, but to play the Old Course. It's a genuine public course, an open course, open to the world's golfers. Some golfers book their starting times three years in advance.

As the home of golf, then, it's appropriate that the Old Course should play host to the most coveted of all tournaments. U.S. golfers Curtis Strange and Tom Kite might say that the U.S. Open is their most important championship, but in their heart of golfing hearts, they know differently and will admit their feelings in private: There is something extraordinary about this event, this Open.

That is why Strange and Kite and 153 other golfers from around the world are here. Professional golfers seek not only fame and fortune at an Open, but a chance to be considered truly great golfers. They are here for history.

"Winning an Open?" Welshman Ian Woosnam asked this week. "This is what I always wanted to win all my life. I regard it as the ultimate championship."

Or how about defending champion Mark Calcavecchia? Here's a fellow whose idea of historical reminiscence is to talk about what movie he saw last week. But he seemed to change after his Open win last year.

"I have spent a great year," he said. "A lot of great things have happened to me because I won the Open. Now that I have won, I want to win another, real bad."

Then there's Greg Norman, 1986 Open winner. What does the Open mean to him? Would it mean more than a win in the U.S. Open?

"I think the Open is the major of majors," Norman said. Notice the way he said it. The Open. Not the British Open.

Even golfers who haven't played an Open before know they are involved in a world championship. Canadian Dave Barr walked off his qualifying course after four holes on Monday when he was well out of it. Barr was encountered walking around St. Andrews that afternoon, looking vaguely lost and obviously disappointed. He was leaving for Vancouver the next day, since he couldn't abide being around the Open without playing in it.

Canadians Danny Mijovic of Unionville, Ontario, and Jim Rutledge of Victoria are playing. Mijovic played a practice round yesterday with Gary Player and his son, Wayne. Rutledge played the Old Course like a student, examining this fold of ground, checking this line of play. This is the Open, and it deserves careful attention.

Yet the Open also calls for a touch of whimsy, as befits a tournament that honours a frustrating game. The officials of the Royal and Ancient Golf Club of St. Andrews who run the championship are sometimes stuffy, but they also know how to have a good time while implicitly suggesting that their championship is the world championship. And they show it here, especially with the draw for the first two rounds.

Therefore, we have the threesome of Spaniard Seve Ballesteros, American Tom Watson and Zimbabwean Nick Price. Ballesteros won over Watson in the 1984 Open at the Old Course and over Price in the 1988 Open at Royal Lytham and St. Anne's in England. Now they're playing together.

But the prize for devilish arrangements must go to the R & A official who decided that Greg Norman must play with Bob Tway and Robert Gamez. Tway holed out from a bunker on the final hole to beat Norman in the 1986 PGA Championship in Ohio, while Gamez holed a 176-yard shot on the last hole to win over Norman in the Bay Hill Classic in Florida this past spring. Ghoulish? Maybe.

Yet it is with such touches that the Open asserts itself as the golf championship of the world. Englishman Nick Faldo starts as

7-1 favourite. He has said that majors are everything to him, and he speaks for all golfers when he says that this major — The Open — is a breed apart.

The PGA Championship

The Globe and Mail, **August 9, 1989**
This is a lament for the loss of match play. Golf's original form of competition has nearly disappeared from the professional scene. This week's PGA Championship is the demonstration case.

The PGA, golf's fourth major, was match play from 1916-1957, after which it switched to stroke play. Match play, of course, pits one player against another in knockout competition. The golfer who wins the most holes in a match advances. Walter Hagen beat Wild Bill Mehlhorn 6 and 5 to win the 1925 PGA at Olympia Fields, Illinois, not far from the Kemper Lakes club in Hawthorn, Illinois, where this week's tournament is on. Hagen was six holes up with five to play. Game over.

Stroke play pits each golfer against the field. Golfers aren't knocked out except at the halfway cut. They add up their scores for 18 holes, total them for four rounds, and there you have it: The winner is the low shooter. It's become the usual means of identifying champions, but it shouldn't be the only one.

The PGA changed from match play to stroke play in 1958 for one reason and one reason only — television. Buoyed by Arnold Palmer's emergence as a charismatic star, networks had begun to cover golf. They didn't want to televise a tournament in which a star might be knocked out early. Better to show him at the end, even if he wasn't doing well.

The thinking seemed commercially sound, but it was born out of fear. Golf needed and needs a match-play championship. The PGA's format had been its strength. Inevitably, the public and players began to see it as more than another weekly event, yes, but less than the Masters and British and U.S. Opens. It's a minor major.

The PGA today is not the tournament it might have been had the ruling body — the Professional Golfers' Association of America — kept it at match play. It also doesn't help that it's the last major of the season, and that it comes too quickly on the heels of the British Open, which was played three weeks ago.

Consider the Masters. The first major of the season arrives three months after the PGA Tour begins, at the beginning of spring. Golf fans are eager, as are the players. The Masters also is identifiable as golf's classiest event; it's golf legend Bobby Jones's contribution to the game, as is the Augusta National Golf Club. The event mesmerizes. It's one to savour.

Next comes the U.S. Open, 10 weeks on. Golfers are well into the season. They've found and lost their games and perhaps found them again. Amateurs across the U.S. and Canada also are well into their season. They're ready for a national championship.

The British Open comes around five weeks later. The time between events is shortening, but no matter. The PGA and European Tours have been in full swing for months. Golfers around the world have tried to qualify. They're ready to gather in a different country of golf for what seems like a world championship. And it's always a doozie.

Who can forget the last day's drama at Royal Troon three weeks ago, when Greg Norman shot 64 to get into a playoff before self-destructing, when Wayne Grady almost came through, when Mark Calcavecchia overwhelmed the grand old links to win? The memories are still fresh.

Nevertheless, here comes the PGA. It's too soon. The PGA ought to be in the fall. Then there might be time to get excited about it.

Even that, however, wouldn't suffice. The PGA should return to match play. So what if Seve Ballesteros and Curtis Strange aren't in the final match? Proper coverage would allow us to follow them in the earlier matches. Besides, golf isn't meant to be a fair game. If Ballesteros is knocked out by a player who couldn't touch him over 72 holes of stroke play, so be it. Match play's unpredictability is its charm.

The irony is that the PGA of America has the example of the Ryder Cup as proof that match play is popular and deserves nurturing. The 1987 Ryder Cup at Muirfield Village Golf Club in Dublin, Ohio, was full of people. The tournament was carried on network television. This year's renewal of the Ryder Cup will be held in September in England. More than the PGA, it seems like the next major on the calendar.

But none of this matters to the PGA of America. The organization has let its championship be diluted. It will get less media coverage than any major. Herbert Warren Wind of *The New Yorker* magazine covers the Masters and U.S. Open, but not the PGA. Scot Sandy Lyle didn't play the PGA last year, though he had won the Masters.

Where have you gone, match play? You're in club championships across North America. You're the main game at clubs in the U.K. But you're not at Kemper Lakes this week, and we miss you.

The Globe and Mail, August 12, 1991

Carmel, Indiana — Forget the ozone. John Daly was the X-zone while winning the PGA Championship at the Crooked Stick Golf Club. The new and completely unexpected golf hero hit the ball into uncharted areas no other golfer came near and in the process set himself a new course in life.

But for a stutter step on the 17th hole yesterday, which he three-putted for double-bogey, Daly was awesome. There's almost no frame of reference by which to assess his 12-under performance while winning his first major, check, his first win in his first year on the PGA Tour. He ran roughshod over the field at Crooked Stick.

This was the story of the year in golf, by far, maybe in years. It was thrilling to watch Jack Nicklaus win the 1986 Masters at age 46. But it was happening out at Crooked Stick, where the midwestern golf fans discovered a golfer who could be a star of international proportions.

"I just feel so wonderful," Daly said. "It's a dream come true. I'm just glad an American won another major."

This American, though, is different. He is not only the longest driver on any tour anywhere, he's the longest accurate driver. Never mind Greg Norman, Mark Calcavecchia and Freddie Couples. Daly's divot on most holes was the only one within 30 or 40 yards.

But Daly, who now gets a 10-year exemption onto the PGA Tour, is more than a long driver. Lots of those have come down the pike and ended up choosing long-driving exhibitions for a living. Nothing dishonourable about that, but the real game is about playing at the highest levels and winning. Daly did so while seeming to mature in one fell swoop, one magical week.

How could you figure it? Daly was ninth alternate in the PGA Championship when the week began. He moved up to first as golfers dropped out for various reasons and drove all night Wednesday from his home in Dardanelle, Arkansas, to Crooked Stick. Maybe he would get in.

Get in he did, after Nick Price went home to be with his wife, who was in labour. Daly didn't have practice rounds with his two pals Hubie Green and Fuzzy Zoeller, outlaws themselves in a conservative game. But Daly did get Price's caddy, Squeaky, and he did have a game tailor-made to Crooked Stick's 7,289 yards.

But come on. How could he win, even after a first-round, three-under par 69? Then he shot 67 on Friday and 69 Saturday. Legends were starting about the pugnacious golfer with the in-genuous blue eyes, the smoke in his hand, the casual flick of the right hand with the putter, a pace so fast he might rival Moe Norman as the game's speediest pro.

Daly once broke a golf ball with his driver. So went story No. 1. Air fizzed out of the ball when he crushed it. He's built like a fullback, but any brute aspect of the fellow is in his movement, not his bulk. Daly was smooth. He rolled the ball into the hole all week as if he had it on remote control.

"I felt like I could make the putt every time I stepped over it," Daly said. "I think the key was that all four days I didn't think. I just hit it."

The crowd loved Daly's attitude. Here was a guy anybody could root for. He talked about how his only goal this year had been to keep his PGA Tour card. He painted a scene of his fiancée, Bettye Fulford, sticking by the phone in Dardanelle when he was out, and vice versa, in case the call came that he was moving up the alternate list.

Then came yesterday. Daly putted before playing and didn't care if he missed a short one. So what? It was practice. Kids high-fived him and adults crowded him for autographs, or maybe just to get near him. Daly couldn't believe all the support fans were giving him.

"I think the fans won this tournament for me," he said. "I really do."

He also won it for them. Daly responded to the fans who surrounded him whenever they could. A phalanx of Indiana State Police protected him, but you thought Daly wouldn't have minded if the folks walked down the fairway with him.

Those fans listened when Daly teed off every hole. They heard something unusual.

"Kill," Daly's caddy, Squeaky, told him whenever he set up with a driver. Daly killed all right. He destroyed the field and the course and turned himself into a folk hero at the same time. It sounds crazy, but old-timers confirmed that neither Arnold Palmer nor Jack Nicklaus ever heard louder cheers or received stronger support.

So it went at Crooked Stick for a golfer nobody knew a week ago. Now the golf world is suddenly a Daly planet, and Crooked Stick a place where a dream came true for a long shot who hit long shots one hole after another.

The Globe and Mail, **August 14, 1991**
John Daly's Rocky-style march to victory Sunday in the PGA Championship has sent otherwise rational people into a frenzy. The reaction to the fairy tale come true has been continuous, even heedless. Yo, Long John.

"Watching John Daly for four hours on Sunday was more exciting than watching man walk on the moon," Toronto physician John Goldberg said the other day. The good doctor might have overstated the case slightly. Then again, maybe not.

Next came businessman Ken Barnes. He mentioned that it was a pleasure to see somebody give the ball such a good whack. Barnes could have been speaking for all golfers who were turned on as Daly averaged more than 300 yards on his drives at Crooked Stick.

Barnes was followed as speedily as Daly hits a putt by a comment from Torontonian Norman Greenberg. This mid-amateur has qualified for next week's U.S. Amateur at the Honors Club in

Chattanooga and will be going for a Rocky-type story of his own. But he wanted only to talk about Daly.

"He was like a bullfighter at a baseball game," Greenberg said. "It was awesome."

Awesome it was. Daly's style could force swing gurus to think again.

Daly's swing arc is so wide and his turn behind the ball so extreme you would think his back muscles could tear. But he generates oodles of potential energy. His backswing ranges wild and free; it's an uninhibited attack on the ball.

That backswing sets up a tremendous coil behind the ball. Daly then rotates to his target so quickly and powerfully that his clubhead lags well behind. Daly produces extreme clubhead speed as his spinning body pulls the clubhead through the ball. And he does so in balance. His gyrating motion is as graceful as it is powerful and efficient.

Then there's Daly's approach to the game. His speed could be mistaken for carelessness. There's no lining up from six angles. Nor does Daly read a putt. One look and he raps the ball. He trusts his instincts.

Daly's task now will be to maintain his carefree approach. The worst thing he could do would be to analyze his method and write an instructional book. But golfers everywhere will want to discern a "secret" in his swing. Who knows, maybe he has one; he wasn't exactly a nobody before the PGA, having won $166,000 for seventy-second place on the money list in his rookie year prior to the PGA.

But nobody should swing like Daly unless he's four years old. That's when Daly, now 25, started on a nine-hole course in Dardanelle, Arkansas. Golfers could, however, adopt his rapid-fire style. He doesn't miss 'em quick, he makes 'em quick.

Yet Daly wouldn't be a candidate for a modern golf hero just because he drives long and straight or plays rapidly. Canadian legend Moe Norman hits the ball straighter and has for 45 years. And Daly himself said that Bobby Wilson, another Arkansas pro, hits the ball longer than he does.

Oddly, Norman and Wilson have been giving clinics this summer across Canada. They're billed as "the longest and the straightest" and will next appear August 22 at noon at the

Lionhead club in Mississauga and at 6 p.m. at the St. Andrew's East club in Stouffville, Ontario. Daly, though, combines the longest and the straightest in one player, and a major championship winner.

He also mixes with the fans, hangs out at football games and just plain enjoys himself. It will be interesting to see how he handles the massive attention he'll get now — his story made the front page of *The New York Times* on Monday, for instance.

But Daly is not the next Jack Nicklaus, as too many people are saying. That's ridiculous.

There was an object lesson at the PGA. Golfer Bobby Clampett, microphone in hand, strode alongside Daly during the final rounds at Crooked Stick and could be seen grinning when Daly responded to the fans as he went down the last fairway. Clampett was heralded as the next Nicklaus when he arrived on the PGA Tour in 1981 with his "Golfing Machine" swing, as it was known. Now he's a struggling golfer who was working for CBS during the PGA.

Still, it's true that Daly is an exceptionally gifted golfer. Bruce Lietzke, who finished second at Crooked Stick, said he could be the next golfer to win seven or eight PGA Tour events a year.

We'll see. Thus far Daly has provided the golf world with a memorable four days. We don't know what he'll do next, but what he has already accomplished was remarkable enough.

The Ryder Cup

The Globe and Mail, **September 26, 1991**
Johnny Miller was relaxing in NBC's broadcast booth at the Honda Classic in Lauderhill, Florida, last March when he casually mentioned that he was already looking forward to the Ryder Cup. Miller said the match-play competition between teams of 12 professionals from the United States and Europe would be the biggest event this year, and that he was excited about his role as analyst on the telecast.

The event is now at hand, and it should be something. The Ryder Cup will begin tomorrow at the new Ocean Course on

Kiawah Island, South Carolina. The United States hasn't won the Cup since 1983, although it is 21-5-2 since the biennial matches began in 1927.

But the United States has not for some time been an automatic winner of these matches that bring team play into a game that week after week is relentlessly individual. Some publications are calling this year's Ryder Cup a "war on the shore," implying that the battle for world supremacy will be waged and won at the edge of the sea on Pete Dye's Ocean Course.

The players themselves agree and tend to calibrate the matches in weighty terms. Lanny Wadkins, for one, is a crucial member of the U.S. team. And Wadkins, who has played six of the past seven Ryder Cups, feels that nothing less than the stature of the PGA Tour is at stake.

"You're representing your country and your tour," Wadkins said recently from his home in Dallas. "We all have a lot of pride in our tour. We think it's the best in the world."

That may be, but the Europeans rather than the Americans have dominated world golf in recent years. The big names have been Nick Faldo, Seve Ballesteros, Ian Woosnam and José-Maria Olazabal. Wadkins and other U.S. golfers have been relegated to almost a second-class status, and the Ryder Cup results have only confirmed the position that lies uneasily on the U.S. team's shoulders. The United States lost in 1985 and 1987 and tied in 1989. Europe therefore still holds the Ryder Cup.

The upshot of it all is that the U.S. team is hungry to bring back the Cup. Golfers on the PGA Tour have been talking about the Ryder Cup all year. Many have visited the Ocean Course. They were humbled in the past few matches and so have prepared themselves as well as possible.

One doesn't have to go far back in the Ryder Cup to understand what it means to the players. Wadkins recalls a wedge shot he hit on the final hole of the penultimate match during the 1983 Ryder Cup at PGA National Golf Club in Palm Beach Gardens. The Ryder Cup hung in the balance.

"Hitting that wedge shot I was probably the most nervous I have felt in my life," Wadkins said.

But the shot was perfect and finished a foot from the hole. Wadkin's birdie won the hole from José-Maria Canizares, tied his

match and won the Ryder Cup for the United States. It hasn't
won since.

"Tom Kite slapped me on the back when I walked on the
green and said, 'Great shot,'" Wadkins recalled. "I turned to say
something to him, but my mouth was so dry nothing came out."

Wadkins also heard that team captain Jack Nicklaus went back
to the spot 72 yards away in the fairway from which he had hit
the shot.

"They say Nicklaus kissed the divot," Wadkins said.

Such extravagant feeling has transformed the Ryder Cup into
a major championship. It's why the 25,000 tickets for the event
were sold out within a week of going on sale in October 1990.
It's why European team member Woosnam says that the players
will be so nervous on the first tee come tomorrow's opening
matches that they'll be hoping just to make contact with the ball.

As tremendous a sporting event as the Ryder Cup is becoming
in North America, it should not be surprising that NBC and the
USA networks will combine for 21 1/2 hours of coverage. No
golf event in North America has been as widely covered.

What is difficult to understand, however, is that Canadian networks in particular have chosen not to pick up coverage. Torontonian Guy Murray held the rights to Canadian coverage, but
was able to place the NBC feed only in the London, Ontario,
Winnipeg and Maritime markets.

"There were two problems," Murray said. "One, most people
in the program and sales departments are unfamiliar with the
Ryder Cup. And two, there's a plethora of sports coverage now
with NFL football, a Blue Jays pennant race and Canadian football having a minor resurgence."

The ridiculous aspect of this was that as of this week most
Toronto-area golf fans were still shut out from seeing the Ryder
Cup. Yet Toronto is one of the top golf markets in North America. Even the Buffalo NBC affiliate, WGRZ, had decided not to
pick up network coverage.

But WGRZ relented after a flurry of calls from Buffalo and
southern Ontario. The station will carry the Ryder Cup from 3 to
6 p.m. on Saturday and 1:30 to 3:30 on Sunday, by which time
the matches will be finished. "We weren't aware of the impact of
this tournament," WGRZ regional sales manager George Correa

said after the station changed its mind. "We just weren't on it. But fortunately we caught our mistake in time."

WGRZ's change of heart will be every southern Ontario golf fan's gain. The Ryder Cup is usually thrilling, as complete in what it provides in emotional range as most weekly events are threadbare because they are mostly about money.

Money is not an issue at the Ryder Cup, because there is no purse. Miller has said the competition will be a "study, a doctoral thesis on handling pressure and nerves." And Nicklaus isn't known to have kissed any divots from any of his 20 major championship wins.

But Nicklaus is said to have done so in the Ryder Cup. Need we know more about the significance of the Ryder Cup? Golfers' eyes will be on the happening in South Carolina this weekend, and rightly so.

The Globe and Mail, **September 28, 1991**

Kiawah Island, South Carolina — Tension in 72-hole golf tournaments doesn't usually start until the last nine holes. But yesterday's opening matches in the twenty-ninth Ryder Cup at the wicked Ocean Course demonstrated that foursomes and better-ball competitions are different. They produced tension from the start to the finish during the first day of the three-day event.

Looking at the end first, the results of the day showed the U.S. on top. They led four and a half points to three and a half after the morning and afternoon matches. The same formats go today, with 8 of the 12 members of each Ryder Cup team playing. The competition concludes tomorrow with 12 singles matches, each match counting for one point.

But back to the beginning, when Seve Ballesteros and José-Maria Olazabal were out against Paul Azinger and Chip Beck in the first of the four foursomes, or alternate-shot, morning matches. Their match, which the Spaniards won 2 and 1, set the tone for the Ryder Cup's to and fro tempo.

Here, for starters, was Azinger on the first hole. He needed to make a short putt to halve the hole since Ballesteros and Olazabal were in with par. Azinger was putting for himself, for Beck and for the U.S. team — a three-in-one deal. No wonder there was something in the ocean breezes that isn't tangible so early at other tournaments.

Azinger holed the putt, and then Ballesteros drove left into the marsh on the next hole. His mistake led to others, and he and Olazabal were lying seven by the time they reached the green. What could they do but concede the hole and laugh, which they did? This was match play, so they only lost the hole. They didn't need to count the score towards a total.

Things went from bad to worse for the Spaniards. Ballesteros was wild with his shots and Olazabal couldn't save the team every time. The Europeans were three down after nine, but they were making some people happy.

Those people were the Americans, of course. They were wearing the stars and stripes on their shirts, sweaters and visors. Chip Beck's wife, Karen, featured stars and stripes on her earrings. U.S. team captain Dave Stockton had said at the opening ceremonies that American pride was alive and well. Who could argue?

That American pride had taken the form of a momentarily confrontational rules discussion on the ninth hole of the match under discussion. Olazabal had lost his ball in a water hazard off his drive, and Azinger was saying that the ball had entered the water in one place. Olazabal and Ballesteros felt differently, and it was left to the match referee to decide from where the Europeans could play their next shot, under penalty of one stroke.

The penalty led to another loss of hole, and then an arcane rules discussion took place on the 10th tee. This extended forum was of no consequence except to rankle Ballesteros. He often plays better in that mood.

Suddenly Ballesteros was transformed, and Olazabal followed. The twosome won the 10th, 12th and 13th holes to draw even, and then Olazabal floated a 30-yard sand shot within three feet of the 15th hole. The Americans three-putted, Ballesteros holed the short putt that Olazabal's golden shot had left him, and the Europeans were one up with three to play. The match had changed quickly.

The teams moved on and halved the 16th with pars before facing long shots over the water into the wind of the treacherous par-three 17th. Pete Dye had placed such a strong hole for maximum match play effect and got his wish. Olazabal backed off his shot, then drilled a longish iron 25 feet from the hole. Beck followed to 35 feet away, and so his side was still in the game.

But Ballesteros sent his putt skimming across the slope of the 17th green and watched as it melted into the hole. That was it; he and Olazabal had won 2 and 1 in a match they seemed to have lost early.

That's the Ryder Cup, and that's match play. Fred Couples's wife, Debbie, led her husband onto every green yesterday during his two wins with Ray Floyd. She waved the American flag all the way. Cheerleading, she knew that every match is a mini-tournament and that every shot counts so much.

Call this the Ryder Cup theme, then, when every shot is its own story. Early evening came and David Feherty holed a 12-footer for par at the 18th to bring himself and Sam Torrance back from a three-hole disadvantage to tie Mark O'Meara and Lanny Wadkins in their better-ball match. And Azinger and Beck would draw water, not blood, on the 17th to lose their second match to Ballesteros and Olazabal.

So maybe it's proper that the Ryder Cup occurs but every two years. Weekly events that provided so many swings of fortune from the first drive might be too much to take. Only two days to go, and who knows what might happen?

The Globe and Mail, **September 30, 1991**
Kiawah Island, South Carolina — Where were the stress-relief experts when the golfers in the Ryder Cup needed them? Every player could hardly catch his breath during yesterday's final single matches, and though the United States came out on top it was apparent at the end that no tournament is more nerve-racking than this biennial elaboration of what golf can demand of its top players.

"As far as pressure goes, there is more here than you can imagine," U.S. player Fred Couples said after the matches ended. "It's a weird experience, people screaming USA, USA."

Couples was speaking for all the players, for the pressure was numbing from the first shot yesterday. Hale Irwin was in the last match and said he could hardly talk during the final nine holes against Bernhard Langer. No wonder; the entire Ryder Cup came down to that last match.

As the day's play was ending, the United States and Europe had each won 13 of the 28 points available in the competition. The United States needed 14 1/2 points to win the Ryder Cup for the first time since 1983. Europe needed 14 to retain the Cup, since it won last time and a tie is, in essence, a win for the holder.

Those requirements translated into at least a victory and a tied match for the United States. Lanny Wadkins and Irwin, in the second-to-last and last matches, were playing Mark James and Langer, respectively.

Wadkins, two up, gained his par-five on the 16th, which was good enough to win when James missed from 15 feet for par. That point ensured the United States at least a tie in the matches. Wadkins couldn't contain his emotion. A towel was his only protection from the tears streaming down his face.

But here came Langer and Irwin, fighting for the last point and the match. Everything rode on their play as they stood on the 197-yard par-three 17th that played into the wind across a pond. The players on both sides gathered there, as did the captains. Langer was one down and needed to win both the 17th and 18th to take the match, tie the over-all competition and re-tain the Ryder Cup for his side.

Langer had played his heart out already, holing an eight-foot par putt on the 15th to get to one down and a five-footer at the 16th to keep the match going. How much could he be expected to do?

Now Langer hit his tee shot just left of the green at the 17th, and Irwin did the same. Irwin, one up at the time, needed but two putts to ensure the necessary half-point to win the Ryder Cup for the United States, but he three-putted. Langer made a gutsy short putt to take the hole.

And so it came down to the last hole, a 438-yard par-four along a greensward cut between the dunes. Irwin pulled his drive, Langer was dead centre and before you knew it the play-ers were surrounded by 20,000 fans. Both players missed the green to the right, Irwin chipped well short of the pin and then Langer putted from the fringe to within five feet of the hole.

Irwin had the putt to win but left it short, so Langer now needed his short putt to win the hole and the match. That would make it 14-14, all square and in many ways a fitting result after three days of thrilling golf.

But Langer missed the putt, and it was over. Fans swarmed the green to celebrate. Champagne bottles popped open. European team captain Bernard Gallacher rushed on to the green to console Langer. Langer had made those difficult putts to send the match down the last fairway and on to the final green, where the entire competition came down to his last putt. But he missed the putt, and that was it.

Yet in other ways that was not it. One remembered the emotion the players showed. Mark Calcavecchia was nearly inconsolable after losing the last four holes to tie Colin Montgomerie. The half-point seemed critical at the time.

Some golfers handled the demands of the situation well. Corey Pavin holed from off the green at the second in his match against new British star Stephen Richardson and was on a high the rest of the way as he won. Paul Azinger handled José-Maria Olazabal and seemed in another world all the way round.

In the end the two teams gathered with U.S. vice-president Dan Quayle at the closing ceremonies had much to be proud of. Gallacher congratulated Langer "for playing so well under tremendously stressful and pressurized circumstances." Both teams stood to acknowledge Langer's courageous play.

But Langer was just not good enough, Irwin just was, and so the U.S. team now holds the Ryder Cup again. Major championships for individual prizes are special, but the Ryder Cup is extraordinary. The U.S. and European players showed why, time after time, even as the pressure told in their often faltering swings.

The Globe and Mail, **October 2, 1991**
Among the many reactions to the Ryder Cup, none has been more intriguing than the observation that the emotion the players showed was surprising.

Those golfers who have expressed this feeling base their idea on the notion of golf as an individual game. And of course, it is most of the time, every golfer for him or herself.

But golf has also been a team game since it began, and continues to be. Club golfers often engage in better-ball matches. British golfers play foursomes, or alternate-shot matches, two to a side. The format isn't popular in North America, but the Ryder Cup may encourage people to try the game.

The Ryder Cup could influence golf positively, should players allow it to. We in Canada and the United States tend to ignore both match play and team play. Individuals to the end, we insist on our right to post a score, no matter how high.

But match and team play allow even the hacker to participate in ways that make sense. Seve Ballesteros and Wayne Levi inadvertently made the point in their singles match on Sunday when they double-bogeyed and triple-bogeyed the par-five second hole, respectively.

Such high scores would have cost more in individual golf than they did by the Ryder Cup format. Ballesteros won the hole and Levi lost the hole, no more benefit or loss than that. But double and triple bogeys deplete one's account in individual medal play. Match play and team play can cushion the blow. Holes can be recovered more easily than strokes, teammates can win points that other members lose.

Team golf, however, is onerous in ways that individual play is not. Hence the burden that Bernhard Langer felt as he stood over his five-foot putt on the last hole that, had he made it, would have kept the Ryder Cup for the Europeans.

The responsibility that Langer shouldered was something every player in the Ryder Cup felt. Nick Faldo admitted to finding the gravity of team play too much to bear. He said he hated being out there during his last match against Ray Floyd. Faldo took the match one up, but not before nearly squandering a four-up lead with four holes to play.

Hours after the match even the members of the winning U.S. side were still quivering. Mark Calcavecchia said it was all too much for him, as was obvious when he lost his last four holes against Colin Montgomerie. He still tied the match, but such is the nature of team play that he felt he had lost.

Hale Irwin said much the same thing. His team had won, but Irwin was more in mind of his poor chip shot on the last hole that effectively gave Langer and the Europeans an opening.

"My disappointment after my pitch shot at 18 was so great," Irwin said. "Thankfully no one on this team will ever have to know [how great it was]."

Irwin referred frequently to the shared responsibility that team play demands.

"Twelve other people [including team captain Dave Stockton] are depending on you," he said. "That we're bringing our collective individual talents to this is something."

That "something" is intangible, yet it's the crux of team golf. Failure can ruin a player's confidence out of all seeming proportion to the error. Conversely, success becomes a massive asset that a player can draw upon. Fred Couples, of all the U.S. golfers, may benefit more than anybody from contributing to his team.

Two years ago at the Ryder Cup, Couples missed the 18th green the final day with a 9-iron in his hand. He lost his critical match to Christy O'Connor Jr. Couples has also failed down the stretch in major championships and has been candid in acknowledging his difficulties.

But Couples won three matches and tied another at the Ryder Cup. He matured as an individual by playing a huge role for his team.

"I can forget about it [making mistakes to lose] on Monday if it's an individual tournament," Couples said. "But not at a Ryder Cup."

Couples redeemed himself on Kiawah Island and was in some fundamental way a new man when he tried to speak at the post-match news conference. But he was so choked up he couldn't complete his first sentence. Such is the effect of team golf.

An hour later Couples accompanied Lanny Wadkins to a tent where U.S. fans were celebrating. Couples stood on a chair to thank people for their support. It would be hard to imagine a person more satisfied than he was then.

Couples was part of a team and he came through. Now he may well go on to win majors. His is a prodigious talent, and he finally showed it in team golf, a format that at the same time protects a player and renders him terribly vulnerable. This double edge makes team golf entirely different from individual golf. And the Ryder Cup is its ultimate expression.

Chapter Ten

WOMEN

THERE'S LITTLE question that male professional golfers get more coverage than do their female counterparts. I'm not sure why this is so, except that it might not be surprising in a society that has always made life rather more difficult for women than for men. The Ladies Professional Golf Association didn't really provide a significant means for a woman making a living at the game until the 1970s, a decade during which purses increased on the LPGA Tour from $600,000 in 1970 to $1.5 million in 1979. By the end of the 1980s the purses had reached $13 million, and so it made sense for a young woman to attend a college on a golf scholarship. There was money to be made in the game, at least on the LPGA Tour in the U.S.

As little money as there was in the early years, that didn't stop women from giving the game their best shot. I think that's because once somebody has the game in their blood, man or woman, he or she feels compelled to play, to turn into a first-rate competitor. That was certainly the case with Sandra Post, the tenacious Canadian golfer who won eight LPGA Tour events in her career before leaving in the mid-1980s, when she turned to teaching. Post was the first female professional I followed. The story that appears in this collection resulted from our meeting at a tournament in Florida in the winter of 1980 and originally ran in *Toronto Life* magazine. I always thought it was smart of the editors at *Toronto Life* to see the merits of a golf story about a woman who was determined to succeed at a professional sport. As recently as 10 years ago, there weren't all that many ways for a female athlete to provide a livelihood for herself.

But the life of a female professional has never been easy. Not that the life of any professional golfer is ever easy; after all, it's an itinerant life, and there certainly are not any home stands. A golfer might play at home once a year, and that's only if her hometown supports a tour event. In any case, a woman on the road is a woman undertaking an often lonely path. I recall the struggles that players on the LPGA spoke of when I spent a week with them at the start of the 1985 season. The piece that resulted appeared in the summer of that year in *City Woman* magazine. It, too, is included here, and as I reread it I am struck by the persistence of the players, many of whom are still on the LPGA Tour. Of course, they do have role models, the main golfer in this regard being Nancy Lopez. Lopez played with gusto and seemed to have the game in the right perspective. It was important to her, as it still is. But Lopez has a balance running throughout her life that has given her a security not always possible to find while leading the life of a professional golfer.

I also include in this chapter a column on that exceptional woman of Canadian golf, Ada Mackenzie. She was a terrific player, and moreover, she started the first golf club just for women in Canada. It still exists near Toronto on its original site, and it is thriving. Mackenzie knew all too well that women in 1925 didn't have access to many good courses. She went ahead and built her own, and even today Canadian women still speak of her intelligence and perceptiveness. Mackenzie was a big factor in moving women's golf along in Canada, at least at the competitive level. She was also a force in world golf and was an example to her contemporaries of the power of a vision. That's why Marlene Streit, Canada's top amateur for years, is involved in a tournament that honours Mackenzie.

In the end, as ever, women's golf is really not that different from men's golf. The common factor is that the game is the thing, at any level. That's why I close this chapter with an account of two magical weeks in Hawaii in 1992, when Canadians Lisa Walters and Dawn Coe won their first LPGA tournaments. The events as they unfolded seemed uncanny. But golf is like that: Remarkable things can happen on the course.

Sandra Post

Toronto Life, **May 1980**
While her swing is pure form, her character is pure spirit. Very few people know her, but she knows herself. Golfing around the world for 13 years, she has made many acquaintances, but golf courses are still among her best friends. All around her able golfers have fallen, but she has persevered. She won early and late with little but energy and hope driving her in between. In 1968, her first year on tour, she won the Ladies Professional Golf Association championship, defeating the game's leading money-winner, Kathy Whitworth, by seven shots in an 18-hole playoff. In her twelfth year, 1979, she won almost $180,000; she was first in three tournaments, including the rich Dinah Shore Winners' Circle for the second consecutive year, and was second in money earnings to Nancy Lopez. In April of 1970 she was married and in January of 1973 she was divorced. In the interval she played only 39 events, winning less than $13,000. After the divorce, self-knowledge replaced blind faith and she made the commitment to what she had always been meant to do.

Her world is composed of such places as Deerfield Beach and St. Petersburg in Florida; Raleigh, North Carolina; Roswell, Georgia; Corning, New York; Mason, Ohio; Lutherville, Maryland; and Jericho, New York. But since 1973 she has been to the Philippines, Indonesia, Australia and 14 times to Japan. Her business has been to make the golf swing she is capable of, shot after shot, day after day, week after week. In quest of the solution to the mystery of hitting a golf ball accurately, Sandra Post has given 26 of her 31 years. Those of us who are neither pursued by nor chase the visions of our best prospects cannot understand what it means to an athlete to sense what he can do, work at his sport and then come through on demand. The concentration required, the relentless application of all one's energies, would amaze most of us. The professional golfer is a professional gambler who rolls the dice every time he tees it up. Sandra Post might have hit the ball an average of 72.3 times per round in 1979, but there is no count of all the balls she hit across all the fairways at the Oakville and Trafalgar golf clubs when she was a child and a teenager.

"The public doesn't understand. You walk off the green and someone will say, 'Smile.' You've just made double-bogey, it's 35 degrees out and the rain's coming at you at right angles and they'll say, 'Smile, it's only a game.' You want to say, 'Hey, mister, at 12 years old I beat golf balls until blood ran down the grip. It might be just a game to you, but to me it's my livelihood. It's pretty hard to eat the irons.'"

Sandra Post spent her first 18 years with her parents and older sister, Suzanne, on the family's 25-acre fruit farm in Oakville. Her introduction to golf came at five, while on vacation in Florida. It was the winter of 1954 when her father took her to a tournament where she met LPGA pro Marilynn Smith, who made a lasting impression by giving her a ball, a glove and some tees. Back home, Post began to spend as much time as she could hitting balls around the Oakville Golf Club. With the instincts of a hermit, she took to the game that gives loners freedom of expression. Excitement built and a dream was generated with every well-struck shot. She astounded even herself with a desire that seemed to have sprung from nowhere. Sure, her father was a golfer, a good player who had competed in the Canadian Amateur. And sure, he was competitive by nature and only too glad to have an athletic, co-ordinated daughter who took to the game at which he had shown flashes of excellence. But none of this accounts for the zeal with which Post approached her golf. At age seven she knew she wanted to become a pro golfer. Under one arm she carried her books to the Linbrook Public School, but under the other she carried a putter.

After she went on to Oakville-Trafalgar High School, Post joined the Trafalgar Golf Club, where she played up to 54 holes a day. In the early and mid-sixties, she went round and round the Trafalgar course with such players as Wayne McDonald, 1969 Ca-

nadian Amateur Champion, and Martin Mason, 1966 Ontario
Amateur winner. By now Post was a teenager and her future
was becoming clear. What had been a spontaneous reaction at
seven to a question about what she wanted to be was taking on
substance and purpose. She learned to handle adversity. The initial test came in 1964 when she lost in the semi-finals of the
Ontario Junior Girls' and was left off the team of two players
who would represent Ontario at the Canadian Junior Girls'
Championship in Calgary. The blow came hard; she could not
understand the reasoning of the Ontario Ladies' Golf Association,
since she had led the field in the qualifying team matches.

"You think about why you've made it and the people who
have helped you. But have you ever thought of the people who
made it hard for you, and how they really did help you? They
made you so angry. They made you have that little coating so
that when things didn't go so well down the road you could
handle them."

A week after the Junior Girls', the Ontario Ladies' Amateur
was played at the Sunningdale Golf Club in London. Gathered
were the province's best players, including Marlene Stewart
Streit, long Canada's leading amateur and winner of the Canadian Ladies' Amateur seven times by 1964. Post got through to
the 36-hole final against Sue Hilton, a Sunningdale member who
had won the Canadian Junior Girls' in 1962. Two down with
two to play, Post birdied both holes to send the match into a
sudden-death playoff. Immediately her concentration and com-
posure were tested: Her father, who had been walking in the
gallery, was being taken off the course. He was being ejected, she
was told, because he had been advising her what club to play by
gesturing from the sidelines. "No one clubs me," snapped Post. "I
call all the shots. I'm going down the 37th and so is my dad."
And on the 37th she made a 15-foot downhill putt to win. "So
now they don't know what to do with me. I'm not on the junior
team, but I've won the provincial championship. They offered
me $100 to get to Calgary. I told them to keep it — $100
wouldn't get me to Bronte. I was really a big hit with them."

She did get to Calgary, though, assisted financially by her parents, who knew how important the tourney was to her. "The only
way I could repay them, I said, would be to win, to bring back the

trophy." That she did, after fighting a 104-degree fever and a strep throat. Loaded with penicillin, advised to withdraw, she won by eight shots, beating the first Ontario Junior Girl by 20.

Inadvertently, the province's golfing officials had helped her. It was evident, given the competitive world she was moving towards, that Post had to be prodded, not protected. Sensing this, her father showed his support by giving her the freedom to play golf, but he withheld the unconditional admiration that might have made her feel too important.

"My father instilled in me the feeling of wanting to make it, the desire. He worked on the farm all day, but after dinner he would come to the course with me and practise. Then after all the practice I would lose some match. And he would tell me I wasn't any good just so I would get the message that I had to work harder."

She was developing the combativeness necessary in pro golf. Perhaps it came through the verbal jousts with her father, but it was tested and fuelled by matches with her sister, Suzanne, five years older and a good player who got down to a handicap of about six. Until Post was 12, Suzanne beat her regularly. "That really irritated me. I couldn't stand her beating me, but it was great competition. Of course she would beat me. She was that much bigger. So I would just practise more and more. I had to win. Once Suzanne won the Hamilton and District Junior and beat me. I was shattered. It didn't matter that she was older. Anyway, being the younger daughter I had to compete just for recognition."

What comes across in any encounter with Post is her fierce determination. It is the product of both a rooted lack of confidence that she has always had to fight and the realization that, yes, she did have a large talent. Post has always been able to respond when pressed, plays well under pressure and bristles at any suggestion she may not be giving her best, a trait that some have mistaken for arrogance. At a recent tournament, she was being interviewed in the press room when a reporter asked in a mocking tone why none of the players seemed to want to play very well that day. Why, he wondered, did they not shoot low scores when the course seemed to be playing easy? "Do you really think nobody wanted to play well?" returned Post. "Do you think we weren't trying? We were out there playing our hearts out. It just didn't happen."

At the same tournament, a struggling professional who had played very well for the first two rounds was standing around the practice putting green, waiting for the groupings for the third day. Being among the leaders, as was Post, she could have been in the same group. When she heard that they would not be together, she was relieved. "I really like Sandra. You couldn't meet anybody nicer. But she's just so competitive. She would intimidate me." Yet at a tournament in the Far East the same pro found herself low on funds, without even enough money for meals. Without being asked, Post made sure the woman had meal tickets (a courtesy provided by sponsors at some tournaments) and assured her that should she need any more help, she should not be too embarrassed to ask. "It's perfectly natural," Post said when reminded of the incident. "If you like people you'll help."

June 24, 1968. Sandra Post and Kathy Whitworth were playing off for the LPGA championship at the Pleasant Valley Country Club in Sutton, Massachusetts. It was Post's eleventh tournament as a professional, but she was playing as if it were her eleventh year. Never worse than tied for the lead since the opening round, she felt ready to play her head-to-head match with Whitworth. "Now there are only two of us left," she thought, "and that makes it match play, in a way. Match play is what I was playing most of the time until just a few months ago, and it won't bother me a bit." Post shot 68, Whitworth 75. After the round Whitworth said: "To beat Sandra I probably would have had to play a career round. She was just great, and for one of her age her poise is almost incredible. I predict she'll be one of our greatest players for a long, long time."

She won $155 in her first tournament that year, picked up an extra $1,000 for a hole-in-one in her third and then won the LPGA a few weeks later, winning $3,000 and a $1,500 bonus from Spalding. Later in the year she was voted LPGA Rookie of the Year and had enough money to buy a condominium on the ocean in Boynton Beach, Florida (just south of West Palm Beach). In 1969 she also played well, finishing twentieth on the money list. Sandra Post was fulfilling the promise Kathy Whitworth had recognized.

February 1980. The fourth tournament of the new season, the Bent Tree Ladies' Classic, is being played in Sarasota, Florida. Post has gotten off to a good start this year and stands third on the money list. I have come down from Toronto to spend a week watching this golfer who had won so many awards in 1979: Canadian Golfer of the Year, presented by *Teeoff Golf News*; the Bobbie Rosenfeld Award as Canadian Female Athlete of the Year; the Ontario Sportswriters and Sportscasters Award as Ontario Athlete of the Year; the Lou Marsh Trophy as Canadian Athlete of the Year. ("I put the phone down and I started doing circles. My father asked, 'What's going on?' 'Athlete of the Year,' I said. 'Thirteen to 12 over Gilles Villeneuve. The Lou Marsh! It's ours!'") And now on the first tee of the Bent Tree Golf and Racquet Club, she hears: "Ladies and gentlemen, next to play will be Sandra Post. Sandra is the 1979 Canadian Athlete of the Year and is one of our finest players." Post acknowledges the applause of the crowd, many of whom are Canadians, and prepares to play, though inside she's transported.

She shoots 69 to tie for the first-round lead with three others. Playing briskly and efficiently, in control, she shoots 71 in the second round and another 71 in the third. On Sunday she will play at 12:03; JoAnne Carner, with whom Post is tied for the lead at five-under 211, will go in the last group, at 12:12. But now it's late Saturday and I'm talking with the Stick, short for Stickman, a sagacious observer on both the men's and women's tours. We find a place near the practice area and I listen.

"Every golfer got to have self-control. If you got that you can avoid adversities; you got to have the desire, you got to want to win real bad, you got to find the confidence, but there's only one place you gonna find it: from experience. A winner's got to come through the hard times when he's got no concentration, when he figures there ain't no way he can get the ball in the hole. When the times is rough and you're not feeling so good and you can't take the club back 'cause your life's all messed up and your girl's left you 'cause you been neglecting her. You got to go through these times. You go through them and they become part of you and you gain confidence. Time and patience. Time and patience gonna give you what you need to win."

I think of what Post had told me about her divorce, the most painful time of her life. The man she married, John Elliott, was also a golf pro; he was trying to establish himself and not too pleased at being the lesser performer of the two. Post was caught between what was expected of her at home and what she expected of herself on tour. The tension pulled the marriage apart. "It was a tremendous hurt for me," Post had told me. "But I just had to accept that this marriage failed. For a while it had been great, but life goes on and this time I was going on alone."

After the divorce she quit playing, didn't touch a club for five months. Eventually she realized that she could not evade the responsibility to bring her talent to its potential. "I had to get back into it. I had something to prove. I was going to make a comeback at 24."

Come back she did, but this time with a friend who understood her need to play golf and who was secure enough in himself to accept the fact that golf had to be her first priority. Leigh Kandar, Massachusetts-born and trained in law, gave her legal advice when necessary but also gave her the anchor she needed. "Leigh was a great inspiration," Post had said. "Gave me a lot of strength. He was a good friend when I was down. I really needed some help. I was getting messed up." They live together now in Boynton Beach — that is, whenever they can make it home from their separate and constant travels. Kandar looks after Post's various endorsement contracts, which include Dodge, Ram Golf Corporation and Lily of France, the New York-based company whose name you see on her visor. He also owns a home on Cape Cod, their frequent retreat in the summer, and a sporting equipment company in the Boston area. Together, they've invested in real estate in Florida and a collection of Corvettes, from as early as 1957 to as late as 1980.

Home, a source of confusion during her marriage, became a significant aspect of the balance that Post now sought to create. "In this business, if you want to have a home and the things that you like you have to manage your life," she had told me. "Your place has to be taken care of and you need to know that. I've got three dogs [Hitchin', Tradin' and Whippin', all Shih Tzus] and they need to be looked after. They're my boys. When I come home, they don't care if I shot 67 or 85." We had been sitting beside the creek that runs through the golf course, Post talking about what she's seen and felt: "I love the life, even though it can be so lonely. Sometimes I'm not sure if I'm ever going to get home again. I've gone weeks without speaking to anybody I really knew and thought, 'Why did I go this far? I've gone too far this time.' But then somebody will say, 'Sandra, how are you? We're from Charlottetown, or Winnipeg, or Thunder Bay.' I can't tell you how good that feels, how much it means."

Now it's the last round at Bent Tree. Payday. Post is practising her sand play as I drive into the club. Yesterday she had misplayed a couple of sand shots on the last two holes. After parking I watch her from a distance, remembering that George Knudson once said he learned so much about the swing from watching players such as Sam Snead from 100 yards. Post, from that distance, swings with the compact efficiency of a skilled fencer. While I continue to watch her and sense the way in which 26 years of practice are distilled into a motion that takes one to two seconds, Elmer Prieskorn, her teacher, walks by. Prieskorn has worked with some of the great women players, including Babe Zaharias, who won two gold medals in the low hurdles and javelin in the 1932 Olympics and then took up golf, winning the United States Women's Open in 1948, 1950 and 1954. I ask him to evaluate Post, with whom he began working seriously in the winter of 1978-79. "When she came to me, she had been trying to lengthen her swing by changing planes," Prieskorn says. "Now she's trying to keep it on the same plane and move the ball around by using her legs." Their work together has obviously been worthwhile. Post's record in 1979 is evidence of that. Remarkably, she admits to having learned about the golf swing only since working with Prieskorn. "My swing came from imitation, from watching good women players. I really didn't think of anything, just swung hard. I always had a short swing and knew that if I wanted to play a long time I would have to lengthen it. But I didn't know how to go about it. I had no understanding of arcs and planes. Now, though, I do. Elmer has given me some key thoughts so now I know what is happening when I'm not swinging well." What effect, I ask Prieskorn, did he think the good year in 1979 would have on Post? "It takes a strong person not to become lazy after all the success. It won't come so easily now. You've got to use reverse psychology with her, or she might get to thinking she won't have to work so hard. Can't pat her on the back too much. But I think she'll be fine. She loves to play; she's got the desire. It's just a question of hard work, keeping aggressive, going right at the hole."

Helping her go right at the hole for five years has been Jabbo, her 33-year-old caddy from Jackson, Mississippi, who lives in Los Angeles. His real name is Johnny Hubbard and he is a prominent, though quiet, part of the Post team. "Isn't that Jabbo nice?" asks Sandra. "He's a piece of work. We're good together. All business out there. He's been so good coming down the line. He knows his job and I know mine. We work together and haven't had a disagreement in our five years." Jabbo provides Post with the security on the course that Leigh gives her away from it. "She played real good last year," Jabbo tells me later. "Everything went nice. All the experience sunk in. In '78 [when she won her first official event since the LPGA 10 years before] I was really glad for her. She'd been trying so hard. Been in position to win so many times. But now she knows *how* to win. That's what it's all about. She did a real good job of overcoming the mistakes. Every year she gets better."

Tenth hole. Final round. Post stands over a long shot to the green. She and Carner have played the front nine in 37 shots and are still tied. Post, indecisive about her club selection, turns away from the ball, leans on her bag and consults with Jabbo. She takes a 4-iron, Jabbo moves back a few paces and Post settles into her stance and swings. "Once I'm committed to the club, that's it. Jabbo helps me settle my mind and I just go ahead and hit it." It was the right choice. The ball finishes 30 inches from the hole and Post birdies. Never for a moment seeming to pay any attention to what Carner is doing behind her, though she is well aware of the situation, she plays on. On 12, a par-three over water, she almost makes a hole-in-one and gets another birdie. But Carner is matching Post birdie for birdie and two more, taking a two-shot lead after birdies on 10, 11, 12 and 14. On the last hole, Post sinks a 35-foot putt for a birdie that gives her second place, both in the tournament and on the money list, behind Carner, who wins this week by one.

I hurry over to the grassy area near the parking lot where the caddies gather to seek out Stickman once more. What, I want to know, does he think of Sandra Post?

"Sandra? The hardest player out here. She's tough; she's gutsy. She's got all the shots; she wants to win, thinks she can win every time she tees it up. She's always at that flag, always giving the full putt. She's gonna take it up there. She's good from the fairways. When she's 45 or 50 yards from the hole, she'll hit that sand wedge real close. She's experienced, knows how to do it all. She can pitch; she can play. Got a scrambling game and a road game. I think she's the soundest player out here. Solid. Week in and week out, pick up the paper and there's her name, Sandra Post, the Canadian, the Golden Canadian. The lady can flat play."

Nancy Lopez

The Globe and Mail, **January 26, 1985**
When the sun broke warm and friendly over the Deer Creek Golf and Racquet Club, site of the $200,000 Mazda Classic of Deer Creek, early yesterday morning, the two pros that make up golf's golden couple were 323 yards apart. Twenty-eight-year-old Nancy Lopez, a winner of 29 Ladies Professional Golf Association events, looked down the fairway of the first hole before hitting a 2-iron dead centre; in the distance, behind the green, her husband, New York Mets third baseman Ray Knight, 32, awaited the arrival of his bride of 28 months.

A few minutes later, Lopez's short-iron approach was sailing towards the hole, finally settling 12 feet to the right, not quite pin-high. Knight, a seven-handicap golfer, positioned himself directly behind the hole on Lopez's line, the better to watch her birdie putt.

Deliberate as ever, Lopez lined up her shot from both sides of the hole. That done, she gripped her mallet-head putter, placed her right forefinger down the shaft as a guide and took a short, slow backstroke. Accelerating the blade through the ball, she hit a putt that looked to be in all the way, but it turned left at the hole as it grazed the edge.

And so, the second round of Lopez's tenth season on the tour began with a routine par-four. On her way to the second tee, she linked arms with her husband, chatted quietly and then birdied the par-five after reaching the green in two. After her opening-round par-72, that birdie put her one under for the tournament. Later, she missed some short putts and finished with another 72.

Lopez and Knight, two athletes who are devoted to each other, their 14-month-old daughter, Ashley Marie, and their sports are embarking on what both hope will be championship seasons. Lopez, having assured herself that she can be mother, wife and golfer, said she is "ready to make some noise on the tour."

Knight, traded from the Houston Astros to the Mets towards the end of the past season, feels his team can go all the way to the World Series, particularly if pitchers such as Dwight Gooden stay healthy. The addition of former Montreal Expos catcher Gary Carter is also a plus.

The biggest bonus for both Lopez and Knight may be their support of each other's careers, and the foundation they feel that having a daughter has given each of them. Lopez, after playing only 12 tournaments in 1983 and 16 in 1984, will play at least 20 this year. Knight, who hit .237 last year after two .300 seasons, said he is over some physical problems and has started hitting and throwing as he prepares for the new season.

"This year is very important to me," the soft-spoken, thoughtful Lopez said. "I'd like to come back and play the golf I think I can. Last year was a bit of an adjustment, travelling with Ashley. But now I'm used to that."

There is no questioning their priorities. It is family first, careers second, although each appreciates that golf and baseball cannot be neglected. Lopez said that Knight, being a professional athlete, has been able to help her understand the importance of her career.

"Ray has been a good influence," she said. "He says that I have all this talent, that I should use it. He thinks I can win five in a row again, like I did in my rookie year (1978, when Lopez won nine tournaments). I fight my inner feelings a lot, wanting to be home with Ashley and looking after Ray, but I'm learning that I also need golf to be happy."

Knight, who knows an athlete's ups and downs, understands his wife's feelings.

"Nancy is such a giving person," he said. "In the last couple of years, while she was pregnant and in the year after Ashley was born, she gave so much. Her golf suffered and she became unhappy. I've encouraged her to play. She needs golf, but sometimes she's afraid that, by being on the course, she'll be taking away from Ashley and me."

Knight feels Lopez can be No. 1 on the tour again, as she was in 1978 and 1979. Both he and Lopez have been married before, so both know they must keep communication lines open. That means acknowledging and attending to their multiple roles: spouse, parent and athlete.

Lopez and Knight have no money problems, which makes it easier to handle their lifestyle. A woman travels with them and also accompanies Lopez and her daughter when Knight is playing baseball. They have the money to stay in first-class accommodations.

Knight begins spring training late next month. In the off season, he and Lopez spend five months together at home near Atlanta, a time, he said, "when nobody comes into our own world."

During the first two rounds at Deer Creek, Lopez has seemed absolutely at ease. Her swing is still special — she sets the clubhead at the top of her swing above her head, well away from the usual plane, and then returns it powerfully through the ball — and she still has a marvellous touch around and on the greens, not to mention with the admiring crowds that follow her and chat baseball with her husband.

From the outside, nothing seems to have changed from Lopez's glory years, but it is clear she has grown tremendously in recent years. She has proved her fears groundless and can concentrate on her sport because she knows she can be much more than just a golfer.

The Globe and Mail, **December 24, 1987**
All right, golf trivia buffs. Which professional golfer has won the most U.S. tour events in the past decade?

Chances are you said Tom Watson or Greg Norman or Jack Nicklaus. If so, you're not even close. You haven't even got the right sex. The answer is Nancy Lopez, winner of 38 Ladies Professional Golf Association tournaments since 1978 and a recent inductee to the LPGA Hall of Fame.

Getting into the LPGA's Hall of Fame is one tough chore. A golfer not only has to complete 10 consecutive years of LPGA membership, she has to win 30 LPGA events, including two different majors; 35 tournaments, with one major, or 40 without any. Lopez made it by winning 35, plus the LPGA championship.

By the LPGA's criteria, only seven men would have made the Hall of Fame on the PGA Tour, if there were one. The LPGA roster shows 11, including Patty Berg, Mickey Wright, Kathy Whitworth and JoAnne Carner. Lopez fits right in.

Lopez made the Hall of Fame faster than anybody. Her thirty-fifth victory was the Sarasota Classic last February, just over 10 years since she came out of New Mexico to give the LPGA a genuine star. In her first year — her first year — she won nine tournaments, including five in a row.

Lopez has dominated women's golf, much as Arnold Palmer and Jack Nicklaus did in their first decades on the men's tour. It doesn't make sense to attend an LPGA event and not spend most of your time watching Lopez.

Last week's Mazda Champions in Jamaica was a good example. Lopez and Miller Barber were partners and walked away with the first prize of $500,000. Lopez was followed all the way by her husband, baseball player Ray Knight. They're far and away the LPGA's most glamorous couple.

Watching Barber and Lopez was quite an experience. Neither has the most orthodox swing. Barber's right elbow flies so far from his side on his backswing that he could hold a coconut under his arm. Lopez swings her club on a path roughly equivalent to flying Toronto to New York via Chicago. But their swings work when it counts, at impact.

Watching them, one golf addict, who has heard more swing theories than he wants to think about, recalled what Tom Watson had said one fine Masters morning in Augusta, Georgia. The topic of discussion, naturally, was the swing.

"Look," Watson said, "there are endless ways to take the club back. All I know is that you'd better be in the right position through impact. You'd better be there."

Lopez has been there for a decade. She's been there even after she's taken time off to give birth. A fella's gotta wonder how a woman could even hit a putt after carrying around a baby for nine months, never mind win tournaments. But it doesn't bother Lopez.

In April of 1983 Lopez, then two months pregnant, won the J & B Scotch Pro-Am. And she said she intended to play three more months, until, as she put it, "I can't swing around my stomach any more."

In May of 1986 Lopez gave birth to her second daughter. She played only four events that year, all after her child was born. And what did she do? Nothing much, just three top-five finishes.

This year Lopez has been a full-time golfer. She even wrote a book called *The Complete Golfer*, in which she includes tips on playing while pregnant. Attractive and talented as she has always been, this year she's glowed, as British photographer Keith Hailey observed last week.

"Nancy has always been lovely to photograph," Hailey said. "But now there is something about her that makes her even more special."

Hailey didn't elaborate, as he was too busy setting up his equipment. But Miller Barber did, having just given his partner the honour of holing the final putt to win the tournament.

"I just see a champion when I look at Nancy," Barber said. "It's the way she reacts to certain situations, the way she spurs you on. And it's not that she ever brags about her abilities. Champions don't. They just play. They play every shot like it's the last shot in their lives."

Barber was a teenager admiring a movie star. He'd seen Ben Hogan and Arnold Palmer and Jack Nicklaus, but for this moment, anyway, he was in awe of Lopez.

"If she's not the best player there ever was," Barber said so softly you could barely hear him, "she's darn near close to it."

Anybody who saw Lopez last week or who has followed her career would agree. If Palmer's the king of professional golf, as he's known, Lopez is the queen.

Caught in the Trap

City Woman, **Summer 1985**

There's an unexpected late-January chill in southern Florida, as the travelling road show called the Ladies Professional Golf Association tour begins the year's first tournament. Like a caravan of gypsies, the women who follow the tour will criss-cross the United States and visit Canada and Japan. The majority are from the U.S., but a smattering are from elsewhere in the world, including six, count 'em, *six* Canadians. That's something of a miracle, considering only four Canadians are playing on the men's PGA Tour this year. From 1968 through mid-1983, only one Canadian — Oakville, Ontario's Sandra Post — had any real chance of succeeding on the LPGA, and only one, or sometimes two, other Canadian players (Cathy Sherk and Jocelyne Bourassa) ever kept her company on tour.

Indeed, for the six who are playing this week for the $200,000 stakes and $30,000 first prize at the Deer Creek Golf and Racquet Club in Deerfield Beach, Florida, and for those among the 20 young Canadian women currently at U.S. colleges on golf scholarships who may eventually join the LPGA, Post pioneered the tour.

Now 36, she began her professional career at 18 with $400 and a car her folks had given her. She drove 45,000 miles her first season and never looked back. "I chose to leave Canada," she says. "I was going to do whatever I had to do — move to Florida, get myself a house, get into a position where I could play golf 365 days a year. Whatever it took, I was going to do it. I didn't care."

Some golfers get rich. Post won eight tournaments in her career and nearly $750,000 in prize money, more than any Canadian golfer ever, male or female.

But what about B.C. golfer Dawn Coe, who won only $19,603 in 1984; or Lynn Parker, from Yorkton, Saskatchewan, who played her rookie season last year at age 30 for a grand total of $8,661? What about Judy Ellis, a 27-year-old from Waterloo, Ontario, whose 1983 take of $34,884 sank last year to half that amount? What of talented young Canadians like Lisa Young,

Nancy White-Brewer and Barbara Bunkowsky, who subject themselves to the gruelling, often bizarre, rigours of a 35-week travelling circus and often barely make enough to clear expenses? What's the attraction for women like them?

So formidable are the obstacles I often wonder why the women continue. Yet they must continue until their passion for the game is spent. Golf for them, as it was for Post, is more obsession than profession.

As Post did for 16 seasons before them, the golfers at Deer Creek are about to spend a year in the toughest professional sport in which to make a living. Just because a player makes it to a tournament is no guarantee she will make money. Golf is a non-salaried, individual sport in which a player is assured of only one thing. Each year she will spend at least $20,000 in expenses. Indeed, if she fails to make the weekly "cut," she makes no money at all for that week, even though she has played in the tournament. It's as if a teacher worked all week only to be told on Friday afternoon she wouldn't be paid because she had had an off week.

Late each Friday afternoon, after the second round of the four-round tournament, golfers congregate around a massive scoreboard to learn whether they have made it into the top half of the field. Though tournaments typically begin with 144 players, the half of the field that scores the highest is finished for the week. At Deer Creek, Judy Ellis is one of the women huddled around the scoreboard. As the afternoon light fades, she learns that she has missed qualifying for the weekend play by one shot.

In no other sport is a turn of bad luck so punishing. Athletes in salaried sports such as hockey are protected by their contracts against their inevitable bad days or prolonged slumps. Tennis players who get into a tournament at least make *some* money, even if they lose their first match. But a golfer is down the road without a cent in her pocket.

Of the 254 golfers who held LPGA playing cards in 1984, only 54 made more than $40,000. Subtract the expenses and not much remains. As for the other 200 women, $8,000 seasons like Lynn Parker's are not unusual.

Obviously, most of the women wouldn't be here without sponsors such as Future Stars Inc., the Texas company that will pay first-year–player Nancy White-Brewer's expenses for two years in exchange for a percentage of her earnings and a share of any product endorsement or other revenue they might generate for her. For Prince Edward Islander White-Brewer, 25, who turned to golf five years ago after missing qualifying for the 1980 Canadian Olympic speed skating team by one-tenth of a second, the deal is her ticket to being here. Others rely on "sweetheart" investors, like the six men at home in Prince Rupert, British Columbia (including her father and brother), who back 25-year-old Lisa Young.

But sponsor or no sponsor, each player has in every sense reached this point in her career on her own. She is her own manager, arranging for her own travel and accommodations, dragging her own bags from course to course. Whereas hockey or baseball players come home for half the playing season, golfers are on the road constantly, rarely returning home, especially Canadians, who tend to establish a southern base from which to practise (Young, despite a promising rookie season last year, with $37,568 in prize money, scraped together the $1,000 in airfare to see her family in British Columbia only once, at Christmas). Each player has been on her own from the time she decided to play pro golf, and she'll be on her own for the nine-month duration of the tour, travelling from golf course to golf course — alone.

The grinding sense of rootlessness extracts its price in personal relationships, too. Barbara Bunkowsky, a 26-year-old from Burlington, Ontario, who some observers feel will replace Post as Canada's next top player (she grossed $71,682 in her second season last year), knows the problem. "Having a relationship is the hardest thing about being out here," says Bunkowsky, whose relationship with pro golfer Kenny Knox fell apart in 1984. "There just aren't that many guys around who can handle a woman on the road so much."

Not even male golfers, it seems, who presumably would understand what they were getting into. Such attachments tend to come apart, especially if the male isn't having much success on the course. Post married golf pro John Elliott in 1970, for example, but he didn't enjoy being called Mr. Post. They were divorced after less than three years of marriage.

No salaries. Loneliness. Failed relationships. At one point last fall, Bunkowsky came off the course in tears, convinced that she shouldn't even be on tour. Yet it's a new season at Deerfield Beach, and she, and the others, are still out there. Why?

The answer is the game itself. Some take to golf early, as if destined to play. When she was seven years old, Post, for one, told her father she wanted to become a pro golfer. When Bunkowsky was 10, she was smashing balls around her father's course in Burlington.

Others more or less collide with golf, and it sticks to them. The game eluded White-Brewer when she played it casually as a teenager, and it galled her that as a natural athlete she could be incompetent at *any* sport. But once bitten, like Post and Bunkowsky, like all the women on the LPGA tour, she became trapped by her own talent. Golf chose these women the way the cello chose Ofra Harnoy, the way writing chose Margaret Atwood and acting Kate Lynch.

A lifetime devotion to the arts is perhaps easier to understand than an obsession with golf — can a small white ball command a human life? — yet one is no less compelling than the other. Though the swing takes only one and a half to two seconds to complete, it is one of the most analyzed motions in sports. To the observer, it seems effortless. To the golfer, however, it's an intricate aggregation of arcs and planes that must connect in proper sequence to form a smooth, fluid whole. Mastering the swing could itself occupy a lifetime, but technique is the easier part. The real challenge is the mental game.

Perhaps the highest discipline a person can impose on herself is to control and use emotions. If that's true, then golf may be *the* ultimate sport. The challenge of golf arises from two elements that distinguish it from nearly all other ball and stick sports: the stationary ball and the slowness of the game. These factors combine to generate the major problem in golf: There's too much time to think.

All golfers have had the experience of standing over a ball and picturing it flying into water hazard. Inevitably, the ball follows the path laid down by the vision. On the golf course, at least, what a golfer thinks and visualizes seems to direct her swing. The mind does indeed influence the body.

It is the golfer's challenge to turn off her conscious processes and simply swing the club. She must learn to play a conscious game unconsciously, or else thought will govern her muscles. That almost Zen-like state of pure concentration, when one *senses* what to do, is a lot easier to achieve in a game like tennis or hockey, when a ball or puck is flying at you at 100 m.p.h. and you react instinctively. Golf is not a game of reaction, but of creation.

The game's mental challenge has given rise to the most sophisticated body of literature in sport. John Updike, in reviewing *Golf in the Kingdom*, the book Michael Murphy (the co-founder of the Esalen Institute in California) wrote in 1972, was inspired to remark on the game's "psychosomatic sensitivity to our interior monologue and the sway of our moods." In Updike's poetic estimation, the game is "like a magic mirror, an outward projection of an inner self." Or, in more pedestrian terms, the swing is an expression of what's going on in the player's mind.

To conquer the mental game and achieve the state of awareness necessary to play it, some golfers have to alter their temperaments on the course. Post had to learn to become a "controlled hyperactive," to slow herself down on the course, a triumph of mind over matter that White-Brewer, as a former speed skater, is still trying to achieve.

The enormous effort of will took its toll on Post. Shackling her automatic responses for up to six hours a day left her drained. "All my energies were out there on the course. I needed them all to control myself and stay consistent. The girl who played golf was so different from the real one who is enthusiastic and excitable. I couldn't let that out on the course. I got so nervous I'd often have to kneel down because my legs felt so weak. Controlling myself took so much out of me that I didn't even have the energy to go out at night."

Post says it took 10 years to get the anxiety out of her body, to reach the state where she could just stand up to a shot and swing freely. Ten years. Golf is a game, right? Tell it to the women of the LPGA.

Such preoccupation with self-discipline subjects the player to constant self-evaluation, with golf bearing down on one side of the scales and little on the other side to balance it. As Lynn Parker says, "Sometimes your entire self-image can be wrapped up in whether you can hit a shot."

Post's ultimate solution was to get out early. In 1983, her right thumb went numb, a particularly revealing ailment for a golfer whose only connection to the club is through her fingers and hands. She returned to her native Oakville to relieve herself of the accumulated toxins of so many years in a pressure cooker and to see a doctor. He told her to take six weeks off. She never went back.

In one sense, she was lucky. She at least has a chance to replace some of her life that, driven by the internal pressure of her own talent, she allowed the tour with all its attendant nerve damage to consume. It's too easy to remain on tour for years, well into one's forties or even fifties, with no real life, no home life, no outside interests. In more active sports you burn out, and then you move home to Flin Flon and go into law or business. In golf, there is no burnout age, which can prolong the delusion that if you keep trying, you'll win. Maybe next week. Maybe next year. Before you know it, you've blown your life.

Attempts to find an anchor amid the tour's helter-skelter existence can take many forms. But one anchor no golfer can do without is her teacher-mentor, and if she's smart, she finds the right one and sticks with him. He is her most important professional ally, a friend to combat the loneliness, a technical adviser to rescue her when her swing goes awry.

White-Brewer has her mentor, Torontonian George Clifton, at her side this week at Deer Creek. In the past four years, he's performed wonders, slowing her down to golf's laboured pace, and at the same time encouraging her to use the strongest part of her athleticism, her speed skater's legs, as a force of power in her golf swing. White-Brewer has been with Clifton since day one. He's her coach and her friend. "I can have a horrendous day," she says, "but then all I need to do is talk to George, and I feel great."

Bunkowsky, on the other hand, has arrived at Deer Creek with the sound of too many teachers ringing in her ears and vibrating down the shafts of her clubs. It shows in her playing. In the first half of last year she won over $60,000, $26,250 of it in a single tournament win in Clifton, New Jersey, in May. Not since Post had another Canadian won on tour. But then, in the second half of the year, she earned only about $10,000. Of the Canadians, she is the most conflicted where teaching is concerned, having worked over the years with at least five teachers, including former boyfriend Kenny Knox, and currently Texan Clay Edwards, who also coaches Canadians Richard Zokol and Jim Nelford. At Deer Creek she seems mixed up. Her mind is a thesaurus of golf concepts; when she thinks of one way to swing the club, alternatives present themselves. She hits the ball well on the practice tee, but by the first tee only 50 yards or so away, she's lost. Unhappily, Bunkowsky, as well as the other Canadians (with the exception of White-Brewer), have to content themselves this week with phone calls to their mentors. That's tough, particularly since there are precious few other shoulders to cry on.

Some of the women do find a haven in a personal relationship, though they are in the minority, and some even manage to have a family while continuing their careers. There's Nancy Lopez, who in her rookie season in 1978 won five consecutive tournaments and led the money list. When Lopez married New York Mets baseball player Ray Knight two and a half years ago, after one failed marriage, she wanted a child immediately. At 28, she is entering her prime golfing years; it also happens, of course, that these are the years when a woman feels the most intense pressure to have children. Having 18-month-old Ashley, who accompanies her on tour, has eased that pressure for Lopez, but there's still conflict.

"Nancy chose to give up some of her golf to have a child, and her game suffered. She became unhappy," says Knight, who is with Lopez on tour half the year when he's not with the Mets. "I've encouraged her to play because she needs it. But she's so afraid she'll take away from us."

White-Brewer and Parker both are married. Says Parker, whose pro-golfer husband, Roger, is based in San Antonio, Texas, where they live, "This isn't a normal way of life. So you try to have some semblance of normality. I get it from having a home now, and from my husband. I really need that. Being on tour is like working in a fishbowl. You forget they're bombing El Salvador, or that there's a world out there."

The need for emotional security is deep, and many of the women, especially those not happily attached to a man, feel compelled to look for it elsewhere. Some 30 women attend weekly Christian Fellowship meetings, a higher proportion of players than on the men's tour — though fundamentalist religion is obviously not for everyone. (When asked if she wanted to be born again, Post replied, "I thought I came out all right the first time.") But for women like 29-year-old American Betsy King, last year's leading money-winner with $266,771, who has been involved in the group since 1980, the fellowship is a psychological salve.

The search for ties also leads some of the women into lesbian relationships. That's a private decision, but the LPGA players are under public scrutiny every week, and the media in particular are always scrounging for the latest scoop on who might be a couple. The tour, in fact, is so sensitive to the issue that it tells golfers to respond to the question with the stock answer "Sorry, we don't do bed checks."

The lesbianism issue underlines the problem of the way male society perceives the LPGA. Regrettably, men in general tend not to look on the women as golfers. They come to tournaments not so much to watch the golf, but to hear any gossip that might be floating in the wind, and to take in the scenery (that's not to say the greens). U.S. player Jan Stephenson and Barb Bunkowsky, by the way, have both been approached to pose for *Playboy*. Asked if they enjoy women's golf, the usual male response is: "Are you kidding? There's no power in it. It's boring. I come out to look at the women."

Unfortunately, the attitude that women golfers are second class — more valued for their physical appearance than for their skill — has an impact on their earning power, for the tour is male-controlled. So are the television networks. Although purses have jumped more than 500% in the past 10 years, the LPGA, unlike the men's tour, doesn't get much network television coverage — only 5 events vs. 28 — and so it can't generate much income from that source. Thankfully, corporate sponsors contribute nearly as much to purses as they do on the PGA tour — in fact, the entire $9 million that the women are playing for in 1985; but the reason the PGA tour is playing for two and a half times that sum ($23 million) is the income it derives from networks.

The women's game isn't taken seriously, and it doesn't help matters that even the LPGA administration fails to promote the talent of its women. *Fairway,* the association's official publication, is given to featuring its players posing in negligees or as characters from Broadway plays. (One photo showed Kathy Baker in a strapless white tulle gown, arms outstretched above a bank of microphones, the image of Eva Peron.) Despite its own double standard, the LPGA might like to think that people come out to watch women's golf because they can learn something from the game. But I can tell you differently. They come out to survey the players.

To spend time on the LPGA tour is to see a world of sharp contrasts painted against the seductiveness of lush greens. It is to witness the struggles of extraordinarily talented women who come up against a lifestyle for which they have had little or no preparation, for even college golf offers the comfort of team play, without the pressure to play for money. It is to feel a palpable desperation in the air: on the driving range, where the flight of the golf ball against a blue sky can crush a player's confidence if the curve is not right; at a motel desk, where a player is telling the check-in clerk that her mother will arrive later in the week, giving her a real connection in an isolated place; in the press room one afternoon, when South African Sally Little enters in a rage after playing poorly, saying, "The first round of the year and already I feel like getting off the tour."

It is to see Bunkowsky in the middle of the 10th fairway at Deer Creek, fidgeting over the ball, then hitting a shot that barely clears the water in front of the green, as she stretches forward, trying to help its course. It is to see far fewer fans than on the men's tour, to recognize that though this is a women's golf tour, it is still a man's world, where the sponsors are corporations run by men, where the people who run the tour are men, where the bulk of the media are men.

But finally, it is to feel stirring within oneself an enormous respect for these women, who traipse from course to course and suffer the indignities of the tour because they feel they can play golf better than they can do anything else. It is to admire them because they are flirting with failure every shot, 70 to 75 times a day, 280 to 300 times a week, for the length of their careers.

I've seen the growth of. the women's tour from a small group of 30 to 40 in Post's early years to the 200 and more playing now. I can feel the women's pride at having their own home and course in a magnificent development at the Sweetwater Country Club near Houston, Texas.

But when away from the LPGA tour, flying back from Deer Creek or thinking of Post, Bunkowsky, et al., I feel a curious complex of aloneness and exaltation. Like them, I have been on that road from course to course too many times for too many weeks of the year, seen too many bad movies in too many shopping malls in too many Deerfield Beaches. But at the same time, I have a lingering memory of an evening early in 1980 when Post returned to the Oakville Golf Club, where she was honoured as Canada's Athlete of the Year for 1979. She was radiant that night, full of the confidence and joy that comes to one who has achieved what the mind must have conceived time and time again, only to be frustrated.

Deer Creek turns out to be an unhappy tournament for the Canadian women of the LPGA. Young is low Canadian in a tie for forty-eighth place, good for $650, a little more than she needs to cover expenses. Bunkowsky ties for sixty-first place, winning $323, while the other four miss the cut and stay on to practise for the weekend.

But the exaltation that Post felt is always possible in golf. There is always the chance this will be a player's week, or perhaps her year. Today, wherever they are, the current crop of Canadians is no doubt working towards those times. They are working to free their talent: Barb Bunkowsky, hitting balls for three hours one afternoon in Deerfield Beach and finding for the time being the rhythm she was seeking; White-Brewer, missing the cut at Deer Creek but bouncing happily into the clubhouse on the weekend to declare, "If I enjoy this so much while I'm missing a cut, imagine how much fun I'm going to have when I do well."

And then, at the end of it all, a picture of the winner at Deer Creek, 31-year-old American Hollis Stacy, holing a long putt on the final green to win by one shot and leaping into the air as the ball falls, dazzled by her own performance. The golf tour is a crucible for all the anguish and joy of things deeply felt. But at moments like these, all the anguish, all the hardships, all the bizarre demands of the life recede. And there is only joy.

Ada Mackenzie

The Globe and Mail, **August 21, 1991**
In a week of national championships, it seems appropriate to celebrate a tournament that doesn't declare a national champion but instead commemorates one. The event is the Ada Mackenzie Charity Tournament, which was held Monday at the Weston Golf and Country Club and which since 1975 has raised some $500,000 for disabled athletes.

This year's tournament was won by the Toronto Golf Club's Jane Moffatt. She won the Ontario Senior this summer and shot 79 at Weston, that with a triple-bogey at the 18th hole. Never mind, though; winning isn't the only thing at the Ada Mackenzie. It will be more important, of course, and should be, at this week's Canadian Amateur at Royal Ottawa and the Canadian Professional Golfers' Association championship at Club de Golf Sorel-Tracy in Quebec.

But something besides competition was going on at Weston, a course that superintendent Thom Charters maintains impeccably. The elements that have made the Ada Mackenzie one of Canada's most respected charity tournaments were there, and readily apparent.

By mid-afternoon, for instance, Canadian champions Marlene Streit and Gayle Borthwick were organizing silent and live auctions that would take place in the evening. Tournament founder Kay Helleur, long a top Canadian golfer, was also busy, but still willing to talk about a tournament so close to her heart.

"Ada was Canada's first outstanding athlete," Helleur said, "and it just happened that she was a golfer. She paved the way for international golf for Canadian women. I felt it was important to carry her memory on."

Mackenzie was influential. She won five Canadian Ladies Amateurs between 1919 and 1935 and captained international teams. She competed at age 81 in the 1971 Canadian Ladies' Golf Association Seniors at the Ladies' Golf Club in Thornhill, Ontario, having founded that club in 1924.

Mackenzie also founded the Ada Mackenzie sportswear shops, and it troubled her that women who worked didn't have full access to golf courses on weekends. The attitudes haven't changed much, sad to say.

Mackenzie therefore started the Ladies' Golf Club in 1924, women only allowed as full members. The club is still thriving. Mackenzie died in 1973, but during her life she influenced such golfers as Streit, Helleur, Borthwick and Sandra Post. And now the tournament in her name is helping disabled athletes.

"I knew her for years," Helleur recalled. "She was a tremendous golfer, especially in match-play. It always seemed she was able to win that extra hole."

Mackenzie's swing was long and flowing, the clubhead falling well behind her back on her follow-through. An old photo at Weston showed her in full swing, and there wasn't much to argue with in her technique.

"It was an old-timey swing," Streit pointed out in the clubhouse, getting up and swinging her arms to demonstrate. Borthwick said that Mackenzie's swing was as fluid as Bobby Jones's, and as long as John Daly's , the new PGA champion. High praise, but all who came up against Mackenzie would agree.

That same praise is now due the women whom Mackenzie influenced and who run the tournament in her name. The beneficiaries are the Canadian Wheelchair Sports Association, the Ontario Track 3 Ski Association and the Ontario Blind Golfers Association. The bulk of the money goes to the Canadian Wheelchair Sports Association, which will send a swim team to Barcelona for the 1992 Paralympics.

"It's so rewarding to help these people," Streit said as scores came in at Weston. "They're such fine athletes."

Borthwick voiced a similar sentiment and also pointed out that the tournament draws 90 of the lowest-handicap female golfers in Ontario. Higher-handicap players had to be refused because of the limited size of the field.

Mackenzie probably would have approved of keeping the tournament a mainly low-handicap affair. After all, she was a seventies shooter most of her competitive career and made plenty of trips into the sixties as well.

"Miss Mackenzie, full of life and gaiety, inspires her team with her youthfulness," a 1953 newspaper report said when she led a group to an event in Wales. "She plays the game with all the vigour of a woman of 40. She is a great competitor and fears no one."

It can't be said better. Mackenzie was a woman to be reckoned with, and the tournament she inspired is one of the most significant of its kind. Long may it continue.

Dawn Coe and Lisa Walters

The Globe and Mail, **March 4, 1992**
Tampa, Florida — The pro shop at the Tampa Palms Golf and Country Club is a sumptuous marketplace for anybody who wants the best equipment and clothing in the game. But today, it's also a gathering place for those who are still excited about the recent accomplishment of their representative on the Ladies Professional Golf Association Tour. Dawn Coe won the Women's Kemper Open last week in Hawaii, and the folks at Tampa Palms are thrilled.

A sign behind the counter in the pro shop recognizes Coe's win, her first in a nine-year career on the LPGA Tour. Coe, a 31-year-old from Lake Cowichan, British Columbia, won the Kemper with birdies on two of the last four holes. Her win came directly on the heels of fellow B.C. golfer Lisa Walters's win in the Itoki Hawaiian Ladies Open. Their duet on the island had more than a touch of magic about it.

"It was spectacular, really storybook," Coe said from San Diego after the first round of the Inamori Classic, where she was one shot off the lead after an opening two-under-par 70. "You'd have a better chance of winning the lottery than having the two of us win one week after another."

At Tampa Palms, Jimmy Jones had made a similar comment. Jones, a low-handicap amateur, is Coe's fiancé. They were engaged at the club and will be married there November 14. He was watching a replay of his fiancée's win at the Kemper Open and pointed out that as Coe putted on the last green, Walters and Nancy Ramsbottom, another Tampa Palms professional, were looking on from the edge of the green.

Walters seemed to be biting her nails, and no wonder. She and Coe are close friends who have long been roommates on the LPGA Tour. After Walters, 32, unexpectedly won her first LPGA Tour event, also in her ninth year, Coe congratulated her immediately.

"Lisa apologized to Dawn," Jones said. "She told her it was supposed to be her winning. Dawn told Lisa to enjoy it, that her time would come."

That it did, and quickly. Walters, speaking from Hawaii last Saturday, the night before the final round of the Kemper Open, had a premonition of Coe's win.

"You're talking to me tonight about my win," Walters said, "but tomorrow you'll be talking to Dawn. She's going to win."

Coe won in high style, as had Walters. She holed a 30-foot birdie putt at the 15th, then putted in from the fringe at the 16th for another birdie. Ahead, Dottie Mochrie had shot an eight-under-par 65 to get to 12 under for the tournament. Coe was at 13 under, and when she came off the 16th green said right into the camera, "Hi, Jimmy."

"I was watching from the kitchen with some buddies," Jones said. "I couldn't get too close to the TV, I was too nervous. But we erupted when the putt went in."

Coe parred the 17th and 18th holes to win. Johnny Miller, golf's most astute television analyst, pointed out that the best thing about Coe's march to victory was that she was winning it "in the classic style," that is, making birdies to win.

"That's what it's all about," Miller said as Coe prepared to tap in her winning par putt. "All the hard work has come to this."

Walters, waiting by the green, was one of the first to congratulate Coe. Her own win was still fresh in her mind and had come in its own classic style.

"I made four birdies in the first five holes," Walters said. "Since I started the round five shots from the lead I knew I was close.

But I didn't worry, even though I was nervous for the middle six holes."

Walters, by her own admission, had been mired in a four-year slump, never finishing higher than ninety-fourth on the money list. Coe had finished 11th, 11th and 25th since 1989, winning some $650,000. The only thing their golf games had in common was that neither player had won on the LPGA Tour, although Coe had won a tournament last year in Korea. But Coe was expected to win and felt her turn was coming. It was different for Walters.

"I went through a lot of problems the last few years," she said. "But I kept trying. Four years is a long time to be in a slump, but as long as I was making a little profit I was going to stay out."

Walters suffered from an inability to control the clubhead, and consequently her shots wavered. But then she took her husband Mike's advice. She gripped the club more tightly and found she was better able to get the clubhead on the ball properly.

"I started hitting the ball at the flag," Walters said. "This year I hit the ball pretty well the first two weeks on the tour, although I missed the cuts."

Walters opened the tournament she won with rounds of 72 and 71. Her burst of birdies on the front side in the last round set the stage for her win. She didn't look at a leader board until she completed her round.

"I couldn't believe it when I saw I had a two-shot lead. I was definitely surprised."

The lead held up. Walters suddenly had her first LPGA Tour win and the $60,000 that went with it. She got the automatic exemption into the Nabisco Dinah Shore in March at Mission Hills in Rancho Mirage, California, a major championship. And she received the invaluable five-year exemption from qualifying that goes with winning.

But still she thought of her roommate and friend as they went on to the Wailea Golf Club's Blue Course on the island of Maui. "It was nice that Lisa and I could see each other win," Coe said. "We've roomed together the last nine years, which makes it sweeter. The support you get from your peers out here is important."

Coe and Walters have become the toast of Canadian golf, and also golf in the Tampa area. Walters plays out of the Bloomingdale Golfers' Club in Valrico, Florida, near Tampa, as do

Colleen Walker and Lee Janzen, already winners this year on the LPGA and PGA Tours. Walker's win came at the expense of Coe, who lost a sudden-death playoff.

"We've been swamped," Coe said this week. "Lisa comes in and says, 'Okay, we're home, let the phones begin.' The phone's been ringing at six in the morning."

Many of the calls have come from Canadians. Jocelyne Bourassa, the executive director of the du Maurier Ltd. Classic, Canada's contribution to the LPGA's four majors, spoke to Coe and Walters on Wednesday. Bourassa won the forerunner of the du Maurier in 1973, when it was called La Canadienne.

Canadian women have been making an impact on the LPGA Tour for some time, more so than the Canadians on the PGA Tour.

Barbara Bunkowsky won the 1984 Chrysler Plymouth-Charity Classic and after a lengthy slump the Burlington, Ontario, player finished twenty-eighth on the money list last year. Montreal-born Tina Purtzer, 29, won the Jamie Farr Toledo Classic in 1990, and such players as Gail Graham, Jennifer Wyatt and Nancy White are showing up on leader boards. They in turn are supported by Canadians Karin Mundinger, Nancy Harvey, Heather Cameron and Tara Fleming.

"You'll see some noise from the Canadians this year," Coe said. "Gail Graham, Jennifer Wyatt and Nancy White are all off to good starts."

The Canadians on the LPGA Tour come from all parts of the country. Wyatt is from Vancouver; Graham from Kelowna, British Columbia; Harvey from Swift Current, Saskatchewan; Mundinger and Fleming from Toronto; Cameron, a non-exempt player who holds her tour card, from Truro, Nova Scotia; and White from Montague, Prince Edward Island.

Sandra Post, for one, knows what it can mean to have a player to root for.

"I never realized until I left the tour that people liked to see if I was in contention," said Post, a winner of eight tournaments on the LPGA Tour, from her home in Oakville, Ontario. "They would tell me that they'd pick up the paper just to see how I was doing."

Post's point was that golf fans in Canada enjoy, even need, somebody to follow.

"Just think what Seve [Ballesteros] did for golf in Spain. It can mean a lot to have people winning on the tour. And the other thing is, we have been short on Canadian women sports heroes. We've had Barbara Ann Scott, Nancy Greene, Elizabeth Manley and Karen Percy for a while. But that's about all."

Post might have included herself as one of those Canadian sports heroes. Her three LPGA wins in 1979 led to her being chosen Canadian Athlete of the Year. She was the only Canadian woman playing the tour full-time in those days. Post set a standard that other women may not reach, but she showed that more than minor accomplishment was possible.

"It's so exciting," Post said about Walters and Coe. "I think it's great for Canadian golf, both men and women. I'm amazed at the number of people who have come in to our school [Post teaches in Oakville] who have asked, 'Did you watch Coe on the weekend?' Let's face it, Canadians love winners, even though we don't have that many."

One might expect Walters's and Coe's wins to translate into more money off the course. Walters has not had an agent or manager, while Coe works with Elliott Kerr of the Landmark Sports Group in Toronto.

"I've got one little offer for the driver I use," Walters said. "The people want to do something. And I might get into some pro-ams because of the win."

Walters and Coe can expect to make some money in corporate outings and the like, but the economic climate could keep them from really cashing in. Both players are personable, however, and sports agents agree that this quality is imperative in generating off-course earnings.

"It will be hard to sell right now," Coe pointed out realistically. "Corporations are making cuts. But who's to say what might or might not happen this year? It's only been a few days since I won. The win does give Elliott some leverage. It makes it easier for him to make presentations."

Those presentations will inevitably be tied to Coe's play. And anything that happens for Walters off the course will reflect her on-course performance. These sobering facts were at the forefront of the players' minds following their wins.

"I like to pace myself," Coe said. "I told Elliott I don't like to do a ton of outings, so we don't. One time I flew from Seattle overnight to Toronto, did an outing all day, sat through dinner, then flew all night to Los Angeles. I went from there to Korea. That won't happen again."

But what could happen is that Kerr, Coe's agent, will make some new deals in the coming months to add to her associations with Budget, Taylor Made golf equipment and Nike.

"We've had talks with a couple of new Canadian clubs," Kerr said yesterday from Hawaii, where he was on vacation. "Both are in Western Canada, and I expect we'll settle something before long. I also met with a car company two days after Dawn won. The timing was unbelievable.

"The win means that Dawn's perceived value is that much greater. This does everything to heighten the awareness of her. She emerges from being the top Canadian to a player of international stature. It also helps that she's No. 1 on the money list. It's still early in the season, but you can bet I will use that in my presentations."

No matter what happens off the course, it seems probable that both Walters and Coe will retain their sensible views of their careers. That their wins were a long time coming may turn out to be to their long-term advantage.

"I still think it's amazing that somebody can make this amount of money playing golf, that people are willing to pay you thousands of dollars for wearing a visor," Coe said. "It almost doesn't seem fair, but at the same time I've worked hard for so many years."

Meanwhile, at Tampa Palms, Coe's future husband is still in dreamland.

"I'm at a loss for words," said Jones, who was overwhelmed by the response to Coe's win, and to the eerie way in which her victory followed Walters's win. There was something in the air in Hawaii.

The magnificent amateur Bobby Jones once said that the longer he played golf the more he felt that destiny took a hand in the game. Destiny turned two weeks in Hawaii into grand occasions for Walters and Coe, and Canadian golf is all the better for their significant accomplishments.